Becoming a SECONDARY SCHOOL SCIENCE TEACHER

Jazlin V. Ebenezer
University of Manitoba

Sharon M. Haggerty
University of Western Ontario

Merrill,
an imprint of Prentice Hall
Upper Saddle River, New Jersey   Columbus, Ohio

Library of Congress Cataloging-in-Publication Data

Ebenezer, Jazlin V.
    Becoming a secondary school science teacher / Jazlin V. Ebenezer
and Sharon M. Haggerty.
        p.   cm.
    Includes bibliographical references and index.
    ISBN 0-02-331312-9
    1. Science teachers—Training of.   2. High school teachers—
Training of.   I. Haggerty, Sharon M.   II. Title.
Q181.A2E24   1999
507.1'273—dc21   98–47306
                    CIP

Cover Photo: © Michelle Bridwell, PhotoEdit
Editor: Bradley J. Potthoff
Production Editor: Mary M. Irvin
Photo Coordinator: Sandy Lenahan
Design Coordinator: Diane C. Lorenzo
Text Design and Production Coordination: Elm Street Publishing Services, Inc.
Cover Designer: Tanya Burgess
Production Manager: Pamela D. Bennett
Director of Marketing: Kevin Flanagan
Marketing Manager: Suzanne Stanton
Advertising/Marketing Coordinator: Krista Groshong

This book was set in Galliard by The Clarinda Company and was printed and bound by R. R.
Donnelley & Sons Company. The cover was printed by Phoenix Color Corp.

© 1999 by Prentice-Hall, Inc.
Simon & Schuster/A Viacom Company
Upper Saddle River, New Jersey 07458

Photo Credits: Wendy Saby, p. xxiii; Anthony Magnacca/Merrill, pp. 52, 86, 90, 98, 133,
212, 355, 372, 394; Anne Vega/Merrill, p. 56; Nova Stock/Photo Edit, p. 87; Michelle
Bridwell/Photo Edit, p. 99; Scott Cunningham/Merrill, pp. 110, 256; David Young-
Wolff/Photo Edit, p. 126; Jazlin Ebenezer, pp. 269, 280; Bart Smith, p. 297; Tony
Freeman/Photo Edit, p. 313.

Printed in the United States of America

10 9 8 7 6 5 4 3 2 1

ISBN: 0-02-331312-9

Prentice-Hall International (UK) Limited, *London*
Prentice-Hall of Australia Pty. Limited, *Sydney*
Prentice-Hall of Canada, Inc., *Toronto*
Prentice-Hall Hispanoamericana, S. A., *Mexico*
Prentice-Hall of India Private Limited, *New Delhi*
Prentice-Hall of Japan, Inc., *Tokyo*
Simon & Schuster Asia Pte. Ltd., *Singapore*
Editora Prentice-Hall do Brasil, Ltda., *Rio de Janeiro*

This text is dedicated to these men and women of noble character, courage, and strength, who have each played a significant role in my academic life:

Sylvia Connor, Luke Ebenezer, Sudesh Ebenezer, Gaalen Erickson, James Gaskell, Dexter Harvey, Jane Jabez, Thambakara Jabez, Joanne Kesselman, Xiufeng Liu, Barbara Marantz, Linda Montgomery, Karen Ogden, Leslie Sisco, Emoke Szathmary, and Jennifer Waroway.

Jazlin V. Ebenezer

I wish to dedicate this text to the following colleagues, advisors, and members of my family, all of whom have contributed in so many ways to support and nurture me in my academic journey:

José Aguirre, Elizabeth Cooper, Gaalen Erickson, Jim Gaskell, the late Bernadine Melanson, and, last but not least, my children, Braden, Megan, and John; my mother; and my grandmothers.

Sharon M. Haggerty

BRIEF CONTENTS

v

CONTENTS

CHAPTER 7

Novel Teaching and Learning Ideas 166

CHAPTER 8

Explanation, Evidence, Relevance 198

PART THREE

Science Curricular Content, Issues, and Trends 235

CHAPTER 9

Contextual Science from a Historical Perspective 236

CHAPTER 10

Interactive Learning with Computer Technology 254

FOREWORD

In 1981, the late Joseph I. Lipson, then Director of Science Education Development and Research at the National Science Foundation (NSF), and I wrote a paper titled the "Crisis in Science Education." The paper was read into the Congressional Record, and excerpts were reported in several national magazines. It was not a popular message at the time, especially within the NSF, but it turned out to be an enduring one. Tremendous effort has been invested during the past 20 years to address problems in science education, and according to the American Association for the Advancement of Science Project 2061, continuing efforts will be required at least until the year 2061. In fact, a system that continually reassesses its progress or lack thereof is the preferred state. The crisis is succinctly summarized in our first paragraph:

> We live in one of the most (if not the most) advanced technological societies in the world. Yet we are not providing the majority of our children with even the most rudimentary knowledge and skills necessary to manage that society.

We were among the first government officials in the United States to notice the problem, but our observations were not original. We were reacting to pioneering research produced by such individuals as Rosalind Driver in England; Gaalen Erickson in Canada; Roger Osborne in New Zealand; Michael McCloskey, John Clement, and James Minstrell in the United States; and Joseph Nussbaum in Israel. These researchers and others were beginning to identify student preconceptions, naïve ideas held by students that remained intact and untouched even after many years of didactic instruction intended to change them. Consequently, the value of "traditional instructional methods" in science (such as large-scale verbal transmission of "facts" and laboratories designed to illustrate "claims") was called into question.

A reform movement was born with an ambitious agenda: to significantly change the ways we teach science at every level of education *world-*

wide. Many countries, states, and provinces began to reevaluate their science teaching, set goals and agendas for reform, and establish standards for science learning at each grade level. The most enthusiastic response to date has occurred at the primary school level where the greatest number of changes have taken place. Some reasons for this are:

- it makes sense to work from the bottom up;
- many students in the United States are "turned off" by science by eighth grade and this needs to be changed; and
- instructional styles advocated by the reform provide a good match to those used instinctively by many elementary teachers.

Learning research has also directed our attention to (or perhaps simply reflected our attention to) the elementary level. There have been thousands of studies of children's preconceptions and the effectiveness of various teaching methodologies to induce conceptual change in the face of these deep-seated naïve beliefs. Yet, there have been few studies of the preconceptions (dare we use the word?) and beliefs of high school and university science teachers about what science is and what aspects of science they consider to be important to convey to their students. Some of the ideas of prospective science teachers are captured in this book, and this may stimulate further research along these lines.

Becoming a Secondary School Science Teacher by Jazlin Ebenezer and Sharon Haggerty moves the bar up a notch. It addresses secondary school science teaching head on. In the spirit of an introductory science text, this book provides a remarkably comprehensive survey of strategies developed to promote authentic, meaningful science learning. The authors avoid the impression of an encyclopedia, however, by drawing on student voices to generate reader interest and illustrate multiple perspectives. The book includes not only a wide-ranging review of educational theories and practices but also many useful science lessons and assessment strategies. I suspect historians as well as science teachers will find this a useful place to review the science education research and reform activities of the past quarter century.

Progress is inevitably cyclical and foretelling the future is always risky. For example, in his recent book, *Consilience: The Unity of Knowledge*, E. O. Wilson describes the Enlightenment of the seventeenth and eighteenth centuries, the groundwork it laid for modern science, and the optimism its proponents felt for human nature and steady forward progress. Yet, many of their dreams were shattered by the political chaos that followed (but fortunately not lost from civilization entirely). With guarded optimism, then, it seems reasonable to expect that *Becoming a Secondary School Science Teacher* will have a significant impact on secondary school science teaching and will contribute to meaningful and much-needed improvements in science literacy among high school graduates.

Kathleen M. Fisher

PREFACE

In recent years, science educators have been working on reforming science education. This reformation has been based on a vision of teaching and learning science in which all students have a greater opportunity to become scientifically literate. To reach this goal, educators must alter the way science is taught and learned. Therefore, the purpose of this text is to help you transform the way you think about teaching and learning science. This text will help you explore your prior ideas about teaching science, understand the true nature of science and scientific inquiry, and provide you with a teaching methodology in which you will learn how to help students construct meaning through scientific inquiry and discourse.

⊠ CONCEPTUAL HIGHLIGHTS OF THE TEXT

To realize the vision of science for all, we emphasize that a teacher must acquire an adequate background of science content knowledge, grasp and understand how children learn, and develop an underpinning of the theoretical aspects of teaching science. In addition, we assert that a teacher must learn how to engage in continuous reflective practice. Throughout the text we provide you with many opportunities to engage in personal and collaborative reflective inquiry about teaching and learning science. Thus, through interaction with this text, you will accomplish the following:

Develop an understanding of how learning occurs and how you can facilitate learning in science. We believe that incorporating children's ideas, beliefs, and questions about science concepts and related societal issues in meaningful science lessons is an effective way to teach science. To accomplish this, you must first seek children's science conceptions. Then you can learn to negotiate science ideas with children and conduct collaborative inquiry so that children will see the struggles and tensions that scientists go through as they invent scientific knowledge. In this manner, children will get a glimpse of the true nature of scientific inquiry.

Explore the nature of science. Modern as well as postmodern views about science presented in this text indicate how much has changed from the time of Bacon and Newton to the present day. However, the reason and logic of Bacon and Newton's day will continue to be practiced in school science, alongside the give-and-take of modern scientific discourse. Classroom discourse will enhance your construction of deeper meanings of scientific inquiry.

Examine curricular issues. Effective science curriculum includes planning for multicultural and gender equity, adapting activities for special-needs students, and utilizing technologies in science to create learning environments to meet the needs of all of your students. In this text, you will view science through a multiple-voice framework so that you may reach students with different backgrounds, interests, abilities, experiences, and motivations. A multiple-voice framework for science teaching enables you to develop learning objectives, review curricular materials, select teaching strategies and learning activities, choose assessment tasks, and engage students in a variety of ways to develop an understanding of science.

Enrich your science content knowledge. In this course you will be exposed to various science themes and the knowledge presented in them. You will also be taught two learning tools, Vee diagramming and concept mapping, to help you develop much-needed science content knowledge throughout your teaching career.

We do not expect you to have a deep understanding of all the sciences. Clarifying and deepening your understanding of science content, however, is part of your teaching responsibility. Hence, this is an area in which your knowledge can evolve through professional development activities even after you leave your university or college.

To have a sound foundation in science and an in-depth understanding, you must continue to seek scientific knowledge throughout your career. Participating in research at science workshops or field settings is a legitimate way to learn science and the nature of science. Why do we stress the importance of continuous learning of science? Teachers are ambassadors of the scientific community in the classroom. As ambassadors, it is important to present an authentic image of someone who engages in scientific inquiry, not someone who is a fountain of scientific wisdom.

Understand that your professional development is a continuous, active process for which you are professionally responsible. We suggest that once you begin your teaching career, you should seek professional activities that will provide you with sustained and contextual participation and reflection in integrating your content and curriculum knowledge, learning, and teaching skills. As researchers and reflective practitioners, preservice and practicing teachers can make significant contributions to the advancement of knowledge of teaching and learning. And through this course you will indeed develop theoretical and practical meanings to shed light on the problems of teaching. You will also develop the skills (journal writing and using audio/video recordings, peer observations, and dialogue) to conduct research in your classroom and carry out a reflective practice.

⟨⟩ ORGANIZATION OF THE TEXT

This text is organized into four parts. The four chapters in Part One set this text in the current reform framework by focusing on science standards, scientific literacy, and science-technology-society-environment issues from the perspectives of preservice teachers. They clearly delineate and summarize the nature of science and current learning theories. Students have the opportunity to explore and develop their own style. Gardner's multiple intelligences model and White's model of learning science provide the preservice teacher with further insights into ways to facilitate student learning.

Part Two provides strategies for science discourse. The Ben Carson story illustrates the importance of reading to learn science. The contrast between conventional labs and inquiry-based labs is illustrated with examples. Journal writing and research reporting are important science inquiry skills. Novel teaching and learning ideas are introduced. Part Two also demonstrates various mapping styles with concrete examples.

Contemporary curricular content, issues, and trends highlight the five chapters of Part Three. The large context problem approach provides important insights into the nature of science, which leads to generating questions and having students approach research based on the history and philosophy of science. Computer technology is described as an interactive tool for learning science. STSE integration and its associated programs for promoting sustainable development and living are recognized. Many authentic-assessment ideas and techniques are developed.

Part Four addresses unit and lesson planning based on many voices. The common knowledge construction model draws upon some of the latest thinking in relational learning, culture, language, and STSE connections. We provide a biology unit developed by Richard Hechter that is based on the common knowledge construction model.

⟨⟩ SPECIAL FEATURES OF THE TEXT

We have incorporated a number of pedagogical elements that will facilitate your learning to teach science:

Preparatory teaching activities for reflective practice, including journal writing and preservice teacher comments

Teacher Practice and Peer Talk activities

Sample lessons and unit plans

Instructions for creating concept maps and Vee diagrams

Preservice Teacher as Researcher (P-STAR) conference papers based on exemplary practicum science teaching experiences and research

Margin notes that provide definitions of important terms, guides for reflection on teaching strategies, and National Science Education Standards

Probes at the end of chapters, which summarize and raise provocative questions

Becoming a strong and effective teacher is a complex, career-long process. No one else can make you a good teacher. You must develop patterns of thoughtful reflection and analysis of everything you do and read. It is our hope that as you read this book and practice the suggested activities, you will feel prepared to begin the process of becoming a better science teacher. After extensive research with our own preservice teachers, we are confident that this text can help and guide you as you develop your knowledge, understanding, and abilities to teach science.

ACKNOWLEDGMENTS

We would like to thank the reviewers of our manuscript for their insights and comments: Patricia A. Giese, Slippery Rock University of Pennsylvania; Fred H. Groves, Northeast Louisiana University; S. Maxwell Hines, Hofstra University; Harold J. McKenna, City University of New York; Herbert H. Stewart, Florida Atlantic University; Rita K. Voltmer, Miami University; and Michael Wavering, University of Arkansas.

Appreciation is extended to the 1994–1998 preservice teachers at the University of Manitoba and the University of Western Ontario for collaborating with us to prepare research-based lessons, activities, units, and strategies. The contributing preservice teachers' names are included along with their work throughout the text.

We extend special thanks and acknowledgment to our colleagues Dr. Joel Bass, Dr. Richard Duschl, Dr. Gaalen Erickson, Dr. Kathleen Fisher, Dr. Xiufeng Liu, Dr. Francis Madrid, and Dr. Fred Ellett and Dr. Arthur Stinner for their expert ideas concerning the Internet, science assessment, interpretive discussion, SemNet concept mapping, concept mapping, sustainable development, and the history and philosophy of science respectively. Art Frankel provided advice on a variety of topics.

From the University of Manitoba, we offer thanks to Eileen Repeta, Scott Wellman, and Jill Wharton for help with computers. Our special thanks to Joel Themmen for helping us create a Web page on which to put the references for students' conceptions. Steve Czyzowski provided computer and e-mail support at the University of Western Ontario.

We acknowledge Tani Cyr for providing us with summaries for the part on current trends and issues in science education. We acknowledge the constant encouragement that preservice teachers Randean Kopytko, Yvonne Manderson, Barbara Marantz, and Jennifer Waroway have given us during this strenuous period of writing.

This text is the outcome of peer reviews by our American colleagues at different stages of its development. We sincerely thank our reviewers for their helpful comments and suggestions.

Preservice Teachers: University of Manitoba. Natalie Bergson, Sandra Bourcier, Kathy Doell, Gustave Foster, Corrine Friesen, Mark Glenwright, Marilyne Hauser, Richard Hechter, Michael Kattenfeld, Len Kerr, Karen Knight, Tamara Kosteki, Mark Krahn, Kevin Lang, Robert Lewin, Christine Loewen, Marcia Loewen, Sofia Lukuszuk, Lucia Luz, Kathleen Madden, Barbara Marantz, Tom Miko, Sharon Mohammed, Kathryn Murison, Ryan Penner, Heidi Plett, Angela Poettcker, Shelby Primmett, Mohammed Razai, Chris Roe, Jerry Semchshyn, Deanna Shanks, Kathryn Slovinsky, Pawel Szponarski, Corinna Turzak, and Kim Wiedenbach. We are proud to say that most of these teachers are teaching at various levels in the school system.

Preservice Teachers: University of Western Ontario. Norina Andrews, Eric Brandsma, Neil Dyal, Jeff Misener, Jason Murdoch, Bart Scollard, and Malcolm Small.

Graduate Students at the University of Manitoba and Practicing Teachers in Winnipeg, Manitoba. Michael Collins, Garry De Blunde, Mary-Ann Fast, Susan Jaworski, Marlene Kroeker, Greg Lupal, Barbara McMillan, Don Metz, Ken Park, Carla Reilly, Rodelyn Stoeber, Ann Walker, Denise Weselake, and Leslie Wurtak.

Graduate Students at the University of Western Ontario and Practicing Teachers in London, Ontario. Joe Calabrese, Zandra Cerpa, Rudi Czekalla, Steve Fernandes, Jon McGoey, Maureen O'Neill, Jim Ross, John Shoemaker, and Alison Yantzi-Sammel.

School Division. Fort Gary School Division, Winnipeg, Manitoba.

This text is also a by-product of many research projects that were financially supported by the Social Science and Humanities Research Council of Canada for both Jazlin and Sharon and the University of Manitoba (Research and Development Office, Faculty of Education, and Communication Systems) and the University of Western Ontario. Without the assistance of these institutions and corporate bodies, this classroom-based research book may not have become a reality.

We would also like to express our sincere appreciation and thanks to Phyllis Crittenden, at Elm Street Publishing Services, for her wisdom and guidance throughout the editing process of this book. Hers was not an easy task, what with Jazlin in Bangladesh and Sharon jetting to and fro across Canada during the production stages. Throughout it all, Phyllis maintained her good humor, questioning, reminding, and encouraging when and where necessary. Much of that which has been done well is to her credit. Responsibility for any remaining errors is ours alone.

Jazlin V. Ebenezer, Ed.D.
Sharon M. Haggerty, Ed.D.

About the Authors

Jazlin Ebenezer is associate professor in the Faculty of Education, University of Manitoba, Winnipeg, Canada. Her experience includes teaching science curriculum and instruction to preservice teachers at various levels during their certification year. At the graduate level, she teaches "The Study of Teaching." Jazlin conducts classroom-based, action-oriented collaborative research, which is supported by the Social Sciences and Humanities Research Council of Canada. Her research program focuses on preservice teachers' voices, attitudes, and conceptualizations; students' perceptions of science concepts and incorporating their ideas into science lesson sequences; environmental ethics and sustainable living; and electronic multimedia within a constructivist framework. She has authored and co-authored a number of articles both in scholarly and professional journals and has presented papers in Russia, South Africa, the United States, and Canada. She carries out ongoing research with universities in Cape Town, South Africa. At the Manitoba Ministry of Education and Training, she is involved with the decision-making processes of science and chemistry curriculum development and implementation.

Sharon Haggerty, shown in the center of the photo below, is associate professor and chair of Graduate Education in the Faculty of Education at the University of Western Ontario, London, Canada. Sharon has taught teaching methods courses for both secondary and elementary science at Western and at three other Canadian universities. She also teaches graduate-level courses in learning science, environmental and global education, and research methods.

Sharon's research, like Jazlin's, focuses on how teachers, including preservice teachers, learn to teach science. The findings of that research have been included in this book, and the voices of many of her former preservice teachers are presented here. The relationship between gender and science learning has also been an important aspect of this research. The Social Sciences and Humanities Research Council of Canada has also funded Sharon's research, some of it in collaboration with José Aguirre.

Learning about teaching and gender and science have been the major focus of Sharon's publications. She was co-chair and editor of the proceedings of the International Conference on Gender and Science and Technology, held in Canada in 1993. She has presented scholarly papers, conducted workshops, and attended conferences throughout Canada, the United States, Australia, and in Israel. She has served as an advisor on curriculum policy and development in two Canadian provinces and is a past president of the Saskatchewan Science Teachers' Society.

INTRODUCTION

Heart to Heart—Preservice Teachers as Researchers

What are your professional attitudes toward and dispositions in learning to teach science? Do you belong to the category of preservice teachers who search for right answers or become impatient when direct answers are not given? Do you agree with a group of preservice teachers who stated to their science teacher educator in frustration, "Show it to me and tell me how to do it" (Stofflett, 1994)? How would you feel about being asked to explore and assess your prior beliefs about science teaching? How will you react when you experience conceptual conflicts and your ideas are challenged? Your science teacher educator is cognizant of your problems and difficulties. Seek opportunities to engage in heart-to-heart talks with your educator about your stages of development as well as concerns that may arise as you become a teacher of science.

What might be some of the stages you will go through in your preservice teaching? What might be some of the anxieties and concerns in science teaching?

⚙ POSSIBLE STAGES IN YOUR PRESERVICE TEACHING

Research shows that the preservice teaching period is marked with successive stages. The projection of "self" is first; the focus is on personal actions rather than students. For example, the notion of self revolves around the question "How do I perform in class?" "How do others view me as a teacher?" In this stage, the preservice teacher seeks the views of significant others: science teacher educator, cooperating teacher, faculty advisor, principal, students, and parents. Inward-looking tendencies and the pursuit of confirmations, validations, and affirmations about one's role as teacher may prevail. Next, the focus is on the science experimental task, the materials, and the best possible delivery of the activity. The question is, "How do I best present this science topic to my students?" Lastly, the move is

FIGURE I-1
Successive stages in
preservice teaching

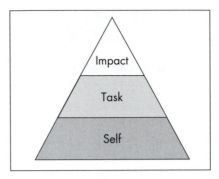

FIGURE I-2
Integration of self, task, and impact

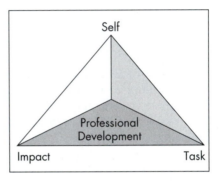

toward the learner: "What impact do I have on the learner?" The preservice teacher begins to look beyond himself or herself and the activity and focuses on what students are learning. Gunstone, Slattery, Baird, and Northfield (1993) point out that successful personal professional development requires that the concerns of these levels (self, task, impact) be addressed in an integrated manner from the start of your teacher education. See Figures I-1 and I-2.

⊗ ANXIETIES AND CONCERNS

There are several concerns that you might exhibit in your preservice period. A common concern is feeling that you do not have adequate science content knowledge. This is understandable because science content knowledge is an important aspect of pedagogical knowledge. This concern is expressed by teachers with science background in one or two areas who may have problems with teaching other areas of science. One way of overcoming this problem is presented in Chapter 3 of this textbook. Another way of looking at this problem is stated by Rose, a preservice teacher:

> I am now beginning to realize that every teacher doesn't have to know everything about every subject he/she teaches. In fact, I think that a great deal of learning can occur for a teacher through the planning and implementing of

lessons. I found that, before I taught my unit on clouds and precipitation, I knew very little about the subject. But, through the research that I did and the experiments also, I learned a lot about the subject with my students. My pre-conceived notion that the teacher must be the possessor of all knowledge has relaxed . . . (Ebenezer & Hay, 1995, p. 97).

A sensitive issue is that you will undoubtedly have alternative concep-tions of science concepts as well as experience conceptual difficulties. Your views about the nature of science may contrast with the contemporary philosophies of science. Additionally, your conceptions of teaching, learn-ing, and assessment might be different from what you will experience in this course. For example, you will experience teaching that is more than simply laying the curricular content on students. It means learning meth-ods that incorporate students' ideas. This may be an additional burden on you. Furthermore, you will be taught from a constructivist perspective (incorporating preservice teachers' ideas about teaching and learning into the science teacher educator's lessons).

Your dilemmas may also include science classroom management, carry-ing out discourse with students, multiple ways of teaching science, and curriculum and instructional assumptions. For example, planning fewer activities, covering less content, and constructing questions that will pro-mote understanding the content in deeper ways may go against the eager-ness to cover too much material in a short time.

Another potential area of concern is that what you learn in your edu-cation courses will not be the same as what you do in your practicum, although both institutions are legitimately teaching you practical aspects of how to teach and how to grow professionally. It is important for you to realize that preservice teacher education cannot prepare you com-pletely; it is only the beginning of your professional development.

Becoming aware of yourself, becoming personally responsible for teaching and making decisions, carrying out personal reflections, and engaging in interpersonal interactions are necessary requirements in learn-ing to teach science, but they are not easy. They are in fact intellectually demanding. Therefore this might be a concern, too.

To alleviate or overcome some of the foregoing concerns we invite you to engage in reflective practice that invites you to study teaching as a com-munity of researchers rather than as an individual. This will also help you to share aspects of your practice with your peers and your science teacher educator in nonthreatening ways. You will recognize, clarify, review, and renew your teaching ideas as you reflect on contextual personal experi-ences and problematic situations. In this model, personal experience is the basis for considering and changing ideas, with educational theories and concepts providing ways of organizing and interpreting your experiences.

To develop a practical philosophy of teaching, you must seek opportu-nities to engage in reflective inquiry and discuss salient principles and major issues of science teaching. You must be committed to examining additional ways of teaching through reading, contemplating, and researching. Commitment to a novel way of teaching is easy to make when you become an active collaborative partner with your peers as well as your science teacher educator in the inquiry of teaching and learning. Seek genuine opportunities for sustained, meaningful, and critical dialogue (Erickson, Mayer-Smith, Rodriguez, Chin, & Mitchell, 1994).

⚙ LEARNING TO TEACH

This book is dedicated to the task of helping you come to the realization that assessing your own prior experiences in science education and your beliefs about teaching, as well as making sense of your personal decisions and actions as you learn to teach, are vital for professional development, growth, and transformation.

Science teacher education literature describes ways of growing professionally. Additionally, it provides methods and strategies for learning how to teach science. In this introduction, we provide you with tools to help you intentionally and systematically trace your professional metamorphosis.

The general methodologies that are appropriate include writing an autobiography, conducting narrative inquiry (focusing in part on the "storied lives" we lead), assessing your conceptions and beliefs, engaging in self-reflective practice, establishing collaborative relationships with one or more trusted friends, colleagues, educators, cooperating teachers, faculty advisors, and students, and researching into your teaching.

Science in My Life: A Narrative Inquiry

Begin a process of self-understanding that specifically includes science and its place in your life, both in and out of school. Recall your experiences as far back as you can. This story form encourages you to recall experiences that might have significant science connections. These stories will raise new questions and allow you to construct powerful insights into science and the teaching of science. Furthermore, it may help to develop a broader understanding of how each of us is connected to others and to the environment in which we live.

The following list is provided to help you focus on what may prove to be some of the more interesting influences, which will help you make sense of science in your life as it relates to your becoming a teacher:

1. Family experiences as a child; experiences with teachers; school experience
2. Meanings of the experiences in item 1
3. Family role models; positive teacher role models; negative teacher role models
4. Ideals of adult-child relationships; ideal instructional strategies; ideal instructional environment
5. Significant recent experiences and people.
6. Your role identity (Grunau, 1994)

Using this list as a starting point may help you reflect on some formative experiences, and may lead to a better understanding of yourself as a teacher of science.

Assessing Your Conceptions and Beliefs

Your autobiography will include personal beliefs about science teaching, images of good science teachers, images of yourself as a teacher, and memories of yourself as a student in science classrooms. For professional growth to occur, these personal beliefs, images, and memories must be brought into the conscious mind and clearly defined. Through structured learning experiences, you should be able to modify and reconstruct your personal beliefs and images.

Seek ways to interact with students and study their ways of performing science activities as well as the decisions they make and actions they take; this knowledge will help you assess your own prior knowledge and beliefs about teaching. This will require assignments consisting of journal writing and action research that allow you to stand back temporarily from your personal beliefs, acknowledge where they are inaccurate or incomplete, and reconstruct them. Take opportunities to work with role models— teachers who question and reflect on their pedagogical beliefs, and teachers whose ideas and practices are somewhat different from your own beliefs—so that cognitive dissonance will be created to question your own personal beliefs. Without cognitive dissonance, learning will be shallow, technical, and imitative (Kagan, 1992).

Self-Reflection in Professional Practice

Professional practice often requires individuals to modify their attitudes, beliefs, and values. Changing behavior involves your personal conceptions of teaching and learning. Conceptions of teaching and learning are influenced by how you learned or how you were taught science. Professional development can take place only if you are motivated to change; reflection is a tool to bring about that change.

Engaging in reflective practice means to intentionally make certain aspects of your practice problematic so that you may gain new insights into that practice (Clarke, 1994). It is a conversation that you carry on within your problem setting. When you openly and actively converse with the social context, you are generating knowledge-in-action (Erickson, 1986; Feiman-Nemser & Buchmann, 1986). Clarke states that according to Schön (1983, 1987), "knowledge-in-action is the raw material on which reflection operates." You may act on the problem while you are carrying out the investigation (*reflection-in-action*). On the other hand, you may plan a course of action after much thought and deliberation when the experiment is over (*reflection-on-action*). Clarke (1994) conceptualizes reflection as "the interplay between framing and reframing experimentation and backtalk in the action setting." If you consider yourself as a reflective practitioner, you will go "beyond curiosity and intrigue to frame, reframe and develop a plan for future action." It is during the reframing stage that you will construct new knowledge about your problem setting.

When you engage in professional practice, you will shift from traditional classroom practices. Initially, you may frame your reflections in terms of "imitating" or "cloning" other teachers. Later, you may reframe your reflections on your own practice by probing into your own beliefs and making these explicit. We encourage you to reflect on your practice to become empowered teachers (independent and autonomous). If you tend to replicate other teachers, you will evolve into a repetitive practitioner! Reflecting on your practice as a whole rather than on particular aspects is important for defining practice that is uniquely yours.

Establishing Collaborative Relationships

As mentioned earlier, the type of teaching that is advocated in this book creates many conceptual demands. Many realities, including the content of the discipline, pose great challenges. Hence, the study of teaching in conventional classrooms must be a collaborative exercise. A collaborative venture will promote reflection and develop both a language of professional knowledge and classroom inquiry that will encourage open communication and criticism between the collaborators to achieve professional growth and improved practice. Conceptual freedom and conceptual unity are two principles that are essential for successful collaborative work. Such things as modeling, coaching, intellectual reflective dialogues, viewing of videos of teaching practices, and joint experimentation are natural components of the collaborative enterprise. Joint explorations must be carried out within ethical frameworks of reciprocity, mutual benefit, and commitment to human caring. Collaborative adventures will help all the key players (you, your teacher educator, your cooperating teacher, your faculty advisor) to contemplate the complexities of teaching and learning. Collaborative relationships will result in shared commitments and concerns and will give all who participate a vision for new ways of looking at science teaching and learning. Collaborative relationships will promote mutual learning, relearning, and sometimes unlearning about "seeing" science classes.

Journal Writing

Journal writing is a tool that is often used in professional practice. Three questions about journals often arise (Connelly & Clandinen, 1988, pp. 36–37). They are presented in Figure I-3.

☒ SCIENCE METHODS COURSE

This course will focus on your understanding of the nature of teaching and learning and the nature of scientific inquiry. Hence, in developing a practical philosophy of teaching science, attention has been given to *postmod-*

1. What should I write?
Write as much as you can in your journal. Describe your students, actions, events, and reactions that you have, both while teaching and after you are finished teaching. Record the feelings you have about your practices and the various events that happen. Be alert to past experiences that come to mind as you react emotionally and morally.
2. How often should I write?
Write regularly. Make an entry every few days or more frequently if you have the time or if something particular occurs to you. To be useful to you as a reflective tool, the journal needs to be an ongoing record of thought.
3. Should I go back and reread it?
It is helpful to reread your journal entries from time to time and try to make sense of the kind of things that suggest ideas. Read carefully to see if you can pick up any threads or themes that seem to recur. Keep an open mind and try to see patterns. Keep comparing these ideas with those from before.

FIGURE I-3
Three questions about journal writing (*NOTE:* From *Teachers as Curriculum Planners* (pp. 36–37), by F. M. Connelly and D. J. Clandinen, 1988, New York: Teachers College Press. Copyright 1988 by Columbia University. Adapted with permission.)

ern theories of knowing* and *postmodern philosophies of science.* Students' personal knowing (students' ideas of a science concept and their sources), the teachers' academic knowing (science content knowledge, science pedagogical knowledge, curricular knowledge) and teacher-students common knowing (shared understandings) are developed through hands-on/minds-on/speech-on reflective collaborative inquiry. To develop professional knowing, this course adopts the following tenets and standards:

- You should approach science pedagogical studies on the basis of your personal beliefs, attitudes, understandings, and values about teaching and learning.
- You should critically explore your perspectives of teaching and learning in a variety of contexts and make these explicit.
- You should come to the understanding that knowledge is personally constructed and socially negotiated.
- You should understand the notion that learning may take one or more forms: learning may be evolutionary (an adaptive process—prior knowledge interacting with new knowledge) and revolutionary (new ideas replacing old ideas—a conversion process).
- You should accept the notion that it is the fusion between your personal conceptions and socially constructed knowledge that eventually forms your practical pedagogy.
- You should be willing to take risks and be open-minded and flexible enough to adopt alternative or additional ways of teaching and learning.
- You must realize that construction and development of a practical philosophy of teaching takes time and commitment.
- You must be ready to encounter personal conceptual conflicts and painful moments as you develop a practical philosophy of teaching.

Patience is a noble characteristic that you must have as small increments of change take place.

- You should acknowledge that teaching is problematic because it is embedded in complex and ambiguous sociocultural boundaries and landscapes.
- You should learn the art of reflective inquiry so that problems in teaching become evident.
- You should attempt to develop a rich repertoire of strategies and ways of making sense of experiences that would account for your competence in dealing with problems of practice.
- As researchers, you should identify and frame the problem; devise, implement, and assess possible ways of solving the problem; based on all criteria, decide to use the best available problem-solving strategy; and take a course of action to solve or reframe the problem.
- You should not expect teacher educators to be transmitters of "knowledge from above." Rather, you should become active collaborative partners with teacher educators (faculty and teachers) in the inquiry of teaching and learning.

On the basis of the preceding assumptions for your development, you will be given opportunities to explore your personal beliefs and understandings of teaching and learning through meaningful practical experiences in the university and school-based classroom contexts. You will create, negotiate, and recreate meanings through dialogue and intentional reflective inquiry. Your learning situation will characterize the spirit of a research forum in which the collaborative members share what they have done and what they claim to know to produce a joint teaching culture.

PART ONE

DEVELOPING A PRACTICAL PHILOSOPHY

"The universe impinges on us, and we are aware of it through our senses. From the sensations we receive we construct objects and incidents and determine causes for effects. Each of us builds a world."

White, 1988, p. x

White notes that each of us constructs or develops our own interpretations and beliefs about the world around us and how it works. Our world views act as a lens or filter as we go through life. So, how we teach science depends on our image of science and our beliefs about the nature of scientific inquiry. Our views of learners, of how people learn most effectively, and of what constitutes good teaching also influence our school science practices. Hence, we begin this book by asking you to consider your **conceptions** of these matters. What do you really mean when you speak about science? What distinguishes science from other ways of knowing about the world? What is the role of theory in science? How do people (both practicing scientists and science students) go about "doing science" and learning about science? What is your view of the students you expect to teach? What is your understanding of what interests motivated them to learn? What is the best way to teach science—or *is* there a best way? If not, why not? You will explore all of these questions as you prepare yourself to become a science teacher. These questions will assist you in developing your own practical philosophy of teaching science.

Chapter 1 explores your science curriculum emphases and provides other preservice teachers' voices about curriculum. Chapter 1 also compares preservice teachers' science curriculum emphases to the National Science Education Standards. An examination of science content standards in Chapter 1 provides

a conceptual lens for science learning outcomes as well as presenting an advanced organizer for the rest of this textbook. We end the chapter with a unit format that mirrors the science content standards and will guide you in learning the information presented in the subsequent chapters.

Chapter 2 invites you to explore your personal conceptions of what is meant by science. Then, in the context of preservice teachers' conceptions, we critically examine the nature of science, by considering the views of some of the major philosophers of science. Through peer talks and practices, you will have opportunities to rethink the nature of science. Since you are the ambassador of the scientific community in your school classroom, the image of science you portray to your students will influence their abilities and understandings of science as inquiry. Therefore, the principles and concepts presented in Chapter 2 are fundamental to your school science practices.

Chapter 3 explores your views of teaching and learning science. Preservice teachers' metaphors are presented and their initial ways of teaching are discussed. Since we believe that teaching involves concept development through inquiry and that learning is conceptual change, we present contemporary conceptual models of teaching. The principles common to all of these models are exploring students' ideas systematically and incorporating them into science lesson sequences. Some examples are provided for you to better understand the models.

Chapter 4 discusses the types of knowledge in science and how these can develop students' multiple intelligences. Howard Gardner's theory of multiple intelligences is illustrated through examples and lesson plans. This chapter also stresses the importance of helping students become consciously aware of the different types of knowledge and be able to use various forms of knowledge to explain science concepts and natural phenomena.

Windows into Science Education

STUDY QUESTIONS

1. What sorts of experiences are reflected in preservice teachers' accounts of what aspects of the science curriculum are emphasized?

2. What are the science content standards for curriculum development, according to the National Research Council?

3. How do preservice teachers' conceptions of curriculum emphases compare with the National Science Education Standards?

4. What are some pedagogical elements that could be included in a unit that reflects the National Science Education Standards?

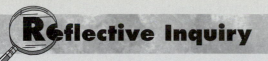

Reflective Inquiry

KIRK'S VOICE

To do what the teacher told you to, isn't cool. And they want instant gratification. What good is this to me now? The problem with that, I guess, is well, they were there in class in body, but they left their minds at home. I mean that quite literally. They simply did not want to be there.

JOURNAL ACTIVITY

School Science Curriculum Emphases

What do you think the science curriculum should emphasize? What were your experiences when you took science in school? Share some of your experiences with one or more of your classmates.

Systemic change refers to total system change—change involving people (from individual practices through organizational levels to senior policymakers), processes, practices, policies, power, and philosophy.

We want you to take special note of the science content standards that appear as margin notes because these are a complete set of outcomes that a science program should emphasize. The science content standards outline what students should know, understand, and be able to do.

The *National Science Education Standards* (NRC, 1996) cover the following areas:

- Science as inquiry
- Unifying concepts and processes in science
- Physical science, life science, and earth and space science
- Science and technology
- Science in personal and social perspective
- History and nature of science

Preservice teachers' emphases for science curriculum mirror most of the *National Science Education Standards,* which are the foundation for curriculum development. Preservice teachers mentioned very little about either "unifying concepts and processes in science" or the "history and nature of science" when they explored their ideas about scientific inquiry. The descriptions of these two science content standards are presented immediately, while others will appear as margin notes in parallel to preservice teachers' accounts.

Paul Hurd, a science teacher educator, hired a taxi driver to interview adolescents to find out about their school life. Adolescents found school science boring, unproductive, and unchallenging (Hurd, 1994). **Systemic change** is currently underway in North America, aimed at improving students' attitudes toward science and shaping opportunities for learning.

This systemic change is a response to declining financial resources and changing student demographics as we approach the next millennium. Learners are required to have sufficient knowledge and skills to work in an increasingly complex world of rapid technological advancements. Scientific knowledge and scientific ways of thinking are necessary for informed decision making. Collective decisions are essential to manage shared resources such as air, water, and forests. The modern workplace expects workers to be creative, to reason, to think, to make decisions, to solve problems, and to take appropriate action.

How can we prepare our students to meet the demands of today's marketplace? In the midst of this whirl of change, how can you make science relevant for all adolescents? Preparing students to cope with their rapidly changing environment is a challenge!

Every boy and girl from every neighborhood and every social class should have access to quality science education. Note what a preservice teacher says about equity and excellence in science education:

SANDY'S VOICE

I believe teachers should introduce, explain, and allow students of all races and capabilities to explore the endless possibilities of science.

Science must be not only for those who want to pursue a scientific career, but also for those who choose to follow other walks of life. The able and the disabled should do science. Regardless of age and gender, all learners should have the same learning opportunities in science. If science is for *all* students, what should be the emphases of school science curriculum? Let us compare the responses of a group of preservice teachers with the science content standards outlined in the *National Science Education Standards* (National Research Council, 1996).

PRESERVICE TEACHERS' SCIENCE CURRICULUM EMPHASES

Preservice teachers who were interviewed believed that a science curriculum should contain the following four emphases:

- Conducting scientific inquiry
- Understanding science concepts
- Integrating science and technology
- Connecting science to self and society

Conducting Scientific Inquiry

Many preservice teachers thought that a science curriculum should provide activities to help students develop scientific attitudes and values, study the natural world, and use evidence to support their arguments. Consider these preservice teachers' conceptions of the purpose of scientific inquiry in school.

JANE'S VOICE

To inspire creativity and imagination, to teach kids to ask intuitive questions about the nature of things (how they operate); to develop reasoning skills such as analysis, hypotheses, and deduction; to develop critical thinking; and to learn to work cooperatively on solving scientific problems.

DON'S VOICE

Students must learn skills and techniques. They should learn to infer and ask questions via the scientific method. They need to learn to explore all possible reasons for why certain results occur.

SARAH'S VOICE

Science should be presented in such a way that students are actively involved in the discovery process—asking questions (knowing what good questions are), testing their hypotheses, and being able to prove that something is the way it is using systematic processes and formulas. Students should engage in higher-order thinking.

DOUG'S VOICE

Students should be able to perform experiments to answer questions or prove their own theories. Science should teach an orderly way of approaching a problem (i.e., objective, hypothesis, etc.).

SHEILA'S VOICE

Students should do many hands-on experiences where they can observe and make judgments according to their observations. Students should always be encouraged to think and to analyze their thoughts and ideas and also to re-evaluate, change, and improve on ideas, and to share ideas. Science should show people how to be analysts and to think through problems.

NICKY'S VOICE

To discuss science as a field that is evolutionary and revolutionary—still growing and with vast amounts of uncertainty; how science is fundamental to our lives (e.g., animal testing; chemical reactions,

Unifying concepts and processes standards for K–12 paint a big picture of scientific ideas—both the conceptual and procedural ideas common to both the natural and the designed worlds; for example, seeking evidence, models, and explanation are all part of scientific inquiry. The integrative principles include systems, order, and organization; evidence, models, and explanation; change, constancy, and measurement; evolution and equilibrium; and form and function.

History and the nature of science standards emphasize that history must be used to help secondary students develop an understanding of science as a human endeavor, of the nature of scientific knowledge, and of science in different historical and cultural perspectives.

Conception A mental image or understanding of an object or group of objects or relationships among objects.

Preconceptions Conceptions that are held as a result of previous experience.

plants and animals, the food chain, Sun-Earth-Moon relationships).

What is scientific inquiry? To our group of preservice teachers, scientific inquiry is multifaceted. Scientific inquiry involves inquisitiveness, creativity, and imagination. Such attributes are called habits of mind. Scientific inquiry requires asking intuitive questions, framing a question in the context of available knowledge and experimental evidence, planning investigations, developing and testing hypotheses through experimental procedures and methods (making observations; gathering, interpreting, and analyzing data; inferring; predicting; making judgments), thinking through problems critically and logically, confirming personal theories, sharing ideas, and examining, improving, and changing personal ideas in the light of available evidence. A combination of doing hands-on science, reading science, thinking science, and speaking science (discourse—words and ideas interacting with other words and ideas) contributes to scientific inquiry. These activities should help secondary students develop their own understanding of scientific ideas, know how scientific inquiries are conducted, and learn how findings are validated.

Understanding Science Concepts

Like most preservice teachers, Marilyne focused on the science content knowledge that should be taught.

MARILYNE'S VOICE

> *The science curriculum as I see it is becoming aware of the world around us—at first students look at animals, then they learn to classify them and study their traits and behaviors. Students also learn about things like states of matter—what causes changes: freezing, melting. This grows into more defined chemistry and physics as the years progress. Students also study the earth, its place in the universe, and its neighbors. They learn about rock formations, water cycles, climate, and environments on earth—how they compare and how they support different life forms. Learning about simple machines and motion—levers, pulleys, gears—helps students learn about forces and energy.*

Learning all the topics that Marilyne has described and more is important in science education. Without a basic foundation in the content area, students' personal and societal roles will be less effective. One aim of science education, therefore, is to teach the core knowledge of science in a meaningful way. In each of the science topics, there are a limited number of core concepts and subconcepts. Helping students identify the core

Science as inquiry standards accent the development of (1) student abilities that are necessary to do scientific inquiry and (2) student understandings about scientific inquiry. Abilities include identifying questions and concepts that guide scientific investigations, designing and conducting scientific investigations, using technology and mathematics to improve investigations and communications, formulating and revising scientific explanations and models using logic and evidence, recognizing and analyzing alternative explanations and models, and communicating and defending a scientific argument. Students should understand that scientists do all of these in their scientific inquiry.

Physical science, life science, and earth and space science standards are framed by concepts, principles, theories, models, and laws. Secondary students should see the relationship between scientific ideas and practice. They should translate scientific ideas in investigations.

concept and subconcepts is important. For example, the core concept in a unit on sound is vibration. Subconcepts are frequency, wave, amplitude, and pitch. Students should be able to relate subconcepts to the core concept.

After doing some activities in a particular topic, you will find that a limited number of conceptual structures underpin them. Therefore, the purpose of teaching is not to do exhaustive numbers of hands-on activities so that students will find science is fun. Rather, conceptual meanings must be systematically developed using a few carefully selected activities that represent the core concepts and subconcepts. More important, science activities should be ultimately connected to the core concept through appropriate teaching and learning methods. Although the methods of carrying out science activities must be practiced and scientific attitudes must be developed, it is also important for you to learn how to help students construct meaningful scientific concepts. In pursuit of this, your professional development as a teacher must include ways of deepening your understanding of disciplinary content knowledge.

Integrating Science and Technology

Anna was one of the few preservice teachers who gave prominence to the relationship between science and technology.

Anna's Voice

Students should be introduced to the concept of technology, and they should recognize how important it is in their lives. For students to be able to conduct scientific research, technological devices are important. For example, a microscope reveals the structures within a leaf—parts that are unobservable to the naked eye. The composition of the stars is known through spectroscopic measurements. Telescopes reveal the nature of distant planets. Technological products are countless. They range from simple tweezers, nutcrackers, and toothbrushes to the Hubble telescope and robots. When students participate in scientific activities, they will begin to see their lives in the greater picture of science and technology.

Science is a way of knowing about the natural world and the universe beyond. Technology is how we modify the world to meet human needs. Science is inquiry, whereas technology is design. Technological products are developed to improve our ability to study the world. They include research tools ranging from pencils to computers and books we use to gather, interpret, and disseminate research. Technological needs such as building a rocket can drive scientific research. Social needs, attitudes, and values shape the direction of scientific and technological research and development in every culture.

Science and technology standards highlight the attitude of developing students' abilities for technological design. These abilities include identifying a problem, proposing designs, choosing among alternative solutions, implementing a proposed solution, evaluating the solution and its consequences, and communicating the problem, process, and solution. Students should also understand *about* science and technology. Decision making is integral to technology and design.

Enabling students to devise technical designs that can improve their science investigation is of paramount importance. Technical designers have many factors to consider—the purpose, user criteria, cost, time, trade-offs, material constraints, a plan, human and material resources, and tools and techniques for measurement and accuracy. Once a device is designed, students should be able to identify the stages of problem identification, solution design, implementation, and evaluation.

Connecting Science to Self and Society

Knowing how to interpret natural phenomena using scientific knowledge is not sufficient. Adolescents should see connections between science and technology and societal issues. Ethical concerns, both personal (drinking bottled water) and societal (selecting a land site for garbage disposal) must be considered in science class. *Sustainable development* issues such as maintaining a river or sustaining a forest must be part of science education. Preservice teachers' ideas about science education and society revolve around three important areas:

The U.N. Commission on Sustainable Development describes *sustainable development* as paths of environmental, economic, social, and political progress that meet "the needs of the present without compromising the ability of future generations to meet their own needs" (Uzwyshyn, 1990, p. v).

Relevance/relationship of science to students' worlds
Science-technology-society connections
Sustainable development

Relevance/Relationship of Science to Students' Worlds

MARK'S VOICE
Rather than presenting isolated facts and unrelated concepts, the curriculum should show students the relevance of science to their world and everyday life. Science is an exciting and integral part of our lives and should be presented as such. Students should be able to understand the connections and the influence humans have on their world. It is critical to contextualize science so that students can see relationships between themselves and their living environments.

Science-Technology-Society Connections

FLORENCE'S VOICE
I believe that the curriculum should be flexible enough to incorporate current events. For example, the meltdown of Chernobyl might be a good entry into the study of atomic energy. At the very least, it would stimulate discussion that would be a valuable learning experience. It is also important to show the development of society through science and technology. You might start with the first human explorations and inventions, such as fire and the wheel. Then progressively study more complex and in-depth

topics such as aerodynamics (How do airplanes fly?) and human biology (How does the human body work? What does the human body consist of?). It is important that students understand that science and technology are part of our society.

Sustainable Development

STEVE'S VOICE

I believe that the science curriculum should help students understand their world and their place in this world. Science study includes human relationships to the natural world as one part of the web of life; the environment as it relates to human decision making (reduce, reuse, recycle); learning to stay healthy and disease-free and to deal with current issues such as environmental pollution and the depletion of the ozone layer. Science must relate to students' ability to be responsible and knowledgeable adults.

Aikenhead (1980) argues that a socially and personally relevant science curriculum is more appropriate than a knowledge-based science curriculum for students, most of whom will be future consumers of science rather than producers of it. Similarly, Hurd (1994) contends that science embedded in social and cultural contexts is necessary to prepare "new minds for a new age." Modern adolescents are increasingly aware of world problems because of current developments in media and communications. Hence, we need a science curriculum that our students can live out. Social values and ethical issues should be recognized as relevant dimensions of their science education. Students must be given opportunities to tap into the expertise that natural and social scientists can offer in terms of recognizing as well as learning how to resolve ethical issues. The time has also come to consider the computer as a member of our students' research team for data collection, analysis, organization, and communication.

With a view to changing the course of science education, Hurd (1987) pointed out that (a) values and ethical questions of both a personal and social nature cannot be avoided in science teaching; (b) science teaching should be extended to include skills that are essential to the processing of scientific and technological information of a personal and social nature; (c) students should have an understanding of how to make decisions by selecting policies for action from alternatives, of what risk means, and of how preferences, ethics, and values influence judgment; and (d) at least a portion of science courses should be organized in terms of problems embedded in a personal and societal context. Despite this, studies indicate that regular science classes deal with very few science-related social issues. Why is this so?

Fleming (1986) perceived that scientific knowledge in the context of social issues may be resisted because of teachers' lack of science background/knowledge. Another science- and technology-related social issue is that students have difficulty relating to the uncertainties of value-based issues because of their perception that science is about bits of truth or right answers. Paying attention to sustainable-development issues could provide a context in which students' perceptions of the construction and validation of scientific knowledge can be examined and explored.

Ebenezer and Zoller (1993) argue that more emphasis must be placed on the science teacher's role and teaching style if educational changes in students' awareness of science, technology, and society connections can be achieved. They also point out that for students to develop rational arguments for decision making and to take actions accordingly, teachers must develop and implement appropriate intervention strategies.

Science in personal and social perspectives standards stress that school activities should provide opportunities for secondary students to develop an understanding of personal and community health, population growth, natural resources, environmental quality, natural and human induced hazards, and science and technology in local, national, and global challenges.

⌖ SCIENCE CONTENT STANDARDS

Reform efforts initiated and led by organizations such as the American Association for the Advancement of Science (AAAS) and the Carnegie

TABLE 1-1
Content Standards, Grades 5–8

Unifying Concepts and Processes	Science as Inquiry	Physical Science	Life Science
Systems, order, and organization	Abilities necessary to do scientific inquiry	Properties and changes of properties in matter	Structure and function in living systems
Evidence, models, and explanation	Understandings about scientific inquiry	Motions and forces	Reproduction and heredity
Change, constancy, and measurement		Transfer of energy	Regulation and behavior
Evolution and equilibrium			Populations and ecosystems
Form and function			Diversity and adaptations of organisms

Earth and Space Science	Science and Technology	Science in Personal and Social Perspectives	History and Nature of Science
Structure of the earth system	Abilities of technological design	Personal health	Science as a human endeavor
Earth's history	Understandings about science and technology	Populations, resources, and environments	Nature of science
Earth in the solar system		Natural hazards	History of science
		Risks and benefits	
		Science and technology in society	

NOTE: Reprinted with permission from *National Science Education Standards* (p. 110). Copyright 1996 by the National Academy of Sciences. Courtesy of the National Academy Press, Washington, DC.

Corporation resulted in a number of documents in the 1980s and early 1990s: *A Nation at Risk* (National Commission on Excellence in Education, 1983), *A Nation Prepared* (Carnegie Forum on Education and the Economy, 1986), *Project 2061: Science for All Americans* (AAAS, 1989), and *Benchmarks for Science Literacy* (AAAS, 1993). These reform documents culminated in the establishment of the *National Science Education Standards* (NRC, 1996). These standards indicate contemporary curricular intentions that assist educators in developing science content that students should know, understand, and be able to do in science, providing contextualized teaching and learning experiences for students, and in preparing appropriate assessment standards and procedures. Tables 1-1 and 1-2 sketch what secondary students should have accomplished at the end of grade 8 and grade 12, respectively (NRC, 1996).

The National Science Education Standards should not be considered prescribed curricula. Standards are proposed goals for educators (administrators, curriculum developers, and teachers) who are in the business of developing science curriculum as well as teaching, learning, and assessment strategies.

TABLE 1-2
Content Standards, Grades 9–12

Unifying Concepts and Processes	Science as Inquiry	Physical Science	Life Science
Systems, order, and organization Evidence, models, and explanation Change, constancy, and measurement Evolution and equilibrium Form and function	Abilities necessary to do scientific inquiry Understandings about scientific inquiry	Structure of atoms Structure and properties of matter Chemical reactions Motions and forces Conservation of energy and increase in disorder Interactions of energy and matter	The cell Molecular basis of heredity Biological evolution Interdependence of organisms Matter, energy, and organization in living systems Behavior of organisms

Earth and Space Science	Science and Technology	Science in Personal and Social Perspectives	History and Nature of Science
Energy in the earth system Geochemical cycles Origin and evolution of the earth system Origin and evolution of the universe	Abilities of technological design Understandings about science and technology	Personal and community health Population growth Natural resources Environmental quality Natural and human-induced hazards Science and technology in local, national, and global challenges	Science as a human endeavor Nature of scientific knowledge Historical perspectives

NOTE: Reprinted with permission from *National Science Education Standards* (p. 111). Copyright 1996 by the National Academy of Sciences. Courtesy of the National Academy Press, Washington, DC.

✪ SCIENTIFIC LITERACY

Science content standards have been developed to empower all students to have equal opportunities to become scientifically literate. *Scientific literacy* means learning the major science ideas and concepts in life, physical, and earth sciences; seeing the reasoning behind the relationships among ideas; understanding how these ideas can be used to explain and predict other natural phenomena; and translating ideas to novel events. How scientific knowledge is constructed and validated is part of scientific literacy. Students should be able to translate the modes of scientific inquiry, rules of evidence, ways of formulating questions, and ways of proposing explanations to make informed decisions in science-related social and ethical matters (NRC, 1996). The following unit format (Ebenezer & Connor, 1998) is designed to implement the *National Science Education Standards*.

✪ A SCIENCE UNIT FORMAT

We have included the following unit format in the first chapter so that you can use it as a framework for what you will be learning in subsequent chapters. Using this framework, a complete unit on photosynthesis is presented in Chapter 15. In relevant chapters we will ask you to focus on Chapter 15 so that you will learn how to incorporate appropriate pedagogical elements in different lesson plans.

Author(s)

Write the author's name.

Curriculum

State the program(s) of science that you are using.

Grade Level

Indicate the grade level for which the unit is intended.

Nature of Students

Know your students. Ask yourself: "Whom will I be teaching?" Describe any special characteristics or considerations you need to make for the unit.

Purpose of Unit

What are the purposes of teaching this unit? Briefly describe.

Overview

Integral to science pedagogy is the teacher content knowledge of the discipline by Shulman (1986).

The *zone of proximal development* is the mental space in which a learner moves from assisted learning of a concept, skill, and the like to individual competence. The expert teacher guides the novice learner in attaining higher conceptual ideas (see Chapter 3 for a detailed discussion of Vygotsky's zone of proximal development).

Describe and justify major goals in the unit. What major ideas need to be developed or addressed? Your justification should reflect scientific knowledge; scientific attitudes; attitudes toward science, technology, society, and environment (STSE) issues; and historical connections. The *National Science Education Standards* (NRC, 1996) and your district program guide should help you determine the preceding goals.

Curricular Content Development

Science Content Knowledge

With the aid of theoretical diagrams, clearly discuss the scientific ideas you wish to teach. This provides focus, organization, and an understanding of the entire topic or unit for both you and your students, which helps students transverse the "zone of proximal development." Include proper references if you are copying experts' science ideas from books, and create a bibliography that cites all references, including page numbers.

Historical Context
Situate your unit within historical and sociopolitical contexts. Identify the scientist(s) who contributed to the development of your unit's scientific ideas. For example, explore the questions, "How did Franklin study the nature of static electricity? What were some of the social, cultural, and political influences in Franklin's work?"

Technological and Societal Context of Inquiry
Identify technological and societal contexts in your unit. How do these contexts relate to your school community? Situate your unit within a local or global problem context. What technological products or processes are relevant to this unit? Grant students opportunities to become inventors.

Teaching and Learning Approaches
What teaching and learning approaches do you plan to use in this unit? For example, you might incorporate the following:

- Collaborative, reflective scientific inquiry in cooperative groups
- Experiments, discussions, argument, negotiation, social consensus
- Journal writing, drawing, research reporting
- Representation of knowledge structures through concept and Vee mapping
- Symbolizing qualitative understandings with quantitative, mathematical problem solving
- Presentation of contextual historical problems
- Issue-centered approach to studying STSE issues
- Multimedia computer technology (CDs, videodiscs, etc.)
- Problem solving and inventions as ways of exploring design technology

The Common Knowledge Construction Model
Phase I: Exploring and Categorizing
Exploration Activities. Design initial activities to find out what ideas, meanings, understandings, views, and questions your students have about a natural phenomenon or a science-related issue. Describe activities and ways of exploring students' conceptions using the **POE method,** for example, or explore students' views of an issue using TV or newspaper excerpts. Include key questions, materials, and procedures.

You can also write the activities and procedures to suit STSE lessons, historical lessons, and design technology lessons. The fundamental notion is that the learning should be *interactive*.

You may organize your content knowledge using analogies, concept maps, and Vee diagrams. (See Chapter 7 for information on charting analogies and Chapter 8 for step-by-step procedures for drawing concept maps and Vee diagrams. Computer software is now available for concept mapping. Try it. You will enjoy! (See Chapter 10.)

The common knowledge construction model, which is the heart of the unit plan outlined in this chapter, consists of four interactive phases:
- Exploring and categorizing
- Constructing and negotiating
- Translating and extending
- Reflecting and assessing

We explore the theoretical frameworks for the common knowledge construction model in Chapter 14. We also illustrate the interplay of multiple voices in a sequence of lessons on oxidation and reduction developed by two preservice teachers.

An exploring and categorizing lesson format may consist of the following pedagogical elements: objectives, materials/resources, exploration activity, categorizing student's conceptions, relating student's conceptions to curricular ideas, teacher reflections, and direction for subsequent work.

POE stands for *predict, observe,* and *explain*. It is a popular method for exploring students' ideas. We will discuss this method in detail in Chapter 5.

Each lesson may not begin with student conceptions. But take every opportunity to use students' questions and ideas.

Exploring and categorizing students' ideas are based on Ferrence Marton's work on *phenomenography* (Marton, 1981), an assessment tool discussed in Chapter 14.

If you are not able to work with students to explore their ideas as part of your methods course, examine the literature on students' conceptions to gather students' ideas of a particular topic. A book entitled *Making Sense of Secondary Science: Research into Children's Ideas* by Driver et al. (1994) is another excellent resource for students' ideas.

Categorizing Students' Conceptions. Make sure you use students' ideas from the initial activities. Organize or categorize students' conceptions/views, providing examples of students' verbal, written, and pictorial responses.

Relating Students' Conceptions to Curricular Ideas. Present curricular ideas, teacher-made categories, and students' ideas in tabular format as follows:

Curricular Ideas	Teacher-Made Categories	Students' Conceptions

In this chart denote the following:

- Students' conceptions that make sense
- Students' conceptions that need to be explored further
- Additional curricular content—science or societal attitudes that need to be learned

Some science education research journals that carry articles on students' conceptions are *International Journal of Science Education, Journal of Research in Science Teaching,* and *Science Education.*

Teacher Reflections. Reflect on what you have learned about your students and their ideas. Speculate about the sources of students' conceptions. Did they use analogies and metaphors? Relate your findings of students' conceptions to previous research findings on the same topic by quoting at least one research article in science education.

Direction for Subsequent Work. Based on your students' conceptions and the research findings, draw general conclusions about direction for subsequent work.

Phase II: Constructing and Negotiating
Design lessons that are relevant to students' initial ideas.

1. The lessons and activities should help students develop strategies to confirm as well as expand upon their initial ideas; this gives them confidence in their own knowledge. For example, if students say that water

consists of one part of hydrogen and two parts of oxygen, use the electrolysis of water to show them the ratio in which hydrogen and oxygen combine to form water.

2. The lessons and activities should help students develop strategies to clarify their own ideas. For example, if students do not understand why water is a good solvent, discuss the polar nature of water.

Title of Lesson. Write the title of your lesson. The title can be very creative and may reflect student ideas or curricular ideas.

Students' Conceptions or Views. Write at least one student conception or view of students from the chart you prepared during the exploration phase. State how you will help students become aware of their ideas. For example, you may wish to display students' ideas on chart paper in your classroom. Point to this chart when you address one or more of their ideas.

Discussion. Write a statement of justification of students' conceptions and curricular ideas. For example, many secondary school students state that plants need energy to grow and that plants get the energy from their food. Many students also believe that plants get their food from the soil via the roots. Hence, the idea that plants manufacture food through a biochemical process known as photosynthesis must be made intelligible.

Objectives. Objectives set the tone and must include specific action verbs. For example, begin each objective by stating that students will *experience, measure, manipulate, build, classify, characterize, speculate, identify, verify, compare and contrast, hypothesize, predict, assess,* and so on. Do not use general terms such as *understand, know,* and *explain* in objectives, for these are embedded in any educational objective.

Teaching and Learning Approaches. State the teaching and learning strategies you will use in this lesson: investigation, POE, journal writing, drawing diagrams, peer sharing, large-group sharing, and so on.

Materials and Resources. List the materials and resources you need for this activity. Items for an experimental activity, such as chart paper, a journal, and books, might be included.

Activities and Procedures. When you write the procedure for the lesson, imagine that you have a class of students. How will you organize the activities and students so that optimum learning will take place? This planning depends on the nature of learners, activities, subject matter, materials and resources, space, and time. Classroom management must be carefully considered to promote teacher-student interaction and peer science "doing" and discussion. In other words, how will you engage students in classroom discourse during scientific inquiry?

Assessment. What is the outcome of this lesson? Have you accomplished your objectives for this lesson? How will you assess student understanding?

Reflection. Based on your lesson plan, speculate on how the lesson will achieve what you have set out to do. Will the lesson motivate students to

You may want to compare students' ideas to early scientists' ideas. For example, most students think and also talk as if heat is a substance that flows from one area to another or into and out of objects: "Heat flows like a fluid." A study of Lavoisier's caloric view of heat would be useful. Then you can present the currently accepted view of heat.

The following headings are important for the lesson plan on constructing and negotiating: students' conceptions, discussion, objectives, teaching and learning approaches, materials and resources, activities and procedures, assessment, and reflections.

Chapters 5–13 include many teaching, learning, and assessment strategies.

learn science concepts? Will students practice some of the processes of science (for example, learn to use a weighing scale or adjust a microscope)? If you have an opportunity to teach, ask yourself the following questions: How did the lesson go? What was puzzling? Were there surprises? What would you do differently? How did the students respond to the lesson?

Phase III: Translating and Extending

The lessons and activities should accomplish some of the following:

The pedagogical elements in an STSE lesson format are the same as in the "constructing and negotiating" phase. However, issue-based STSE lessons must reflect problem-solving attributes such as decision making and action taking. Design technology–based STSE lessons should incorporate problem-solving elements of the design process (see Chapter 9 for details).

Carry out your plan. Be flexible! Remember, science is not smooth and structured. Your unit will change as you continue to incorporate students' ideas. Always remember to check whether the students have made meaningful connections to your activities, teacher-student jointly planned activities, textual materials, and multimedia representations.

1. *Make STSE connections.* How does solution chemistry relate to societal issues such as pollution?
2. *Recognize cultural contributions.* A chemistry unit on solutions could easily result in exploring the uses of solutions in the world of medicine and in the manufacturing of soft drinks in different cultures.
3. *Incorporate design technology.* Lessons could revolve around design technology.

Phase IV: Reflecting and Assessing

Assess as you go along (continuous assessment). Have students gather or collect their notes in one journal; store concept maps, diagrams, and the like in an ongoing portfolio. Use this feedback to structure your lessons. Plan to assess each activity and the topic or unit according to the most appropriate method for the occasion. Select methods of assessment that will help students reflect on what they have learned, and tie the concepts together. Some examples are performance-based tests, concept mapping, student-teacher conferencing, written tests, oral presentations, self-evaluations, peer evaluations, anecdotal records, and classroom charts.

Prepare specific culminating (end-of-unit) assessment activities and strategies for your unit. These may consist of performance activities such as investigations, projects, or creative drama.

⊠ CHAPTER REVIEW

In this chapter we have given a "big picture," or a conceptual view of what school science should look like. We have introduced the concept of "science for all" and outlined how science education can help secondary students be lifelong learners in the pursuit of scientific literacy. We have also discussed what is involved in becoming a scientifically literate person. From the preservice teachers' point of view, we have focused on four main curricular emphases: the nature of scientific inquiry, the understanding of science concepts, the relationship between science and technology, and the relevance of science to personal and social issues. We have also highlighted the science content standards of the National Research Council. These standards are illustrated with a unit format that will be a framework for your subsequent learning.

PROBES

1. How do you propose to reach *all* students?
2. What would you like to emphasize in science education?
3. What voices in science education do you recognize in the unit format presented in this chapter? Think about your teacher education program to answer this question.

CHAPTER 2

Science and Scientific Inquiry for Understanding

STUDY QUESTIONS

1. What are some words that come to mind when you think about scientific inquiry?

2. What are some of the major contemporary views of scientific inquiry?

3. How is scientific inquiry carried out in schools?

Reflective Inquiry

JOURNAL ACTIVITY

Conceptions of Science

Record your conceptions of science (what does science mean to you?) by considering the following questions:

1. What would you say is the goal of scientific inquiry?
2. What do you think is the role of theory in science?
3. Explain your view of how scientists pursue scientific inquiry.
4. How would you say scientific knowledge is evaluated and accredited?
5. What do you think it takes to be a good scientist?

All but the second question are similar to those proposed by Claxton (1991, p. 59). Claxton suggests that "what science is" is addressed by these five questions, each of which should be considered separately.

On the first day of class in a science teaching methods course, preservice teachers were asked to write what science meant to them. During subsequent class discussions five major issues were identified: What is the goal of scientific inquiry? What is the role of theory in science? How do scientists pursue scientific inquiry? How is scientific knowledge evaluated and accredited? What does it take to be a good scientist? We will consider these issues in this chapter. Before you read further, please complete the journal activity on the previous page.

In this chapter we explore views of the scientific enterprise. We begin by looking at the issues raised in the preceding questions, considering what other preservice science teachers have said about these matters. The latter part of the chapter briefly considers four key philosophers (Bacon, Popper, Kuhn, and Lakatos) and looks at some of the implications of their views of science for teaching.

⚛ THE NATURE OF SCIENCE AND SCIENTIFIC INQUIRY

YVES'S VOICE
Science is everything around us.

MARK'S VOICE
Science means the scientific method.

Each of these statements by preservice teachers contains one of the two common notions of science that characterized most of the responses: (1) science is the study of everything around us, and (2) science is using the traditional scientific method. Did you include one or both of these ideas in your statement of what science means to you? We have seen that preservice teachers like you often have a number of different views about the nature of science. Similarly, science teachers, science educators, scientists, and philosophers of science have put forward different views. Why is this so, and what does it mean for you as a future science teacher?

Knowing Science, Understanding Science

Philosophers and others have written extensively about the nature of knowledge, that is, about *epistemology*. Greene (1994) lists the following issues of concern to those who would explore such ideas:

> what constitutes knowledge, what validates knowledge claims, how "truth" is to be defined, how social and cultural conditions affect scientific investigations, how "understanding" differs from "knowledge," what "meaning" signifies, and what belief systems and locations in the world have to do with the determination of what is taken to be "real" and "true." (p. 425)

Early philosophers differed on the source of knowledge and hence on what constitutes knowledge. Plato and Descartes, for example, believed that reason was the source, whereas Aristotle and John Locke believed that only experience could lead to knowledge.

Fenstermacher (1994) described a range of views about what it means to *know*. A traditional epistemological view of knowledge is that three conditions must be met before one can be said to know something. A person *S* knows *p* if and only if

p is true;
S believes *p;* and
S had valid justification for believing that *p* is true.

In contrast, Alexander, Schallert, & Hare (1991) have suggested that

knowledge refers to an individual's personal stock of information, skills, experiences, beliefs, and memories. This knowledge is always idiosyncratic, reflecting the vagaries of a person's own history . . . [it] encompasses all that a person knows or believes to be true, whether or not it is verified as true in some sort of objective or external way. (p. 317)

These authors suggest that it is not necessary to distinguish between beliefs and knowledge, that it does not matter whether a belief is true. However, Fenstermacher (1994) concludes that truth is important if one wishes to make any "epistemic claims" about a statement. He gives an example similar to the following: If Susie were to state, "Harry's car is in the garage," there are various levels of certainty that might be behind her statement. Susie may have seen Harry park his car in the garage moments before; she may know that Harry always parks his car in the garage; or she may believe that a person like Harry would not leave his car sitting out on the street. The justification for the truth of the statement that Harry's car is in the garage is strongest in the first instance and weakest in the third.

Similarly, learners have different levels of justification for the knowledge they acquire when learning science in school (or any other learning). For example, a ninth-grade student may memorize a definition of thermal energy and believe he knows what thermal energy is. However, if he is unable to solve problems that require an understanding of thermal energy, the limitations of his "knowledge" are revealed.

 PEER TALK

Understanding Science

A ninth-grade class was studying a unit on heat and temperature (Haggerty, 1986). A major objective for the unit was for the students to learn to distinguish between heat and temperature. Their textbook offered definitions similar to the following: Temperature is a measure of the average mechanical energy of the particles; heat is a measure of the total mechanical energy of the particles. The students duly memorized the textbook definitions. When they wrote the usual test at the end of the unit, most were able to state the definitions correctly, but very few were able to apply their "knowledge" to explain the following correctly:

> A large ice cube and a small ice cube were left on the counter. The small ice cube melted faster than the large ice cube. Does that mean that the large ice cube took more heat to melt than the small ice cube? Explain your answer.

How would you explain why the large ice cube took longer to melt? Did the students "know" the difference between heat and temperature? Did they "understand" the difference? Do you?

The students in the preceding example believed they "knew" about heat and temperature. They were able to correctly define them on the test. However, a traditional philosopher/epistemologist would say their belief was neither true nor justified. Alternatively, if those same students were asked if they "understood" the difference between heat and temperature, most of them would agree they did not. Students readily distinguish between knowing and understanding. For them, knowing means being able to give the correct answer, even if what they "know" has been learned by rote and they do not understand what it means. They believe it because an authority—their textbook and/or their teacher—has told them it is so.

Elgin (1996) has considered this dilemma of the contrast between knowledge and understanding. She examines the traditional usage of the term *knowledge* to refer to what people know about science:

> [To use the term] "knowledge" would be unwise on several counts. . . . [B]y tradition, knowledge is a permanent achievement, its justification unconditional and insensitive to changes . . . knowledge by tradition implies truth. So a falsehood, however reasonable and illuminating, is never knowledge. But a falsehood might well be incorporated into a system . . . to good effect.
>
> Objects in a vacuum fall toward the Earth at a rate of 32 ft/sec^2
>
> is not strictly true since it neglects the gravitational attraction of everything except the Earth. Still, it provides genuine insight into the behavior of falling bodies. . . . It is . . . valuable, even if its falsity disqualifies it as knowledge. . . . "Understanding" is a better term. . . . Not being restricted to facts, understanding is more comprehensive than knowledge ever hoped to be. (pp. 122–123)

For science learners, simplifying a phenomenon often makes it much simpler to understand and to work with. If the learner had to take account of all of the relevant variables in his or her calculations on falling objects, it would be quite incomprehensible.

As a prospective science teacher, you may wonder why the nature of knowledge and knowing should be of such concern. Surely all that is needed is to define what we mean when we use the term *knowledge* and then get on with it. However, as for the ninth-grade students learning about heat and temperature, it is one thing for us to be able to repeat a definition of *knowledge,* and quite another thing to internalize or understand its meaning sufficiently to act consistently upon that meaning. Such action is important because research about teaching suggests that our views of knowledge and knowing may be related to how we represent and teach science (Brickhouse, 1990; Gallagher, 1991) and that the language we use to present scientific ideas may have an impact on our students' conceptions of the nature of science. If our underlying views have not been made explicit, their impact on our thinking is likely to be unconscious, and that may lead to inconsistencies in how we approach our teaching (Zeidler & Lederman, 1989). In a literature review, Lederman (1992) examined a number of studies that investigated views of the nature of science and concluded that "it appears that the most important variables that influence students' beliefs about the nature of science are those specific instructional behaviors, activities, and decisions implemented within the context of a lesson" (p. 351). It is important that the strategies we use in our teaching reflect an appropriate view of science and scientific inquiry.

In this book we will think of learning science as learning to *understand* science, and the results of that learning process will be refered to as *understanding* rather than *knowledge*. That is, we consider the goal of school science to be understanding science. Now let us look at how science is viewed in science textbooks and classrooms.

School Science

Nearly four decades ago, the noted science educator Joseph J. Schwab observed that in most textbooks, science

> is taught as nearly unmitigated rhetoric of conclusions in which the current and temporary constructions of scientific knowledge are conveyed as empirical, literal, and irrevocable truths. (Schwab, 1962, p. 24)

Is this true of today's textbooks? By reading between the lines we can infer the view of science that is being portrayed in science textbooks. In most cases textbooks present science knowledge as if it were factual and permanent. They may state that scientific theories and ideas have changed in the past, but the tentative and open-ended nature of knowledge is not reflected in the description of current scientific knowledge (Gallagher, 1991).

As an alternative, Schwab (1962) advocated a "narrative of inquiry" (p. 88) view of science, in which problems are posed, actual scientific data are presented, and scientists' interpretations of the data are given. The student is thus taken on a scientific journey, along with the scientist. Although Schwab expressed this concern so many years ago, most textbooks still reflect a "rhetoric of conclusions" view of science, or what Gallagher refers to as "revealed truth" (1991, p. 123).

TEACHER PRACTICE

Portrayal of the Nature of Scientific Inquiry in Science Textbooks
Choose any science textbook that is currently used in your local schools and examine how the science content is presented. Is there any indication of the tentative nature of current scientific knowledge, of science as a narrative of inquiry? Or is science presented as a rhetoric of conclusions? Find some examples in the textbook you have chosen that illustrate how science is portrayed.

DON'S VOICE

[In my science classes] I was used to the speech, the person getting up there, putting two words on the chalkboard all day and just talking.

Don's memories of his high school science classes were memories of listening to his teacher talk and copying notes from the board. This is a common experience for secondary science students. With increased public demands for accountability in education, teachers have become increasingly conscious of pressure to "cover the content." The safest way to ensure that the required content is covered seems to be to transmit "science facts," and to ensure that the students have "good notes." Once again we see science presented as a rhetoric of conclusions, rather than a narrative of inquiry. This approach denies the critical spirit of science.

One frequently taught aspect of science content is "*the* scientific method." As Gallagher (1991) notes, the scientific method is often presented as one of the first topics in a course. It is typically presented as a specific set of stages (hypothesis, experiment, conclusion) and is then ignored throughout the remainder of the course unless it surfaces as a format for writing up science "experiments."

School science is different from research science, or "scientists' science." Research science is what scientists do. The way school science is presented is important because it conveys a message of what research science is about.

THE ROLE OF THEORY IN SCIENCE

The role of theory is probably among the least understood aspects of the scientific enterprise. This question elicited a variety of responses from the preservice teachers, and a number of interesting ideas appeared in these responses. Did your response to the theory question agree with any of the following ideas about the role of theory in science? Think about whether you agree or disagree with each of these ideas and compare them to your own response before reading on:

QUENTIN'S VOICE

*The role of theory in science is to give the base knowledge to the
student so he or she can understand why something is happening.*

FRAN'S VOICE

*Theory is an attempt to explain the phenomena of science in words
to support ideas of science. Theory presents ideas concerning the
world of science.*

Quentin seems to be saying that theory is the basic scientific knowledge or content that is taught, and that providing students with the
content results in student understanding. Fran's response is similar—that
theory is the verbalization of scientific ideas. This view is reflected in a
common approach to teaching science: some "theoretical" information is
taught or presented to the students (for example, the role of chlorophyll
in a leaf) so that they will learn that content. Students then perform an
"experiment" that illustrates or "proves" that the content (that is, the
"theory") is true (perhaps covering a portion of a leaf for a few hours
and then testing for starch). The students recognize that there is a correct answer that they are expected to find as a result of their experiment.
Essentially, the experiment is used to verify what has already been
accepted by the scientific community.

YVES'S VOICE

*Theory is often the first attempt to describe a naturally occurring
event. Following theory, experiments can be devised to hopefully
prove the theory.*

URSULA'S VOICE

*The role of theory in science is to be the starting point from which
investigations will be made. A theory is an explanation of why
things are the way they are. Based on theory, applications of science
are made to improve the quality of man's life.*

ERICA'S VOICE

*Theories are essential to science. They give a basis from which we can
hypothesize and test scientific phenomena. Theories can lead to laws
and total understanding of how a system works.*

LEN'S VOICE

[Theory] is the proven model that is a universal truth.

Yves and Ursula suggest that theory is the basis for experiments that attempt to prove the theory to be true. These responses refer to the role of theory in research science, rather than in school science. However, experiments are still viewed as attempts to *verify* theories, as often occurs in school science activities. An extension of this idea is seen in the claims made by Erica and Len. Erica says that theories "can lead to laws and total understanding" and Len says that theory "is the proven model that is a universal truth." This notion—that hypotheses form the basis of experiments whose results lead to theories, and that theories are then subjected to further experimentation, finally becoming proven laws—is a common view of how research science is conducted. This view of science implies an experiment-based teaching approach, with the purpose of the experiment being to test a hypothesis or a theory in order to prove it to be true. As before, verification is the objective.

Vic's Voice

Theory is necessary in order to give some explanation of the processes behind some phenomenon.

Nancy's Voice

Theory in science is needed to explain what you see in a hands-on experiment. When you hypothesize something and then results occur, theory is what helps you to understand the why/how/etc.

Vic and Nancy view theory as a basis for explaining various phenomena. In Nancy's view, the experiment comes first, and then theory is used to explain the results of the experiment. A fundamental difference in this view is that there is no predetermined correct answer. Rather, observations are made and then the theory is drawn upon to provide an explanation for the findings.

Facts and Theories: A Spectrum

Science is filled with ideas—theories and explanations that help us understand how and why things came to be. Claxton (1991) suggests that theories consist of "hypothetical influences and invisible entities" (p. 61) such as quarks, gravity, momentum, and continental drift. For example, we know that apples fall to the ground as evidence of gravity.

Science may be thought of as consisting of two types of knowledge: "facts" that have been discovered as a result of observation and experimentation, and "theories." A common-sense view is that facts precede theories. School science teaches us to first arrive at facts and then to account for those facts: Perception (observing) comes first and then comes conception (thinking). Thinking is when we interpret what we have seen; our interpretations are based on our experiences and our needs.

Claxton does not distinguish between fact and theory, seeing and interpreting, or observation and interpretation. These are not at two opposite poles; rather, they exist on a spectrum or continuum. Statements such as "The heart pumps blood around the body," "Wires of different thickness have different electrical resistance," and "Copper sulfate crystals are blue" may seem like statements of fact. But these were novel ideas when they were first proposed. For example, 350 years ago, William Harvey proposed that the heart was a pump. It was not a self-evident fact at the time; "The heart is a pump" was a startling hypothesis and it took several years for scientists to accept this novel idea. Similarly, the rotation of the Earth and other planets in the solar system around the Sun is a fact to us. But to sixteenth-century intellectuals, this idea was preposterous, and they had valid arguments for their beliefs. We speak of electrical resistance in terms of an intrinsic property of wires, and yet "it is equally a theoretical notion which expresses the relationship between the 'potential difference' applied to the ends of the wire, and the strength of current which then flows through it" (Claxton, 1991, p. 63). Similarly, the fact that copper sulfate crystals are blue can be given meaning only within the conceptual frameworks of "compounds" and "crystalline structure." To a high school student, the chemical conceptual structures underscoring the observation that copper sulfate crystals turn white when heated may seem to be a fact. But to a chemist, the idea that "the crystalline structure breaks down when the bound molecules of H_2O are driven off as steam, leaving an anhydrous powder which does not absorb light of same wavelengths [is only a theoretical proposal]" (Claxton, 1991, p. 63). Hence, science to most of us is observations or self-evident descriptions, but to scientists the reasoning or the *why* of things is theory. In people's minds, theoretical ideas are truths. Scientists have shown what matter is really like, although we cannot see it. "[L]ittle balls of negative electricity that revolve around a tiny but very dense core in definite orbits, like the planets around the sun" (Claxton, 1991, p. 63) is only the textbook representation of the atomic model that helps individuals understand the structure of the atom.

You may now wish to revise your journal response to the question about the role of theory in science. If so, please make a note about why you changed your mind.

THE PURSUIT OF SCIENCE KNOWLEDGE

The preservice teachers were also asked: How do scientists go about doing science? Most of their responses dealt with experimentation and testing theories. For example:

VIC'S VOICE

People in science are trying to better understand the nature of their universe. They go about it by proposing theories and testing the theories with experiments.

URSULA'S VOICE

People in science have a theory. They experiment to prove or disprove this theory. From the results of their investigations they modify the theory or add to it.

Vic and Ursula seem to hold Popper's view of scientific knowledge generation—that is, to look for observations that would disconfirm an idea or conjecture and make one abandon his or her idea, modify it, or make it more precise. Popper's view is one view of how scientific knowledge is generated and will be discussed later in this chapter. Lakatos, whose views will also be discussed, addresses the notion of modifying theories when anomalous experimental results are obtained.

Claxton pictures the scientific method as consisting of several layers (see Figure 2-1). The core of a scientific activity involves a certain type of thinking, the interaction of three focal activities: observing, generating ideas, and testing ideas. The activities and ideas vary in different fields of science and go on under the influence of three surrounding contexts: the personal context (personality and temperament of the indi-

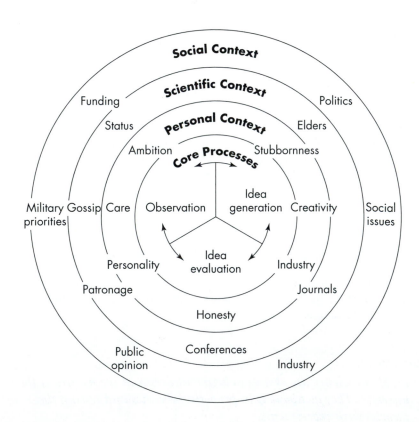

FIGURE 2-1

The nature of scientific activity (*NOTE:* From *Educating the Inquiring Mind: The Challenge for School Science* (p. 69), by G. Claxton, 1991, London: Harvester Wheatsheaf. Copyright 1991 by Harvester Wheatsheaf Reprinted with permission.)

vidual scientist), the scientific context (the scientist working within his or her community of expert scientists), and the social context (scientists working amid the influences of social pressures and political/economic decisions).

Claxton (1991) notes that science is not clearly defined. Scientists attempt to generate accounts for natural phenomena that provide a basis for accurate predictions. Scientific inquiry involves reflective and intuitive thought, as well as creativity, logical thinking, rational problem solving, and hypothetico-deductive thinking. School science has the option of focusing on many different or interactive aspects of science.

The National Research Council (1996) has included the study of the nature of scientific inquiry as one of the seven standards. They advocate making a conscious effort to teach authentic ways of conducting science. The standards also suggest that the "true" nature of scientific inquiry should be part of students' school experience in science class, in lessons, in labs, and in projects. Idea generation and the evolutionary nature of science, the influence of nonrational personal and social factors, and the special skills of "messing about" and reflection in action must be stressed in high school science.

What image of science should students have? To what extent is it "necessary and appropriate for secondary school students to be introduced to the complex world of real scientific activity" (Claxton, 1991, p. 58)? Claxton also asks whether teachers should address the nature of science, or whether "an image of science is better conveyed by practice, example, and demonstration" (p. 58). These are questions for you to ponder as you read through this chapter.

☒ THE EVALUATION AND ACCREDITATION OF SCIENTIFIC KNOWLEDGE

BECKY'S VOICE

Science is to hypothesize about a particular process or principle; and to support theories, experimentation is done to prove whether an idea is correct or not.

FRAN'S VOICE

[Scientists] approach science in a sequential way. Step by step. Logic and reason, without emotional interference.

How do scientists decide what scientific knowledge, understandings, and theories are valid or credible? Becky suggests that experiments "prove" whether an idea is correct. She does not consider the possibility of ambiguity in experimental results themselves. But what if experiments conducted by different people or at different times yield different results? Fran believes that science is completely logical and rational. There is no potential for ambiguity because there is no "emotional interference" in doing science. Upon reflection, most of us recognize that it is not that simple! How do scientists decide when it is appropriate to accept some claims and to reject others?

According to Popper and Lakatos, scientific knowledge is never certain, although it steadily comes closer to reality. The quality of scientific ideas should gradually improve; those that survive experimental testing linger, and those that are refuted do not. The process of scientific development has been compared to natural selection, or "survival of the fittest." A theory or a new line of inquiry becomes established and accepted on the basis of the quality of research as well as on how it is promoted.

What counts as scientific knowledge is influenced by decisions and actions of communities of scientists. Scientific papers are submitted to academic journals and to scientific conferences; they are judged by rational criteria that underlie the currently accepted theoretical assumptions, and must be within the parameters of those established tacit presuppositions to gain acceptance. Editors and referees of academic journals, academic colleagues, publishers' academic consultants, and graduate student committees and examiners all exercise quality control over whose work is promoted and what gets published. Whether a scientific paper is accepted for publication is determined by members of a committee that evaluates how the research was conducted. The primary focus is on the actions of the experimenter rather than on the results of the experiment per se.

Scientific ideas are tested on the basis of their consistency and coherency as well as their ability to account for what is already known. From scientific ideas we should also be able to predict or expect the unknown. Popper's hypothetico-deductive theory of logically extrapolating from known ideas to derive predictions about unknown or unexplored phenomena is important in the evaluation of scientific ideas. However, the Popperian scientific method, although important, portrays only one approach to scientific thinking and does not give us any guidance in how we should judge between two or more competing scientific theories or explanations. As we will see later in the chapter, for that we must turn to Thomas Kuhn.

There are also, of course, external, nonscientific influences on scientific progress. Social attitudes determine the topics that society considers worthwhile. For example, funding is currently available to conduct applied research in areas such as AIDS and cancer, whereas pure theoretical research is not being adequately supported. Different priorities and mechanisms for funding scientific research depend on the views of the politicians in power. Scientists, like the rest of us, live in a world of financial fluctuations and constraints.

✖ WHAT DOES IT TAKE TO BE A GOOD SCIENTIST?

MARK'S VOICE

> *[It takes] curiosity about all that we see, questioning those things we do not understand. Science for me is a continuous process of learning about those things in our world.*

FRAN'S VOICE

> *Trying to prove theories of why things work the way they do. [Scientists] approach science in a sequential way. Step by step. Logic and reason, without emotional interference.*

Mark considers curiosity and questioning to be the most important attributes of a good scientist. If the scientist cannot recognize a problem, there will be no efforts to solve that problem. He believes attitudes are important. Fran, on the other hand, rejects any "emotional interference" in doing science. Science is logical, like *Star Trek*'s Mr. Spock.

The Role of Reason and Rationality

Although science is overlaid with social control and personal investment, Claxton (1991) suggests it is "characterized and finally judged by its ability to see where ideas lead, in terms of observable implications rather than to direct them and promote them in terms of one's personal preferences" (p. 70). Needs and desires come into play in science. But the value of scientific thinking, although fallible, lies in its commitment to account for observations. Scientific thinking claims to be dissociated from personal motivation, relevance, and gain. However, as history shows us, the pursuit of knowledge based on scientific thinking disconnected from human values and purposes can produce ideas and inventions that are harmful, with dangerous and life-threatening side effects.

F. Ellett, Jr. (personal communication, December 22, 1997) suggests that Aristotle's rational virtues provide a solid basis for recognizing good science. Those virtues may be described as follows:

Practical wisdom: The ability to exercise sound judgment and discernment
Justice: The capacity to consider all alternatives fairly
Courage: The strength of character required to risk embarrassment, criticism, and alienation to advocate what one believes in
Temperance: The trait that keeps one pursuing scientific values in one's work, undeterred by external concerns
Hope: The mean between despair or cynicism and presumption

Faith: Trust in genuine authority and willingness to speak on its behalf
Love: A deep commitment to the internal values and standards of the scientific endeavor

The last three of these virtues (faith, hope, and love [or charity]) are particularly well known and are frequently cited in western culture.

Claxton (1991) identified three core processes of science: observation, evaluation, and generation. The latter two have already been discussed, and the first warrants consideration as well.

The Role of Empirical Observation

Scientific thinking is inextricably linked to observation. Scientists develop their ideas with respect to ongoing observations. Formal deduction is important, but it is the habit of careful observation that distinguishes the scientist from the logician or the mathematician. However, what scientists observe and record is by no means clear-cut and unbiased. There are always questions, hunches, theories, and hypotheses behind their observations, and these guiding frameworks are not necessarily well formulated or conscious. Observation is continually driven by human interest and motivation. It is critical that we recognize the significance of human preconceptions and how these influence our perception of the world, including our scientific observations. Scientists, like everyone else, are influenced by their beliefs and assumptions as they conduct their scientific inquiries. Bacon and other inductivists ignored the human inclination to view the natural world in terms of personal theories and beliefs, but this notion can no longer be considered credible. Now we will look at some of the key philosophers and sociohistorians of science in more detail and consider the implications of their views for how we teach science.

 TEACHER PRACTICE

Analyzing Science Activities

Electricity makes many people uneasy; we are raised from infancy to fear electricity. Here are three examples of how the topic of electrical circuits might be taught. The first two examples are from science textbooks, for grades 9 and 10, respectively. The third is taken from the Elementary Science Study, a program developed in the 1960s for elementary classrooms, but equally appropriate for preservice teachers who have already completed a degree in science. The third activity was used with a group of preservice biology teachers, some of whom had previously taught a unit on electricity during their practice teaching, using a standard textbook approach.

Grade 9 Textbook Example

ACTIVITY 2-1

BUILDING A FLASHLIGHT

PART A

Problem

How can you make a simple flashlight?

Materials

2 D-size cells
holder for 1 cell
holder for 2 cells
small lamp
1.5 V bulb
2 V bulb
3 V bulb
connnecting wires

Procedure

1. Connect the small lamp to a single cell as shown.

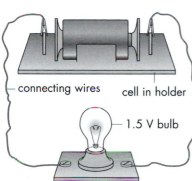

— connecting wires   cell in holder

— 1.5 V bulb

2. Substituting first a 2 V bulb and then a 3 V bulb for the 1.5 V bulb, repeat Step 1. Observe any difference in bulb brightness.

3. Using whichever of the materials you require, experiment to create a cell and bulb arrangement that will make a 3 V bulb glow brightly.

PART B

Problem

How can you vary the brightness of your flashlight?

Materials

2 D-size cells in holder
small lamp with 3 V bulb
connecting wires with clips
very fine nichrome wire (50 cm)

Procedure

1. Connect the lamp and cells as shown.

Caution: The nichrome wire may become too hot to touch while it is connected.

2. Slide one clip back and forth along the nichrome wire. Observe what happens to the bulb as the clips are moved closer together and further apart.

Analysis

1. What was the effect on the brightness of the 3 V bulb when you
   (a) added more cells?
   (b) moved a clip on the nichrome wire?

Further Analysis

2. Which type of wire allows more current to pass, copper or nichrome?

3. If you want to increase the current passing through nichrome wire, should you increase or decrease the length of the wire?

4. Which combination of cells, bulbs, and wires would you use to make the "best" flashlight? Explain your answer.

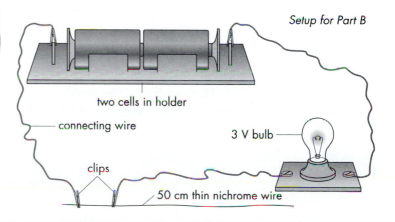

Setup for Part B

two cells in holder

— connecting wire

3 V bulb —

clips

50 cm thin nichrome wire

NOTE: From *Science directions 9,* Activity 4-5 (p. 183), by D. A. Roberts, M. K. Winter, D. Bullard, A. J. Hirsch, G. R. Gore, E. S. Grace, B. Emerson, and L. W. McClelland, 1991, Toronto: Copyright 1991 by John Wiley & Sons Canada Limited. Reprinted with permission of ITP Nelson.

Grade 10 Textbook Example

ACTIVITY 2-2
THE ELECTRIC CIRCUIT

In this activity you will construct a simple electric circuit, and determine the function of each of its parts.

Materials

dry cell
switch
light bulb (screwed into holder)
connecting wires (conductors)

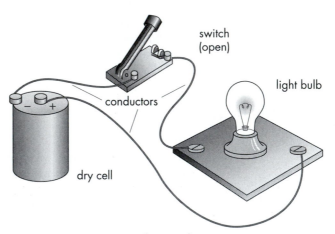

pictorial circuit diagram

desk, in the positions shown in the figure.

3. Connect a wire from the negative terminal of the dry cell to one side of the switch. Draw a line on the circuit diagram in your note-

Procedure

1. Draw the diagram of the electric circuit shown in the figure.

2. Place the dry cell, the (open) switch, and the light bulb on your

book to show which wire has been connected. (See the figure.)

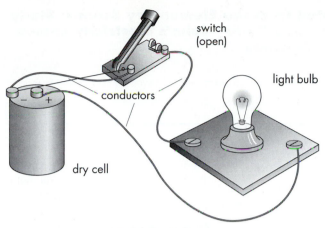

switch
(open)

light bulb

conductors

dry cell

pictorial circuit diagram

4. Connect a wire from the other side of the switch to the bulb. Draw the appropriate line on your circuit diagram.

5. Connect a wire from the other side of the bulb to the positive terminal of the cell. Draw the appropriate line on your circuit diagram.

6. Close and open the switch several times. Record what happens. Touch the light bulb.

7. Close the switch. Disconnect and then reconnect each end of all three wires in turn. Record what happens.

8. Close the switch. Unscrew the bulb, and then screw it in again. Record what happens.

9. Remove the switch from the circuit, and connect the bulb to the dry cell. Find as many ways as possible to turn the light bulb on and off. Record each method.

Discussion

1. What happens to the stored chemical energy in the dry cell when the switch is closed?

2. What energy changes occur in the light bulb?

3. What is the function of (a) the dry cell, (b) the switch, (c) the light bulb, and (d) the wires?

4. Which one of the four parts of the circuit can be omitted? Why is it usually included in a circuit?

5. List three different ways of turning the light bulb on and off.

6. Would the circuit operate differently (a) if the connections on the switch were reversed? (b) if the switch were connected on the other side of the light bulb? Explain your answers.

7. List three simple electric circuits used in the home that have the four parts identified in this activity.

NOTE: From *Heath science connections 10,* Activity 17-1 (pp. 495–497, by J. L. Candido, E. S. James, R. E. Phillips, B. D. Kaufman, and G. W. Wiley, 1988, Toronto: D. C. Heath Canada. Copyright 1988 by D. C. Heath Canada Ltd. Reprinted with permission of ITP Nelson.

Activity Adapted from the Elementary Science Study Unit *"Batteries and Bulbs"* John's Electricity Lesson for Preservice Teachers

ACTIVITY 2-3A

WILL THE BULB LIGHT?

Problem

How many different ways can you find to light a bulb?

Materials

2 "D" batteries
bare copper wire
bulb

Explain

Explain why the bulb lights, or does not light, each time.

Predict

Predict which of the arrangements in Prediction Sheet 1 will cause the bulb to light. After making your predictions, test some of them to see if you were correct. Explain why the bulb lights, or does not light, each time.

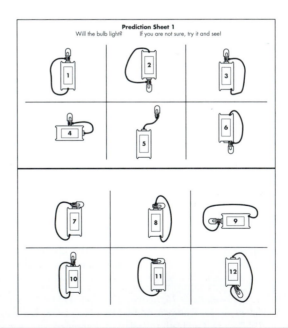

NOTE. From *Teacher's guide for batteries and bulbs: Introduction to electricity and magnetism,* Prediction Sheet 1 (p. 15), by D. Alberti, R. J. Davitt, T. A. Ferguson, and S. O. Repass, 1968, St. Louis, New York: Webster Division, McGraw-Hill. Copyright 1968 by the Educational Development Corporation. Adapted with permission.

ACTIVITY 2-3B

WILL THE BULB LIGHT?

Problem

Can you light a bulb with two wires and one battery: (a) without touching the two wires together? (b) without touching the bulb to the cells? (c) without doing either (a) or (b)?

Materials

2 "D" batteries
bare copper wire
bulbs

Explain

Explain why the bulb lights, or does not light, each time.

Predict

Predict which of the arrangements in Prediction Sheet 2 will cause the bulb to light. After making your predictions, test some arrangements. Explain each of your results.

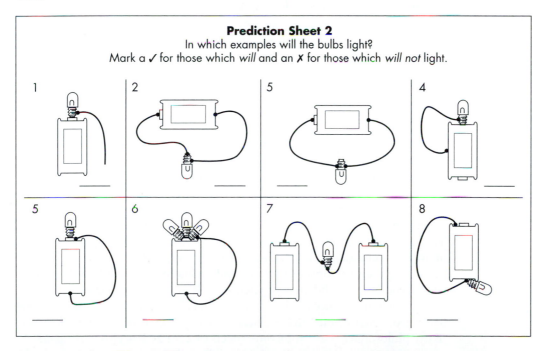

Prediction Sheet 2
In which examples will the bulbs light?
Mark a ✓ for those which *will* and an ✗ for those which *will not* light.

NOTE: From *Teacher's guide for batteries and bulbs: Introduction to electricity and magnetism*, Prediction Sheet 2 (p. 29), by D. Alberti, R. J. Davitt, T. A. Ferguson, and S. O. Repass, 1968, St. Louis, New York: Webster Division, McGraw-Hill. Copyright 1968 by the Educational Development Corporation. Adapted with permission.

When the preservice teachers did this activity in their methods class, some were unable to get their bulbs to light. They assumed that their bulbs were faulty and tried several different bulbs, all to no avail. The difficulty was that they were not touching each end of their wire to the two different ends of the bulb circuit (that is, one end is the little knob at the end of the bulb, and the other end is the metal sleeve that gets screwed into a bulb holder). When the teachers had taught tenth-grade students about electrical circuits, they had used a bulb holder, as the textbook examples do, and they did not realize that the circuit continues *through* the bulb, not just *to* the bulb. Using bulb holders covers up an essential aspect of the circuit. In the class discussion following the activity, many preservice teachers found that they understood electricity for the first time in their lives.

For additional background on student difficulties with understanding electricity concepts, see Osborne and Freyberg (1985).

 PEER TALK

Messages about Scientific Inquiry
Examine each of the three activities on electrical circuits. What approach to scientific inquiry is represented by each activity?

PHILOSOPHERS' VIEWS OF SCIENCE

At the beginning of this chapter you answered questions about your view of science. Unless you have taken a course in the history or philosophy of science, you may not have previously thought about what science is and how it is conducted. You probably worked out your tentative answers to the questions by thinking about science courses you have studied and science books you have read.

A person's view of science is important in determining his or her interest in science. Many people reject studying science because they consider it to be unemotional, impersonal, objective, and irrelevant to their lives. Given the massive impact of science and technology on modern life, is this an appropriate or valid view of science? Is it an appealing view?

Not only do science students and teachers have a variety of views of the nature of science, but philosophers of science also have different views. Early philosophers have sometimes been categorized as either *rationalists,* those who believed that the basis of knowledge is reason or rational thought, or *empiricists,* those who believed that knowledge develops through experience and sensory observation. Two kinds of scientific reasoning have been described: deductive and inductive. Here is a simple example that is often used to illustrate deductive reasoning:

All swans are white.
This animal is a swan.
Therefore, this animal is white.

If we assume that the first two premises are true, then the third *necessarily* follows. We accept this conclusion; it is a valid deductive argument.

Deductive arguments lead to inescapably true conclusions as long as they derive from premises that are true. However, there is no mechanism for evaluating the truth of the initial premises. Thus a deductive argument and its conclusion may be valid, but false!

Alternatively, suppose we have tested many metals for electric conductivity and find that all those tested were good conductors. If we were to then conclude that a new unknown metallic object is a good conductor (because all metals previously tested were good conductors), the conclusion would not be logically valid. In this case, we are unable to establish the truth of the premise in the same manner in which we established the premises in the deductive argument in the example of the swan. The case of metal conductivity involves inductive argument—we reason from a limited set of observations to a generalization that may or may not be true. Inductive arguments lead to probable inference, rather than to logical truth, as is the case for deductive reasoning.

Consider the following premises of an inductive argument:

All fish are cold-blooded.
This animal is cold-blooded.
Therefore, this animal is a fish.

The conclusion is not valid. It may be a fish, but the animal is equally likely to be a reptile or an amphibian, as these animals are also cold-blooded. Had our first premise stated, "All fish and only fish are cold-blooded," then our conclusion would have inevitably and necessarily followed that the animal indeed was a fish and could be nothing else.

We can often develop generalized (inductive) arguments from very few instances. Additional instances or evidences do not sufficiently strengthen the commitment to the generalization, as we saw in the case of all metals being good conductors of electricity. On the other hand, deductive arguments originate from human intuition and observations based on this intuition. We first draw generalizations from which it is possible to make deductive inferences. For example, from Newton's laws we can "deduce" the periodic motion of a pendulum as well as the elliptical motion of the planets. From the theoretical framework of atomic theory and the theory of spectroscopy, we can "deduce" that the outer atmosphere of the sun contains helium. From Euclid's premises (postulates), we can deduce all the propositions in his thirteen books of geometry. If the postulates are true, then all the deductive propositions must be true.

Francis Bacon: An Inductivist View of Science

Until relatively recently, natural science was considered a branch of philosophy. Scientific knowledge was the product of rational thought, what today might be called "theorizing." The sixteenth and seventeenth centuries marked a turning point in how science was conducted. Until that time, scientific activity was dominated by rational thought; now the importance of observation came to be stressed. Francis Bacon (1561–1626) attempted to make sense of this new way of thinking about scientific

A remnant of this tradition is still seen in universities today, where the most advanced science degree is the Ph.D., or Doctor of Philosophy degree.

reasoning. He determined that science, which had been referred to as "natural philosophy," was distinguished from other forms of philosophy by its method, and therefore it was critical to define that method. Science's method consisted of careful, unbiased observation and experimenting aimed at developing inferred generalizations (induction). Bacon stressed that scholars must strive to overcome their preconceptions and theories to ensure pure, accurate observation. As experimentalism came to prevail as the basis for science, science as a field of study became separate from other forms of philosophy (although there continues to be an area of philosophical inquiry that addresses questions concerning the nature of science and scientific knowledge).

Inductivist views of science have been criticized by many. Charlesworth (1982) has summarized some of the major concerns, including the following:

- Observation can have meaning only within the framework of a theory; otherwise it is meaningless.
- The "problem of induction" is to determine how one can justify "inferring unlimited general laws" (p. 19) based on a limited number of observations.
- Induction can yield only simple generalizations. It has no means for deriving more complex theories.
- Bacon's views on "pure" observation neglect the role of social and cultural circumstances.

 PEER TALK

Bacon's View and Science Teaching

In a small group, compare your ideas about the questions posed at the beginning of this chapter. Find some statements that reflect Bacon's view of science.

Choose a science textbook and examine some of the laboratory and other activities in the book. Find some examples of activities based on induction, that is, in which students are asked to observe (and/or experiment) and then draw generalizations based on their observations.

How do Bacon's views fit into the common view of the "scientific method"? Is this approach to school science a reasonable approach? Why or why not?

Karl Popper: A Deductive-Falsification View of Science

One of the better-known contemporary philosophers of science, Sir Karl Popper (1902–1994), believed that only deductive arguments, such as those in geometry, lead to certain conclusions from self-evident premises. Popper wanted to "solve" the problem of induction in science in a novel way. Like Bacon, Popper believed that science was characterized by a unique method. He maintained that we do not use any kind of induction to solve problems in our environment. Popper's argument makes sense when he says that there must always be a framework of expectation because, as we saw in the case of "all metals are good conductors," repetition of instances cannot in any way prove that a generalization is true. Attempting to solve the problem of induction, Popper proposed that if an accepted theory fails to survive a test, we reject that theory or hypothesis. That is, his notion of constructing scientific theories is to eliminate false ones. Scientific activity then involves imaginatively inventing theories or conjectures that have a high ability to be *falsified,* or proven false. Rational thinking, for Popper, consisted of detecting errors, eliminating them, and learning from them.

Popper's method of falsification as a scientific process seems plausible. However, in this view, one "not true" instance falsifies the entire theory, thereby leading to the rejection of that theory. For example, one example of a levitating heavy object on the surface of the earth would topple Newton's theory of gravitation. Moreover, Kuhn and others have claimed that Popper's view does not fit the way science is actually done. That is, Popper's view of science is false!

 PEER TALK

Popper's View and Science Teaching

In your small group, compare your ideas about the questions posed at the beginning of this chapter and the preservice teacher responses quoted in this chapter. Find some statements that reflect Popper's view of science.

Choose a science textbook and examine some of the laboratory and other activities in the book. Find some examples of hypothetico-deductive, or hypothesis-testing, activities.

How do Popper's views fit into the common view of the "scientific method"? Is this approach to school science a reasonable approach? Why or why not?

Thomas Kuhn: Science as a Sociohistorical Tradition

Thomas Kuhn (1922–1996) is probably best known for his introduction of the term *paradigm* to refer to a tradition or school of thought in science, and for his contrasting of normal science and revolutionary science. Kuhn began his scientific career as a physicist, but he soon became intrigued by the history of science. When reading Aristotle he was disturbed that a man who was so brilliant in other philosophical and scientific endeavors, could be so "wrong" in his physics. In Kuhn's words:

What my reading of Aristotle seemed . . . to disclose was a global sort of change in the way men viewed nature and applied language to it, one that could not properly be described as constructed by additions to knowledge or by the mere piecemeal correction of mistakes. That sort of change was shortly to be described by Herbert Butterfield as "putting on a different kind of thinking cap." (Kuhn, 1977, p. xiii)

A paradigm is a unique research tradition or model that is based on certain assumptions about basic underlying principles and techniques and about the key questions to be addressed by science.

Normal science is ongoing when the current research in a particular field takes place within a single paradigm.

Revolutionary science occurs when researchers begin to uncover anomalies that cannot be dealt with using existing theories, and minor adjustments to those theories will no longer resolve the anomalies. Major changes in the theories are proposed.

Kuhn was highly influential in bringing about radical changes in the philosophy of science. Until the appearance of his book *The Structure of Scientific Revolutions* (1962), philosophers of science generally looked upon the history of science in terms of a logical and rational reconstruction of the evolution of scientific thought. Science was thought to consist of one standard approach, rather than a variety of traditions.

Kuhn came to realize that Aristotle's physics was not wrong in the context of his time; it was just different. Aristotle's physics was based on observation—he described what he saw, but what we can see is often not the whole story. Suppose you push a book on a table and it moves. You cannot see the frictional force between the book and the table that explains why the book stops moving when you stop pushing it. However, if you push an ice cube that is sitting on a larger block of ice, the opposing friction is so small that it moves for a long time before coming to rest. Aristotle believed that a force was needed to keep a body moving, that the natural place of an object is at rest. For example, he tried to explain the flight of an arrow as the air rushing from front to back and pushing from behind. Aristotle's view of force was different from Newton's view. His understanding was different.

Kuhn proposed that most practicing scientists work in "normal science." During periods of normal science, scientists learn to identify problems and techniques associated with a particular research tradition. Scientists become members of a research tradition as well as "believers" in a paradigm by virtue of their training and education, the literature they read, and what they recognize as standard models and solutions of their craft. The activity that Kuhn calls normal science, however, can continue only as long as the solutions to the problems posed by the paradigm are accepted by the research community. When solutions to important problems are challenged, debates may ensue over legitimate methods, problems, and standards of solution. Attempts to identify and then question the foundations and the presuppositions of a tradition may signal the beginning of a crisis and should signal the beginning of change or revolution if someone can create a promising alternative.

Kuhn admits that the rationality of revolutionary science, however, cannot be easily defended. According to Kuhn, when a theory such as Einstein's theory of general relativity replaces Newton's theory of gravitation, the two theories become incommensurable; that is, there is no way the two theories can be compared because, as we have already noted, such fundamental notions (or terms) as *mass* and *energy* take on new meanings in the new tradition.

According to this view of science, there is no logical way anyone can prove that one theory is superior to another. However, Kuhn (1977) has espoused five epistemic values or criteria, which he suggests can be used for evaluating the validity of theories or explanations. When two theories both claim to provide the best explanation for a phenomenon, they can be compared to determine which best fulfills the following values:

- A theory should be accurate (p. 321); that is, findings that can be predicted from the theory should be consistent with known observations and experimental results.
- A theory should be consistent, not only internally or with itself, but also with other currently accepted theories about related aspects of nature (pp. 321–322).
- A theory should have broad scope: its consequences should extend far beyond the particular observations, laws, or subtheories it was initially designed to explain (p. 322).
- A theory should be simple, bringing order to phenomena that in its absence would be individually isolated and confused (p. 322).
- A theory should generate new research findings; that is, it should disclose or predict new phenomena or previously unnoted relationships among those already known (p. 322).

Kuhn claims that these criteria or values are sufficient to allow scientists to "choose between an established theory and an upstart competitor" (p. 322) that provides alternative explanations for a phenomenon or group of phenomena. Members of the "old tradition" may be either *persuaded* or *converted* to accept a new way of seeing. Persuasion, however, may or may not be followed by conversion. Persuasion, according to Kuhn, is connected with one's resignation to the obvious superiority of one theory in solving outstanding problems over the other's. For example, Einstein's relativity theories can solve all the problems that Newton's theory could, and also "explain" such anomalous behavior as the precession of the perihelion of Mercury.

Conversion, on the other hand, refers to whether one can make a total switch when embracing the new theory. For example, scientists who had received their scientific education based on Newtonian physics were often able to intellectually accept quantum mechanics and relativity, but were not "converted" to it. Kuhn likens such a person to the translator who, translating a theory or **world view** into his own language, is unable to make it his own. In this sense, we must remember, however, that Kuhn does not say that absence of logic can be equated with absence of reason.

There are problems, however, with Kuhn's picture of how science progresses. Unlike Bacon and Popper, Kuhn does not view science as steadily progressing toward reality. Kuhn argues that normal science, alternating with periodical revolutions, is the way a mature science such as physics grows. For example, some might interpret Einstein's special theory of relativity as an attempt to reconcile Newtonian mechanics with Maxwell's electromagnetic theory. However, Einstein did not develop these theories as a response to an accumulation of commonly perceived problems and

World view A broad, general belief system derived from previous cultural experiences that subconsciously determines how we think and behave.

anomalies. It is not necessarily clear why some anomalies precipitate a revolution in science and others do not.

In what sense, then, can we talk about scientific progress, given Kuhn's picture of normal and revolutionary science? According to Kuhn, science can "progress" on both levels: during the long period of normal science and also during the shorter period of a successful revolutionary science that ushers in a new tradition. On the first level, scientists trained in a common intellectual tradition attempt to solve the problems that the tradition generates, which then are expected to be soluble on that tradition's terms. On the second level, a mature science such as physics progresses with a succession of traditions (for example, Aristotelian, Galilean, Newtonian, Einsteinian), each with its own methods of research (disciplinary matrix). Each tradition guides a community of scientists for a period of time, and each in the end is abandoned.

The need to abandon a tradition in favor of a new one is signaled by the accumulation of long-standing problems that prove unyielding to the research methods of the old tradition, however cleverly applied by the most skillful "puzzle solvers." With the piling up of such problems, a crisis period is reached when scientists actively look for alternative ways of solving them. Eventually one of these, based on a new set of ontological assumptions and new methods of solutions, wins the allegiance of most scientists. A new disciplinary matrix develops that is able to solve these problems. What counted as a scientific world view in the old tradition is reconceived, reevaluated, and sometimes discarded, but it is often retained on the "back burner" to re-emerge later in a new guise and under a new paradigm. Textbooks are rewritten, science education is changed, and, as Kuhn argued, the scientist sees the world differently.

 PEER TALK

Kuhn's View and Teaching Science

In your small group, review your ideas about the questions posed at the beginning of this chapter and the preservice teacher responses quoted in this chapter. Look for statements that reflect Kuhn's view of competition among alternative theories.

Choose a science textbook and find descriptions or examples of normal science and of revolutionary science. What paradigms are reflected in the text?

How do Kuhn's ideas fit into the common view of the "scientific method"? Is this a reasonable approach to use in teaching school science? Why or why not?

How might you introduce Kuhn's approach of shared decision making by a community of inquirers, based on the five epistemic values, into the science curriculum? How would adopting that focus affect your science teaching?

Imre Lakatos: Core Theories and Auxiliary Theories

Imre Lakatos (1922–1974) recognized the validity of Kuhn's arguments against Popper, but he was sympathetic with Popper's notion of falsification. Popper had talked about "crucial experiments," or experiments that prove that existing theories are false. As we have noted, Popper's view was that no theory could ever be proved to be true; it is only possible to prove that a theory is false. Lakatos presented several arguments that were intended to modify Popper's notion of falsification:

1. It is not possible for a crucial experiment to decide between competing theories at any particular time; that can be achieved only through a value system that provides criteria for determining which theory is most powerful.
2. If there is a conflict between an observation and a theory, it is usually more reasonable to modify the protective belt of *auxiliary theory* than the *core theory*.
3. Theories are often retained by members of the scientific community long after they have been falsified. No theory should be abandoned until a better theory is available to replace it (Avegelis, 1989).

Lakatos believed that in reality scientists do not consciously attempt to invent theories that are easily falsified. He argued that high-level theories, such as Newton's gravitational theory, should be thought of as *core theories*. Core theories are so fundamental that they are "protected" by a layer of *auxiliary theories*. If an experimental result cannot be explained in the light of a core theory, scientists tend to adjust the protective layer of auxiliary theories in order to fit the experimental result to the core theory. This is often successful; however, it is not always possible to protect a core theory.

Contrary to Bacon's view of the need for all scientific observation to be pure and uninfluenced by existing views, today we recognize that scientists are immersed in tacit and largely unconscious core assumptions that serve as a "framework of presuppositions within which theories are developed, but which are only occasionally themselves unearthed and submitted to scientific scrutiny. For example, [the idea that] matter is made up of combinations of a limited number of 'fundamental particles' is such an assumption" (Claxton, 1991, p. 65).

Claxton (1991) likens Lakatos's view to a large tree (see Figure 2-2) in which the roots or core assumptions are paralleled to presuppositions that provide the language, perspectives, and priorities that scientists accept and adopt within a certain area of science. The trunk of the tree represents basic facts that appear to be uncontroversial and are found in textbooks. Most people take these for granted. For example, "neurons communicate at synaptic junctions by the release of neurotransmitters" (Claxton, 1991, p. 67) is the kind of scientific knowledge claim that is rarely questioned or challenged. At the top of the tree trunk, speculative ideas or theories

FIGURE 2-2
The tree of scientific
knowledge (*NOTE:* From
*Educating the Inquiring
Mind: The Challenge for
School Science* (p. 66), by
G. Claxton, 1991, London:
Harvester Wheatsheaf.
Reprinted with permission.)

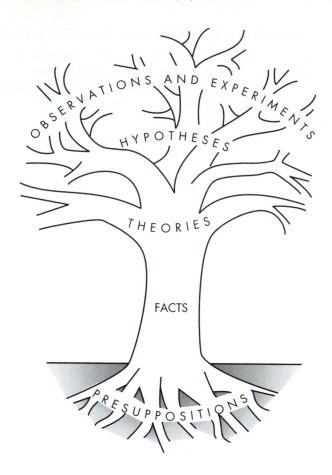

proliferate. The branches of the tree represent hypotheses. The leaves are observations and experiments.

 **PEER TALK**

Lakatos's View and Teaching Science

In your small group, review your ideas about the questions posed at the beginning of this chapter and the preservice teacher responses quoted in this chapter. Can you find some statements that reflect Lakatos's idea of adjusting auxiliary theories in order to protect core theory?

Choose a science textbook and look for descriptions or examples of auxiliary theories and core theories.

How do Lakatos's ideas fit into the common view of the "scientific method"? Is this a reasonable approach to use in teaching school science? Why or why not?

How might you introduce the idea of auxiliary and core theories into the science curriculum? How would adopting that focus affect your science teaching?

☒ ALTERNATIVE NATURES
OF SCIENTIFIC INQUIRY

Scientific inquiry involves an interaction of observation, rational thinking, and creative thinking. Science is a disciplined activity, but it is not always clearly analytical in nature. Therefore, the notion commonly referred to as "the scientific method" is only a generalization. Science is neither a single straightforward method for collecting and distilling facts to be used to derive generalizations (Bacon's inductivist view), nor a process of conjecturing and refuting (Popper's hypothetico-deductive view). Rather, scientific inquiry is an intricate mixture of activities of different types, whose composition may vary from topic to topic or as a topic evolves.

Until recently, it was widely assumed that "real" science draws on the Western European traditions we have discussed in this chapter. However, the notion that "different cultures may have different images of what science is, or that the image within a culture may alter radically during certain crucial periods of scientific progress" (Claxton, 1991, p. 73) is now widely accepted. The recently published *Encyclopedia of the History of Science, Technology, and Medicine in Non-Western Cultures* (Selin, 1997) provides a very comprehensive overview of non-European science. Consider the following examples of scientific achievements we never hear about: The Chinese were aware of the circulation of blood 1,800 years before Harvey, and they had developed a seismograph over 1,800 years before the one first developed in France. The efficacy of Chinese medicine is also now being more widely acknowledged. A thousand years ago, Muslim science was far advanced over that of Europe in fields such as engineering and astronomy, to name only two. It scarcely needs pointing out that we use arabic numerals today, not roman numerals! Native American astronomy is well known. Less familiar, however, is their approach to agriculture, which, in marked contrast to today's agriculture, did not result in the destruction of the soil ecosystem. MacIvor (1995), among others, is calling for a dramatic change in how science is taught to Native American students. The changes being demanded would undoubtedly make science more appealing to many non–Native American students as well; we recommend that our readers consult MacIvor and other recent authors who are working in this area.

Not only have non-Western cultures presented alternative views of science, but there has also been a substantial questioning of the traditional scientific value of objectivity, particularly by feminist scholars (Harding, 1991; Hubbard, 1989). It is now reasonably well accepted that science cannot be confined to a single, well-defined method. But this does not mean that it is devoid of methods. We have looked at some common approaches to scientific development in this chapter.

When a new problem is investigated in as neutral a way as possible to allow the data to speak for themselves, without considering the role that preconceptions play in influencing observations and interpretations,

Bacon's view is in play. The process of observation and the generation of ideas run freely and simultaneously without critical thought.

The initial stages of scientific inquiry may also involve less deliberate and more contemplative types of thinking such as intuitions, hunches, and images. This reflective phase may lead to a period of greater activity—a period of "messing about" in which various hunches are subject to preliminary probing to see where this will lead or what might happen. Scientists' journals are often characterized by wild jottings during this stage. Usually they spend time reading and discussing the topic under investigation with fellow scientists, which may lead to clarification or to further confusion. At this stage a specific line of inquiry is not undertaken.

When experimentation is in full swing, analytical, logical thinking is in play. Attention is given to methodological detail. Variables are manipulated more directly and their effects are seen more clearly. Generation, observation, and testing of ideas is tighter; new ideas emerge as a result of modification of existing models, rather than through leaps of imagination. A research program consists of evolving, interdependent sets of studies arising out of reflection on their predecessors, rather than out of a collection of isolated experimental studies.

Science is many things, and scientific inquiry has many facets. In this chapter we have barely scratched the surface, mentioning but a few characteristics of the thinking of some key scholars and searching for evidence of their ideas in school science. A review by Koulaidis and Ogborn (1995) suggests that most studies of science teachers' philosophical assumptions reveal an empirical-inductivist view of science. Popperian-style hypothesis testing is also seen, but Kuhn's views seem to have had little impact on science teachers. Are these conclusions consistent with the observations you made about your own ideas and about science textbooks as you read through this chapter?

☒ CHAPTER REVIEW

Many preservice teachers believe in a specifiable "scientific method." They also believe that if the elements of the scientific method can be characterized, described, and taught, then students will arrive at appropriate scientific knowledge. Such popular beliefs could lead preservice teachers to teach science according to an empiricist-inductivist view of science, a view commonly held by many members of the educational community—teachers, science educators, scientists, and the public. In this chapter our discussion of the nature of scientific inquiry points to several important implications for how science teachers can help their students develop a more realistic view of the nature of scientific inquiry:

1. Encourage students to construct imaginative theories to account for observable data (natural phenomena).

2. Help students understand the underlying meaning of science concepts, both from their own perspectives and from previously learned theoretical frameworks.
3. Provide students with alternative theories (scientists' theoretical frameworks) to think about and develop appropriate meanings. Science teaching should not necessarily focus on diagnostic work.
4. Enable students to be puzzle lovers and solvers.
5. Help students understand that science is not an isolated activity; rather, it is a social enterprise with socially informed, formulated, and accepted commitments in a given community.

PROBES

1. What are your conceptions of science and scientific inquiry after reading this chapter?
2. What are your perceptions of your own science education with respect to the issues discussed in this chapter?
3. Compare and contrast your conceptions of science with the accounts that are presented in the chapter.
4. Critically examine your own internal conflicts about the nature of science.
5. What steps do you think that you, your cooperating teacher, and your science educator should take to provide you with a contemporary view of science?
6. How do you feel today about what you have learned in your science methods class about the nature of science?
7. What puzzles do you have about how you would portray the nature of science in your science teaching?

CHAPTER 3

Conceptions and Models of Teaching and Learning

STUDY QUESTIONS

1. What are some ways of exploring personal views of teaching and learning?

2. What are the dominant learning theories?

3. What is meant by conceptual change?

4. What are the foundations for conceptual-change teaching models?

5. What are the common assumptions of conceptual-change models?

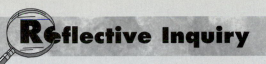

Reflective Inquiry

MARK'S VOICE

Teaching is like a traffic officer. One must direct the process (learning process) of various people (students) to their destination (prescribed student goal) as efficiently as possible.

JOURNAL ACTIVITY

Metaphors for Determining Personal Conceptions of Teaching and Learning

Describe your conceptions of teaching and learning by choosing a metaphor and explaining why and how your metaphor illustrates the nature of teaching and learning.

A **metaphor** extends ideas by making a comparison of two things usually not compared. Metaphors are one approach teachers may use to explore their personal ideas about teaching. A discussion of the metaphor leads to a more thorough analysis of personal views and clarification of ideas.

Preservice teachers were asked to suggest a **metaphor** for the teaching learning process (Gurney, 1995). Some of the metaphors they suggested were: a traffic officer, a journey, a symphony orchestra, a playground, and a catalyst in a chemical reaction.

☒ PRESERVICE TEACHERS' METAPHORS FOR TEACHING AND LEARNING

When we interpret teaching and learning metaphors, the first thing we consider is who has the major role in the metaphor. Is it the teacher or the learner? Often the teacher has the major role, and so we suspect that this person sees teaching as the central part of teaching and learning. For example, consider Mark's voice in the section titled "Reflective Inquiry." In Mark's view, the teacher is responsible for ensuring that both teaching and learning occur. Mark's metaphor does not consider an active role for the student. The teacher has an active role; the student's role is passive. Some metaphors have an active, central teacher, but the teacher's role is less directive than that of a traffic officer. Once we decide who has the major role in the metaphor, we next consider the *nature* of the roles.

A common metaphor for teaching and learning involves a garden or a journey. Again the teacher has the central role, but that role is one of nurturing or guiding the students. In Jerrod's metaphor, there is a shift from the teacher as leader (and hence the students as followers) to the students' taking responsibility for their own journey as they learn:

JERROD'S VOICE
Teaching students is like taking a hiking trip with them. You show them the start of the path and help them along, but they also

must do the work and learn what they can as they travel the path. Eventually they will continue the hike on their own or with someone else.

Ivan's metaphor portrays a central teacher role with the students actively involved in their learning:

IVAN'S VOICE

A puzzle: Small pieces fit together to form a larger picture. The teacher presents small ideas for the student to fit together and form an overall picture.

Here the teacher does not tell the students how to put the puzzle together, but gives the pieces to the students. However, keep in mind that there is only one correct way to put a puzzle together. In Ivan's metaphor, the students' task is to learn the correct way.

Less common are metaphors in which the learner has the central role, and the role of the teacher is defined in relation to the learner. In Fran's view, the learner takes responsibility for learning and the teacher is there to provide assistance:

FRAN'S VOICE

Learning is like a frog swapping up a bug with its tongue. The learner must reach out and grasp it and devour it so that it becomes part of him or her forever, through understanding. Teaching then is like the wind, which facilitates the grasping of the bug.

Metaphors also allow us to compare students' views over a period of time. The preservice teachers who participated in this study chose teaching and learning metaphors on both the first and last days of their methods course. Ivan chose the puzzle metaphor at the beginning of his preservice program. At the end of the program he wrote:

IVAN'S VOICE

The teacher paints a picture. The learner views the painting and may get various meanings from the picture.

Again we have the teacher setting something before the students, but there is an important difference. Instead of a puzzle, which can be completed or interpreted in only one way, we have a painting, which can be interpreted in many different ways. The learner's views are very important in this metaphor; when the learner creates his or her own meaning from the picture, based on past experiences, we say that the learner has constructed his or her own learning. The learning task is no longer to merely reproduce what the teacher intended. As we continue to explore preservice teachers' views of teaching and learning, we will keep in mind these alternative roles for teachers and learners.

 PEER TALK

Metaphors for the Roles of Teacher and Students
Compare your metaphor with the preceding examples. Discuss with your peers how your metaphor portrays the roles of the teacher and the learner.

⚛ PRESERVICE TEACHERS' WAYS OF TEACHING SCIENCE

You have visualized the nature of teaching and learning through personal metaphors. Now you will be given an opportunity to explore your ways of teaching by actually teaching a lesson in science.

 TEACHER PRACTICE

Exploring Personal Conceptions of Teaching
Choose a topic from your science curriculum (something you can teach in fifteen minutes or less). Prepare a science lesson and teach it to one or two of your peers, recording the lesson on video or audiotape (preferably on video). Review the tape with someone you trust. What was your approach to teaching? What assumptions about how students learn best lie behind your approach? How did you expect the students to demonstrate that they had learned something? Submit an interpretive report about your teaching methods and your conceptions about science teaching and learning.

There are many different ways to teach science. Perhaps your lesson used one or more of the strategies discussed in this chapter. In this section we will present brief examples of lessons and reflections of other preservice teachers. Teachers use many different strategies for teaching, not only to provide a variety of different kinds of activities for students, but because different strategies are appropriate for different purposes. We will discuss each strategy in terms of its assumptions and what it can and cannot achieve.

Lecture

Becky chose the topic of ecology. She wrote:

BECKY'S VOICE

> *The basic principles should be taught in order to understand this dynamic system. Then it should be related to humans as a part of ecology. Laws governing this system should also be discussed.*

Becky proposed a *transmission* approach to teaching about ecology. In this approach, the teacher determines what knowledge is to be learned and presents it to the students, either in a lecture or via a textbook, film, or other media (that is, it is *transmitted* from the teacher or some other authoritative source to the learners).

This is a common view of teaching among beginning student teachers, as the following remarks about the characteristics of good teaching reveal:

VIC'S VOICE

> *The characteristics of good teaching involve the ability to convey concepts and ideas simply and clearly. The ability to inspire students and obtain their confidence is also essential.*

JERROD'S VOICE

> *[I had a] naive notion before I started here, you know . . . just get up and tell them what, how it was, and they would swallow it all, and spit it back, and that was all there was to teaching.*

Jerrod's approach is often useful when a teacher needs to provide specific information about something. It can be an efficient means of transmitting necessary information. It assumes that the students will acquire and understand what is transmitted. Students frequently respond to this approach by memorizing (laboratory procedures, definitions, formulas, diagrams, and so on). In Chapter 2 we saw that memorizing does not guarantee understanding. Moreover, memorized abstract ideas are easily forgotten. Thus, this strategy is most appropriate for learning information that is easily understood; it is not as appropriate for complex or abstract concepts. Students who have memorized and then reproduced information may believe that they have learned that information and that they *know* all there is to know. They may not really *understand* what they have "learned." When the transmission approach is used for teaching more complex concepts, it often results in essentially mindless reproduction of what has been transmitted.

Experiments and Controlled Experiments

Will suggested using a practical laboratory activity to teach about the effect of temperature on chemical reactions. He identified the following steps for the activity:

1. Set up an experiment in triplicate, using three different temperatures: (1) very high, (2) medium, (3) very low.
2. Examine which setup gives the best yield (quality and quantity).
3. Repeat the experiment to find the optimal temperature.

The purpose of Will's activity is to *replicate* existing knowledge. It is assumed that the teacher and/or the textbook know the correct answer, and the student's task is to find that answer. If students complete the activity carefully and correctly, they will find the correct answer. If they do not get the correct answer, they have failed to satisfactorily complete the activity. There is no expectation that the students will have any prior knowledge that is of use in this activity, other than having mastered basic laboratory skills such as measuring and setting up the apparatus. This is a very common approach in most science programs, both at the school level and in university science courses.

As in the previous example, the student is seen as a passive learner, receiving information to be stored for future needs (such as examinations). This model differs from the lecture approach in that students are responsible for following instructions (which are transmitted by the teacher or the lab manual) to perform an activity that provides them with the knowledge to be learned.

Analogies and Models

Quentin proposed using a physical analogy to model characteristics of electron flow, which would help students understand this rather abstract concept:

QUENTIN'S VOICE

I would like to see this concept taught with the help of physical objects that the students can touch and feel, for example, Ping-Pong balls for electrons and a tube for the conductor.

Again we have an example in which the teacher provides the knowledge that students are to learn. The student's task remains that of acquiring the desired knowledge.

Quentin recognizes that electron flow is a difficult concept for many students to understand, and suggests using a hands-on model to illustrate the phenomenon. He also notes that it may be helpful to draw on many senses: touch and sight as well as hearing.

Many learners do find it difficult to understand abstract concepts, especially if they are explained in a transmissive mode, whether that transmission comes as an explanation by the teacher in class or by the textbook. Often the use of an analogy or model does facilitate understanding, although the use of analogies requires more than just presenting a model and explaining how it models electron flow or any other concept. Treagust (1995) and others have studied how to use analogies effectively to help learners understand science concepts.

Treagust (1995) has developed a three-phase approach: focus, action, and reflection (FAR). This approach will be discussed in more detail in Chapter 7.

Socratic or Large-Group Discussion

Diane chose teaching the concept "What is a living thing?" She proposed beginning the lesson by having some examples of living things at the front of the class, such as a plant and a mouse. She would then have the students list all the characteristics of living things they could think of. The characteristics would be discussed, and then the teacher would add any they missed.

Diane chose an approach in which the teacher plays a different role, that of a facilitator. We sometimes hear preservice teachers make comments such as, "I haven't really done any teaching yet, just facilitating." Such comments reveal that the person feels as if he or she isn't really teaching unless he or she is providing the information to be learned, that only transmission teaching is "real teaching."

Until this point, all of the strategies we have considered assume that the teacher is the provider of knowledge to the learner. However, the *Socratic approach* assumes that learners already have a wealth of relevant knowledge; the teacher's role is to establish a situation that will help the students identify their prior knowledge and share it with one another. The teacher uses questioning to help the students organize and evaluate their existing knowledge.

Diane's final sentence is revealing, however. She seems to believe that particular characteristics constitute a correct and complete answer, and she wants to be certain that students receive the correct answer; thus, the teacher adds any characteristics the students missed! A more consistent approach would be to have the teacher use further questioning to guide the students to identify the additional characteristics. Even so, we still have the assumption that there is a correct set of characteristics that the learners should know. Not all teachers would feel comfortable with that notion, and it is not characteristic of a truly Socratic approach.

 PEER TALK

Analysis of Preservice Teachers' Voices
1. Look back to the ideas of the preservice teachers for teaching a science concept. Which of these lessons would you prefer to participate in? Why?
2. Which of the preceding metaphors of teaching science are present in each of the examples of how preservice teachers would teach a concept? What can be inferred about these preservice teachers' conceptions of teaching and learning from these brief excerpts?
3. What would you identify as the advantages and disadvantages of each of these approaches to teaching science?

CONTEMPORARY VIEWS OF LEARNING SCIENCE

As we have seen in the previous section, each of the strategies we have looked at is more useful in some situations and for some learning goals than for others. Not only must teachers consider the intended goals of a lesson when choosing how to teach a particular concept, they must also consider how the students in their classes learn best. As teachers and learners, we all tend to prefer teaching strategies that reflect how we best learn and understand a concept. It is important to remember that not everyone learns the same way, and we must consider a variety of alternative approaches to teaching if we are to meet the needs of all or most of our students. Learning theories are useful for illuminating teaching practice.

What Can a Learning Theory Do for Me?

Why do we spend time on learning theories? Is learning about theory just one more useless thing for an overworked preservice teacher to have to deal with? How can discussing and thinking about learning theories help you become a better teacher? According to Shapere (1974), theories can have three functions:

- Provide a consistent framework for future action
- Allow us to predict what will happen under particular circumstances
- Provide a possible explanation for how and/or why something occurs as it does

Thus, learning theories provide us with a set of guidelines that make it easier for us to plan our teaching. They help us to predict which approaches will be successful and to adjust or adapt less successful approaches. Learning theories also help us make sense of how learners respond and behave when they are in a situation where we expect learning to occur. They provide a framework for analyzing why particular activities are or are not successful. Learning theories also help us predict how particular learners or groups of learners will respond to certain activities and certain kinds of teaching strategies.

Many different theories have been proposed to account for how people learn. They are often classified as falling into one of two major areas: behaviorist or cognitive. Most educators prefer one of these approaches. Educational psychology books that review different approaches to learning theory usually emphasize one over the other. We cannot possibly consider all of the established learning theories, but we will look at well-known examples of each type and discuss the contribution each can make to helping us develop a personal theory of learning.

Behaviorist Theories of Learning

One of the best-known learning theorists is B. F. Skinner, whose name has become synonymous with behaviorist or **stimulus-response** learning. When mice are trained to run a maze that has food at the end, the food provides a stimulus for successful completion of the desired response: learning to run the maze. The behaviorist makes no attempt to determine how the mouse learns how to complete the maze. He or she is concerned with how efficiently it runs the maze. Similarly, parents may reward their children for completing their homework by allowing them to watch TV (the stimulus). The parent is concerned that the child completes the homework (the response); how the child accomplishes that is not relevant to whether or not the child is allowed to watch TV.

As we have noted earlier, behaviorist approaches to learning are sometimes used in education as well. For example, if everyone in a class has completed the lab report (the response), a teacher may allow the students a few minutes of free time at the end of the period (the stimulus), or students may not be allowed to go on a field trip if they have not completed certain tasks. Much modern computer-assisted instruction is based on behaviorist theories of learning (when the student gives the correct response, the computer plays a little jingle or provides an animation).

Stimulus-response learning is characterized by observable or overt behavior that results as a response to a particular stimulus.

Extrinsic rewards are awarded based on students' performance rather than on reasons that prompt them to respond or act in particular ways.

Intrinsic rewards are based on learning that is self-motivated and self-fulfilling, such as a feeling of satisfaction or pride or recognition of one's improved understanding of what was learned.

Some people believe that behaviorist strategies are manipulative. Behaviorism focuses on what is learned and what stimulus will increase the chances that the learning will occur, using **extrinsic rewards** (Skinner, 1953). There is no provision for the nature of the task itself to provide a reward or for the learner's self-satisfaction to serve as an **intrinsic reward.** Behavioristic learning strategies were formerly more popular in schools than they are now. Most teachers today prefer cognitive strategies (except in particular and unique situations, such as with children with severe behavioral problems). However, as we shall see, behaviorist theories do underlie some current educational practice. Can you think of some examples?

Instructional Implications of Behaviorism

A well-known definition of learning is "a change in behavior." If behaviorism is primarily concerned with what is to be learned, rather than how it is learned, then learners must be told what they are expected to learn. It becomes the teacher's responsibility to prescribe what is to be learned. Thus, typical teaching strategies would include lecturing and other transmissive approaches. The teacher's role is to indicate *what* is to be learned, rather than *how* the student should learn. The student's role is to learn and then to demonstrate that learning has occurred.

Cognitive Theories of Learning

In *cognitive theories,* a major emphasis is on *how* learning occurs. Here the teacher is concerned with how a student processes information in order to learn, and is responsible for providing the conditions necessary for the student to learn. We will look at two different approaches to cognitive theories. In the first of these, the major emphasis is on the developmental level of the learner and how that affects learning. Piaget is undeniably the best known of the developmental theorists. Other cognitive theorists, such as Ausubel and Vygotsky, believe that the learner's background knowledge and experiences are more important than developmental level.

Ausubel's meaningful theory of learning will be developed in detail in Chapter 8.

Jean Piaget: Human Development

Jean Piaget (1896–1980) began his career as a biologist studying snails. He became interested in how snails learn, and concluded that stimulus-response theory did not adequately account for his observations. After completing his Ph.D. at age 21, Piaget held a number of positions, including one at the Binet Testing Laboratory in Paris, standardizing intelligence tests. Piaget became intrigued by the incorrect responses students gave, particularly with the consistencies he found among incorrect answers. Later he became research director of the Jean-Jacques Rousseau Institute in Geneva and continued with his lifelong passion of studying children's thinking. He was intrigued by how his own children learned, and, like many enthusiastic parents, began to keep extensive records of his children's development. These observations led him to study children's thinking in greater depth, ultimately leading to his theory of intellectual development.

Piaget's field of study is known as *genetic epistemology*. Epistemology is the study of knowledge. Genetic epistemology refers to the study of how individuals come to acquire knowledge. An extensive review of Piaget's work is beyond the scope of this book, but can be found in most books on learning theory or educational psychology. For our purposes, we are interested in two areas of his work: his notions of assimilation and accommodation, and his stage theory of intellectual development.

Assimilation is a process by which an individual takes in knowledge that is consistent with his or her existing knowledge. For example, if you are familiar with the distinguishing characteristics of mammals (that they have hair, give birth to live young, and feed their young with milk produced in mammary glands), you will readily identify a cat as a mammal, even if you have never seen a cat before. That is, you assimilate cats into your understanding of mammals, without having to change your understanding of what a mammal is, because you observe mammal characteristics. However, if you have never heard about the unusual mammals of Australia, you will not be able to assimilate a platypus (which has hair, lays eggs, produces milk, and has a beak and feet similar to those of a duck) into your understanding of mammals. You will have to broaden your understanding of what a mammal is to *accommodate* the characteristics of a platypus. (It is not surprising that when Europeans first saw platypuses, they thought they were a hoax!) Your understanding of what a mammal is has now changed.

Piaget also proposed that all individuals proceed through a number of stages of intellectual development: the sensorimotor stage (birth to about age 2), the preoperational stage (ages 2 to 7), the concrete operational stage (ages 7 to 12), and the formal operational stage (age 12 and over). This theory caught the eye of educators, because it seemed to account for many of the learning difficulties teachers had already identified. For example, many students have difficulty understanding density when it is taught in grade 7. This could be explained if the learners had not yet made the transition from concrete to formal operations, as the concept of ratio quantities (such as density) requires formal operations. During the 1970s, Piaget's ideas were increasingly embraced by educators throughout North America and other parts of the world.

 TEACHER PRACTICE

Influence of Piaget's Thought

Examine a science program guide or materials for the influence of Piaget's theory.

Vygotsky: Zone of Proximal Development

More recently, science educators have become interested in the theory of Lev Vygotsky (1896–1934). Especially important for science, it is a theory of the social aspects of mental development and reasoning. Language is a major tool in this personal development. Believing in the developmental nature of content knowledge and the role of language in human development, Vygotsky (1968) proposed that higher knowledge will transform the meaning of lower concepts. Vygotsky envisioned an expert-novice relationship, where the expert assists the novice to reach the higher ground in a particular knowledge domain. We may liken this to situations in which scientists assist their graduate students to reflexively learn the higher knowledge structures not by simply telling them, but by helping them with problem-solving activities. Let us translate this to school science. The teacher is the expert and the student, who is the novice, collaboratively learns with the teacher. The teacher's function is to assist the young person to move from his or her current level of performance to the maximum level that the learner can achieve with assistance. The distance between the learner's existing level and the target level is known as the *zone of proximal development*. For Vygotsky, "[h]uman learning presupposes a specific social nature and a process by which children grow into the intellectual life of those around them" (Vygotsky, 1968, p. 88). Vygotsky uses the term *scaffolding* to describe the process by which the teacher helps the child to grow intellectually.

In his book entitled *Actual Minds, Possible Worlds,* Bruner (1986) states that his view of learning has changed. Formerly an ardent follower of Piaget, Bruner now supports Vygotsky's perspectives of learning. We will focus on what Bruner has to say about learning through the eyes of Vygotsky. According to Bruner, scaffolding occurs when

> the transmission of mind across history is effected by successive mental sharings that assure a passing on of ideas from the more able or advanced to the less so. And the medium in which the transmission occurs is language and its products: literacy, science, technology, literature. (Bruner, 1986, p. 74)

This transmission of mind is not viewed in a traditional sense, in which the teacher puts the pieces of knowledge into the student's head; rather, the transmission involves a "negotiable transaction" between the teacher and the student, a "microculture" (p. 76). The student must borrow the knowledge and the consciousness of the teacher to enter into the language and culture of science. In scientific knowledge acquisition, procedures for helping the learner enter and progress across the zone of proximal development are in the hands of the teacher. Through this process, modes of discourse play an important role.

Piaget versus Vygotsky: Bruner's Version

For Piaget, human development was the appropriate nourishment of the present. About Piaget, Bruner states:

[T]he drama was the child's reinvention of the world, a constant and recurring process achieved through action on the world in the present that, with time, transformed the child's pervious logic into a new logical *structure d'ensemble* that (as noted) included the old as a special case. . . . [G]rowth happened naturally. . . . The drama consisted in honouring its natural growth, not in comparing its present status with what it would later be or might become under some special curricular dispensation. (Bruner, 1986, p. 141)

Concerning Vygotsky's view of human development, Bruner notes that

the mind grows neither naturally nor unassisted. It is determined neither by its history nor by the logical constraints of its present operations. Intelligence, for him [Vygotsky], is readiness to culturally transmitted knowledge and procedures as prostheses of mind. But much depends upon the availability and the distribution of those prosthetic devices within a culture. (p. 141)

Vygotsky saw the social support system for leading the child across the zone of proximal development to be essential, and this could be achieved in a progressive medium through language. The method uses either a well-conceived tutorial or a small discussion group. One of Vygotsky's central metaphors is the "notion of two separate streams of development that flowed together: a stream of thought and a stream of language" (Bruner, 1986, p. 143). For Vygotsky, language had the powers to alter thoughts and give new ways of describing the world. Language became the coffer for new thoughts. In contrast, Piaget believed in the logic of thought and felt that language only reflects thought, thus subordinating language to thought. Vygotsky stated that language has a cultural past and a generative present. He believed that language plays the role of a nurse and tutor of thought. For Piaget, growth is nurturing of intrinsic logic; for Vygotsky, growth is reaching to a higher concept level.

Bruner (1986) points out that Piaget's structuralist views of the child's mind fall apart if we trace the history of science and compare it to the growth of the child's mind. Piaget neglects particularity of an individual's knowledge, locality of knowledge, the tinkerer's creativity, the role of negotiations in establishing meaning, and historical opportunity.

Bruner talks about the possibility of many worlds. Meaning and reality are created and not discovered. Negotiation is the art of individuals constructing new meanings to regulate their relations with each other. Change is not in the solo child. The child is not by himself or herself. Rather, the child is part of the culture that he or she inherits and then re-creates.

Vygotsky (1968) emphasized that learning takes place in social and cultural contexts. On this basis, Bruner affords a "cultural posture" for a theory of intellectual development. Bruner relates the growing of an individual to the culture in which he or she belongs and to the relationship between the individual and the culture. In Bruner's words (1990),

it is culture . . . that shapes human life and the human mind, that gives meaning to action. It does this by imposing the patterns inherent in the culture's symbolic systems—its language and discourse modes, the forms of logical and narrative explication, and the patterns of mutually dependent communal life. (p. 34)

PEER TALK

The Difference Between Expert-Novice and Teacher-Student Relationships

How does Vygotsky's expert-novice relationship differ from the traditional science teacher-student relationship?

Learning theories described in this chapter and philosophies of science described in Chapter 2 have provided the basis for the development of many useful teaching models. We describe a few popular teaching models in the next section.

CONCEPTUAL-CHANGE TEACHING MODELS

Conceptual change is based on the Piagetian principles of assimilation and accommodation (Driver, 1983).

Since the late 1970s, science educators have been developing teaching models that promote conceptual change. These teaching and learning models have borrowed ideas from developmental and cognitive psychology and from the philosophy of science. Conceptual change has been characterized as evolutionary and revolutionary. In Chapter 2 we learned that the development of scientific knowledge involves evolutionary (assimilation) and revolutionary (accommodation) conceptual changes. From a historical perspective, Toulmin (1972) characterized scientific progress as evolutionary change—conceptual systems change as individuals change their meaning because of the influence of their cultural environment and political processes. This view of scientific progress is similar to Piaget's biological model of adaptation (assimilation and accommodation). The argument from a historical perspective is that early scientists changed their conceptions gradually. For example, Galileo believed so strongly in the Aristotelian idea of the circular motion of the heavens that he simply would not consider ideas that were inconsistent with that belief. Considering conceptual change as revolutionary is based on Kuhn's idea that the choice of a theory is not by rule but by the decisions of a community, influenced by shared professional, social, and psychological values (Kuhn, 1970). Conceptual change is like a gestalt shift. It is a paradigm shift—one paradigm replacing another paradigm (as when Einsteinian physics replaced Newtonian physics). Scientific progress is a relative notion.

Considering conceptual change as evolutionary and revolutionary, in this chapter, we will describe and analyze some of the popular conceptual-change teaching models that have appeared in science education literature. You will realize that within the conceptual-change tradition, there are several approaches to science teaching; each approach has different purposes and intentions, although some of the differences are subtle. We will begin with the learning model called the learning cycle, developed by Karplus and Renner in 1977.

The Learning Cycle

Karplus (1977) and Renner (1982) proposed a three-stage model as follows (see Figure 3-1):

1. *Exploration Phase.* The teacher gives students materials or demonstrates events related to the topic and encourages them to explore and phrase questions about things they do not understand. For example, a teacher might set up a clock that ticks or might pop a balloon. Students' questions may include "How does sound travel from these sources to our ears?" and "How do we hear the clock ticking or the pop sound?"
2. *Concept Introduction Phase.* The teacher introduces and explains the key concepts. The teacher might explain concepts such as vibrations and waves. Through models such as a pendulum, water waves, and

Unidirectional arrows indicate the relationship between the phases of the learning cycle or how one phase leads to the next one. Ideally, the concept application phase of one lesson can lead to the exploration phase of a new lesson. The bi-directional arrows indicate that evaluation and discussion can be integrated into any part of the cycle.

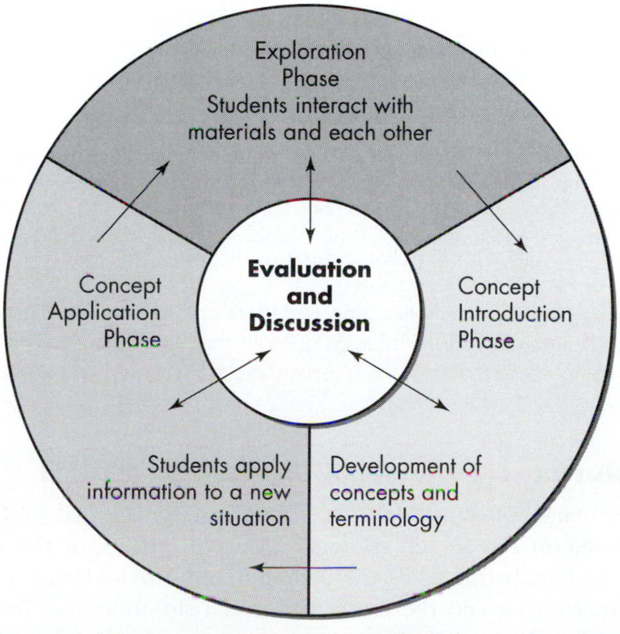

FIGURE 3-1

The learning cycle (*NOTE: From "Bridging the Gap between the Old and the New: Helping Teachers Move towards a New Vision of Science Education," by C. R. Barman, 1996, in R. Rhoton and P. Bowers (Eds.), Issues in Science Education, p. 156. Arlington, VA: National Science Teachers Association. Copyright 1996 by NSTA. Reprinted with permission.)*

springs, a teacher might discuss how sound travels or the transmission of waves. The teacher will illustrate how we hear sound with diagrams of the outer, middle, and inner ear. A diagram may help explain how the brain interprets sound. Based on their questions, the teacher may refer students to their textbooks. The textual reading becomes more purposeful.

3. *Concept Application Phase.* The teacher helps students apply the newly learned concept to new situations. In terms of understanding the concept of waves, students can use an oscilloscope to examine a vocalist's voice to determine the characteristics of sound, such as pitch and frequency.

The learning cycle is based on Piagetian learning principles of self-regulation, in which learners develop new reasoning patterns as ideas are assimilated and accommodated. Students reflect on their ideas as they explore and interact with materials and with other learners. Learning is achieved by repetition and practice, so that ways of thinking become consolidated. Elements such as repetition and practice are recognized in this case as procedures to improve cognition rather than to improve behavior, as in the case of behaviorism.

 TEACHER PRACTICE

The Learning Cycle

The following excerpt discusses teaching materials on complete and incomplete metamorphosis. In a small peer group, determine which phases of the learning cycle are missing. Modify the teaching materials to conform with the learning cycle.

> The teaching materials contain information about the stages of complete metamorphosis. There are excellent illustrations to explain each of these stages. At the end of the presentation of both forms of metamorphosis, the text has an activity that has the students use hand lenses to observe different stages of a mealworm's life cycle (for example, larva, pupa, adult) (Barman, 1996, p. 158).

In peer groups, select science teaching materials and use the learning cycle checklist to evaluate them (see Table 3-1). With the aid of resource materials, add the missing components of the learning cycle.

Nussbaum and Novick did not label their learning model. Hence, we have given their model a title based on its underpinning philosophy.

Underpinning the conceptual-change model developed by Nussbaum and Novick is Toulmin's idea that scientific progress is evolutionary and is based on the biological principle of adaptation (Nussbaum, 1989).

The Evolutionary Conceptual-Change Model

The evolutionary conceptual-change model was developed in 1979 after Joseph Nussbaum researched students' conceptions about the earth as a cosmic body (Nussbaum, 1976). Nussbaum and Novick were surprised to find that children viewed the earth in a much different way from adults. Children's conceptions led these researchers to develop a teaching style

TABLE 3-1
Learning Cycle Checklist

Exploration Phase	Yes	No
A. The lesson contains an exploration phase that is activity-based.	___	___
B. Ample time is provided for the exploration phase.	___	___
C. The exploration activity provides student-student and student-teacher interaction.	___	___

Concept Introduction Phase		
A. The concept(s) is named or appropriate vocabulary is developed after an exploration activity.	___	___
B. The concept(s) and term(s) are an outgrowth of the exploration phase.	___	___

Concept Application Phase		
A. The students extend the concept(s) to one or more new situations.	___	___
B. Appropriate activities are used to apply the concept(s).	___	___

NOTE: From "Bridging the Gap between the Old and the New: Helping Teachers Move towards a New Vision of Science Education," by C. R. Barman, 1996, in R. Rhoton and P. Bowers (Eds.), *Issues in Science Education,* p. 159. Arlington, VA: National Science Teachers Association. Copyright 1996 by NSTA. Reprinted with permission.

that would help modify the incorrect ideas. Their strategy involved activities that would produce cognitive dissonance (activities that produce results that conflict with students' existing frameworks), thus helping children change their ideas.

Subsequently, using the particle theory as an example, Nussbaum and Novick (1981) developed the following model of teaching based on the idea that conceptual change is evolutionary:

1. The teacher demonstrates a science-related phenomenon that would create cognitive dissonance and challenge children's ideas. The students hypothesize about the natural phenomenon.
2. Discussion follows in which students give reasons for their hypotheses. The teacher categorizes the reasons.
3. Students debate the pros and cons of the different categories of views.
4. The teacher carries out a new activity (usually a demonstration) that, hopefully, will lead to an accommodation in students' cognitive structures. Students create a new model that takes the observed phenomenon into account.
5. Further demonstrations and much discussion take place.

The evolutionary conceptual-change model and the learning cycle are similar in that both involve puzzling activities or events. Although both models use cognitive dissonance, the purpose of each model is different. In the learning cycle, the puzzles are used to initiate students' questions so that the teacher can clarify and name concepts developed in the exploration phase and develop questions for further investigation. In the evolutionary conceptual-change model, the puzzles are used to challenge students' ideas and to intervene in students' original thinking with further puzzle-producing activities and demonstrations.

An example of the evolutionary conceptual-change approach is Nussbaum and Novick's series of lessons on the particulate model of matter (Nussbaum, 1985).

Step 1:   The teacher shows students a flask containing air and an evacuating pump and demonstrates its operation (see Figure 3-2). Students are then asked to pretend they are wearing a pair of "magic magnifying spectacles" that allows them to see the air in the flask. Then they make two drawings: one flask filled with air, and the other flask half-filled with air (half the air is removed by the pump). The teacher then selects representative samples of the drawings and puts them on the chalkboard.

Step 2:   Students are asked to state their reasons for their hypotheses and draw their pictures. Fourteen-year-olds gave a variety of responses (see Figures 3-3a and 3-3b).

STUDENTS' REASONS
– "Air is made up of particles."
– "The particles are not scattered evenly in an enclosed container but they were concentrated in some part of a confined space."
– "There is empty space between the particles."
– "Dust and other particles; other gases such as oxygen and nitrogen; the particles are closely packed—there is no space between them; air, dirt, germs; unknown vapors; particles expand into empty space."

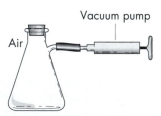

FIGURE 3-2

Apparatus for removing air from a flask (NOTE: From "The Particulate Nature of Matter in the Gaseous Phase," by J. Nussbaum, 1985, in R. Driver, E. Guesne, and A. Tiberghien (Eds.), *Children's Ideas in Science*, p. 127. Philadelphia: Open University Press. Copyright 1985 by Open University Press. Reprinted with permission.)

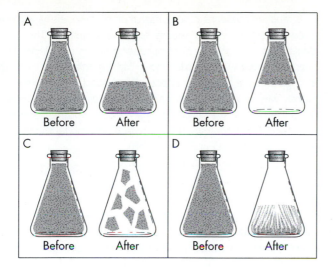

FIGURE 3-3a

A continuous representation of air structure (*NOTE:* From "The Particulate Nature of Matter in the Gaseous Phase," by J. Nussbaum, 1985, in R. Driver, E. Guesne, and A. Tiberghien (Eds.), *Children's Ideas in Science*, p. 128. Philadelphia: Open University Press. Copyright 1985 by Open University Press. Reprinted with permission.)

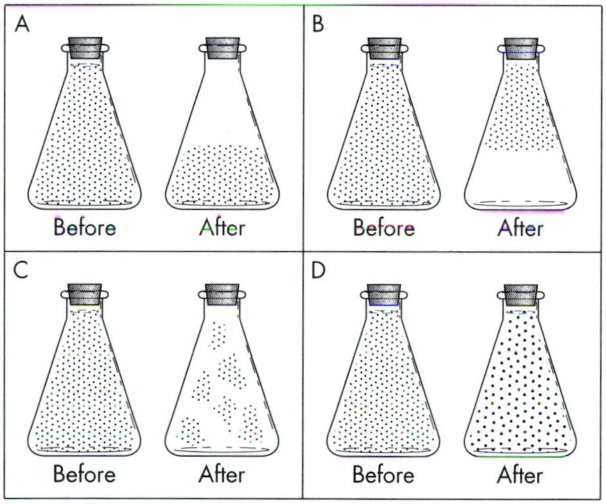

FIGURE 3-3b

A particulate representation of air structure (*NOTE:* From "The Particulate Nature of Matter in the Gaseous Phase," by J. Nussbaum, 1985, in R. Driver, E. Guesne, and A. Tiberghien (Eds.), *Children's Ideas in Science*, p. 128. Philadelphia: Open University Press. Copyright 1985 by Open University Press. Reprinted with permission.)

– "Particles in gas in intrinsic motion."

– "The particles want to rise; the particles weigh very little and therefore rise; . . . air floats in space because of its low specific gravity (i.e., the natural tendency of air is to float up into space—this is the natural place of air); [i]f all the particles fell to the bottom, there would be a vacuum and this is impossible in air (i.e., a vacuum is impossible—matter is always sucked into the vacuum to fill it up)." (Nussbaum, 1985, pp. 130, 131).

Step 3:   Students take part in an open debate arguing the merits of each view.

Step 4:   The teacher presents a demonstration that, hopefully, will lead to an accommodation in the students' cognitive structure. The demonstration consists of compressing gas in a syringe. Students then are faced with the dilemma of forcing half of the air in the syringe into the remaining space already occupied by air. In other words, why is air so compressible? Much discussion follows as students debate the validity of the various hypotheses they originally proposed. Students may then create a new model that fits the data better (see Panel D in Figure 3-3b).

Step 5:   More demonstrations and discussions follow (see Figure 3-4).

The evolutionary conceptual-change model represents a beginning of the conceptual-change frameworks that followed in the 1980s. Nussbaum and Novick believed that confronting students with discrepant phenomena and creating cognitive dissonance would gradually (evolutionarily) change students' conceptions. In this type of conceptual change, Nussbaum (1989) suggests that learning is "an evolutionary pattern in which the student maintains substantial elements of the old conception while gradually incorporating individual elements from the new one" (p. 538).

The CLIS Model

The Children's Learning in Science (CLIS) project was developed in the 1980s under the guidance of Rosalind Driver. CLIS involved over 30 science teachers who worked in collaboration with project researchers to develop trial teaching schemes using a constructivist view of learning. This view acknowledges that children hold beliefs about the world that they have constructed through personal interaction with natural phenomena and through social interaction with other people. They come to the classroom with these pre-existing conceptions and, when exposed to a range of learning activities, may modify their own ideas toward the intended learning outcome (Needham & Hill, 1987). The CLIS project is based on the following seven principles:

1. What is already in the learner's mind matters.
2. Individuals construct their own meaning.
3. The construction of meaning is a continuous and active process.
4. Learning may involve conceptual change.
5. The construction of meaning does not always lead to belief.
6. Learners have the final responsibility for their learning.
7. Some constructed meanings are shared (Scott & Dyson, 1987, pp. 7–8).

The CLIS teaching sequence is divided into five main phases: (1) orientation, (2) elicitation of ideas, (3) restructuring of ideas, (4) application of ideas, and (5) review of change in ideas. Table 3-2 illustrates the CLIS constructivist teaching sequence.

Lesson 1–2	Experiments with air and with specific gases (air occupies space; identifying O_2 and CO_2; air has weight, air can perform work: lifting objects, moving objects), air is a mixture of different gases.		
Lesson 3	Exposing SAFs about the structure of air in a reduced pressure situation. Pretending that they can use magic eye glasses, pupils imagine how air would look in the flask 'before' and 'after' partial evacuation of the flask.		Particles + Empty Space
Lesson 4	Conceptual conflict and change: discrepant event— air compression. Pupils "invent" the particle idea for the structure of air.		
Worksheet 4	Draw and explain what you believe *now* about the structure of air in a reduced pressure situation (Lesson 3).	before after	
Lesson 5	Short discussion on some functions of various visual models.		
Lesson 6	Exposing SAFs about the mechanism of gas diffusion. Experiment: smell—what makes it travel?		Particle Motion
Lesson 7	Cognitive conflict and change: discrepant event— diffusion of bromine in air and in a vacuum.	bromine tubes / no air air / dry ice	
Worksheet 7	Draw the air and explain what made the balloon inflate.	heating	
Lesson 8	Consolidating the particle model and making a list of claims representing aspects of the model.		
Lesson 9	Reinforcement of the idea that the kinetic behavior of particles is responsible for air expansion: (1) when heating; (2) when adding particles.	(2) (1)	Reinforcing Particle Motion
Worksheet 9	Draw the air and explain what made the soap film rise.	soap film / heating / the bottom / in warm water	
Lesson 10	Reinforcement of the idea that air pressure is dependent on the number and the velocity of particles.		
Worksheet 10a	True/False evaluation of statements representing SAFs and ScF.		
Worksheet 10b	True/False evaluation of statements representing SAFs and ScF.		

FIGURE 3-4

Teaching sequence of particle model (*NOTE:* From "The Particulate Nature of Matter in the Gaseous Phase," by J. Nussbaum, 1985, in R. Driver, E. Guesne, and A. Tiberghien (Eds.), *Children's Ideas in Science*, p. 128. Philadelphia: Open University Press. Copyright 1985 by Open University Press. Reprinted with permission.)

TABLE 3-2

Constructivist Teaching Sequence

Phase	Purpose	Methods
I. Orientation	To arouse interest and set the scene.	Practical activities, real problems to solve, teacher demonstrations, film clips, videos, newspaper clippings, problems, discrepant events.
II. Elicitation of ideas	To enable students to become aware of prior ideas.	Practical activities or small-group discussion, followed by reporting back.
III. Restructuring of ideas	To create an awareness of an alternative viewpoint—the scientific one—to: a. modify b. extend or c. replace existing ideas with a more scientific view.	Small-group discussion and reporting back.
i. Clarification and exchange	To recognize alternative ideas and critically examine one's own.	Teacher demonstration, performing personal experiments, worksheets.
ii. Exposure to conflict situations	To test the validity of existing ideas.	Discussion, reading, teacher input.
iii. Construction of new ideas	To modify, extend, or replace existing ideas.	Practical work, project work, experimentation, teacher demonstration.
iv. Evaluation	To test the validity of newly constructed ideas.	
IV. Application of ideas	To reinforce newly constructed ideas in familiar and novel situations.	Personal writing, practical activity, problem solving, project work.
V. Review	To gain an awareness of the change of ideas and familiarization with the learning process to allow students to reflect upon the extent to which their ideas have changed.	Personal writing, group discussion, personal diaries, reviewing work, posters, etc.

NOTE: From *Teaching Strategies for Developing Understanding in Science* (p. 7), by R. Needham and P. Hill, 1987, Leeds, England: Centre for Studies in Science and Mathematics Education, University of Leeds.

In this learning process, students are involved in freely expressing and exchanging their ideas, reporting on the results of their investigations, writing their reports and journals, and testing their ideas in investigations. Teachers must provide a supportive environment and ample time for discussion, adopt a nonjudgmental role, develop suitable activities on which the students can test their ideas, acquaint the class with scientific ideas, and allow them to explore these ideas along with their personal ideas.

The CLIS constructivist view of learning and teaching has been used widely at the middle school and high school levels. Topics such as plant nutrition, the particulate theory of matter, and energy have been thoroughly researched and taught by CLIS teachers. Some would argue that a major weakness is the lack of an explicit or built-in assessment aspect, when assessment is one of the most important considerations in any instructional program. However, in a constructivist program, the distinction between teaching and assessment is blurred, as ongoing assessment is required in all planning and therefore becomes an integral part of teaching.

 TEACHER PRACTICE

The CLIS Model

Follow the CLIS model to develop a science lesson sequence. Consider using science concepts such as photosynthesis and energy.

Thus far we have examined conceptual-change models from a psychological perspective. Now we will look at two models that espouse historical approaches: the conceptual-change model (Posner et al., 1982) and the logical-evidential-psychological (LEP) model (Stinner, 1992).

The Conceptual-Change Model

While the model proposed by Nussbaum and Novick is based on Toulmin's idea of conceptual change as evolutionary (gradual change), Posner's group at Cornell University in 1978–1979 developed a model based on Kuhn's (1970) characterization of science as normal science and revolutionary science. As noted in Chapter 2, *normal science* occurs when practical scientists work within a research paradigm that is bound by specific science concepts and methods of inquiry. *Revolutionary science* is when challenges are made to scientists' basic assumptions. Posner and colleagues (1982, p. 212) compared scientific research progress to learning. From a cognitive psychological point of view, these authors paralleled normal science to assimilation and revolutionary science to accommodation. In other words, sometimes students use existing concepts to handle new ideas (assimilation); other times students must replace or reorganize their main concepts (accommodation). As well, they believed that inquiry and learning depend on the conditions of the learners' present concepts. These concepts influence their understanding of new ideas.

Posner and colleagues (1982) also believed that learning takes place within a conceptual context or environment that greatly influences what the learner does. This is indeed based on Kuhn's idea of sociohistorical context. This conceptual context or "conceptual ecology" consists of cognitive artifacts that learners are likely to possess—anomalies, metaphors, metaphysical beliefs, learned knowledge, and personal commitments.

The model developed by Posner et al. (1982) characterizes conceptual change from scientific knowledge development. Art Stinner, a science teacher educator of the University of Manitoba, Winnipeg, Canada, developed the LEP model (Stinner, 1992). Stinner uses examples from history to teach scientific concepts.

Based on Kuhn's views of science, particularly with respect to the principle of revolutionary science, Posner and colleagues (1982) believe that several important conditions must be fulfilled before new ideas can be internalized by individuals (p. 214):

1. There must be dissatisfaction with existing conceptions.
2. A new conception must be intelligible.
3. A new conception must appear initially plausible.
4. A new concept should be fruitful.

With respect to this model of learning, Hewson (1981) argued that a necessary condition for learning is that learners must first realize that their present conceptions are unsatisfactory for explaining an observation or event. However, dissatisfaction with a viewpoint is not a sufficient reason to change a viewpoint. A newer and better idea must be there to replace the original conception. The newer idea must be *intelligible,* in that the new idea must appear coherent and internally consistent. The newer idea must be *plausible,* in that the new idea is reconcilable with other aspects of the child's view of the world. And the newer idea must be *fruitful,* in that the new idea is preferable to the old viewpoint on the grounds of perceived elegance, parsimony, and economy. Hewson also emphasized the dynamic nature of the views children hold, so that any change in the viewpoint is generally gradual, affecting different aspects of a changing viewpoint at different times. Social pressures may support and legitimize a subsequent change of viewpoint.

Champagne, Klopfer, and Anderson (1980) provide an example of this model on the topic of falling bodies. Students in a class all accepted the idea that "objects accelerate when they fall freely" (concept 1). Some of these students also believed that "the faster an object moves, the greater the force acting on it" (concept 2). For these students, concept 2 is both intelligible and plausible, as they know what it means and it seems to apply to everyday experiences; if a car is to drive faster, the engine must exert more force. Concept 1, although accepted by the students, is neither intelligible nor plausible because of their belief also in concept 2 which conflicts with concept 1. In order for concept 1 to become intelligible, plausible, and fruitful, the teacher will have to provide experiences that will cause the students to discard concept 2 and retain concept 1. As well, students will have to find concept 1 useful for interpreting data they have assembled from other investigations.

The model developed by Posner et al. (1982) has served the purpose of introducing conceptual change as revolutionary in the Kuhnian sense within the constructivist framework. However, a review of research on the learning of science by Gunstone, White, and Fensham (1988) has revealed that students are quite reluctant to change their conceptions even in the face of conceptual-change instruction. Students often hold several conflicting views about the same broad concept and merely select the one that seems appropriate in any particular context.

TEACHER PRACTICE

Development of a Lesson Sequence Using the Posner et al. Model

Some examples of secondary students' conceptions:

Acid: "Acids eat material away" (Hand & Treagust, 1988).
Condensation: "Coldness caused oxygen and hydrogen in the air to form water" (Osborne & Cosgrove, 1983).
Plant nutrition: Trees grow because of the food taken through the soil (Bell & Brook, 1984).

Use the Posner et al. model to develop a lesson sequence to address one of these conceptions.

In their original conceptual-change theory, Posner and colleagues (1982) set out a central construct for their theory: the learner's *conceptual ecology.* Later, Strike and Posner (1992) expanded their definition of the range of factors that compromise the learner's conceptual ecology to include psychological factors such as the learner's motives and goals. They also noted that students' conceptions are not always clearly articulated. They may have only vague ideas about how something works or may have "body language" about how it works (p. 156). As well, students may not have any relevant prior conceptions, but develop ways of talking about an event only when it occurs. Thus, it is important to try to understand the causes and the character of a particular conception. Strike and Posner also stress that a person's scientific conceptions and personal conceptions are part of the conceptual ecology, and all parts of this system are dynamic and in constant development.

The LEP Model

Stinner (1992, 1995) brings together the works of Carnap (1966), Holton (1980), and Posner et al. (1982) to develop a conceptual model for teaching science. Stinner convincingly argues for a historical approach to answer the question: "What are good reasons for believing . . . ?" He maps out an action plan for teaching a science concept on three planes. As illustrated in Figure 3-5, the three planes of activity—the logical (L), the evidential (E), and the psychological (P)—constitute the LEP conceptual model.

The Logical Plane

The logical plane consists of concepts, theories, laws, facts, and principles of science. The concepts of chemical valence, specific heat, Newton's second law of motion ($F = ma$), the principle of conservation of energy, the Bohr

THE LEP CONCEPTUAL DEVELOPMENT MODEL

What operation(s) (from pencil-and-paper to instrumental) will link the concept to the evidential plane?

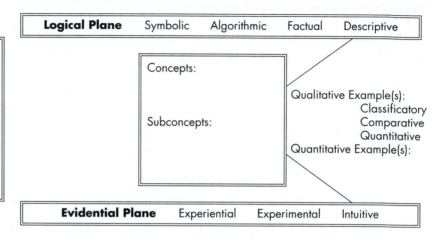

Is the activity, argument, question:

Intelligible?

Plausible?

Fruitful?

Q_1: What are good reasons for believing that . . . ?

Q_2: What are the diverse connections of the concept?

Suggested arguments, questions and activities:

Diverse connections:

Classroom implementation of your LEP model design:

Always keep in mind that conceptual development is the result of the appropriate iteration (back-and-forth) movement between the logical and evidential planes of activity, filtered through the requirements of the psychological plane.

Write a summary, giving good reasons for how you would use the activities, arguments, and questions you set for Q_1 and Q_2 in planning and implementing them. Respond to such questions as:

• On what plane of activity would you first introduce the concept?
• How would you test the preconceptions students have?
• How would you sequence your activities?
• How would you test whether a student finds the activities, arguments, and questions *intelligible, plausible,* and *fruitful?*

FIGURE 3-5

A model for concept development in science (*NOTE:* Adapted from "Science Textbooks and Science Teaching: From Logic to Evidence," by A. Stinner, 1992, *Science Education, 76,* p. 9. Copyright © 1992 by John Wiley & Sons. Reprinted by permission of John Wiley & Sons, Inc.)

model of the atom, Mendel's laws of inheritance, the Hardy-Weinberg law in genetics, the kinetic molecular theory of gases, and the notion that the electron is the basis of electric charge are situated on the logical plane. The key question on this plane is, "What operation(s) will link the concept to the evidential plane?" The solution to this question determines the extent to which activity on the logical plane relates to the evidential plane.

The Evidential Plane

The evidential plane consists of observational evidence. Experimental, intuitive, experiential connections are made to support laws, principles, and facts on the logical plane. The first question asked on this plane is, "What are good reasons for believing that . . . ?" A teacher looks for evidence that makes sense to students. The second question asked on the evidential plane is, "What are the diverse connections of these conceptions?" Students must be shown that the concept is valid in many instances.

When Newton's second law is studied, students should consider everyday examples of motion and forces. Simple experiments can be designed by both students and teacher to answer questions such as, "Is a force required to produce motion?" "What are good reasons for believing that only an unbalanced force produces an acceleration?" and "What are the diverse connections that led Newton to his second law?"

The Psychological Plane

The psychological plane involves students' personal constructions of scientific knowledge. The parallel planes (logical and evidential) meet the same vertical plane (psychological), indicating the significance of the interaction between students' personal meanings and understandings and what is taught through logic (argument) and evidence. The most important focus of the LEP model is *conceptual development*. This is achieved by linking prior knowledge to a new concept using Posner et al.'s (1982) last three conditions of conceptual change. The conception presented by the teacher must be *intelligible*. That is, $F = ma$ must be intelligible to students. Through evidence, $F = ma$ should be made *plausible*. $F = ma$ becomes *fruitful* when Newton's second law of motion is applied in a variety of situations such as linear motion, circular motion, and simple circular satellite motion. The three conditions must be met before a teacher engages students in the actual calculation of force given the quantities for mass and acceleration.

From Qualitative Understanding to Mathematical Relationships

Central to the LEP model is the notion that concepts exist in networks. For example, Newton's second law of motion is a higher-order concept that subsumes the concepts of force, mass, and acceleration, and is expressed mathematically as $F = ma$. Students must understand the concepts of force, mass, and acceleration before drawing a mathematical relationship among these concepts. It is necessary to develop qualitative ideas

A teacher can approach the third question historically by making empirical connections such as the motion of the pendulum, the results of collisions between hardwood balls attached to two pendulum, and the motion of the conical pendulum.

"Cookbook" type experiments such as verifying Newton's second law should be discouraged. The presentation of the mathematical formulation, $F = ma$, should be delayed.

through empirical procedures before assigning them symbols. A learner is believed to *know* a concept only when he or she can specify its operations and apply the concept in a concrete situation, determine quantitative relationships and assign numerical values, and make diverse connections to all aspects of science.

Carnap (1966) grouped scientific concepts into three categories: *classificatory* (qualitative), *comparative* (for example, warmer, heavier, longer), and *quantitative* (for example, assigning a number to the weight of the object). Qualitative and comparative concepts can be operationalized and are often precursors to quantitative concepts. For instance, before the concept of weight was described quantitatively, it was denoted comparatively with concepts such as heavier, lighter, and equal in weight.

Figure 3-6 maps out the relationship of the concepts of density, mass, and volume ($d = m/v$) using the LEP model.

 TEACHER PRACTICE

The LEP Model for the Development of Historical Ideas

Use the LEP model to plan a course of action for teaching $F = ma$, chemical valence, or the circulation of blood. Follow Figure 3-6, which illustrates a teaching sequence for the concept of density. Describe in detail some of the historical activities in your teaching sequence.

Much of the recent literature in science education is based on contemporary philosophy of science and the psychology of learning. The main concern has been, "How can the science teacher help students undergo conceptual change?" Extensive classroom research has shown that students do not readily change their views. The process of learning is very complex and teachers must be aware of many issues and considerations. Therefore, teachers must combine their personal practical knowledge and academic knowledge to teach science meaningfully. To successfully implement conceptual-change models, White (1993) has outlined some conditions for both teachers and students.

The Metacognitive Model

White (1993) believes that metacognition greatly influences conceptional change. He suggests that a number of conditions are necessary for the development of metacognition and conceptual change in both teachers and students. White argues that when teachers and students develop metacognitive attitudes, it is not difficult to change their way of thinking—about science concepts in the case of students and about a different way of teaching science in the case of teachers.

Although we have included the LEP model with the conceptual-change models, it appears to be different from the other conceptual change models. As the name implies, LEP begins with the expert's concept. Evidence is provided for the logical concept. In the psychological plane, Stinner has omitted the first condition that Posner and colleagues (1982) identified. The model does not explore students' prior conceptions or attempt to change conceptions. Rather, the model provides historical evidence for students to come to believe the logical concepts provided by the school textbooks. We have described the LEP model in detail because the principles of conceptual-change teaching can be easily included. The LEP model is useful because of the development of historical ideas in science.

Operational Definition of Density: [variations of] the quantitative comparison of the mass of an object with the volume it occupies.

$$D = \frac{M}{V} \; ; \; M = D \times V \; ; \; V = \frac{M}{D}$$

Mass is in kg.
Volume is in m^3
Volume = l × w × h

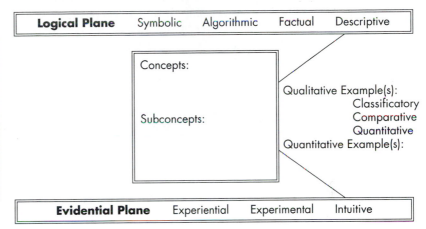

Logical Plane   Symbolic   Algorithmic   Factual   Descriptive

Is the activity, argument, question:

Intelligible?

Plausible?

Fruitful?

Psychological Plane

Preconceptions

Personal knowledge

Concepts:

Subconcepts:

Qualitative Example(s):
    Classificatory
    Comparative
    Quantitative
Quantitative Example(s):

Evidential Plane   Experiential   Experimental   Intuitive

Q_1: What are good reasons for believing that . . .

    objects float or sink in liquid according to their density?

1. How would you separate mercury, gold, and iron?
2. Discrepant events:
   a. How is it that pins can be made to float?
   b. Can you make a large piece of aluminum float?
   c. How is it that a steel ship can float?
3. Find the volume of a regular solid. Determine mass and volume.
4. Archimedes' "Eureka" story: How do you find the volume of an irregular solid?
5. How would you find the density of a sponge?
6. Design a simple hydrometer to determine the density of a liquid.
7. How would you find the density of a piece of driftwood?

Q_2: What are the diverse connections . . .

    of density?

1. Density can be determined for solids, liquids, and gases.
2. What is the density of the earth? a proton? a black hole? space?
3. The best way to determine the fat content of the human body is by flotation methods. How could this be done?
4. Hot air balloons can float in air.
5. The highest density of water occurs at 4°C. Therefore deep lakes never freeze solid.

FIGURE 3-6

The LEP model for teaching *d = m/v*. (NOTE: Adapted from "Science Textbooks and Science Teaching: From Logic to Evidence," by A. Stinner, 1992, *Science Education, 76*, p. 11. Copyright © 1992 by John Wiley & Sons. Reprinted by permission of John Wiley & Sons, Inc.)

1. *Acceptance*. The teacher and students must perceive that there is a need to change, to break away from traditional routines, and to teach and learn with purpose and responsibility.
2. *Commitment*. Attainment of metacognition and conceptual change requires commitment from both learners and teachers. Both must feel ownership of the endeavor.
3. *Support*. A supportive atmosphere must prevail, both in the classroom and with colleagues and the school administration.
4. *Power*. Teachers need to be familiar with appropriate techniques in order to bring about change. Knowledge of appropriate assessment measures that will promote quality learning is necessary.
5. *Reflection*. Students and teachers need time to look at what they are doing and why they are doing it. The teaching techniques and processes need to be shared with the students so all will be partners in the enterprise (White, 1993, pp. 13–14).

⊠ CHAPTER REVIEW

In this chapter we have discussed preservice teachers' conceptions of science teaching and learning through their metaphors and practice. We have answered the question, How do humans construct knowledge? We have explored this question by examining the psychological, sociolinguistic theories of learning. We discussed major perspectives of learning with respect to their philosophical roots, illustrated selected theories of learning with examples, and drew implications for teaching, learning, and curriculum development. Essentially, this chapter has served two purposes for preservice teachers: (a) learning about science teaching, and (b) learning about students learning science.

As you can see, we have been translating psychological and sociocultural linguistic theories of learning into science education. No one theory seems to fit perfectly with all aspects of science education. The learning theories were developed in different periods of history. Although Piaget and Vygotsky were contemporaries, they are of different origins and backgrounds—Piaget believed in the world of the senses, and Vygotsky believed in the world encoded in language. Piaget believed that we are all a product of our biological nature, whereas Vygotsky believed that we are a product of both biological nature and culture.

Learning theories convey powerful meanings for science education and should not be treated as trivial. As we have mentioned before, an understanding of learning theories does indeed help us to re-examine our beliefs about teaching and learning.

A major portion of this chapter has described conceptual-change models of teaching science—models based on psychological, philosophical, and historical theories of science. Teachers in many countries have tested these models in their classrooms. Although implementing these models takes time and energy and requires an in-depth knowledge of science, we encourage you to try these out in your practicum. Preservice teachers who have tried some of these models in traditional classrooms have found them to be very rewarding, not only for themselves but also for their students. Successful teachers are not afraid of taking risks in experimenting with teaching models, recognizing that making mistakes is an opportunity for further learning and professional growth.

PROBES

1. Based on what you have read in this chapter, what metaphor would you now give for how students learn science?
2. Which learning theory or theories would you use for your science teaching? Give reasons.
3. Observe a secondary teacher teaching science. In this teacher's practice, what learning theories are obvious? Give reasons.
4. What does a model of teaching mean to you? Describe a model of teaching that you believe one of your former teachers used (or one a present teacher uses).
5. What common assumptions are exhibited by the models in this chapter?

CHAPTER 4

Developing Learners' Multiple Intelligences

STUDY QUESTIONS

1. How does Howard Gardner conceptualize intelligence?

2. What are the different types of intelligences proposed by Howard Gardner?

3. How can we use multiple intelligences in science teaching and learning?

4. How can we promote bodily-kinesthetic and musical intelligences in science?

5. How can we promote interpersonal and intrapersonal intelligences in science education?

6. What are the different elements of memory in science as theorized by Richard White?

7. How do memory elements contribute to the development of the multiple intelligences modeled by Howard Gardner?

Reflective Inquiry

JOURNAL ACTIVITY

Your Thoughts about Students' Intelligences

How would you describe intelligence?
Could an individual have more than one form of intelligence?
If so, what might they be?
How would you justify the idea that a person can have several intelligences?
How would you propose to teach science to help students develop their different intelligences?

✪ THEORY OF MULTIPLE INTELLIGENCES: HOWARD GARDNER

One framework for looking at various ways that learning occurs has been described by Howard Gardner (1983, 1985, 1993) in his theory of multiple intelligences. Gardner's *theory of multiple intelligences* challenged the view that intelligence could be objectively measured and reduced to a numerical IQ score. Gardner questioned the validity of determining intelligence by taking students out of their natural setting and expecting them to work on isolated tasks. Gardner conceptualized human potential broadly and initially mapped out the variety of human abilities into seven intelligences:

Linguistic intelligence
Logical-mathematical intelligence
Spatial intelligence
Bodily-kinesthetic intelligence
Musical intelligence
Interpersonal intelligence
Intrapersonal intelligence

More recently, Gardner has identified an eighth intelligence, called *naturalist intelligence,* which is important to science.

Gardner (1983) arrived at the first seven intelligences by studying the capabilities of individuals with brain damage, savants, and prodigies, as well as exceptional individuals. He examined studies that pertain to individual growth and developmental patterns in a culturally valued activity, borrowing from the works of Jean Piaget (logical-mathematical intelligence), Erik Erikson (development of personal intelligences), and Lev Vygotsky (developmental models of linguistic intelligence). Gardner traced their historical evolution to understand spatial intelligence (from cave drawings to present-day computer and television technologies) and musical intelligence (from evidence of early musical instruments to present-day electronic instruments). Although Gardner does not favor decontextualized standardized tests, he analyzed these to identify the seven intelligences. Thus, his theory of multiple intelligences is supported by psychometric findings. Through studies in experimental psychology, he has concluded that intelligences can be identified separately. For example, some people have well-developed verbal intelligence and others have mathematical intelligence. Gardner believes that there are core operations that underlie a specific intelligence. For example, some individuals exhibit sensitivity to pitch and rhythm, thus displaying musical intelligence. Gardner claims that symbols underlie intelligences. For example, the language of science is a system of symbols (linguistic intelligence). Likewise, design and technology use graphics (spatial intelligence).

We will examine each of the seven intelligences as well as the most recently identified eighth intelligence, naturalist intelligence, with examples taken from science. Although these eight intelligences interact in complex ways in culturally diverse situations, we will examine them separately for the purpose of indicating how they can be developed in a science class.

Linguistic Intelligence

In Chapter 3 we learned that Vygotsky was interested in the developmental models of linguistic intelligence. Words have power because they express our thinking. Much of science is taught through words, both orally and in writing—the teacher talks and writes and students listen. There is even greater value when students talk and write science, attempting to convince others of their ideas. When we do labs, the experiment is discussed in words and reports are written. Thus, the development of language facility in science enables one to communicate effectively. Science is not always "hands-on." There is thinking involved in any hands-on activity, and those thoughts are expressed in words, either spoken or written. Reading, writing, and talking about science and listening to science talk must be encouraged.

In a science class, linguistic intelligence may be developed in a variety of ways: brainstorming for ideas about a science concept and recording them on the board, chart paper, or an overhead transparency at the start of the unit; exploring students' understanding using a task or diagram or by writing journals about a phenomenon; students talking with the teacher and their peers about what they know in science; telling stories about scientists by weaving in essential ideas and concepts that scientists discovered; debating scientific issues; writing research papers; carrying out scientific discussions in small and large groups; and communicating science using proper vocabulary.

Logical-Mathematical Intelligence

Science has been primarily considered a subject that requires reasoning capability and sensitivity. Science is filled with logical patterns of reasoning, relationships, statements and propositions, functions, and abstractions. We are familiar with scientific processes such as classification, inference, generalization, and testing hypotheses that involve logical thinking. Students who exhibit logical-mathematical intelligence show interest in new developments in science, conduct "what if" experiments (What if I double the volume of water? What happens to the concentration of solute?), give rational explanations for events, often think on an abstract or conceptual level, ask questions about how things work, and experiment using higher-order cognitive thinking processes. They also like to conceptualize, think critically, measure, categorize, analyze, and quantify. They enjoy problem solving, conduct experiments confidently using science equipment, and engage in **Socratic questioning.**

Students with logical-mathematical intelligence also engage in "science thinking." Global issues such as the greenhouse effect, ozone depletion, and AIDS require science thinking and science background knowledge.

In **Socratic questioning,** the teacher questions the students' point of view. In this method of teaching, the teacher does not talk *at* students; instead, he or she talks *with* students in an attempt to get at students' deep-seated beliefs.

In science, students learn to translate qualitative ideas into mathematical relationships. For example, we often use a toaster to toast bread. The coil in a toaster is made of nichrome wire. The coil provides a resistance to the current producing enough heat to make the wire red hot. The radiated heat then toasts the bread. Using the mathematical relationship among potential difference, current, and resistance (Ohm's Law: $V = IR$, where V is the potential difference, I hr is the current, and R is the resistance), we can find the resistance of a conductor in the toaster if we know the numerical values for potential difference and current.

Spatial Intelligence

Spatial intelligence involves pictures: "the images in one's mind or the images in the external world" (Armstrong, 1994). The three-dimensional representation of chemical structures is an example of images in one's mind. Tracing the nervous system during the dissection of a frog can be considered an image of the external world. A *picture metaphor* expresses an idea in a visual image. *Idea sketching* is using a simple drawing in developing a powerful idea. Armstrong (1994) reminds us that the notebooks of many eminent scientists in history, including Charles Darwin and Thomas Edison, contained simple drawings the scientists used in developing many of their powerful ideas. Armstrong's admonitions to teachers are as follows:

> Teachers should recognize the value this kind of visual thinking can have in helping students articulate their understanding of subject matter. The Idea

Sketching strategy involves asking students to draw the key point, main idea, central theme, or core concept being taught. . . . ask students to draw the concept or idea you want to focus on in a lesson. This strategy can be used to evaluate a student's understanding of an idea, to emphasize a concept, or to give students ample opportunity to explore an idea in greater depth. . . . Following up the drawing activity with a discussion of the relationship between the drawings and the subject matter is important. Do not evaluate the drawings themselves; instead seek to "draw out" students' understanding from the sketches . . . graphic symbols that depict the concepts to be learned . . . showing the three states of matter by drawing a solid mass (heavy chalk marks), a liquid mass (lighter curvy marks), and a gaseous mass (little dots). (1994, pp. 73–74)

Modern computer technologies are very useful in developing visual thinking. For example, with computer programs, students can create concept maps, mind maps, cluster maps, and the like to generate and clarify ideas. Students also use computers to represent their ideas graphically. Read Chapter 10 to learn how computers can aid in spatial intelligence.

Bodily-Kinesthetic Intelligence

Development of bodily-kinesthetic intelligence involves hands-on experience and whole-body movement. Hands-on activities are an integral part of science. Students who engage in numerous laboratory experiments and investigations actually have a feel for what they are doing. Hands-on science is an active process when every sense is brought into action. Thinking is also involved.

Science can be also taught through whole-body movement. Students can gain understanding of various scientific phenomena through role playing, which is discussed further in Chapter 7. As their bodies move through a simulation activity, they are better able to visualize the process. In another example, in ice skating the pressure of the skate melts the ice,

forming a thin layer of water between the skate and the ice and reducing friction. Through a skating activity, which involves body movement, students can learn about the concepts of pressure and friction. Figure skating is also an example of body movement in which students can discuss the concept of centripetal force.

Musical Intelligence

Musical intelligence may be developed through science. Students can be encouraged to compose poems and write songs using scientific ideas and concepts. Expression of scientific ideas through music could be an interesting way to teach science.

The concept of waves is useful in determining the properties of various sounds. Different types of instruments such as the piano, clarinet, trombone, and violin can be played and the characteristics of sound (frequency, pitch, and intensity) can be taught, thus drawing on and enhancing the musical intelligence of a learner. For example, Angela Poetteker, a chemistry preservice teacher, composed the following song to illustrate musical intelligence.

ACID RAIN IS GONNA FLY
(To the tune of "Fly" by Sugar Ray)
> All around the world, statues crumble 'cause of me,
> I've been here since 1733.
> Everywhere I go people deny they've caused me.
> 2000 years old, the Colosseum's got to go.
>
> *Chorus 1:*
> All the lakes will die.
> Unless you neutralize me, baby,
> Unless you neutralize me, baby.
> (2 times).
>
> You can't contain me, 'cause I've got no boundaries.
> Unless you do something, my cycle will start again!
> There's no time to think of my beginning or my end,
> You've got to have a plan, or I'll acidify the land.
>
> *Chorus 2:*
> All the lakes will die.
> Unless you minimize emissions,
> Unless you minimize emissions.
> (2 times).
>
> All around the world, statues crumble 'cause of me.
> I've been here since 1733.
> The people of the Earth have been so good to me.
> 2000 years old, the Colosseum's got to go.
>
> *Chorus 1*
> *Chorus 2* (Angela Poetteker, 1998 P-STAR Conference)

Jerry Semchyshyn, a preservice teacher, composed the following song about force, pressure, and buoyancy.

Force, Pressure and Buoyancy

Jerry Semchyshyn

Interpersonal Intelligence

Learning is an act of observing, listening, and speaking. Thus, learning is a social phenomenon. These social attributes of learning thrive better when cooperation among class members is promoted and systematically practiced. Studies indicate that cooperative learning improves achievement, self-esteem, and social skills (Johnson & Johnson, 1989; Slavin, 1990, 1995).

In conceptual-change models of teaching, there are many opportunities for cooperative learning. Students learn to compare ideas, consider different interpretations and responses, achieve consensus, and agree on an approach to a problem (Yager, 1995). Interpersonal relationships among students will continue to develop when group members freely share their ideas about science concepts. They can also collectively set goals to conduct investigations and report on scientific issues such as the origin and structure of the universe, the ethics of cloning, and transplanting organs. The shared goals are then accomplished through a negotiation process that requires group planning, decision making, and action taking.

Open communication and dialogue are fundamental when students work as a community of researchers. Students can each bring their knowledge and skills to the task at hand. The group takes interest and pride in each member's accomplishment (Johnson, Johnson, & Holubec, 1993). Thus a science class may serve as a context to develop interpersonal communication skills, skills in building and maintaining trust, controversy and conflict management skills, leadership skills, and peer mediation skills (Putnam, 1997).

The development of interpersonal skills in a science class is important so that students may understand the nature of scientific inquiry. Longino (1990) proposed that the primary method of objectifying knowledge involves interpersonal negotiation aimed at achieving social consensus. Scientists work in a social context, answerable to and influenced by members of the larger society. Members of a society often dictate what knowledge will be sought, what research will be done, and what research will be funded. Hence, science is a complex social enterprise.

Intrapersonal Intelligence

Social interaction is critical in developing scientific knowledge, but so is the work of the individual scientist operating alone to resolve a discrepancy that perhaps no one else has yet recognized. Einstein seems to have been somewhat of a loner. He recognized a problem with electromagnetic theory when he was about sixteen years old. He wondered what one would see or experience if he or she traveled alongside of a beam of light. In his autobiography he talks about the years before 1905, when relativity was his life. His resolution of the problem came in 1905 from individual insights about the nature of time. In his autobiography he speaks of the importance of conversations with an engineer friend. But it is not clear whether the friend's support was emotional or intellectual. From Einstein's insights about his own construction of knowledge, we see that scientific knowledge resides in individual insights and perseverance as well as in social practice.

A science class can serve as a context in which to develop intrapersonal intelligence. Students can explore their own ideas about a natural phenomenon and be involved in self-assessment. Personal attitudes and feelings of individual students may be explored in a science lesson so that the teacher can examine his or her teaching practice. When studying a scientific issue, each student can identify problems, suggest possible explanations, and engage in self-analysis and reflection (Yager, 1995). Science must have personal relevance. To be successful in science each student must commit to learning.

Johnson, Johnson, and Holubec (1993) suggest that the success of cooperative learning depends on its individual members. Each member of a cooperative group must faithfully carry out the task until the task is completed. When one or two members shirk responsibility, the group efforts suffer. Every member should participate in learning the material. To develop interpersonal relationships, individual accountability is necessary.

Naturalist Intelligence

In a 1995 article Gardner examined seven "myths" about multiple intelligences. The last of the seven was the myth that there are other intelligences, in addition to the seven listed above. Gardner suggested that if he were developing his theory at that time he would probably add an eighth intelligence—the intelligence of the naturalist. He described this

FIGURE 4-1

Multiple intelligences (*NOTE:* Adapted from *Multiple Intelligences in the Classroom* (pp. 2–3), by T. Armstrong. Alexandria, VA: Association for Supervision and Curriculum Development. Copyright © 1994 ASCD. Reprinted by permission. All rights reserved.)

Linguistic intelligence: ability to use language, both written and oral
Logical-mathematical intelligence: ability to understand and use numbers and to reason logically
Spatial intelligence: ability to perceive the visual-spatial world accurately and to transform perceptions spatially
Bodily-kinesthetic intelligence: ability to use both the whole body and the hands to manipulate objects and materials and to express ideas and emotions
Musical intelligence: ability to interpret, discriminate, and express musical forms
Interpersonal intelligence: ability to be aware and sensitive to the needs and emotions of others
Intrapersonal intelligence: ability to have a realistic knowledge of one's own abilities, limitations, needs, etc. along with a capacity for self-discipline

intelligence as the ability to readily recognize flora and fauna, to make other consequential distinctions in the natural world, and to use this ability productively (Gardner, 1995). This is an intelligence of critical importance in learning science.

Figure 4-1 presents a summary of multiple intelligences.

⊠ DEVELOPMENT OF INTELLIGENCES THROUGH SCIENCE LESSONS

Every child has several or all of the eight intelligences in varying capacities. Intelligences in each individual child interact in complex ways. In a science class, these intelligences can be developed to various levels of competency.

Gardner's theory of multiple intelligences can help us ensure that we are meeting the needs of all of our students by providing a variety of activities that draw on all of the different intelligences. Figures 4-2a, 4-2b, and 4-2c illustrate how a teacher might draw on a variety of intelligences in different activities and strategies during units on heat and temperature, neutralization of acids and bases, and phase change, respectively.

FIGURE 4-2a

Development of multiple intelligences: heat and temperature

Linguistic: Students complete written reports on the conduction of heat; students present results of a lab activity on a topic such as the specific heat of water to the whole class.
Logical-mathematical: Students calculate the expected final temperature of water when two cups of water of known volumes and at a known temperature are combined.

continued

Spatial: Students visualize the spacing and motion of molecules during phase change of matter (solid water, liquid water, gaseous water).

Bodily-kinesthetic: Students role-play the kinetic molecular theory—they are molecules and demonstrate the differences in molecular motion in the three phases (solid, liquid, and gas).

Musical: The teacher plays a recording of a song by Flanders and Swan about the kinetic theory of heat.

Interpersonal: Students work in small groups to prepare posters that demonstrate some aspect of heat and temperature.

Intrapersonal: Students are asked to propose an explanation about heating a substance. For example, some students believe that particles melt when a substance is heated, thus extending macroscopic properties to molecules and submicroscopic particles.

Naturalist: Students explain adaptations found in arctic (or desert) plants and animals that allow them to live in an extreme climate.

Linguistic: Students complete "Writing to Learn" journal entries to demonstrate their conceptions about solving titration problems; students complete lab reports based on a *Vee diagram* event.

Logical-mathematical: Students develop graphs for the Vee diagram activity and STSE report; students write down chemical formulas as an extension of the Vee diagram event; students calculate the concentration of hydrochloric acid as requested in the Writing to Learn activity; students complete a "Word Cycle" based on acids and bases as a unit review.

Spatial: Students visualize their inventions during the developmental stages of the "Design Technology" project; students follow a multimedia computer simulation; students figuratively represent acids (or bases) on the "Concept Overview Frame"; students diagram concepts related to acids and bases on the "Three-Point Approach frame for Words and Concepts"; students are asked to visualize the setting of the reading that precedes discussion during the STSE activity.

Bodily-kinesthetic: Students role-play the neutralization of HCl and NaOH; students actively complete the Vee diagram event.

Musical: Students listen to the reading on acid rain; students listen to the song "Acid Rain Is Gonna Fly"; students are encouraged to write their own songs about acids and bases.

Interpersonal: Students work in small and medium-sized groups to analyze the positive and negative aspects of acid rain; students complete "Exit" slips to be shared with the teacher to demonstrate their knowledge and understanding of concepts in the unit on acids and bases; students are encouraged to use chemistry chat rooms and tutorial sites on the Internet to seek responses to their questions about acids and bases.

continued

FIGURE 4-2b
Development of multiple intelligences: neutralization of acids and bases (*NOTE:* From M. Kattenfeld & A. Poetteker, 1998 Chemistry P-STAR Conference.)

Teaching strategies that the preservice teachers have used to illustrate multiple intelligences—for example, Vee diagrams, brochures, role play, writing poems, journaling, and analogy mapping—will be discussed in subsequent chapters. The Concept Overview Frame and Three-Point Approach for Words and Concepts are not described in this book.

FIGURE 4-2b
continued

Intrapersonal: Students are asked to explain what happens when antacids react with stomach acid; students individually reflect on the effects of acid rain before sharing with group members in a "Think-Pair-Share" arrangement; students complete the Writing to Learn journal activity; students respond to teacher-generated questions through Exit slips.
Naturalist: Students propose and discuss solutions to combat acid rain during the STSE activity.
Creative: Students use creativity in the development of their Design Technology project; students generate their own R.A.F.T. activities.
Intuitive: Students are asked to propose hypotheses as to the most effective antacid, based on their knowledge of pH; students must use their intuitive powers in the designing and development of their Design Technology projects.

FIGURE 4-2c
Development of multiple intelligences: Phase changes (*NOTE:* From R. Hechter, S. Primmett, & R. Urbanik, 1998 Chemistry P-STAR Conference.)

Linguistic: Have students write and map an analogy for the phase changes of water at the molecular level. Have students read an article on the impact that global warming has had on the melting of glaciers. These activities will develop understanding of the concept on a personal and global level. It may be important to take the time to teach students how to map analogies so that they can take this strategy to other concepts.
Logical-mathematical: Have students perform an experiment that measures the change in temperature as ice changes its state to water and then to steam. Then have students draw a graph and interpret the results. This allows students to take analytical measurements and make predictions prior to the start of the experiment.
Spatial: Have students draw at the molecular level using computers to show what happens when water begins to boil (inside the bubble). This activity, which can also be used with solids and liquids, addresses students' conceptions of phase change. This can be an initial activity that leads up to the analogy writing in the linguistic category. This activity encourages students to look beyond and visualize what they see.
Bodily-kinesthetic: Role-play or dance the process by which the rates of molecules move from one phase to the next. Manipulate everyday materials to show phase changes of substances other than water (diffusion of liquid perfume, increasing vapor pressure with a soft drink bottle).
Musical: Encourage students to borrow the tune from a well-liked song of their choice and write a song about phase changes. If possible, have students perform the song! It is very important to show students that writing a song can be an attainable goal. Composing a song also encourages creativity with science concepts and a little silliness.
Interpersonal: Have students work in small groups to develop a technological design that incorporates phase changes. Incorporate cooperative learning methods with large concepts, such as environmental issues.
Intrapersonal: Have students write a poem about content-related words. Encourage students to keep a reflective journal on the different types of

continued

FIGURE 4-2c
continued

activities and concepts that they like and dislike. Have students develop a poster or brochure for a company that incorporates phase changes (travel agency, foodservice company, clothing manufacturer, and the like).

When we describe how people are different, we refer to race, language, appearance, and attitude, to mention a few. However, we rarely refer to a person being different by the way he or she learns. Gardner's theory of multiple intelligences provides a framework on which to structure lesson plans. It also helps teachers view students as individuals who learn in different ways.

TEACHER PRACTICE

Gardner's Theory of Multiple Intelligences
Illustrate how you would teach a certain science topic using Gardner's theory of multiple intelligences.

PEER TALK

Desirability or Possibility of Basing Lessons on Multiple Intelligences
Advocates of the theory of multiple intelligences tend to suggest that each lesson should have a multiple intelligences component. What do you think? Is it desirable or possible for each science lesson to have a multiple intelligences component? Why or why not?

In the next section we describe different types of knowledge in science and how they contribute to developing multiple intelligences. White (1988) has described elements of memory that denote different types of knowledge in science. In fact, memory is just one part of intelligence, but White's description of several memory elements seems to tie into multiple intelligences.

The scientific research literature contains many different types of established scientific knowledge, distilled from many years of research. Our inquiry in Chapter 2 concerned how such knowledge is generated. We also asked: Does our knowing depend on the external physical world? Do we use our prior beliefs, knowledge, and understandings to view natural phenomena? The ancient Greeks came to know the visible world through their senses. For empiricists, all knowledge originates in the sensory apparatus. Currently, science philosophers hold the view that scientists' beliefs, expectations, and social environment play a major role in shaping their observations. Both empirical and conceptual knowledge are handed down to each generation; print and electronic media are sources of "passed-on" knowledge, and students are expected to learn the core ideas of science. What different types of knowledge occur in science? And how do we learn these?

⊗ WHITE'S MODEL OF LEARNING SCIENCE

Memory is believed to be at the core of learning. White (1988) suggests seven different elements of memory to describe learning science: strings, propositions, images, episodes, intellectual skills, motor skills, and cognitive strategies. The following margin notes indicate multiple intelligences that are related to each of the memory elements.

Strings

Logico-mathematical intelligence

Strings are sequences of words or symbols that are "given" and cannot be readily paraphrased. Physical laws and definitions, such as "For every action there is an equal and opposite reaction" and "The angle of incidence is equal to the angle of reflection," are referred to as strings. Chemical formulas and equations, such as "$2H_2O \rightarrow 2H_2 + O_2$" are also examples of strings. Students of science are expected to learn and use a number of strings. Students' memory of science strings can be placed at one end of the continuum that ranges from rote learning to deep understanding.

Propositions

Logico-mathematical intelligence

Propositions are sequences of words or statements that describe properties of concepts or draw relations between concepts: "Acids neutralize bases," "Fish have gills," "Matter is made up of mass and space." Unlike strings, propositions can be expressed in an equivalent form. For example, the formula, $d = m/v$ is a string, but when a learner transposes it to an equivalent form, $m = d \times v$, to determine the mass of an object, it becomes a proposition for this learner. For this individual, both formulas express the same element of knowledge. Propositions are therefore relations that can be expressed in various forms.

Our memories consist of many propositions: the things that we read, know, and tell each other. Propositions can be both facts and beliefs. In science, facts are socially accepted beliefs. However, the degree of social consensus about a proposition lies on a continuum and may be culturally distinct. Whether a proposition is accepted as common knowledge depends on the demonstration of consistency. While the number of seasons is arbitrary, the belief that the Earth rotates around the Sun is a fact because the latter can be shown in consistent ways. All beliefs are social constructs or inventions that describe the perceived world. *Sun, Moon, Earth, rotation, revolution,* and *eclipses* are all concepts that humans have invented to help us understand each other as we communicate about the world we see. As teachers we ought to understand how propositions in science are constructed, changed, and discarded by our students.

Images

Images are mental pictures. Strings and propositions can be seen as images. Images are not only visual but relate to all five senses. We can mentally picture licorice candy by its color, smell, taste, and touch. We can also imagine the sound of a school bell, a hand bell, or an electric bell. For our study, what is important is "the function images play in the learning of science" (White, 1988, p. 29). Images can be self-invented or taught by others. Usually images are socially transmitted and then personally constructed. Studies indicate that "people vary in the intensity with which they experience imagery. . . . [Their] imagery powers may vary across the senses" (p. 30). Since images are triggered readily in most minds, it is important to use imagery in science class.

Spatial intelligence

Episodes

"Episodes are our records of experience, memories of events, occurrences we took part in or witnessed" (White, 1988, p. 31). We store and recall episodes when they are important to us. The ability to store and recall episodes varies from person to person. Only the episodes we bring to memory are available to us for a long time. An episode can be a real event, a **transformed event,** or an **imagined event.**

There are idiosyncratic and generalized episodes. The latter type are called *scripts* because they guide behavior to deal with similar events (Schank & Abelson, 1977). In science we come across many scripts, which are necessary to meet standards and expectations as well as to further our studies and prepare for our careers. For example, we use microscopes in certain commonly accepted ways, or follow procedures for folding filter paper and placing it in a funnel in a distinct way. In learning science, episodes are important. Teachers have cultivated scripts for situations that should be taught to students so that communication is more effective between teachers and students. Episodic memory is different from semantic memory; episodic memory is based on experience, whereas semantic memory (strings and propositions) is conceptual.

A **transformed event** is a real event that is recalled differently by a person at a given time.

An **imagined event** is invented by someone who gradually comes to believe in it.

Bodily-Kinesthetic intelligence

Intellectual Skills

Intellectual skills are "knowing how," in contrast to propositional knowledge, which is "knowing that." Propositions are discrete facts, whereas an intellectual skill consists of knowing how to perform a series of related tasks. The acts of discriminating, classifying, and following rules are examples of three different forms of intellectual skills that are important in science.

Logico-mathematical intelligence

Not all white powders or clear liquids are the same to a chemist. Similarly, not all rocks and trees are the same to a geologist and biologist, respectively. *Discrimination skills* must be taught so that students know how to identify substances through specific properties or special features.

Science is filled with classification systems—for example, classification of the elements (the periodic chart) and classification of living things (the animal and plant kingdoms); thus, students must be taught *classification skills*. Sometimes we classify instantaneously using all our senses. However, we cannot depend on perceptions to classify everything immediately. Sometimes we must use definitions and run tests to be able to classify, especially when we are not familiar with objects or they are not readily perceivable. A beginner must run through a list of properties to classify rocks as igneous, metamorphic, or sedimentary. A geologist does it quickly and easily. When matter is not directly observable, we must run tests to determine its properties. For example, different colorless gases are distinguished using specific tests—hydrogen gas extinguishes a flame by making a popping sound, while oxygen gas supports combustion.

Classification is hierarchical and leads us into finer and clearer distinctions. A beginner usually learns to classify from more general to specific, but the direction of learning can be either way. "Classes are a human fractioning of a continuous universe" (White, 1988, p. 37) and therefore the use of classes can be idiosyncratic. However, in science this is not so, because scientists have agreed upon their classification systems; therefore, they are able to communicate through a common language. In a secondary science class, students must be given ample opportunities to classify the continuous world by reaching consensus. They must be also taught

that concepts such as *force, solution,* and *magnetism* have a specific meaning in science, and therefore the contexts in which the language is used
becomes very important. In a science class, students should aim to reach
the scientific interpretation for a given terminology to reduce the discrepancy in communication between a teacher and students. To achieve this
goal, students' classification systems or meaning of a concept must be initially considered by the teacher.

Following rules is another intellectual skill. Rules are part of our memories and we apply rules in learning science. Rules are procedures or algo-
rithms applied to a system of tasks. Being able to balance chemical equations, calculate the number of moles of reactants and products, add vectors
graphically to find velocity at a point on a position-time graph, and draw
Punnet squares to determine genes are all *rule-following* intellectual skills.

Motor Skills

Science is a human activity. Therefore, thinking can occur while all the
senses are in play. Using the microscope, balance, pipette, and burette all
involve motor skills. Motor skills are memories of how to make complex
muscle movements.

Bodily-Kinesthetic intelligence

Interpersonal and Intrapersonal
Intelligences

Cognitive Strategies

Cognitive strategies, which are essential for problem solving, are not highly specialized intellectual skills like those we described previously. They are general skills that we use in our thinking, learning, and doing. In learning science we use general skills such as setting aims and goals, considering and working out different possibilities, choosing the best option, and generalizing across related contexts. Problem solving is a complex performance that involves applying a combination of the memory elements, particularly by using cognitive strategies.

White's summary of the seven types of memory elements for learning science is presented in Figure 4-3.

PEER TALK

White's Memory Elements

Think of a science task or question that involves each of the memory elements.

or:

Analyze a chapter in a science textbook for various memory elements.

The example of density is taken from White (1988). We use this specific example in this chapter because in Chapter 5 we provide a laboratory activity done by an eighth-grade student. You may readily see some of the elements being played out and how they contribute to the development of various intelligences of students.

In your analysis of a science task or a chapter, did you notice the association of the memory elements in a complex network? Concept labels such as *acids, freezing, density, electricity, force, photosynthesis,* and *genes* can bring all the elements into play. How can we apply each of the memory elements to the concept of density (see Figure 4-4)?

When we say a student "has the concept of density," we mean that the student has associated or linked the different memory elements—strings, propositions, images, episodes, intellectual and motor skills, and cognitive strategies—to understand the label *density*. No two students will have identical concepts of density. "The similarity of their concepts is a function of the overlap, the intersection, between their sets of elements" (White, 1988, p. 46). To assess a student's knowledge, the teacher's question is, "Is there a sufficient intersection and overlap between what the students know and what I know?" Hence, the teacher must involve students in the association of all the memory elements for understanding a variety of concepts in science. "Why?" questions must be asked and explanations must be given for propositions, procedures, and skills. Imagery and episodes play a major role in understanding. Simply using the language labels does not increase understanding; to engender greater understanding of a concept, the amount and the nature of knowledge as well as the pattern of association between its elements are important. Much propositional knowledge may not enhance the quality of learning. Propositional knowl-

Element	Brief Definition	Example
String	A sequence of words or symbols recalled as a whole in an invariate form	"To every action there is an equal and opposite reaction"
Proposition	A description of a property of a concept or of the relation between concepts	"The yeast plant is unicellular"
Image	A mental representation of a sensation	The shape of a thistle funnel; the smell of chlorine
Episode	Memory of an event one took part in or witnessed	An accident in the laboratory; the setting up of a microscope
Intellectual skill	The capacity to perform a whole class of mental tasks	Balancing chemical equations
Motor skill	The capacity to perform a whole class of physical tasks	Pouring a liquid to a mark
Cognitive strategy	A general skill involved in controlling thinking	Perceiving alternative interpretations; determining goals; judging likelihood of success

FIGURE 4-3

Seven types of memory elements (*NOTE:* From *Learning Science* (Table 3.1, p. 23) by R. T. White, 1988, Oxford, England,: Basil Blackwell. Copyright 1988 by Basil Blackwell. Reprinted with permission.)

String: Density is the mass per unit volume of a substance: $d = m/v$.

Propositions: The density of water is 1 g/cm^3. Solids float in liquids that are more dense. Oil is less dense than water.

Images: Picture icebergs or wood floating on water; a picture of dots representing atoms, close together for a dense substance and far apart for a less dense one; the feel of a dense object when lifted.

Episodes: Have a half-gallon milk carton filled with lead and leave it standing on the bench. Ask a student to get it and pass it around, to construct a long-lasting experience with the concept of density. Then pass another milk carton filled with polystyrene foam pieces that are painted silver-gray so they look like metal.

Intellectual Skills: Classify objects according to density, using the formula to calculate density (mathematical procedures).

Motor Skills: Find the mass and volume of the regular and irregular objects in the laboratory.

Cognitive Strategies: Translate the concept of density to everyday life. Why do we learn about density? Frequent oil spills by ocean tankers enable us to think about the relative density of oil and water. The relative density of various syrups gives us information about the sugar content.

FIGURE 4-4

Association of memory elements (*NOTE:* From *Learning Science* by R. T. White, 1988, Oxford, England, Basil Blackwell. Copyright 1988 by Basil Blackwell. Reprinted with permission.)

edge combined with episodes is a more powerful way of learning science. It is no wonder that demonstrations, laboratory activities, and field work are emphasized in science teaching. For example, students can learn the kinetic theory of heat at a subjective level when they observe Brownian movement. Understanding a concept is a continuous function of the knower. The assessment of this understanding is based on the person who is judging (the teacher) and the status of the person who is being judged (the student).

⊗ SYNTHESIS OF MULTIPLE INTELLIGENCES AND TYPES OF KNOWLEDGE

In the process of teaching and learning, it is helpful to understand how the various memory elements contribute to the development of learners' multiple intelligences. Armstrong (1994, pp. 177, 178) gives an example of a lesson plan to teach the concept of Boyle's law for secondary chemistry students. We denote Gardner's multiple intelligences in original form using square brackets and White's corresponding elements of memory using curly brackets.

LEVEL: HIGH SCHOOL

SUBJECT: CHEMISTRY

OBJECTIVE: TO TEACH THE CONCEPT OF BOYLE'S LAW

- Students learn Boyle's law: "For a fixed mass and temperature of gas, the pressure is inversely proportional to the volume." They discuss the definition. [Linguistic] {String}
- Students are given a formula that describes Boyle's law: $P \times V = K$. They solve specific problems connected to it. [Logical-Mathematical] {String}
- Students are given a metaphor or visual image for Boyle's law: Air mattresses and pillows are examples of air being compressed. [Spatial] {Images}
- Students do the following experiment: They breathe air into their mouths so that their cheeks puff up slightly. Then they put all the air into one side of their mouth (less volume) and indicate whether pressure goes up or down (it goes up); then they release the air into both sides of their mouth (more volume) and indicate whether pressure has gone up or down (it goes down). [Bodily-kinesthetic] {Motor skills}
- Students rhythmically repeat the following musical mnemonic:

  > When the volume goes down
  > The pressure goes up
  > The blood starts to boil
  > And a scream erupts
  > "I need more space

Or I'm going to frown"
The volume goes up
And the pressure goes down. [Musical] {Proposition}

- Students become "molecules" of air in a "container" (a clearly defined corner of the classroom). They move at a constant rate (temperature) and cannot leave the container (constant mass). Gradually the size of the container is reduced as two volunteers holding a piece of yarn representing one side of the container start moving it in on the "people molecules." The smaller the space, the more pressure (that is, bumping into each other) is observed; the greater the space, the less pressure [Interpersonal, bodily-kinesthetic] {Motor skill}
- Students do lab experiments that measure air pressure in sealed containers and chart pressure against volume. [Logical-mathematical, bodily-kinesthetic] {Propositions, Motor skills}
- Students are asked about times in their lives when they were "under pressure": "Did you feel like you had a lot of space?" (Typical answer: lots of pressure/not much space.) Then students are asked about times when they felt little pressure (little pressure/lots of space). Students' experiences are related to Boyle's law. [Intrapersonal] {Episode}

In this lesson plan, we notice that White's *cognitive strategies* memory element is missing.

⚙ CHAPTER REVIEW

In this chapter we have discussed Gardner's theory of multiple intelligences through a number of illustrations and examples. We have also analyzed science content to indicate different types of memory elements according to White. Although memory is enhanced in science class through the development of the first three intelligences proposed by Gardner, paying attention to other forms of intelligence may aid in retention. We paralleled White's work on memory to Gardner's theory of multiple intelligences. The more meaningful the learning is in terms of multiple intelligences, the more memorable it is, and most likely the memory will be stored in one of the forms listed by White.

Through Gardner's and White's work we realize that there are different types of knowledge and that teachers should make every effort to help students recognize their multiple intelligences. Teachers should also help students become aware of and use the strategies and tools that develop their multiple intelligences. The next few chapters provide you with many teaching, learning, and assessment strategies that will develop students' multiple intelligences.

PROBES

1. What are your thoughts about learning and teaching science to meet the needs of your students' many intelligences?

2. Would you have learned science more easily if your teacher had been more aware of your various intelligences?
3. Observe a teacher teaching a unit in science. What kinds of knowledge are students asked to demonstrate?
4. Critique a teacher's way of connecting the different types of knowledge in science.
5. Develop a conceptual-change sequence of science lessons. In this lesson sequence, indicate how you would attend to multiple intelligences.

PART TWO

STRATEGIES FOR SCIENCE DISCOURSE

In Part One we considered some of the broader issues associated with learning and teaching science—topics that preservice teachers sometimes refer to as "the theory." We saw that many preservice teachers found it difficult to think of teaching except in the context of presenting information to be learned, or practical lab activities to be performed. We now turn to strategies for teaching science that will encourage our students to learn for understanding rather than being content with the ability to repeat definitions and facts about science.

In Chapter 5 we consider some of the more traditional teaching strategies, but perhaps with a new twist. The importance of reading is sometimes overlooked in science teaching, but a brief look at Ben Carson helps us recognize the critical importance of reading. We next consider how practical activities can help our students develop a better understanding of science. Variations of investigations are also considered: group investigations, activity stations, demonstrations, and a strategy often called POE (Predict-Observe-Explain).

Chapter 6 considers the use of journals and other forms of writing and how writing contributes to learning science for understanding. Chapter 7 considers the use of analogies, and a number of other strategies that are more commonly used in language arts and fine arts courses: letter writing, poetry, cartooning, role plays, and brochure writing.

Chapter 8 concludes the strategies section by describing concept maps and vee diagrams: two heuristic strategies for helping learners structure and organize their knowledge to facilitate meaningful learning.

CHAPTER 5

Strategies for Scientific Inquiry

STUDY QUESTIONS

1. Why are reading skills necessary for science learners?

2. How do contemporary approaches to school science laboratory activities compare with conventional approaches?

3. Why is cooperative learning important in school science inquiry?

4. How are science activity stations used?

5. How can a teacher apply cooperative learning strategies to a laboratory investigation?

6. How is the Predict-Observe-Explain strategy conducted?

7. What is a discrepant event? Give examples.

Reflective Inquiry

ANGELA'S VOICE

In today's society, it is important that students become scientifically literate in order that they might understand scientific claims and correctly interpret research findings reported in the mass media. By reading, students can not only develop their linguistic and intrapersonal intelligences, but through example can learn how to effectively and accurately communicate scientific information.

Eliot Eisner has said that "[l]iteracy is not limited to text but relates to the ability to construe meaning in any of the forms used in a culture to create and convey meaning." Thus, it is important that students be able to "read" chemical labels (for example, MSDS sheets), scales of measurement (for example, thermometers), graphs, charts, and diagrams for the safety of everyone in a laboratory.

Using a textbook in the science classroom can serve as an invaluable resource to the science teacher. Appropriate readings may be used to link students' prior knowledge with new concepts, while contrasting the most common student conceptions with a "correct" conception. The textbook provides an interesting way to seek answers to student-posed questions, introduce chemical vocabulary, expand students' learning experiences, and demonstrate how science has historically impacted upon society.

Traditionally, textbooks have been used in science classrooms to search for additional information and to reinforce knowledge presented by the teacher. Today, reading may be used as a learning tool with (as opposed to from) which students can learn and construct meaning while verifying and comparing facts. Used in this way, there is a greater opportunity for students to develop an appreciation of reading that might be extended to all facets of their personal lives.

All self-regulated learners, thinkers, and problem solvers know how to use reading and writing to learn. The same skills that make good readers (engaging prior knowledge, forming hypotheses, establishing plans, and so on) make good scientists. Therefore, reading is important in the science classroom so that teachers can help students develop the skills to become scientists in the laboratory and in society.

JOURNAL ACTIVITY

Preferences for Learning Science
How do you best learn science? List your ways of learning. Rank-order them.

Educating all students to achieve scientific literacy and preparing students for scientific careers are two major goals of science education. We need scientifically literate citizens who can understand and deal with scientific issues. We also need an ongoing supply of professionals in the fields of science to compete in worldwide scientific endeavors. These two goals may be reached by helping students acquire a love for reading science books and literature and understand the methods and frameworks that are unique to science.

Discourse consists of conversations and/or writing used to persuade human thinking.

Scientists read, conduct investigations individually or collaboratively, and engage in ongoing conversations and **discourse** with fellow scientists to generate and validate their ideas. Just as scientists conduct science, students need to explore their ideas through investigations, communicate with their peers about their observations, argue and debate about their ideas, and rethink their interpretations of the phenomena they observe. Discourse can evolve and revolve around reading, investigating, demonstrating, writing journals, writing research papers, analogical reasoning, and role playing. Collaborative and cooperative learning enhances teacher-student as well as student-student discourse. In the following sections, each of these classroom activities is illustrated with examples and/or P-STAR (Pre-Service Teacher as Researcher) conference papers.

It is chiefly through books that we enjoy intercourse with superior minds. In the best books, great men talk to us, give us their most precious thoughts, and pour their souls into ours.
—William Ellery Channing

⚉ READING

Passion for Reading: Dr. Ben Carson, a Role Model

Disgusted with her son Ben's fifth-grade report card, Sonya Carson laid down the rule that he should be reading two books each week and write a book report. To begin his program of reading, Ben Carson asked a librarian for books on animals. One day when a science teacher asked his class about obsidian, the so-called dumb child, Ben, gave a detailed description. The teacher was happily surprised at Ben's in-depth knowledge. Ben's peers, who had been ridiculing him and calling him names, looked at Ben with wonder. This was the beginning of Ben's upward trend in his school grades, until he reached the top of the class. Simultaneously, attitudes toward Ben changed. Ben continued reading science to become a world famous neurosurgeon at age 33. Upon completing his internship, Dr. Carson became the director of the pediatric neurosurgery unit at Johns Hopkins.

In his public addresses in schools, he continues to admonish youth to read, read, and read. Many children have followed Ben's example and achieved success. A member of one of the many Ben Carson (BC) reading clubs in the United States once said to Dr. Carson: "Dr. Carson, I wanted to tell you what I learned about myself . . . I never thought I could learn so much in such a short time." (Carson, 1992, p. 209)

For Dr. Carson, listening to lectures was far down his list; during his four years at the University of Michigan Medical School, he cut many lectures so that he could stay in his room and not be disturbed. He "read constantly and insatiably." (p. 223) His reading began with the required material, then he added other books related to the same topic. To get an in-depth view, he wanted more than one writer's perspective. If the class was studying the nervous system, he used three different texts. Dr. Carson achieved in-depth learning through reading.

In his book *Think Big* (1992), Dr. Ben Carson speaks of how people learn:

- Some have such developed audio skills that they take in information more easily through the ear than the eye.
- Others find that their best learning comes from talking over a topic with someone else. The give-and-take dialogue sharpens their thinking, causes them to reflect, [and] raise questions, and enables them to hear opposing viewpoints.
- Still others do their best learning by the rote system—repetition and drill.
- I have friends who have to actually do something—what we now call hands-on learning. (Carson, 1992, p. 242)

Although Dr. Carson learned best by himself and through reading books, he points out that the best-disciplined learners combine all the methods in some form.

For people who want to become scientifically literate or to become professional scientists, reading is fundamental. Some students feel that most science content is irrelevant for their immediate life. To these students, Dr. Carson suggests that reading activates and exercises the mind, forces the mind to discriminate, pushes us to use our imagination, and makes us more creatively inclined. What might seem unimportant for most youngsters in school these days happens to be the bread and butter for their lives. Hence, Dr. Carson counsels every young person to develop a passion for reading. Science teachers are one instrument to help students nurture the habit of reading and to teach them how to become better readers.

"In-depth learning means learning as much about a topic as possible—learning for the sake of knowledge and understanding itself as opposed to learning for the sake of passing a test with high grades or trying to impress people" (Carson, 1992, p. 241).

Creative means using one's imagination to come up with innovative ideas, or finding new ways to look at old problems.

Strategies to Facilitate Textbook Reading from a Conceptual-Change Perspective

In most science classes, students learn by reading. Whether students like it or not, some teachers focus most of their teaching on textbooks. After their lectures, teachers assign end-of-the chapter questions and certain page numbers to find answers. Science textbooks present cultural products—models, theories, principles, concepts, and experiments—so that students can easily read and understand them. Is it any wonder that science

teachers depend very much on textbooks to convey the cultural givens in science?

A Science Educators' Method of Reading for Conceptual Change

Roth (1991) takes advantage of this standard classroom practice to introduce textbooks for science discourse and conceptual-change teaching. She illustrates the use of textbooks by considering students' conceptions of photosynthesis. Most students believe plants obtain food through their roots. The textbook, however, may read thus: "In the presence of sunlight, plants make food from nonfood materials such as water and carbon dioxide." It is obvious that there is a discrepancy between the student's idea and the conceptual structure presented in the textbook. The student will not recognize this conflict unless the teacher points it out. A structured experience is necessary to help students confront the discrepancy between their view and the idea presented in the textbook. The following guidelines for conceptual-change reading (a) offer teachers a purpose for using a textbook in class, and (b) offer students a method to monitor their conceptual development:

- Consider a critical issue.
- Challenge students to think about the issue.
- Elicit students' conceptions by asking probing questions.
- Make students aware of their conceptions.
- Help students realize that their conceptions are often different from scientific explanation.
- Present text versions of scientists' ideas to contrast with students' personal ideas.

- Help students generate additional questions for further exploration and analysis (Roth, 1991, p. 57).

Becoming a Better Reader

Science teachers must take the time to teach students how to read science materials such as textbooks, journals, magazines, newspaper articles, graphs, and charts. Reading is more enjoyable when students learn to be selective and understand the content. By choosing appropriate teaching strategies and modeling reading techniques, teachers can help students acquire the skills they need to access, read, and process scientific and technical information.

When it comes to plugging in values to solve a formula in science, students do not usually face major difficulties. However, students struggle the most when they face questions that require deeper understanding or an ability to interpret results. It is important for science teachers to recognize that reading belongs not only to English class but also to science. It is essential for teachers to emphasize reading in their science classrooms to promote analytical thinking.

Good readers skim text features such as titles, graphic illustrations, introductions, and summaries. They are able to analyze the content and recognize how it fits with what they already know. Good readers read for detail to see how the new information interrelates with their prior knowledge and ideas (Jones, Palinscar, Ogle, & Carr, 1987). Good readers also read at three levels:

1. reading on the lines (understanding is literal—recalling and remembering facts by analyzing, organizing, and categorizing material);
2. reading between the lines (ideas must be interpreted—seeing relationships between ideas and elaborating them by creating examples or paraphrasing); and
3. reading beyond the lines of questions (translating what is read—interrelating concepts, creating analogies, and solving problems).

Consider Figure 5-1 and the questions that follow, which illustrate the three levels of reading and, consequently, the level of understanding of the passage among students:

ON THE LINES
What was Galileo's postulate regarding the fall of heavy and light bodies in the absence of air resistance?

BETWEEN THE LINES
In a fish tank filled with water we drop two steel balls, one with a mass of 50 grams and the other with a mass of 100 grams. Which ball will hit the bottom of the tank first? Provide a reason for your answer.

BEYOND THE LINES
A piece of paper is placed on top of a regular textbook. They are dropped from a 2-meter height. Which one of the two will fall faster?

FIGURE 5-1
A passage to illustrate the three levels of reading (*NOTE:* From *Physics: Principles with Applications* (3rd ed.), by Douglas C. Giancoli, ©1991. Reprinted by permission of Prentice-Hall, Inc., Upper Saddle River, NJ.)

Falling Bodies

One of the commonest examples of uniformly accelerated motion is that of an object allowed to fall freely near the earth's surface. That a falling body is accelerating may not be obvious at first. And beware in thinking, as was widely believed until the time of Galileo (Fig. 2-12), that heavier bodies fall faster than lighter bodies and that the speed of fall is proportional to how heavy the object is.

Galileo's analysis made use of his new and creative technique of abstraction and simplification—that is, of imagining what would happen in idealized (simplified) cases. For free fall, he postulated that all bodies would fall with the *same constant acceleration* in the absence of air or other resistance. He showed that this postulate predicts that for an object falling from rest, the distance traveled will be proportional to the square of the time (Fig. 2-13); that is, $d \propto t^2$. We can see this from Eq. 2-10b, but Galileo was the first to derive this mathematical relation. In fact, one of Galileo's great contributions to science was to establish such mathematical relations and to insist on their importance. Another great contribution of Galileo was the proposing of a theory with specific experimental consequences that could be quantitatively checked ($d \propto t^2$).

To support his claim that the speed of falling objects increases as they fall, Galileo made use of the following argument: a heavy stone dropped from a height of 2 m will drive a stake into the ground much farther than if the same stone is dropped from a height of only 10 cm. Clearly, the stone must be moving faster in the former case. As we saw, Galileo also claimed that *all* objects, light or heavy, fall with the *same* acceleration, at least in the absence of air. Now common sense may say that the ancients were perhaps closer to the truth. For if you hold a piece of paper horizontally in one hand and a heavier object, say, a baseball, in the other and release them at the same time (see Fig. 2-14a), surely the heavier object will reach the ground first. But if you repeat the experiment, this time crumpling the paper into a small wad (See Fig. 2-14b), you will find that the two objects reach the floor at nearly the same time.

Galileo was sure that air acts as a resistance to very light objects that have a large surface area. But in many ordinary circumstances this air resistance is negligible. In a chamber from which the air has been removed even light objects like a feather or a horizontally held piece of paper will fall with the same acceleration as any other object (see Fig. 2-15). Such a demonstration in vacuum was of course not possible in Galileo's time, which makes Galileo's achievement all the greater. Galileo is often called the "father of modern science," not only for the content of his science (astronomical discoveries, inertia, free fall), but also for his style or approach to science (idealization and simplification, mathematization of theory, prediction of testable consequences that must be checked by experiment).

Galileo's specific contribution to our understanding of the motion of falling objects can be summarized as follows:

at a given location on the earth and in the absence of air resistance, all objects fall with the same uniform acceleration.

Students will learn the content better when there is a purpose for the reading. First, what are students' prior conceptions? Explore prior conceptions, perhaps using the POE strategy described later in this chapter. How does the selected reading connect with their ideas? Choose an appropriate textual passage for conceptual change, and compare and contrast the scientific concepts with students' ideas. In Piaget's terms, provide a schema-building (assimilation and accommodation) experience. Second, students must interact with the material and each other as they read (**collaborative reading**). Third, students should be able to read for meaning by connecting details to the overall idea, making new relationships, and translating ideas to real-world phenomena (use a graphic organizer, such as a concept map—see Chapter 8 for details).

Reading specialists offer additional guidelines for how to become a better reader. One well-known strategy is: *T notes,* which students can create as follows: Draw a line across the page one inch from the top. Then divide the page in half with a vertical line down the center of the page. Label one side "Science Ideas" and the other side "students' ideas." The top of the page is the top of the T. Draw a box under the T to allow students to add other ideas, questions, and conflicts. The teacher asks questions. Students record their own answers and then record science ideas from their text and compare the two.

Len notes that he likes this approach to using the text, that it allows students to use the textbook based on their ideas. However, he points out that this approach took a long time.

Collaborative reading occurs when each student in a small group reads a passage in turn and stops along the way to express a rational opinion, connect the reading to prior experience and related literature, and ask a question. Others in the group also contribute to this discussion.

LEN'S VOICE

I approached it with some hesitation. In fact, I only used it with one of my classes. I believed that it would take far too long and, quite frankly, that it would be a waste of time. In one way I was right. It did take a long time to use this approach. In the class I used, it took three periods to teach the concepts, whereas the other class covered the same area in one-and-a-half periods. But, was that the extra time wasted? No! Both groups wrote the same quiz. The group that used this method scored far better.

In science class, teachers must teach reading skills so that students become voracious readers of science. "Students who excel academically, read extensively" (Carson, 1992, p. 214). Although Dr. Carson learned best by reading, he suggests that students first identify their preferred learning style and work toward strengthening it. A point in Dr. Carson's list of "learning styles is learning by doing." Learning by doing is an important part of science, with its emphasis on practical work in the laboratory and in field settings.

P-STAR CONFERENCE PAPER (5-1)

Don't Throw Out Your Science Textbooks

Len Kerr

Based on Roth's guidelines for conceptual-change reading, preservice teacher Len Kerr used T notes to see the relationship between his students' ideas and science ideas. Len asked two questions about the concept of "life functions." Figure 5-2 represents Len's questions, the corresponding answers or ideas given by a group of eighth-grade students, and a T note a student prepared.

FIGURE 5-2

Life functions: Science ideas versus students' ideas

LIFE FUNCTIONS

Science Ideas	Students' Ideas
obtaining and using energy (food)	eating, hunting, farming, getting food
removing wastes	going to the bathroom
movement response	hunting, moving
growth and reproduction	having babies

Students' ideas that were not covered by the life function science ideas: warmth, shelter, happiness, sleep.

1. What do living things need to survive? (answers: food, warmth, shelter, happiness)
2. What do living things have to do to survive? (answers: eat, sleep, get food, farm, prepare shelter, go to the bathroom, hunt, move, have babies)

 PEER TALK

Reading to Learn Science

In his school days, Dr. Ben Carson read two books a week and wrote book reports for his mother. He amazed both his teachers and his peers with detailed answers to questions asked in class. At college, Dr. Carson read from six in the morning to eleven at night. During his medical studies he skipped classes to read. When he was doing his neurology rotation, his exacting chief resident listened to him open-mouthed because, unlike other interns, Dr. Carson was able to go into detail about the underlying mechanisms of the disease process.

What are your views on Dr. Carson's extraordinary commitment to reading science books?

How will you promote reading in your science class?

Why do you think taking time to teach how to read science reading materials is useful?

What reading skills would you stress?

⚛ INVESTIGATION

Laboratory work is activity based and inquiry oriented, a hands-on approach to science teaching and learning that promotes science discourse. A laboratory activity emphasizes "learning by doing" and appeals to the senses. In a laboratory exercise, students conduct an investigation to find solutions to real-life or novel problems or to draw conclusions for previously studied problems. In an investigation, students are actively involved in the experimental process.

The Conventional Laboratory

A well-rehearsed system of inquiry known as the scientific method is usually followed. Typically, there are six sequential steps in this method:

1. identifying a problem (usually the problem is identified by the teacher and is aimed at verifying existing knowledge)
2. formulating a hypothesis (when appropriate)
3. experimenting
4. observing and recording results
5. interpreting results
6. drawing conclusions

Students generally write up a lab report that details these steps. The scientific method is a structured approach for scientific investigation in school science.

A Science Teacher Educator's Reflections

Students have spent many days learning how to determine the density of a solid through a hands-on experience. According to the laboratory report in Figure 5-3, students in this eighth-grade class have acquired propositional and procedural knowledge as well as intellectual skills in conducting a laboratory exercise. They have learned how to determine the density of a solid using systematic experimental and mathematical

P-STAR CONFERENCE PAPER (5-2)

Measuring Mass, Volume, and Density

Ryan Penner

Doing hands-on activities in a laboratory motivates students because they are actively involved in the learning process. Students are generally excited about conducting actual experiments using lab equipment. A methodical problem-solving approach is followed.

Teachers must ensure that students discuss and understand lab safety procedures, because the lab is a potential safety hazard. Teachers must also closely monitor students in a laboratory setting. Often this becomes an opportunity for misusing equipment (for example, using medicine droppers to shoot water at others). Before starting any experiment, teachers must ensure that students have been taught the proper way to use all equipment so that the experiment will run smoothly. It is also important for science teachers to convey the idea of management and responsibility in their classrooms.

It is important to set up the lab stations in such a manner that the teacher has good control of the classroom. The stations must be placed so that all are easily accessible in case of a possible emergency. The best way to arrange the stations is to place them in one U-shaped format. Some teachers will not have the luxury of making this choice because of the classroom setup. The U-shaped format makes it easier for teachers to eliminate any management problems, check students' progress, and have easy access to all stations.

Figure 5-3 is a lab report submitted to preservice teacher Ryan Penner by a student.

Conventional lab experiments are very structured, in both their conduct and the written report. There is very limited opportunity for student creativity or expression. An alternative would be to allow students to design the experiment themselves, developing their own procedures.

There is usually an opportunity to integrate science labs with mathematics. Many labs contain mathematical calculations, and teachers can deal with matters such as significant figures and precision of measurements, As well, every lab deals with collection, organization, and analysis of data.

1. Problem: How accurately can the physical properties of mass, volume, and density be measured for common rubber stoppers of different sizes? Specifically:
   a. How accurately does a Harvard trip balance measure mass?
   b. How accurately does a graduated cylinder measure volume?
   c. Using the equation *density = mass/volume*, or $D = M/V$, determine the accuracy of the calculated value for the density of four rubber stoppers.
2. Procedure
   a. Part 1: Measuring Mass
      – Apparatus: Harvard trip balance, four sizes of rubber stoppers
      – Procedure: Harvard trip balances are precision instruments and must be handled carefully, as outlined in these steps:
      1. Carry the balance with two hands by the base.
      2. Adjust the balance to zero by putting the riders to zero.
      3. If necessary, turn the balance adjustment knob to put the balance indicator needle exactly at zero.
      4. Place the object of unknown mass on the left pan.
      5. Glide the 10-g rider along the beam to try to balance the object being measured. Return to zero if this is not enough.
      6. Try to balance within 10 g using the 200-g rider (some objects may need extra weights on the right pan).
      7. Finish balancing with the 10-g rider.
      8. Add all the masses together, rounding the total to the nearest tenth of a gram.
      9. Remove the specimen and return the riders to zero.
      10. Carry the balance by the base and return it to storage.
      – When the balance is prepared each rubber stopper is weighed and the mass to the nearest 0.1 g is recorded in the Chart of Observations for Part 1.

Mass
Chart of Observations

Stopper Size	measured mass			average mass
	own	other 1	other 2	
2	8.9	8.0	10.4	8.9
4	14.4	13.5	10.3	12.7
6	22.0	19.2	19.2	20.1
8	36.6	34.0	36.6	35.7

☆ - 1 hole
☆ ☆ - 2 holes

(a)

continued

FIGURE 5-3
An eighth-grade student's laboratory report on determining the density of a solid

In any situation where a mathematical formula is required, the emphasis should be placed on the relationships that exist between the variables rather than just an algebraic manipulation of the formula. For instance, it is more important for students to know what happens to density when volume changes than for them to be able to use the formula.

b. Part 2: Measuring Volume
   – Apparatus: graduated cylinder, water, beaker, medicine dropper, rubber stoppers, paper towels
   – Procedure: Fill the graduated cylinder about halfway with water. Then place the cylinder on a table and add drops of water with the medicine dropper from the remaining water in the beaker. Carefully raise the water level until the *meniscus* is at a known and easily read *graduation*. Note that on a 250-mL cylinder, each graduation is equal to 2 mL.
       This is a method of finding volume by water displacement. When you have adjusted the meniscus, tilt the cylinder at an angle and allow the first rubber stopper to slide down into the water. Read and record the meniscus at the new level. Then, empty the contents of the cylinder into the beaker to retrieve the stopper. Refill the cylinder sufficiently and repeat the process for each of the remaining three rubber stoppers, recording each volume in the Chart of Observations for Part 2. When you are finished, put all apparatus away and clean up any spilled water.

Volume
Chart of Observations

Stopper Size	Starting Volume	Finish Volume	Stopper Volume	Other 1	2	Average
2	60 ml	66.5 ml	6.5 ml	7	6.6	6.7
4	130 ml	140 ml	10 ml	10	9	9.6 ml
6	170 ml	187 ml	17 ml	16	18	17 ml
8	600 ml	628 ml	28 ml	28	28	28 ml

☆ - 1 hole

☆ ☆ - 2 holes

(a)

c. Part 3: Determining Density
   – Apparatus: Results of mass and volume experiments
   – Procedure: Calculate the density of each rubber stopper by using the equation *density = mass/volume*, or *d = m/v;* record your results in the Chart of Observations for Part 3.

continued

Density
Chart of Observations

Stopper Size	Average Mass	Average Volume	Density = $\frac{M}{V}$
2	8.9 g	6.7 ml	1.32
4	12.7 g	9.6 ml	1.32
6	20.1 g	17 ml	1.18
8	35.7 g	28 ml	1.27
		Average	1.27

Array

Row 1	Row 2	Row 3	Row 4	Row 5
1.25	1.23	1.34	1.30	1.25
1.37	1.31	1.27	1.25	1.29
1.25	1.35	1.28	1.30	1.23
1.28	1.22		1.28	1.40
	1.33			
1.29	1.29	1.30	1.28	1.29

Average = 1.29
1.34

continued

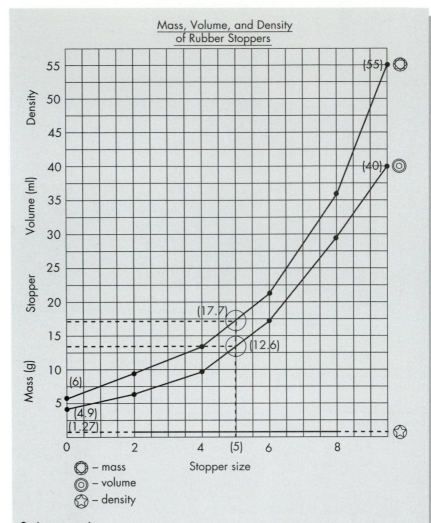

Mass, Volume, and Density
of Rubber Stoppers

3. Interpretation
   a. How could values for the mass, volume, and density of stopper sizes 0
      and 10 be found without using the measuring tools?
         The best method would be to extend the graph lines in the directions
      that they appear to be traveling. Then dotted horizontal and vertical
      sight lines are constructed to help find the corresponding values. This
      method of finding unknown values beyond the limits of the experiment is
      called *extrapolation* (see the graph).
   b. How could values of mass, volume, and density for stopper size 5 be
      found without actually measuring?
         Although a mathematical method could be used, the most convenient
      is to read the graph for an unknown between two known values by
      drawing a horizontal dotted sight line to find the unknown correspond-

continued

ing value. This method of finding unknown values on graphs is called *interpolation*.

c. How do methods of extrapolation and interpolation compare for accuracy?

The best comparison would be with actual measured values when possible, as shown in the Chart of Comparisons.

Chart of Comparisons

		Stopper sizes		
		0	5	10
Mass	Estimated	6.5 g	15.7 g	50 g
	Measured	6.5 g	14.7 g	55.8 g
	Difference	0 g	0.3 g	5.8 g
Volume	Estimated	5.3 ml	10.3 ml	31.3 ml
	Measured	4.3 ml	10.3 ml	40 ml
	Difference	1.0 ml	0 ml	9.3 ml
Density	Calculated	$\frac{m}{v} = 1.51$	$\frac{m}{v} = 1.42$	$\frac{m}{v} = 1.84$
	Actual	1.34	1.34	1.34
	Difference	0.17	0.08	0.50

Interpolation should be quite accurate because the estimate is between known measured values. Extrapolations may be less accurate because they are more of a guess. Accuracy decreased as stopper size increased, especially for volume, because volume measures were less accurate in the larger graduated cylinder. The graduations mark larger volumes, and because the mass and volume lines curve upward, there is more room for error when extrapolating. Interpolating and extrapolating for density should be more accurate because the graph is almost a perfect straight line.

4. Conclusion

From the graph, we know that mass and volume increase by greater amounts as the sizes increase. Because the density line stays almost perfectly flat, we know that the density of the stoppers is a constant. This is because density depends on the material, not the size of the object. Our overall average of density for all classes:

1.29 g/cm^3
1.38 g/cm^3
1.42 g/cm^3

continued

$\dfrac{1.43 \text{ g/cm}^3}{5.52/4} = 1.38 \text{ g/cm}^3$

When we compare our result to the known density of 1.34 g/cm^3, we see that our methods of measuring were very accurate.

5. Applications (Uses) of Density
   A knowledge of density can be useful for:
   1. comparing amounts of matter in a certain volume (cm^3)
   2. separating fluids of different densities
   3. mixing fluids of similar densities
   4. knowing when something will float or sink (buoyancy)
   5. constructing floating objects from materials that sink
   6. understanding why a layer of ice floats on a lake instead of sinking to the bottom
   7. knowing how much of an iceberg is below water

– Problem: Are hockey pucks made of the same rubber material as the rubber stoppers whose densities we determined?
– Steps to Solve:
   1. Find the mass of the hockey puck.
   2. Find the volume of the puck using the formula $V = \pi r^2 h$.
   3. Calculate the density $D = M/V$.
   4. Compare the density of the puck with the density of the rubber stoppers.

Puck # 11				
Mass	Volume			Density
1687	$\pi = 3.14$ 101.5			1.66
	$r = 3.75$			
	$h = 2.0$			
	$d = 7.5$			
Array of Puck Densities				
Row 1	Row 2	Row 3	Row 4	Row 5
0.72 [13]	1.49 [6]			
Sponge				
1.64 [7]	1.50 [4]	.50 [4]	1.50 [4]	1.52 [14]
1.72 [12]	1.66 [11]	1.66 [11]	1.29 [15]	1.29 [15]
1.71 [3]	1.71 [3]	1.66 [11]	1.58 [5]	1.52 [14]
	1.56 [2]	1.42 [9]	1.42 [9]	1.45 [8]
1.64	1.58	1.53	1.44	1.44
		final		
		1.53 g/cm^3		

By determining the density of both types of objects, we have found that most hockey pucks are made of a rubber material with a little higher density than the rubber stoppers, as these averages show:

Rubber stopper density = 1.38 g/cm^3

Hockey puck density = 1.53 g/cm^3

procedures. Students have followed procedures in taking care of the equipment (for example, the Harvard trip balance) and recording accurate measurements (reading the level of water at the meniscus). In other words, students know the parts of a balance and how to use the balance to determine the mass of a solid, as well as how to use the graduated cylinder to determine the volume of a solid. They know how to distinguish between the variables and controls in determining density. They have had practice in drawing tables, entering experimental results, and constructing and interpreting graphs (extrapolation and interpolation), thus enhancing their visual skills. Students have performed appropriate calculations to determine the volume (puck) and density of solids (rubber stoppers and puck). Their conclusions are based on the graphs and also refer to the evaluation of experimental accuracy (their results compared to the known value). They have considered the applications of density. Students translated what they have learned to solve a similar problem (by determining the density of a hockey puck—something that they are familiar with—they have experienced episodic learning). They have learned how to write a formal lab report: problem, hypothesis, test of hypotheses, laboratory procedures, data collection, transformation of data (charts and graphs), interpretations, conclusion, and application.

Although this laboratory activity may be considered a "cookbook" method (except for the results, all students had written the same procedures), it combines some of White's memory elements (described in Chapter 4) to develop students' intelligences. Therefore, it is an essential step in guiding students to take on their own personal inquiry or undertake investigations based on their own conceptions.

Much laboratory work, which is fundamental to science learning, focuses upon practice in using scientific instruments, applying correct methods, and verifying concepts, principles, and laws of science (Hofstein & Lunetta, 1982; Tobin, 1990; Tobin & Gallagher, 1987). For instance, Novak (1988) notes that most students in laboratories gain little insight either regarding the key science concepts involved or toward the process of knowledge construction. He contends that experiments are shown to be ways to "prove" or "falsify" hypotheses rather than methods to construct or generate new conceptual-theoretical meanings. With regard to interactions among students in the laboratory, Lehman (1990) found that during a lab activity, students interacted with one another mainly to confirm or clarify the directions/procedures of the activity.

When conducted appropriately, laboratories do promote intellectual development and develop motor skills and problem-solving skills, or cognitive strategies. Laboratory activities are "the source for episodes and images that give meaning to propositions that students have already learned or will acquire" (White, 1988, p. 186).

Work that takes place in a school laboratory seems to be smooth and well organized. White (1988) argues that the laboratory should be a place to plan for linking knowledge or propositions and to create long-lasting images with specific and sometimes spectacular episodes. Students attach more meaning to statements of different chemical reactions and writing chemical equations when reactions are actually carried out prior to the propositional forms.

For a laboratory activity, teachers should forge the knowledge-episode links by making students write their own statement for the purpose of the experiment. Students should first be trained to write the purpose, with guidance and criticism, as a paragraph or two in their own words, rather than writing one sentence. White (1988) notes that at the end of the laboratory activity, students should be asked to write all the propositional knowledge that they used for the experiment. Students can then compare and discuss their lists. Such learning would be more meaningful than simply performing the laboratory exercise.

Teachers must also provide opportunities in the laboratory for students to connect what they learn in school science to common materials and experiences. For example, students can determine the vitamin C content of fruits and vegetables found in the local grocery store. They can determine pH of samples of water collected in the home or school vicinity. Likewise, students can investigate electricity using common materials (fuses, switches, bulbs, batteries) at home. They can also develop cognitive strategies by linking knowledge to real-life problems that involve technology (see Chapter 11 for an in-depth treatment of technology in science).

Figure 5-4 gives a structure for laboratory work that promotes scientific inquiry (Lunetta & Tamir, 1979).

FIGURE 5-4

A structure for laboratory work (NOTE: From "Matching Lab Activities with Teaching Goals," by V. Lunetta and P. Tamir, 1979, *The Science Teacher*, 46(5), pp. 22–24. Copyright 1994 by The National Science Teachers Association. Adapted with permission.)

1. Plan and design an investigation
   - formulate a question or frame a problem
   - predict results
   - formulate a hypothesis to be tested
   - design an observation or measurement procedure
   - design the experiment
2. Perform the experiment
   - carry out qualitative and quantitative (measurement) observations
   - manipulate apparatus and develop techniques
   - record results and describe observations

  - perform numeric calculations
  - explain the experimental technique
  - work according to design
3. Analyze and interpret the results
  - transform results into charts and graphs
  - determine qualitative and quantitative relationships
  - determine the accuracy of experimental data
  - discuss limitations and assumptions that underlie the experiment
  - propose a generalization or model
  - formulate new questions and problems based on the results of the investigation
4. Apply the results
  - predict and formulate a hypothesis based on the results of the present investigation
  - apply the experimental technique to a new problem or variable

 PEER TALK

Elements of a Laboratory Investigation

Consider Ryan's eighth-grade student's laboratory report. Identify the principles of Lunetta and Tamir's structured laboratory in this report. Are any elements described by Lunetta and Tamir missing in the report? If so, what are they?

Expanding the Limits of Knowing and Understanding

Science investigations also enable students to generate their own questions; research study materials and resources; plan, design, and perform experiments; record observations; analyze and interpret observations; share and discuss observations and results; and report and disseminate findings. Haury and Rillero (1994) illustrate how to expand students' limits of knowing and understanding using a *learning episode*. This episode, led by Haury's favorite science teacher from his own school years, involved a field trip to nearby smelly, clam-filled mud flats along a coastal estuary. The topic of study was respiration, and students had learned several interesting laboratory techniques for determining respiration rates and estimating the volume of oxygen being respired for a given biomass; "It all seemed very understandable in the controlled, aseptic conditions of the laboratory," Haury recalls. In the field setting the teacher asked, "How much oxygen is being respired by organisms of these mud flats?" To answer this large question, he followed with simple questions such as

"What organisms might be living in the mud?" "How many of each kind are there?" "How large are they?" "How could we find out?" A hands-on lesson began with "sampling with hula hoops, application of physiological principles learned in the laboratory, and learning how to learn."

Students can read more books and articles for science content and experiments about living organisms in the mud flats. They should plan, design, and conduct a series of experiments to answer the teacher's as well as their own subsequent questions. Students may record their observations in a systematic manner by preparing investigation sheets prior to the investigation; they may also share and debate experimental observations, conclusions, and results with their peers. Students can also present formal papers at a science meeting and submit articles to the school community paper.

This learning episode is a contextual problem inquiry. Chapter 9 describes teaching science using *large context problems* (Stinner, 1993).

 PEER TALK

Investigation outside the Laboratory

Examine the teacher's activity at the mud flats. How does it compare with the laboratory structure provided by Lunetta and Tamir?

Laboratory and field investigations lead to insights from reading and perceptual learning. *Insight* occurs at the *aha!* stage in a scientific inquiry (Carson, 1992). Carson portrays this principle using the three stages that

Herman Helmholtz, a German physiologist and physicist, described 100 years ago. The three stages are as follows:

1. *Saturation*. Helmholtz conducted research, finding out everything he could about the subject.
2. *Incubation*. This was the reflective time that he spent thinking and mulling over what he learned through research.
3. *Illumination*. Helmholz faithfully gave his full concentration to saturation and incubation. Then, he said, he arrived at a sudden solution (Carson, 1992, p. 186).

Investigations provide opportunities for direct experience with natural phenomena by observing through our senses and our instruments. Thinking, interpreting, and reflecting are also involved in investigations. Sensory data, "experiences with phenomena, exploratory talk and teacher intervention" (Driver, 1989) give meaning to students' conceptions and aid in the construction of new knowledge. Carson (1992) believes that most successful people either are naturally keen observers or they develop that ability. These observers conduct research, know what to watch carefully, reflect by asking questions or try to figure out what might happen, continually scrutinize the experimental process to see the development of relationships, expect specific results, and use each piece of scientific knowledge to develop more sophisticated knowledge. Detailed research and analysis show how researchers developed insight into DNA and the whole genetic structure. These concepts and theories are built around reflected observations.

TEACHER PRACTICE

Preparing a Scientific Investigation

Form small groups and choose a topic. Then plan a mini–scientific investigation of that topic. What are the components of the investigation you have prepared?

How does it compare with the laboratory structure provided by Lunetta and Tamir?

How does it relate to the mud flat teacher's work?

Damon and Phelps (1989) describe **cooperative learning** thus:

A collaborative grouping involves a situation in which two or more students assumed to possess the same knowledge or skills work together to solve a problem with which neither has had previous experience. Students share ideas, acting as sounding boards for ideas, without any division of labor.

A cooperative grouping is a situation in which members pool unique knowledge or skills for the purpose of resolving a problem.

 ## COOPERATION AND COLLABORATION

Cooperative learning and social collaboration provide opportunities for students to clarify their understandings during scientific investigations and of their readings. Ideas are elaborated, justified, and assessed through an interpretive process. *Learning Together* is a cooperative learning model that influences laboratory learning and scientific investigations.

Learning Together in a Laboratory

Figure 5-5 illustrates the Learning Together model's cooperative learning goals, procedure, and other criteria for conducting scientific inquiry.

Group Investigation in Science

In group investigations, students actively engage in carrying out an investigation, integrate their findings, and make presentations to the class. Group investigations help students determine *what* they will study and *how* they will conduct their investigation. The *what* and *how* of the investigation are unique features of group investigation (Sharan & Sharan, 1992). These authors have identified four features of group investigation:

FIGURE 5-5

Learning Together model in the laboratory (From *Cooperative Learning in Diverse Classrooms* by JoAnne Putnam, ©1997. Adapted by permission of Prentice-Hall, Inc., Upper Saddle River, NJ.)

Task: To conduct a scientific inquiry

Cooperative Goals: Each group will complete the project. All members will sign the project to indicate that they have contributed their share of the work, agree with its content, and are able to present and explain it. Each group member should also be responsible for taking care of one of the materials, such as microscope, slides, samples, and so on.

Procedure:
1. Place students in small learning groups of two, three, or four. Assign students an initial problem to solve. Give each group the required materials.
2. The group, with input from the teacher and also based on their own research, solves the problem and prepares a preliminary written report. This report will include theoretical ideas and procedures.
3. Give a more complex problem so that students can translate their learning. Observe group work and coach students when appropriate.
4. Have each group write and submit a report—their solution to the problem.
5. Pair each group member with a member of another group. Have each present their group's solution to the other.
6. Have the group reflect on how well they worked together.

Individual Accountability:
1. Have each group member present his or her group's report to a member of another group.
2. Observe the groups to ensure that all members are actively participating.
3. Give an individual test on the content covered by the problems.

Criteria for Success: A defensible solution to each problem that all members can explain.

Expected Behaviors: All students participate actively in solving the problems and explain their group's solutions to a member of another group.

Intergroup Cooperation: If there are any questions about the assignment or procedures, ask other groups for help.

investigation, interaction, interpretation, and intrinsic motivation (also known as the 4 I's).

Investigation

The teacher poses a multifaceted problem (it has no single answer and is relevant both in and outside of class). Based on their own initiative and group assistance, students research various sources to find a solution to the problem.

Interaction

Each student investigator interacts with his or her peers to address the group's problem, thus creating an *inquiring community*. The community of inquirers discusses the approach to the problem, determines the sources they will use, exchanges their ideas and information, discusses ways of synthesizing their findings, and makes plans for class presentation.

Interpretation

Although students conduct their inquiry individually, they interpret their findings *cooperatively*—by sharing, organizing, confirming, and consolidating their findings. Cooperative interpretation occurs during regular meetings with group members as they exchange information and ideas to analyze what they have learned about different aspects of the topic.

Intrinsic Motivation

Motivation and personal interest increase when students are able to decide what and how they will investigate. Positive interaction with one another also increases motivation.

There are six stages to group investigation (Putnam, 1997, pp. 150–152):

> *Stage 1: The class determines subtopics and organizes into research groups.* Together the teacher and the class pose a problem. Students formulate questions they wish to investigate. With the help of the teacher, they categorize the questions to develop subtopics for investigation. Students then select the subtopic they are most interested in and form into groups to investigate their chosen subtopic.
>
> *Stage 2: The groups plan their investigations.* Members of each group discuss, as well as decide on (a) the sources they will use in their investigation, (b) the approach of the investigation, and (c) the division of responsibility to each group member.
>
> *Stage 3: The groups carry out their investigations.* Students work individually or in pairs. They identify and gather information from a variety of sources. Students share their information with group members. They then discuss, interpret, and integrate their findings; more information may be sought based on the group discussion.

Stage 4: The groups plan their presentations. Each group determines the mode of presentation: videos, boards, papers, posters. Each group also prepares a handout containing findings and sources for the participants.

- Have ready all the materials and equipment.
- Focus on the main ideas and conclusions of the inquiry.
- Each group member must be an active participant.
- Set time limits for each group presentation.
- Involve classmates actively in the presentation.
- Allow time for questions.

The teacher must review plans for the presentations with the students. Each group should also plan for successful sharing of findings.

Stage 5: The groups make their presentations. Each group presents its findings in a meaningful way. Peers may assess the presentation based on criteria predetermined by the teacher.

Stage 6: The teacher and students evaluate their projects. A variety of methods are used to assess students' understandings of the main ideas, construction of new knowledge, and solutions for the various problems. For example, students can provide a set of questions from their project for a class test. Students are asked to reflect on their performance as investigators and as group members depending on a set of criteria. Students can also set goals for the improvement of the group dynamics.

SCIENCE ACTIVITY STATIONS

Science activity stations and demonstrations are popular forms of hands-on activities for thinking and classroom discourse. Several practical activities are arranged on tables in the classroom or laboratory. Each station focuses on a specific objective. It may be as simple as observing two earthworms to distinguish between male and female and recording each of the characteristic features in a notebook; it may be as complex as dissecting an earthworm to locate and label the digestive organs or the reproductive system. Students may draw the system in their notebook and label it.

Students may work in groups of two or three. A limited amount of time is given for each station, depending on the objectives and questions asked. Stations are very useful when there is not a sufficient amount of material for each student or group of students. Stations are sometimes used for performance-based tests (see Chapter 13 for examples).

Organizational issues to be considered when using stations include the following: What type of activities are good for stations? How much time should be allotted to each station? How many students should be working at a station—individually or in a group? If in groups, how do we form the groups? How many stations should there be?

TEACHER PRACTICE

Science Activity Stations
Design a variety of practical activities for a number of stations at the junior high level. Outline procedures for managing station activities.

⌗ DEMONSTRATION

A popular method for stimulating classroom discussion is demonstration. Demonstrations can be performed by the teacher or by students. Most demonstrations are teacher driven. A demonstration attracts the attention of students (for example, the *pop* sound of hydrogen gas) and motivates and maintains interest for constructing knowledge (Why do two balloons kiss?). Through demonstrations, teachers can show students how to use an apparatus (taking a burette reading), illustrate an observation technique (accurate reading of the meniscus), perform a test (the flame test), or conduct an experimental procedure (setting up the apparatus and collecting oxygen gas). A science principle, concept, or natural phenomenon can be developed via a demonstrated activity, thus linking theory and practice (for example, expansion and contraction of a metal with a ball-and-ring activity). A demonstration may introduce a topic (collapsing a metal can to introduce "pressure") or function as an opener to a particular lesson or unit (rolling a ball to discuss forces), as it can stimulate independent thinking and evoke curiosity and inquiry on the part of the students (for example, the decrease in the volume of balloons placed in nitrogen gas). Demonstrations may illustrate or clarify a point during a lecture or discussion (the difference between melting and dissolving, using an ice cube and a sugar cube in water), introduce as well as solve a problem (the law of the lever and the situation in which the lever is balanced), serve as a climax (placing some marshmallows in a vacuum pump and watching them increase in volume), promote inquiry (changing the size of a force using a pulley), and act as a review (showing how the force needed to pull an object up an inclined plane increases as the angle of inclination increases). A demonstration can illustrate an STSE-based principle (water erosion on soil for conservation practices). A science activity may be demonstrated by a teacher rather than being conducted by everyone in the class for several reasons:

- large class size (insufficient space and materials)
- costly materials and equipment (for example, electrolysis of water using Hoffman's apparatus)
- safety and management issues (for example, using concentrated acids or organizing materials to eliminate management problems)
- laborious teacher preparation

The teacher can observe whether all students appear to be on task. It is easier than wandering around the classroom, checking on individual or group progress, or asking appropriate questions and observing students. Note, however, that the teacher's attention may be focused on doing the demonstration while students in other parts of the room are off task.

Having the teacher do the activity will save time and be quicker than having students doing it.

Demonstrations that are less complex can be carried out by an individual or a group of students. The advantage to this is that it provides variety in the classroom and also provides a chance for students to be a part of the lesson (an ownership of sorts).

- ease of organization (because you are the manager)
- lack of time
- no lab assistant to set up the activity

Conventionally, in a science class, the teacher demonstrates an experiment while the students observe. For example, the teacher may demonstrate the conductivity of various solutions using a conductivity apparatus. The students observe and classify various solutions as conductors and nonconductors in a chart in their notebooks. A disadvantage of a teacher demonstration is that students do not have the opportunity to engage in hands-on inquiry. Too much reliance on teacher demonstrations may result in students becoming bored and uninterested by simply watching the teacher conduct the activity. Student participation may be limited to a few of the most verbal students. Some students may have difficulty seeing the demonstration and therefore be denied the opportunity to observe what is going on. The teacher may use too much direct influence, illustrating teacher problem solving rather than involving students in the problem-solving situation.

It is important to remember when doing a teacher demonstration that students must still be involved. You can have them assist you in the demonstration, but they must also be verbally involved. It is very important that students still have the opportunity to add their predictions, comments, questions, and observations during the demonstration. A particularly useful strategy for actively involving students in a demonstration is the Predict, Observe, Explain strategy (White & Gunstone, 1992).

⊗ PREDICT, OBSERVE, AND EXPLAIN (POE)

For Piaget (1974), creating conceptual conflict is essentially the first step in learning. In resolving a conceptual conflict via assimilation or accommodation, a learner becomes intellectually enriched.

Currently in science education, the Predict, Observe, Explain (POE) model is considered a popular type of teacher demonstration that involves students in making predictions, proposing explanations for their predictions, observing the activity, and advancing their personal ideas or theories for their observations. This procedure follows the classic model of scientific research. The POE procedure was originally developed by Champagne, Klopfer, and Anderson (1980) to probe understanding of real situations (White, 1988). Understanding of the concepts related to the situation are revealed by the students' predictions. This means that deeply held beliefs about scientific concepts, principles, and natural phenomena can be uncovered more effectively than by using tests that evoke knowledge at the surface level.

The POE activity may be straightforward in that the experimental observation is what most students expect. Some activities, however, are contrary to what one might expect. The latter type is known as a *discrepant event,* and creates a state of mental imbalance, disequilibrium, or conceptual conflict. If the event is discrepant, students are asked to explain "any discrepancy between what they predicted and what they saw happen"

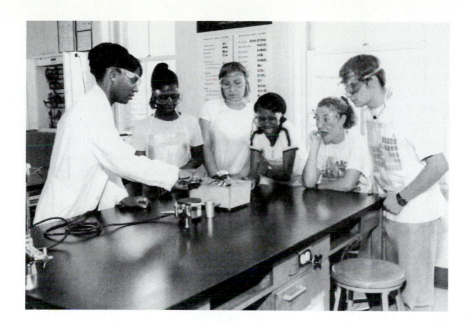

(White, 1988, p. 63). Conflicts are resolved by asking questions (what is happening and why), considering theoretical ideas, and other factors involved. *Invitations to science inquiry* (Liem, 1991) contains over 400 discrepant events that will create cognitive dissonance. Examples of discrepant events in Liem's book are: the crushing pop can, making milk from water and oil, the magnetic finger, and the ammonia fountain.

POE activities encourage in-depth learning. A POE may be used to explore students' ideas, uncover uncommon or odd beliefs, and intervene in students' thinking by negotiating with them. The POE model may be used for student-centered and/or teacher-students communal learning.

How to Conduct PEOE

1. *Introduce the phenomenon, briefly stating the specific context and conditions. Ask a general question: What do you think will happen?* What do you think will happen if I place this wooden "brick" into the bucket of water?
2. *Have students predict (P).* It will float. It will sink.
3. *Ask students to explain (E) the reasons for their predictions.* Students' reasons might be (a) it will float because it is water resistant, (b) it will float because of buoyancy, (c) it will float due to equal force, or (d) it will float because it has air in it.
4. *Conduct the activity. Have students record their observations (O) as the event occurs.* The wooden "brick" floated to the top of the bucket of water.

Student-centered means that students do the activity in small groups in the POE format, whereas *teacher-students communal learning* refers to teacher demonstration with students participating in the discussion.

We have our students think **PEOE** to better emphasize the need to explain their predictions. PEOE is our adaptation of the original POE.

5. *Have students explain (E) their reasons for what happened.* Students might give the same reasons as they gave before, or they might think of other reasons.
6. *Ask students to give examples.* Have students give examples of other objects that might float in water. This will bridge their prior knowledge to the new material being learned. They will relate what they have experienced outside the classroom to the understanding they have developed in the classroom. (This is a very low level of relating school experience to everyday experience. However, this real-life extension should not be neglected. More sophisticated levels of real-life problem solving are discussed in Chapter 11.)
7. *Ask students to make comparisons.* Have students make comparisons between objects that float and sink according to their physical characteristics, such as weight, mass, shape, and volume. These comparisons could be put into a chart at the end of the session.

Suggestions for PEOE Talk

The PEOE strategy fosters interactive and interpretive talk between the teacher and students. Ian Mitchell and the Monash Children's Science Group have devised a strategy for running interactive discussions successfully (Erickson, 1992). The suggestions outlined in Figure 5-6 will assist in developing skills associated with PEOE activities.

FIGURE 5-6
Guidelines for interactive/interpretive discussion during POE (*NOTE:* From "Some Suggestions for Running an Interpretive Discussion," by G. Erickson, 1992, *(SI)²* Newsletter, *5*(1), pp. 1–2. Copyright 1992 by the University of British Columbia. Adapted with permission.)

- Encourage students to offer as many ideas as possible.
- Allow enough time for students to think about what they are going to say.
- Listen carefully to students and, if necessary, check your understanding of their meaning: "Do you mean . . . ?"
- Accept all points based on the topic at hand without judgment. If a student brings up an important but unrelated point, ask him or her to hold the point until discussion on the present topic is finished. Then attend to the second issue.
- Keep the discussion going until you have obtained a range of student views.
- Ask students to take a stand and commit to one point or another by explaining their reasons.
- Recall all related comments and help students link them together, or summarize what has been discussed.
- Use an idea as a basis for another subsequent idea.
- Announce, explain, or approve the "best" possible solution or answer.
- Use the expressed ideas to form the basis for further exploration.
- Divide students into small groups for further investigation and discussion of issues. You may suggest an activity that will help them clarify their ideas, or they may conduct an investigation to address their own question.

- Encourage classroom discussion, not person-to-person talk.
- Encourage all students to participate and express themselves, including the quiet ones.
- Announce an order of speaking if several students raise hands or try to talk at once.
- Encourage students to finish their comments.
- Intervene if a student interrupts or puts down another.
- Repeat the comments that are not heard by all students.
- Use written feedback if dominant students take over the discussion, or have small groups report their views.

FIGURE 5-7
Management skills for class discourse (*NOTE:* From "Some Suggestions for Running an Interpretive Discussion," by G. Erickson, 1992, *(SI)² Newsletter, 5*(1), p. 2. Copyright 1992 by the University of British Columbia. Adapted with permission.)

Management Skills for Classroom Discourse

Erickson (1992) also offers management skills for effective classroom discourse (see Figure 5-7). Interpretive discussion requires mutual trust and understanding. The students should believe that they will be listened to with respect and interest by the teacher and their peers. The students should not feel uncomfortable when the teacher intervenes with critical questions, alternative ideas, and constructive disagreements. The students should realize that the teacher will come around to deal with most questions. They should also recognize that there will be temporary confusion, which is necessary for learning to take place. The students should understand the value of listening to other students' ideas and views. They should also be willing to react to others' ideas by developing an argument.

This level of trust and understanding develops in time. Teachers should be sensitive to students' growth and seek opportunities to help students develop skills in carrying out interpretive discussion.

In a teacher-demonstrated PEOE activity, students are involved through observations and discussions, not through a hands-on approach. A PEOE activity can be more student centered if the students do a hands-on activity in small groups and record their observations, explanations, and drawing diagrams. At the end of the student activity, the teacher must still gather the students together for teacher-students negotiated learning discussion.

Preservice Teachers Practice PEOE during Practicum

The following papers presented by our preservice teachers at the annual P-STAR conference illustrate the PEOE strategy.

 TEACHER PRACTICE

Carry Out a PEOE Discourse

Choose a simple science activity from one of the activity books and carry out a PEOE discourse with a group of students. Make an audio or video recording of the discussion. Transcribe and analyze the discussion. Discuss what you might have done differently to promote improved learning, with reference to Erickson's guidelines for carrying out an interactive discussion.

Carry out a discrepant event with the PEOE format.

P-STAR CONFERENCE PAPER (5-3)

Teaching the PEOE Strategy to Students

Natalie Bergson

Notice how Natalie frames her questions to explore her students' idea about flotation. These questions resemble open-ended questions, where there is no *one* right answer. The answers to these questions are usually detailed, as students are required to provide a rationale for their response or give an argument in order to defend their response. In other words, these questions make students think critically.

Currently, Natalie is a practicing teacher, and she uses the PEOE strategy with her middle school students. After a year of teaching, Natalie wrote the following message about the PEOE strategy to her science teacher educator:

> I also thought you'd be interested in knowing that I use the PEOE strategy quite a lot. I really like it and so do my students. It gives a lot of structure to the lesson. Thanks. (N. Bergson, personal communication, March 10, 1997)

When I conducted the PEOE strategy with my students, I went through each step (prediction, explanation, observation, and explanation) with them each time we did a part of the activity. I told my students that it did not matter if their predictions ended up being right or wrong. I emphasized that what mattered was their involvement and their input in the process. I always encouraged my students when they were making predictions and explaining their observations. Furthermore, I questioned students as they were making their predictions. I would say, "Tell me what you mean by that," "Why?" and "Why do you say that?" When I did this, both my students and I were able to come to a clearer understanding about what the student was trying to say.

Figure 5-8 represents a PEOE flotation journal written by one of Natalie's students.

Fluids and Buoyancy
— Experiment —

	(Draw a Picture) Prediction	Reason for it	(Draw a Picture) Observations	Explanation for Observation
(1.) Styrofoam "brick" is lowered into bucket of water and person holding "brick" lets go of it.	I think that the "brick" will stay above the water.	There are air holes. The air will keep it up.	It stayed above the water. 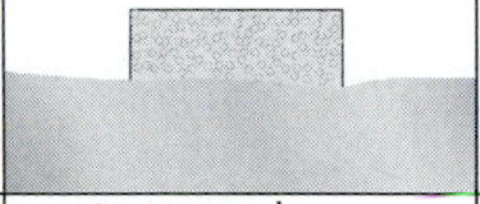	Air trapped in the "brick" kept it up.
(2.) How styrofoam "brick" feels when you are holding it down.	You will feel pressure. 	Air pushes it up.	It popped up. 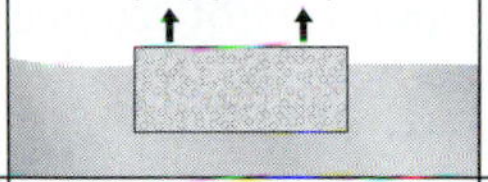	Air is trapped inside.
(3.) What happens when styrofoam "brick" is quickly let go of.	It pops up. 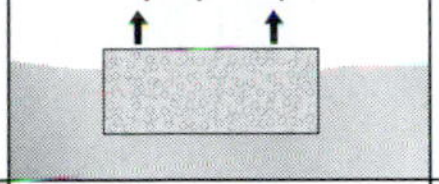	Air is inside.	It pops up. 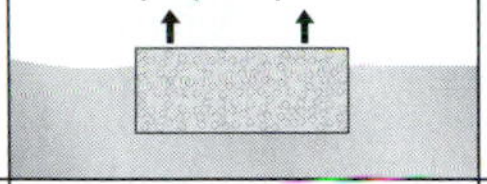	Air inside.
(4.) Wooden "brick" is lowered into bucket of water and person holding "brick" lets go of it.	It will float. 	It's water resistant.	It floats. 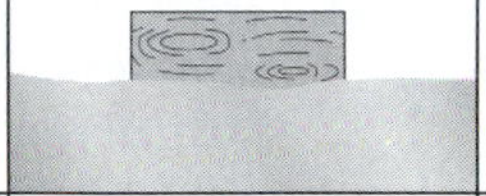	Water resistant.
(5.) How wooden "brick" feels when you are holding it down.	Slight pressure, not much. 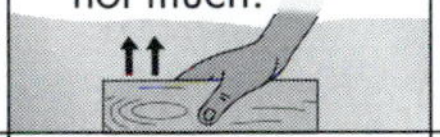	Kind of water resistant. Gets slightly.	It pushed up. 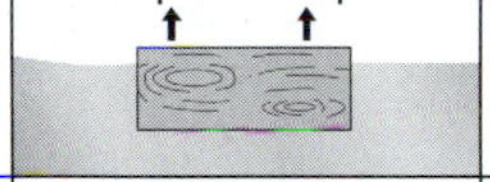	Air inside.
(6.) What happens when wooden "brick" is quickly let go of.	It pops up. 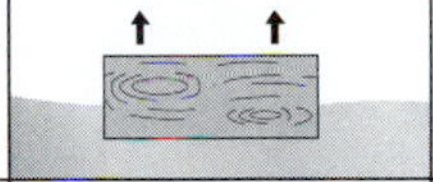	Air inside.	It flew up. 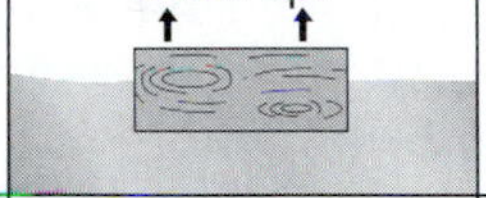	It's buoyant.
(7.) Clay brick is lowered into bucket of water and person holding brick lets go of it.	It will sink. 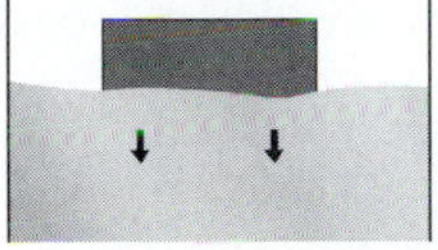	Not enough air in it.	It sunk and stayed. 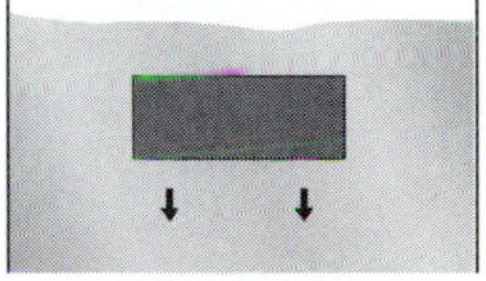	Not enough air.

FIGURE 5-8
Student PEOE chart on flotation

P-STAR CONFERENCE PAPER   (5-4)

PEOE Lessons on Kinetic Molecular Theory (KMT)

David Gardner

As a preservice teacher, would you take the risk that David took in his science class? Comment.

The risk David took in his science class needs to be admired and encouraged. However, these lessons usually take up an entire class period. It is important for science teachers to use a variety of teaching strategies in their classrooms, but it is also important to keep the time factor in mind. Students require enough time to construct their own understanding of the newly learned materials and to reflect on their learning.

I utilized the PEOE strategy extensively in my lessons through the use of physical examples in the classroom. In a normal class, perhaps four or five different PEOE strategies would be evident, and my desk was a museum of science artifacts, whereupon I might pluck a piece at any time in order to illustrate a particular difficult point.

I certainly learned the necessity of making the science class a forum wherein students must explore the pursuit of knowledge on their own. Virtually every student commonly had his or her hand up and would enthusiastically participate in classroom activities. My technique was fashioned to make science an interesting, informative, and question-raising environment, all of which were achieved.

At times, my success proved to be a detriment to my lessons. Where I had hoped to elicit interest and raise questions, my students began asking impressively mature questions relating to KMT anomalies, including the expansion of water at subzero temperatures. I did not want to discourage such insightful questions, yet I had no readily available answers. I was consistently challenged in the lesson. (See Figure 5-9 for a sample lesson.)

FIGURE 5-9
PEOE lesson: Gravel and Styrofoam balls and KMT (there are spaces between particles of matter)

Teacher-Students Discourse
Prediction (P)

MR. GARDNER: Tom, how much Styrofoam would you say is in this beaker?

TOM: About 400 mL.

MR. GARDNER: How much gravel in this other one?

TOM: 200. Around 200 mL.

MR. GARDNER: Do you agree, Danny?

DANNY: Close enough.

MR. GARDNER: What do you think will happen if I pour the 200 mL of gravel into the 400 mL of Styrofoam?

SHELLY: It'll go up to 600 mL.

MARY: No, it'll go up, but not all the way up to 600.

Explanation (E)

MR. GARDNER: It seems there are mixed opinions about this. Please write down what you think will happen and give reasons for your predictions.

Observation (O)

MR. GARDNER: What did you see?

PETER: It's 400 mL! When you poured it [the gravel] in, it [the total volume] stayed the same!

Explanation (E)

MR. GARDNER: Peter has correctly observed that the combined matter equals 400 mL. What happened?

MARY: The bigger Styrofoam balls had big gaps in between them. When you added the gravel, instead of just piling on top of the other, it filled the gaps. It didn't raise the level at all.

MR. GARDNER: Congratulations! This illustrates the second point in KMT. There are spaces between the particles of matter, just as there were spaces between the styrofoam balls.

I found that the more difficult it was to visually explain a concept, or the more complex an explanation, the more students were intrigued and asked questions. Many questions related to the fact that solids are composed of particles with spaces in between. The students found it difficult to understand that a piece of wood, as solid as it was, has spaces between its particles. I explained the concept using Styrofoam and rock, and with a microscopic view of tree bark. In this way, the essential questions of physical inquiry were being asked with genuine interest, and I explained using energetic and innovative examples and models.

A testimony to the learning that came out of this lesson can be seen in student-group lists of "things we learned in this science section," written after four small-group labs in KMT (see Figure 5-10). Notice that there is very little straight regurgitation of textbook knowledge. Students have learned from demonstrations combined with questions and answers. Their own confidence, competence, and interest in the subject matter are evident in their sensible list of what they have learned.

FIGURE 5-10
Students' ideas about KMT

Nathan, Bryan, Lindsay

What was learned - Everthing except energy
consists of matter.
- There are particles in matter
and they move at different
speeds.

What models were used - The spray to demonstrate
gas has particles.
Foam balls and fish rocks
to demonstrate liquids
and solids, and gases have
air spaces.

Definitions - Matter - Anything with a mass that takes up
space.
Models - A simplified version of an object.
Energy - The ability to make things move.

Additional points - Heat makes things speed up.
- All particles are always in motion.
- Hot water dissolves things much
faster than cold water and faster
than water at room temperature.
- All matter is made up of tiny
particles.
- Gas particles move faster than
gas and liquid particles.
N- When heat is added to ice, it melts.

What we learned
- all states of matter consist of particles
- states can be changed by heat
- we learned how models work
- we learned about matter
- we learned about the 3 states   liquid, solid, gas
- we learned about the nature of solids and liquids
-   "   "   "   "   distance apart of particles
- we   "   that all matter is in constant motion.
-   "   "   "   "   speed of motion.
-   "   "   "   energy causes particles to
speed up.

PEER TALK

Analysis of David's PEOE Discourse
Based on Erickson's suggestions for classroom discourse, analyze David's PEOE
conversation with students.

✲ CHAPTER REVIEW

Classroom discourse can provide critical opportunities for students to actively construct meaning in scientific inquiry. Scientific inquiry involves two important types of talk: exploratory and presentational (Barnes, 1988). In exploratory talk, students discuss their ideas as in PEOE and investigation activities; in presentational talk, they report on their investigations. Possible contexts for classroom discourse include interpreting readings, investigations, and demonstrations. Scientific discourse facilitates clarification, explanation, elaboration, and negotiation of scientific concepts and ideas.

In this chapter we examined the importance of reading in science by considering Ben Carson's testimonies. We discussed various methods that can help a student become a better reader. For conceptual-change reading we analyzed Roth's study.

Scientific inquiry can be based on activities such as laboratory investigations, stations, and demonstrations. Each of these methods of inquiry has been illustrated with pertinent examples. We described how an eighth-grade student determined the density of solids in a laboratory. We also highlighted how skills can be taught in this type of laboratory learning. In addition, through literature, we pointed out some of the neglected areas of a laboratory activity. Students should be *doing* investigations and *reasoning* about their investigations (Gitomer & Duschl, 1995).

In this chapter we also presented a popular activity we call the PEOE. How to carry out an interpretive discussion during PEOE activity is a special feature! PEOE involves writing about science ideas; writing in journals is the focus of the next chapter.

PROBES

1. Design a conventional laboratory in the school setting. What is your format? What aspects did you stress? How did you prepare your students for the laboratory? What did you do after the laboratory activity to follow up the ideas being addressed in the activity?

2. In small peer groups, carry out a demonstration in the conventional manner. Do the same demonstration using the PEOE format. Compare and contrast these two types of demonstrations using your example.

3. Consider the following example of teacher-students PEOE discourse.
   a. Identify the PEOE elements of the discussion.
   b. Examine Mr. Gardner's questions carefully. How would you reword some questions?
   c. At the end, Mr Gardner gives his own explanation about air escaping through the tiny hole. How would you help students to word Mr. Gardner's explanation?

Teacher-Students PEOE Discourse

MR. GARDNER: What will happen when I put a tiny hole in this inflated balloon?

TINA: The air will be forced out the hole.

MR. GARDNER: Why do you say that, Tina?

TINA: Because there is an opening in the balloon.

MR. GARDNER: How do you know?

TINA: When you held the balloon onto my face, I could feel the air pushing out.

MR. GARDNER: Harry, if you could actually see air, how would you explain to me what happened?

HARRY: The particles of air inside the balloon were pushed together too tight. So, when you left an opening, the air went out.

MR. GARDNER: Do you agree, Byron?

BYRON: Yeah. There's more pressure inside the balloon than outside, so it'll go out.

MR. GARDNER: Could we say, then, that particles move from areas of high pressure, or concentration, to areas of low concentration?

BYRON: When they can.

MR. GARDNER: Good, when they can?

BYRON: Yeah.

MR. GARDNER: Does this make sense to everyone?
(general nods and "yeahs" of agreement)

MR. GARDNER: Super! You've just explained diffusion, an important aspect of the KMT!

4. Do a discrepant PEOE event with students. Discuss the "*aha*s" and issues. *Invitations to Science Inquiry* by Tik L. Liem (1991) is an excellent book of discrepant events.

CHAPTER 6

Journal Writing and Research Reporting

STUDY QUESTIONS

1. What is journaling?

2. Why do scientists keep a log or journal?

3. What are some different types of journals and how can they be used in school science?

4. What are the key components of a scientific research paper?

5. How can cooperative learning approaches be used for writing research papers?

CATHERINE'S VOICE

Journaling provides a window into student learning for both teacher and student. The writing of thoughts clarifies the student's own ideas and makes the teacher aware of prior conceptions that the student possesses. Many experiments done by students in schools can only be described as cookbook recipes that the students perform but do not truly understand. Making predictions in a journal before actually laying hands on lab equipment forces students to think about the purpose of the experiment and possible outcomes. Teachers can follow up a lab by having students comment on their reactions to experimental results in their journals and make comparisons with their original predictions. If used regularly, journals can allow teachers and students to monitor both short-term and long-term progress. Journaling is an indispensible tool in today's science classroom.

JOURNAL ACTIVITY

Journal Writing

"Journal writing is not keeping a diary of events; rather, journal writing is writing about your journey in life, your relation to something." Comment on this statement.

⚙ VALUES OF JOURNAL WRITING

Journal writing encourages students to think and record personal notes rather than copying notes provided by the teacher. It provides a strong base for expressing, communicating, and validating ideas. Frequent and in-depth entries allow students to demonstrate their knowledge and provide a means of communication between student and teacher that is personal, confidential, and one-to-one.

The values of journal writing include the following:

- Freedom to write personal opinions without fear of being penalized
- Active involvement: figuring things out as opposed to memorization
- Visible progress in learning
- Ideas are more important than the "appearance or format" of the write-up
- Students' ideas are valued (Kuhn & Aguirre, 1987, pp. 269–271)

Journal writing helps students think critically and leads them to higher-level thinking skills such as application, analysis, synthesis, evaluation, and metacognition (Edwards, 1991). Teachers are given a good indication of how a student is doing—the student's frustrations, confusions, understandings, questions, and conceptual development. Moreover, journals provide feedback that will help the teacher plan further instructional activities. As Sanders (1985) states, "[Journals] provide a simple 'educational pulse'" (p. 7).

Journal writing is not merely a description but an interpretation of experience.

An important result of journal writing is that as students practice writing journals with an intent, they become engaged in scientific inquiry just as scientists do.

Scientists engage in informal writing and scribbling in their journals throughout their research. They record their scientific experiences and interpretations. Their journals are an essential precursor to formal papers, conference presentations, and scholarly publications. For instance, scientists record their intuitive ideas, gut reactions, feelings, expressions, confusions, pitfalls, and tinkering. They frequently draw pictures and diagrams to illustrate their theoretical frameworks. Journal writing can also facilitate teaching and learning in school science. Journal writing is an integral part of all scientific inquiry, as journals encourage learners to be active thinkers rather than recipients of scientific knowledge.

⚙ JOURNAL TECHNIQUES

Journals can be booklets, notebooks, or folders where students keep personal reflections about their science laboratory activities, reading, writing, and learning. Journal writing for a science activity may include the following (Pradl & Mayher, 1985; Tompkins & Hoskisson, 1991):

- Predictions or hypotheses about a natural phenomenon
- Observations over a period of time

- Summary and interpretation of results
- Personal responses and reflections about the outcomes of the investigation
- Explanations and illustrations of concepts
- Recordings and/or reactions to what they have learned in class
- A personal record of independent reading
- Reflections on personal thoughts and feelings about the information they have received

The following questions may help students with their journal writing:

- What are my prior ideas for this event?
- What do I think will happen?
- What did I do?
- What happened?
- What did I observe?
- What was puzzling?
- What if I change this variable?
- What other questions can I ask?
- What concepts, principles, laws, and theoretical diagrams help me understand this activity?
- How do I propose to solve the problem?
- How does my present understanding compare with my prior conceptions?

To answer the last question on the preceding list, after the teacher intervention students should go back to their journals and add new ideas. They should also edit anything they feel needs changing in light of what they have just learned.

In the case of a problem-solving activity, journal writing gives students the opportunity to frame a problem after researching existing knowledge, state their own lines of inquiry about solving a problem, record their observations, draw inferences from possible solutions, make decisions about their choices, and reflect on their problem-solving procedures and consequences.

Journal writing encourages students to assume the role of scientists and to participate in activities similar to those of scientists—finding out where they still lack knowledge, connecting new understandings to previous learning and experience, and sharing their findings with others. Keeping journals encourages students to think about their own understanding and learning. It also helps teachers see the types of meanings students are constructing.

Learning Events

We saw how Natalie used journal writing with her students when she did the PEOE flotation activity in Chapter 5. In the PEOE model of journal writing, students' conceptions may be determined when students give their predictions and explanations of an event. Learning Events, a journal format designed by Ken Kuhn, a science teacher at Argyle Secondary School, North Vancouver, Canada, is also used primarily to probe into students' conceptions. It is a welcomed alternative to writing a conventional laboratory report.

The main feature of this journal method is the incorporation of learning events as reported by each student from his or her personal view. The student makes a written report of every activity carried out for a given science topic. Students report their intuitions, predictions, observations, explanations, and conclusions. The students are given a cover sheet at the beginning of each topic. This sheet contains "prequestions" and introduces some of the activities to be carried out by students. Students' responses to the prequestions shed light on their conceptions of the topic. The journal cover sheet and an example are described in Figure 6-1.

FIGURE 6-1

Learning Events journal method (NOTE: From "The Journal Method," by K. Kuhn, 1989, (SI)² Network Newsletter, 1(2), p. 2. Copyright 1989 by the University of British Columbia. Adapted with permission.)

Focus students' interest and attention on the task at hand.

Students write their responses to prequestions. Incorporate some of these responses into the lesson sequence.

Students record their observations and descriptions of experimental phenomena carried out by the students themselves.

Students are required to look back and reflect upon observations and explanations, particularly in terms of what they knew before.

JOURNAL SHEET FORMAT
1. *Name:* _____
2. *Date:* _____
3. *Topic:* The electromagnetic spectrum
4. *Prequestions:* State these as given by your teacher; feel free to add any additional ones.

EXAMPLES
– What does the word *radiation* mean?
– What is the electromagnetic spectrum?
– What forms of light can't you see?
5. *Preconceptions:* Answer the prequestions from your experience. Don't worry about "right" answers.

EXAMPLES
– Make a list that is as long as possible of words that sound like *radiation*. (Give a time limit.)
– Combine your list with those of four other students and put it on the board.
– Have your group classify the words on the board—that is, put them in groups.
– Answer the second and third prequestions.
6. *What happened:* Describe your observations briefly.

EXAMPLE
– Describe your observations of the spectrum and of the apparatus.
– Assignment: Read pp. 70–72 in your textbook and make a copy of the spectral chart. Find out what color temperature in photography is.
7. *Assessment:*
   a. What were some things that you already knew about what you observed?
   b. What result(s), if any, surprised you?

continued

> c. State some questions you have about what you observe or that relate to it. (These will usually be required for the beginning of the following period.)
> d. State any everyday examples or applications of what you observe.
> 8. *Personal notes:* Make any notes for yourself that come out of the debriefing discussion.
> 9. *Your conclusions:* Briefly state the main points of the exercise.

Students are asked to report on personal views, new and unanswered questions, or any insight that they consider relevant.

Students review the objectives and activities of the topic, and briefly state the main findings.

Thus far we have introduced you to PEOE journal writing and the Learning Events journal method. The educational literature suggests a number of journal-based approaches to learning. Not all types are described as preservice teacher activities. However, you might wish to try out some of the different forms with your students. Two of these, learning logs and dialogue journals, are discussed through the experiences of two preservice teachers.

Learning Log

One type of journal writing is the science learning log, which is a written expression of a scientific investigation. For example, students may make daily or periodic journal entries in which they describe changes they observe. They may make an observation chart to record weather patterns, or draw diagrams. Students may take notes during presentations by the teacher or after reading, after viewing films, or at the end of each class period. Students record explanations and examples of concepts presented in class, react to concepts that they are learning and those with which they are having problems.

Lab reports listing the materials and procedures used in an experiment are another type. Questions such as, "What did we do in this investigation?" help students clarify their ideas and allow a teacher to monitor their meaning making. PEOE can be a part of the learning log.

Dialogue Journal

Another type of journal is the dialogue journal. In a science class the dialogue journal provides the student an opportunity to share privately with the teacher or a peer, in writing, his or her understandings, questions, issues, views, concerns, and attitudes about science experiences. In other words, the dialogue journal gives the teacher insight into what each individual student is doing and thinking and then to offer counsel. Journal writing helps students to make meaning from what they read and learn in the science class; the dialogue component enables teachers to monitor students' thought processes or metacognitive abilities.

A major characteristic that distinguishes dialogue journals from other forms is the importance given to communication between the student and

P-STAR CONFERENCE PAPER (6-1)

The Learning Log

Sandra Bourcier

One way of formatting an observation chart in a learning log is to begin with a question. For example, I wanted my students to determine their heart rates. I asked, "What do you think would happen to your heart rate after jumping rope 100 times?" They began by making predictions and explaining the basis for their predictions. A dated log was maintained to record their activities and observations. Finally, students drew conclusions about what they had learned based on their observations and experimental results.

Outline of Activity

1. Introduction to heart rate, and what it is.
2. Locate pulse on wrist.
3. Calculate heart rate when resting.
4. Calculate and compare heart rate after 25, 50, and 100 jumps.
5. What makes heart rate increase (which factors)?
6. Discuss and explore students' conceptions of what factors change their heart rate.

Predictions

The majority of the students predicted that their heart rate would go faster after jumping rope. The more they jumped, the faster their heart would go. Some said that their breathing would also increase and they would sweat. They predicted that it was breathing heavily that would cause the increase in their heart rate, not the movement of their body.

Observations

See the example of the students' chart in Figure 6-2. Students graphed their results in math class after observing sweating, heavy breathing, red face, and pain in the legs.

Explanations

After their observations and recordings, some students stated that their predictions were correct. They noted, for example, that "weight and how good of shape that person is has a great deal with their heart rate." On the other hand, students who predicted that breathing was the cause of accelerated heart rate knew they were wrong and decided that a variety of fac-

Student	Heart Rate			Active Heart Rate	
	25 Jumps	50 Jumps	100 Jumps	Total	Average
#1	108	186	210	504	168
#2	96	150	180	426	142
#3	114	198	228	540	180
#4	102	144	234	480	160
#5	120	204	216	540	180

Resting heart rate: 72 beats per minute

FIGURE 6-2
Observation chart

tors were the cause. The factors they identified were: weight, height, exercise (moderate or fast), type of exercise, being in good or bad shape, how well someone was, and what his or her at-rest heart rate was.

Personal Reflection

This was a simple exercise for students that allowed them to learn more about themselves and their bodies. Heart rate is an important factor in a person's life. A person's heart rate is affected by many factors: a person's weight; what he or she eats; active or nonactive lifestyle; and inherited or noninherited disease. By calculating how much we are exerting ourselves, we should be able to tell when to stop or continue with the activity.

Students were interested in this topic because it directly related to them and they knew they were going to do a hands-on activity. To begin, I prompted them with a few questions. I was surprised when they responded "The heart rate changed because of your change in breathing." Of course, they found this to be unrelated when they tried it out.

I learned here that teachers should not underestimate the variety of answers that students can give; they should be given opportunities to explore their ideas to see if they are valid.

The students and I first calculated our resting heart rates so that we had these values to refer back to after doing our activity. We recorded these findings and went down to the reserved multipurpose room, where we conducted the activity. Each student recorded his or her data on a chart after doing twenty-five jumps, fifty jumps, and one hundred jumps. After the students observed each other and shared records, the activity was open for discussion. I listed the students' observations on the board as they explained what they now thought changed their heart rate.

I used this activity and extended it into the math class that followed. The students used their own data to construct graphs. This made the math class more interesting and involved for the students. The math class was a success. This leads to my belief that science activities can be integrated into various subjects. The students learned far more and were much more interested when they had input to what they were learning in class. This made both the science and math class an enjoyable experience!

Sandra was surprised that her students thought breathing was related to heart rate. She suggests that students' ideas must be explored to see what kinds of ideas they have about science concepts. What is your opinion about Sandra's commitment to exploring students' ideas?

the teacher. Dialogue journals are more like a daily letter or memo to the teacher. While the teacher need not respond to every entry, the intent of dialogue journals is to have students write to the teacher and to have the teacher write a genuine response to the student. It is often quite open-ended, and the student includes ideas and musings about all sorts of scientific matters.

When students are given opportunities to function in a dialogue-oriented classroom, they work in partnership with their teacher and peers. Journals give students a voice in their work; when they put ideas down on paper, they are often better able to recognize and understand them. They develop a sense of pride because they are able to generate their own ideas. Student writing may also empower readers to collaborate with an author or subject as they create uniquely personal meaning together. Teachers can monitor the interaction taking place between their students and the text. On a one-to-one basis, the teacher and student can share ideas to a much greater extent than they would normally have time for.

To help students respond in a scientific manner, teachers should urge them to be more specific with their comments, to make predictions, to be critical thinkers rather than mere reporters, and to write in first-draft formats. This is where the value of the dialogue between the teacher and student becomes important. The teacher's response to what the student has written can help probe or push the student to think more critically and to speculate about what he or she is learning.

There is no standard about choosing an appropriate time for journal writing. Every teacher finds his or her own way or time to let the students write their journals. Some choose the first ten to fifteen minutes of the class time for this purpose. Most teachers prefer this way because they do not have to deal with management problems that often occur in the beginning of each class.

Other teachers allocate the last ten to fifteen minutes of a class for journal writing. The advantage is that students have more familiarity with the topic they are writing about, if it is a topic that was discussed that day.

Some students resist journal writing. Some students find the task boring. Some students may be very withdrawn or not sufficiently introspective to talk "to themselves." If journal writing becomes a preoccupation, then both the students and the teacher will likely find the experience a chore.

Overall, it is the writing process that has the major effect on learning, not the amount of time that is designated to it.

Thus far we have learned about PEOE-type writing (in Chapter 5), learning logs, and dialogue journals through P-STAR papers. Now we will examine a few more journal types.

Personal Journal

Personal journals are private records of personal observations, random jottings, or a daily record of thoughts and feelings. These are not read by anyone unless the individual requests it.

P-STAR CONFERENCE PAPER (6-2)

Conceptualization and Practice of the Dialogue Journal

Christine Loewen

I chose to use dialogue journal in a unit on ecology and ecosystems. I feel the dialogue component will allow me to communicate better with my students and monitor their learning in ecology. My responses and questions to their thoughts will also provide direction and structure for their journal responses.

From the start of the ecology unit, students were asked to keep a dialogue journal to record their personal responses, diagrams, interpretations, questions, or ideas on the concepts outlined in class. At least twice a week, the journals were handed in for my responses. My dialogue to the students probed and pushed their thoughts further. Questions were posed to encourage students to further examine ideas they were having problems with. As well, I asked them to include diagrams and other interpretations from their thoughts on the subject.

After introducing the activity "Food Webs and Food Chains" and discussing the key ideas, I used journal writing as the culminating event. The students were asked to explain in their journals what had happened during the activity and the class discussion and pose any questions that were left unanswered by the lesson. The students were given ample time to write and respond in their journals.

The sample journal entries (see Figure 6-3) reveal the students' ideas and conceptions about food webs and food chains. In both cases, I provided feedback and posed questions relating the students' ideas to real-life situations. I tried to probe their thinking and check for meaning through the application of their conceptions.

I also had the students respond to my question(s). This dialogue continued back and forth between the students and me, over time, until the topic eventually changed and proceeded in new directions.

> Uninterrupted time must be put aside during class for everybody to write in his or her journal.

Dialogue Journals Are Not Only for Language Arts

One of the most valuable aspects that I learned about journals is that they can be valuable tools not only in language arts, but also in science. The activity concerning food chains and food webs within the exploration of journal writing forced me to look at journals in a new way and to see their potential for use in different curricular areas.

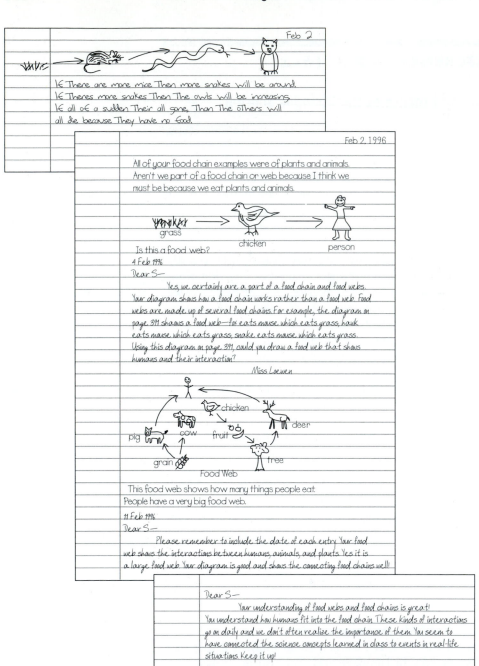

Feb 2

If There are more mice Then more snakes will be around. If Theres more snakes Then The owls will be increasing. If all of a sudden Their all gone, Than The oThers will all die because They have no food.

Feb 2, 1996

All of your food chain examples were of plants and animals. Aren't we part of a food chain or web because I think we must be because we eat plants and animals.

grass → chicken → person

Is this a food web?

4 Feb 1996

Dear S—
    Yes, we certainly are a part of a food chain and food webs. Your diagram shows how a food chain works rather than a food web. Food webs are made up of several food chains. For example, the diagram on page 391 shows a food web—fox eats mouse which eats grass; hawk eats mouse which eats grass; snake eats mouse which eats grass. Using this diagram on page 391, could you draw a food web that shows humans and their interaction?

Miss Loewen

chicken   deer
pig   cow   fruit
grain   tree

Food Web

This food web shows how many things people eat. People have a very big food web.

11 Feb 1996

Dear S—
    Please remember to include the date of each entry. Your food web shows the interactions between humans, animals, and plants. Yes it is a large food web. Your diagram is good and shows the connecting food chains well!

Dear S—
    Your understanding of food webs and food chains is great! You understand how humans fit into the food chain These kinds of interactions go on daily and we don't often realize the importance of them. You seem to have connected the science concepts learned in class to events in real-life situations Keep it up!

FIGURE 6-3
Student-teacher dialogue journal

Previous Instruction Is Necessary

Another valuable lesson I learned from this activity was that a teacher cannot expect students to respond through journal writing without any previous instruction. Students need to be informed of the teacher's expectations and have some practice with the technique in order to become independent writers and learners. Formal instruction should be provided to allow the students to practice some freewrites as their first entries. Class collaboration and peer responses are also valuable resources during formal instruction. Finally, students should be given the guidance and preparation they need to write their journal entries independently.

Overcoming Time Constraints

Rather than requiring students to write an entry every day, where entries would consist of just putting information down for the sake of writing something, students could choose to write about lessons that were exciting for them, were meaningful to them, or that need further clarification in their own minds.

This experience has provided me with a good start to learning about using dialogue journals within the science classroom (see Figure 6-3).

Response Journal

Response journals, also known as *reading journals* or *literature logs,* allow students to keep a record of personal reactions to, questions about, and reflections on what they read, see, write, or listen to. These could include lists of words a student wants to learn, goals for reading, predictions made before and during reading, notes or comments during reading, and reactions, thoughts, or feelings after reading.

Double-Entry Journal

Double-entry journals have pages that are divided into two parts. On the left-hand side of the page, students make notes, list predictions, and draw diagrams before and during reading. On the right-hand side, they write responses to their reading.

Simulated Journal

In simulated journals, students write from another person's perspective (Tompkins & Hoskisson, 1991, p. 199). For instance, Isaac Newton probably was not hit on the head by an apple. However, he did compare the motion of a falling apple to that of the orbiting moon. Newton based his ideas about gravity on the work of earlier scientists such as Galileo. If you were Isaac Newton watching two balls, one solid and one hollow, dropped from a tower, what would you predict about the outcome? That is, which ball will fall faster? Write your reasoning.

Through a simulated journal, students may be taught the history and the nature of science.

In studying early astronomers, students could take on the role of a character such as Galileo. At that time, the scientific community strongly believed that the Earth was the center of the universe. What thoughts would characterize a man who faced so much opposition to his belief in the Copernican system, where the Sun was the center of the universe? Such simulated-journal activities help students empathize with the feelings of the men and women who have shaped science, thereby bringing the human dimension into the world of science.

Freewriting

Freewriting may be used to explore students' ideas before a unit of study, during the unit, and at the end of a unit. In this manner conceptual change may be traced.

In freewriting, "students simply begin to write and let their thoughts flow from their minds to their pens without focusing on mechanics or revisions" (Tompkins & Hoskisson, 1991, pp. 210–213). Freewriting helps alleviate the "blank page syndrome" and can be used to elicit students' ideas on a particular science topic, identify students' understanding of a topic, and encourage them in general. At the beginning of a unit, freewriting stimulates interest and allows students to relate personal experiences about a topic; it can be used again at the end of the unit and the two freewrites compared to display learners' conceptual growth. The difference between learning logs and freewriting is that freewriting is even more personal and may take place in the absence of teacher questions. A student might have to be really motivated to do this type of freewriting.

Quickwriting is a form of free writing. Students reflect on what they know about a topic and then write about it for 5 to 10 minutes. Focusing on mechanics or revisions is not the objective. Quickwrites provide a good way of checking on what students are learning and are an opportunity to clarify misconceptions. Quickwrites are usually shared in small groups.

Dialectical Journal

Edwards (1991) describes two types of dialectical journals: interpretation journals and application journals. These journals help students learn to think critically about what they read or hear. In the *interpretation journal*, students paraphrase what they read or hear and then write what it means to them—making the meaning personal. In the *application journal*, students state in their own words the meaning of what they have read or heard and then write about how they can use it. As Edwards comments, "[The application journal] asks them to look outside the text" (p. 314). Students are pushed beyond interpretation and application of what they have read or heard to analyzing a problem and coming up with a solution for it "by applying meanings from within and beyond the text" (p. 314). Edwards labels this "synthesis-level thinking" and points out that this **synthesis** can also lead to evaluation-level thinking, as students argue for or against their particular solution.

Synthesis Weaving together component parts into a coherent whole (Bloom, 1956).

Many of these journal forms overlap in some fashion. For example, freewriting, a method useful for learning logs and cubing (described in Chapter 7) also involves the higher-level thinking skills fostered by dialectical journals. What is important about all of them is that they encourage active thinking rather than accepting scientific knowledge.

⊗ HOW WOULD YOU ENCOURAGE JOURNAL WRITING?

Teaching and Modeling

It is not sufficient to simply tell students to do journal writing. Teachers must both model clearly and teach the journal formats. Model the benefits and enjoyment of a journal—begin one yourself and share your journal with your students. Explain its purpose until students have mastered the art of journal writing. For example, to encourage clarity, ask students to write their journals as if they were writing for someone who knows nothing about the content. Encourage students to think about what they are reading, thinking, and learning and to share their thoughts with you and their peers. Writing their thoughts allows students to experiment with the written language and try to make sense of what they intend to write.

Collaborative and/or Independent Entries

Begin the practice of journal writing as a structured, collaborative activity. For example, organize students to conduct a PEOE activity in small peer groups. Have one student in the group write the group members' explanations of their predictions and observations. After students have sufficient practice in journal writing, it can become an independent exercise (Edwards, 1991; Tompkins & Hoskisson, 1991). Eventually allow students to select the format they prefer when the situation lends itself to this.

Sharing Journal Entries

Encourage sharing of journal entries and raising questions about specific points. Through sharing and peer response, students gain additional feedback to help improve the quality of their writing. Sanders (1985) states, "Several times weekly students can share excerpts of their entries with the class. They can discern similarities and differences in one another's learning experiences, as well as difficulties and attitudes" (p. 7). You can also write and share your entries with students. This will help students see that you practice what you preach. They will recognize that you are also continually learning and have personal discoveries, queries, and reactions with regard to science ideas and phenomena. Students will view journal writing not only as their responsibility but also as the teacher's.

Diagrams and Drawings in Journal Responses

Using students' drawings to uncover their ideas is not new. Psychologists, child psychiatrists, art therapists, and counselors have used spontaneous drawings as a window through which to explore children's feelings, values, and attitudes for many years. As long as people have been drawing pictures, they have been using pictures to tell a story. Prehistoric hunters, for instance, recorded their deeds on the walls of caves. Before the written word, human beings used drawn symbols.

Children first explore form, shape, and ideas in their drawings. Educators such as Maria Montessori have recognized children's drawings as a rich source of valuable information about all facets of the developing child. Drawing is another language that children intuitively use to express feelings, ideas, clues, and attitudes. As children grow and develop, they shift from drawing to the written word. Often, however, a simple drawing can express an idea that would be very difficult to express in words.

Science teachers often engage students in drawing diagrams to see what information students have acquired: "Draw and label the structure of a flower or the process of mitosis or the circulatory system of a frog." In some studies, science education researchers have asked students to "draw how sugar and water would look if you were to look under an 'imaginary' microscope"; "draw how sound travels"; and "draw how current flows in a circuit" (Driver, Guesne, & Tiberghien, 1994). Researchers have students draw to provide another way of expressing their thinking. Drawings also help teachers interpret students' conceptions of science ideas. For example, a classic study by Nussbaum (1985) illustrates how Nussbaum traced secondary students' conceptions of the particulate nature of gaseous matter.

Drawings are visual representations and communicate knowledge and understanding: What is happening in this picture? How much detail has the student included in his or her prediction? Does the drawing represent a clear understanding of the concept? Drawing forces attention to detail, such as characteristics used to classify leaves. When students draw something, they personalize their exploration and knowledge. When they use drawings to make meaning of concepts (for example, refraction, flotation, or photosynthesis), they are forced to move from the abstract to the very concrete.

Drawing can be more difficult than writing. As a student begins to represent his or her ideas through drawing, a process begins. Drawings tell stories, just as pieces of writing do. Students' drawings provide a springboard for sharing and lively discussion. Students can take turns "reading" their "text" (drawing) to the class. Drawings can help clarify problems. Data can be added to drawings on a continual basis. How students choose to add and/or delete aspects of their drawings reflects their thinking and their level of scientific understanding. Gardner (1983) suggests that drawing in the classroom promotes higher-level thinking and access to all students, especially students who may be weaker in the literacy skills of reading and writing.

Teachers may use students' drawings and diagrams in many situations. At the beginning of a unit, the students' diagrams reveal existing conceptions. Such drawings could be categorized in the same manner as verbal responses to questions or written comments. Exploring students' conceptions through drawings helps the teacher to see into the mind of the learner and to plan for teaching that will accommodate different learning styles. During a unit, diagrams can help students explain their understanding of the concepts. Students can compare their drawings and diagrams with those of their peers to discuss similarities and differences. At the end of the unit, having students draw and label diagrams can be useful in assessing their comprehension and knowledge of concepts taught throughout the unit.

By including students' personal drawings and diagrams in our tool box of learning, teaching, and assessment strategies, we empower students by inviting them to explore their own knowledge using another vehicle (forming images about a topic), be creative and imaginative (using both sides of their brain), take ownership, actively participate, track continuous learning (identify problem areas) or build on learning (adding drawings to a portfolio, where change over time can be assessed).

Teacher Assessment and Feedback

When assessing journal entries, it is important to provide informative and positive feedback to help students improve the quality and completeness of their responses (Pradl & Mayher, 1985). Make students aware of components that need to be addressed and remind students to use their own words and relate the science information to their own personal experience. Do not focus on mechanics or take a right/wrong view when considering responses unless specific content criteria were determined prior to journal writing, because this restricts students' freedom to express their ideas about a science activity or topic. Realize that learners require time to understand and accept the scientific viewpoint (Tompkins & Hoskisson, 1991).

Journal writing provides a medium for helping to share viewpoints, attitudes, and dispositions appropriate to scientific enterprise (such as curiosity, honesty, openness, tolerance, and reflection); methods of inquiry (such as prediction, observation, interpretation, and conclusion); and team skills (such as collaboration, communication, and responsibility) that we wish to cultivate in our students. This is not to say that semiformal or formal lab reports should never be required. However, extensive journal writing must precede formal lab reporting (just as scientists spend more time developing their thoughts in their journals than they do writing final reports). The classroom must be a place for personal inquiry and social discourse; as such, journal writing rather than formal lab reporting should be the main concern.

⊠ WRITING RESEARCH PAPERS

Scientists engage in both primary and secondary research. Primary research involves studying a subject through firsthand observation and investigation, such as conducting a survey or documenting interview data, keeping personal thoughts in a journal, or carrying out a laboratory or field experiment. Secondary research involves examining studies that others have made of the subject. Both of these resources are important when writing more formal research papers. Scientists write proposals and reports, share insights from their journals, and refer to their findings in lab reports to "insiders" as well as when they present research papers to local, national, and international conferences. Similarly, in a science class students are often required to read science literature, write journals and lab reports, and incorporate information from these sources in their research reports and papers.

A research paper is a unified, coherent, adequately developed, original composition drawing on written sources as well as investigations. The term *original* may be somewhat puzzling. A research paper is a unique contribution because the researcher chooses the supporting details that he or she uses as evidence of the thesis (main idea) and puts the ideas, paragraphs, sentences, and words together in a unique manner. No two people make the same choices and express the same viewpoints. Hence, a researcher can contribute something truly original (through systematic self-critical inquiry) in a finished product even if it is based on other people's ideas and information.

It is important to teach science students how to write research papers. Conducting research gives students opportunities to develop essential lifetime skills such as independent and collaborative learning, initiative, and responsibility, as well as a deeper understanding of how to learn. Other desirable skills that students learn during research activity include identifying problems and important issues, framing research questions, using the library, discriminating information, taking notes, organizing information, rephrasing information, and compiling a bibliography. What are some of the steps to do research? Assiniboine South School Division's "Info Zone" Web page at http://www.mbnet.mb.ca/~mstimson/ (1998) offers the following steps for conducting research and writing papers:

> *Wondering* about something (defining the need for information)
> *Seeking* information (locating and accessing resources)
> *Choosing* information (understanding and appraising information)
> *Connecting* useful information (organizing information)
> *Producing* information of your own in a new form (communicating the information)
> Judging the entire process and your product (evaluating the process and the product)

Things students need to do when *wondering and planning:*

- Select a topic or a problem that interests them and is worthwhile to research.
- Explore personal concepts and ideas about the topic by brainstorming and making a list of ideas they already know about the topic. Cluster these ideas.

- Identify and clarify relevant and worthwhile questions about the topic: What is it that students want to know?
- Identify information sources.
- Identify the audience.
- Decide on when and how to present findings.

Things students need to do when *seeking and choosing information*:

- Explore different sources of information (community, Internet, library).
- Locate information in a variety of formats (books, newspapers, databases).
- Assess the information for relevance, currency, freedom from bias, and reliability.
- Keep clear notes of all information search results and sources.
- Comply with copyright restrictions.

Things students need to do when *connecting and organizing the information*:

For graphical representations of knowledge, see Jonassen (1996).

- Compare the information collected from various sources.
- Include only the most important points.
- Organize the information in a new, logical order.
- Summarize information clearly, using personal words.
- Review the topic, problem, or question.
- Organize information graphically using a web, a chart, or a table.

Things students need to do when *producing new information*:

Information can be presented using multimedia, overhead transparencies, seminars, roundtables, and video or audiotape.

- Finish the product.
- Return to polish the product after leaving it for a while.
- Edit and revise as necessary.
- Consider the audience and orient the product to a particular audience.
- Decide how, when, and where to share the product.
- Consider the best way to present the findings.
- Answer the research questions.
- Communicate information clearly to others.
- Acknowledge sources.

Things students need to do when *judging*:

- Look for strengths and weaknesses of the project by evaluating at frequent intervals while researching and preparing the project.
- Look back on the research process and think about what worked and what did not.
- Consider the advice you would give someone doing this project.
- Gather feedback from others (peers, parents, teacher, librarian).
- Seek ways of making the project even better after leaving it for a while. (Are you satisfied with the results of your effort?)

- Judge the project and/or presentation and consider what might be changed to improve it.

Students need to be provided with the following information before they begin their research:

- A choice of topics within a subject domain based on personal interest
- The format of the presentation: written, oral, multimedia, posters
- Location of resources: library documents, science investigations, personal experiences, experiences of others through interviews, Internet
- How to summarize (warn about plagiarism)
- How to organize a research report (web, flow chart, concept map, and so on)
- How to cite and follow a standard format for references
- Due date
- Standards, checklists, and grading criteria.

Often, teachers expect students to give an oral presentation as well as submit a written report of their research. Research reports must include an introduction, body, and conclusion and reflect the three C's: clarity, coherence, and consistency. Self and peer editing are essential for clear writing. Visuals such as charts, pictures, and diagrams must be used to illustrate content. Present interview excerpts, data and journal entries from science investigations, and evidence from audio or video tapes. Cue cards, overhead transparencies, multimedia, and practice will all improve the oral presentation. Research reports may be rated *excellent*, *satisfactory*, or *poor*, based on the steps for conducting research described earlier. Grades may be allotted. Assessment criteria can include originality, clear writing, evidence of adequate research, content presentation, illustrations, records of data, transformation of data, interpretation, knowledge and value claims, articulation of ideas, adequate references, and complete references.

 TEACHER PRACTICE

Critical Examination of Research Papers

In secondary science, student research is often based on science-, technology-, and society-based topics and issues. For example, a practical research topic that can be given to a tenth-, eleventh-, or twelfth-grade chemistry class is acid rain. The research should include the following:

1. What are the causes of acid rain?
2. What effect does acid rain have on the environment and on living things?

3. What is being done to reduce the causes of acid rain and to reduce its effects as much as possible?

Some other possible research projects include the following:

Determine whether the color of a food dye added to water affects how much energy the same quantity of clear water absorbs when exposed to the sunlight.

Is there a relationship between the color of an object and the amount of solar energy it absorbs?

What is the forensic use of pH? How is pH used in forensic science?

The Web page at http://rampages.onramp.net/~jaldr/topics.html (Aldridge, 1995) provides a long list of research topics in chemistry, including colloid chemistry, chemistry of electronics, synthetic gem-stones, scent chemistry, iron processing, irradiation of foodstuffs, photographic chemistry (color), superconductors, carcinogens, and rocket fuels.

Have students write a research paper on any of these topics or a topic of your choice. Observe students presenting these research papers in class. What procedures do students follow?

Collect the research papers and evaluate them based on the criteria described earlier.

Learning Together Model

Use a cooperative learning group when you assign a research paper. Ask students to submit a revised paper on the basis of two reviews by members of their cooperative learning group. Figure 6-4 presents an approach to using cooperative groups for writing research papers.

Jigsaw for Science Comprehension

The jigsaw method is a modified version of Student Team Learning, developed by Slavin (1990). Each student is assessed for individual work. Each team is also rewarded based on the progress that it has made. The following is a typical jigsaw activity:

1. Divide the class into 4 groups, labeled 1, 2, 3, and 4.
2. Assign a different topic to each group.
3. When each member of the group is ready to discuss their topic, the groups are rearranged.
4. Each member of group 1 pairs up with someone from group 3. Similarly, members of groups 2 and 4 pair up.
5. In dyads, members take turns sharing their topic with their partner.
6. Students return to their original groups (1, 2, 3, and 4) and report back on what they have learned from their partners.

An alternative plan is as follows:

1. Place students into groups of three or four.

FIGURE 6-4
Writing a research paper together (*NOTE:* From *Cooperative Learning in Diverse Classrooms* by JoAnne Putnam, ©1997. Adapted by permission of Prentice-Hall, Inc., Upper Saddle River, NJ.)

Task: Writing a research paper

Cooperative Goal: All group members must make sure that each member's paper follows the criteria set by the teacher.

Procedure:

1. Group students into pairs or dyads. Ensure that at least one student in each pair is a good reader.
2. Student A describes to student B what he or she is planning to write. Student B listens carefully and probes with a set of questions. The students then switch roles. Based on the feedback given, students write an outline of the research paper.
3. Students individually research resources needed for their paper. Students may share materials that are relevant to their partner's work.
4. Students write their papers individually.
5. When finished, the students proofread their partners' papers for content development, grammar, punctuation, spelling, and language usage. Suggestions for revisions are encouraged.
6. Students revise their papers, taking the suggested revisions into account.
7. The teacher monitors the work of the dyads, offering suggestions based on the academic and cooperative skills.
8. Students write about how effectively they worked together, listing the specific actions they engaged in to help each other, making suggestions for improvement in the next paired writing assignment, and acknowledging the help they received.

Criteria for Success: A well-written research paper by each student.

Individual Accountability: Each student researches and writes his or her own paper.

Expected Behaviors: Explaining, probing, and listening.

Intergroup Cooperation: Check procedures with another group if it is going to be helpful.

2. Assign each team member a specific topic.
3. The students study their particular material and then meet with students from other groups who have been assigned the same topic. These new groups are referred to as the *expert groups*.
4. Once the expert groups have shared and discussed what they have learned, students return to their original groups to discuss their findings.

A science class should provide a context for developing cooperative group skills. At the same time, cooperative skills are used to enhance science learning. When science discourse takes place in a cooperative environment, social and interpersonal skills are cultivated and can later be transferred to the workplace, in science or elsewhere. The development of interpersonal relations and other social aspects of learning must not be neglected when teaching science content. Science classrooms must promote intellectual, emotional, and social skills. In a cooperative environment, students learn the art of getting along and serving unselfishly: caring, understanding, helping, and tolerating. In our view, these human tendencies and qualities constitute interpersonal intelligence (Gardner, 1983). These social skills can be "taught just as purposefully and precisely as academic skills" (Johnson & Johnson, 1994, p. 59).

⊠ CHAPTER REVIEW

This chapter discussed how journal writing leads to writing and reporting formal research papers. Journaling is a natural activity for scientists. Likewise, student scientists must engage in the practice of journal writing. Special consideration was given to Learning Events, a specially designed journal format that may be thought of as an alternative format to conventional laboratory reporting. The learning log and dialogue journal were discussed through preservice teachers' eyes. Language arts–type journals were considered worthwhile additions to the science class. Journal writing alone is not sufficient; students must engage in writing and presenting formal research papers.

PROBES

1. Practice a type of journal writing as you learn about becoming a better science teacher, using the following topic: "You are an oxygen molecule about to enter a person's nose. Write brief journal entries for each two-minute slot in the next half hour" (McClintock Collective, 1989, p. 72).
2. Implement cooperative learning in writing a research paper. Write a reflective report on implementing a cooperative approach.
3. Conduct a jigsaw activity with your students. What are your perceptions of this type of cooperative learning?

CHAPTER 7

Novel Teaching and Learning Ideas

STUDY QUESTIONS

1. What are some novel teaching and learning strategies that can be used in a science class?

2. Are these legitimate forms of teaching in a science class? Justify your answer.

3. Why is it important to develop analogical reasoning?

4. Should we humanize science concepts? Defend your position.

5. What are some creative approaches to teaching and writing poetry?

6. What might be some reasons for cartooning in science class?

7. Name several ways of using brochures in science.

Reflective Inquiry

BETSY'S VOICE

I was really impressed with one teacher. She even brought in poetry to the science lab! I thought, "Hey, that's really interesting! I think you could really do a lot with that." And I started thinking about maybe bringing in music, making songs out of scientific theories, stuff like that.

JOURNAL ACTIVITY

Unusual Teaching Ideas and Practices

Have you heard of or experienced any unusual teaching ideas and practices in science? What are they? Write about your experience and share it with your peers.

In this chapter, we will discuss additional strategies that may be used for concept development and discourse in science, including analogy mapping, humanizing science concepts, cubing, letter writing, concept stories, poetry, comics, and brochures.

✖ ANALOGICAL REASONING

Science teachers and students naturally use analogies to explain science concepts and phenomena. Science textbooks are also filled with analogies. For example, sound travel is often paralleled to water ripples.

Analogies are frequently used in science discourse. They are explanatory tools that facilitate understanding. Treagust (1993) defines *analogy* as "a process of identifying similarities between two concepts" (p. 293). The familiar concept is referred to as the analog. The unfamiliar concept is called the *target*. Usually the target relates to the scientific concept. The analog is often one from everyday use. The analog concept and the target concept (the science concept) have *shared attributes*. The analog and the target may have some attributes that are not shared. Good mapping should indicate where this breakdown occurs.

Through extensive classroom-based research on analogies, Dr. David Treagust from Australia has developed a guide that focuses on three aspects of teaching and learning with analogies. They are focus, action, and reflection, or FAR (Treagust, 1993). See Figure 7-1.

Analogies and Students' Worlds

Analogies are a part of students' worlds, and they play a powerful role in the students' making sense of an idea. It is important for teachers to analyze students' analogies to determine what types of sense they are making about science concepts and their physical world.

Students should be given opportunities to employ their own analogies to explain a scientific model or a phenomenon. For example, Cosgrove

FIGURE 7-1

The FAR guide (*NOTE:* From "The Evolution of an Approach for Using Analogies in Teaching and Learning Science," by D. Treagust, 1993, *Research in Science Education, 23,* p. 299. Copyright 1994 by the Australasian Science Education Research Association. Adapted with permission.)

FOCUS	
Concept	Is it difficult, unfamiliar, or abstract?
Students	What ideas do the students already have about the concept?
Analog	Is it something your students are familiar with?
ACTION	
Likes	Discuss the features of the analog and the science concept. Draw similarities between them.
Unlikes	Discuss how the analog is unlike the science concept.
REFLECTION	
Outcomes	Was the analogy clear and useful, or confusing?
Improvements	Refocus as above in light of outcomes.

P-STAR CONFERENCE PAPER (7-1)

The FAR Guide for the Ball-and-Ring Activity

Vernon Eby

Preservice teacher Vernon Eby used analogies when he did the ball-and-ring activity with middle school students. He followed the FAR (focus, action, reflection) guide for analogical reasoning.

The pedagogical elements of analogical reasoning are set in bold face and are supported with the ball and ring activity.

Focus

Concept:

In the ball-and-ring activity, the concept is "a change in volume when metal is heated."

> *Is the concept difficult, unfamiliar, or abstract?* "A change in volume when metal is heated" is an idea that will be familiar to some students. For example, one student told the others why bridges are built with cracks in them rather than in one solid piece. Her dad, who was an engineer, had previously told her that expansion and contraction are due to heating and cooling, respectively. "The expansion of metal when heated" is rather a difficult concept because students may not know the "microscopic" reasoning for it. This reasoning may be considered abstract because we cannot actually see the ball get bigger; the observation of the ball passing through the metal ring is accounted for by kinetic molecular theory.

The term microscopic is in quotes because the molecules are really sub-sub-microscopic, which can be confusing if students expect to be able to see them under a microscope.

- Molecules in solids vibrate about a certain point; they are held in position because of the attraction between the nearby molecules.
- The amount of vibration depends on the temperature of the metal.
- Heating causes the molecules to vibrate faster and move farther apart.
- The molecules push each other apart and increase the volume of the metal.

Students:

What ideas do the students already have about the concept?

> *Predictions:*
> – Nothing will happen because the ball won't get hot enough.
> – The ball will grow because it is getting hotter.
> – The ball might melt like an ice cube.
> – The space between the ball will get bigger because the ball will melt.

Observations:
- The ball barely fit in the ring before we heated it.
- After heating we couldn't get the ball back through the ring until it cooled.
- We didn't actually see the ball get bigger.

Explanations:
- The ball got bigger so it wouldn't fit in the ring anymore.
- Things in the ball moved faster pushing out the sides.
- The atoms were getting hotter and they wanted to get away from each other, so the ball got bigger.

Analog:

Is it something your students are familiar with?

Vernon used the verbal/pictorial analogy shown in Figure 7-2. He told his students that the molecules in the metal are much like people. Like molecules, when people are cold they like to huddle close to each other in a tight ball to keep warm. However, when the metal starts to get hot, the molecules, like people, tend to move faster and farther away from each other to stay cool. The students can relate to this analogy.

Action

Likes:

Discuss the features of the analog and the science concept. Draw similarities between them.

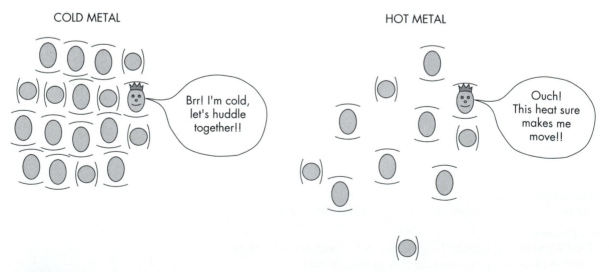

FIGURE 7-2
Verbal/pictorial analogy

Unlikes:

Discuss how the analog is unlike the science concept.

For example, we can compare the movement of the atoms to the movement of people:

Analog Features (movement of the molecules)	Comparison	Target Features (movement of human beings)
The movement of the molecules closer to each other when the metal is cold	is compared to	the tendency of people to move closer together when they are cold.
The movement of the molecules faster and farther away from each other when the metal is hot	is compared to	the tendency of people to move farther away from each other when they are hot.
The theoretical entity (the molecules)	cannot be compared to	real people.

Reflection

Outcomes:

Was the analogy clear and useful, or confusing? The analogy is clear and useful, but students must be told that molecules cannot be properly characterized by comparing their movement to human behavior. It may be useful to some students. One of Vernon's students linked this idea to heat bubbles on the highway: "when the road gets hot and the cement pops up." An analogy can also be confusing. Another student raised a question about freezing. He wanted to know why, when he put his jug of water in the freezer, it popped the lid off. He was confused because Vernon had told him that when objects get colder they also get smaller.

The outcomes of the ball-and-ring experiment were useful because the use of expanding and contracting metals is evident in today's society. Thermostats and thermometers are both based on the thermal expansion of liquids and metals. Engineers must be knowledgeable in this area when building roads, railways, bridges, buildings, and power lines.

The students' questions are useful: Why can't we see the ball get bigger? What would happen if we left it in the flame? Would it melt? What happens if you heat the ring at the same time? If it gets bigger, does that mean it weighs more?

Improvements:

Refocus as above in light of outcomes. The principle of expansion and contraction in metals is different from the expansion of solid water (ice). The intermolecular hydrogen bonding in ice creates more space between the water molecules in ice. This type of bonding is not the case with any other solids. How is ice like other solids? When ice is heated, these bonds are broken and the atoms move freely, forming liquid water. Another difficulty is that some materials, like the metal, are solids at room temperature, whereas ice melts to form a liquid at room temperature. Although the metallic ball expanded when heated, this expansion was not very clear because it was not visible to the naked eye.

(1991) related how fourteen-year-old boys constructed a valid model for an electric current using their own analogies to indicate how electricity travels (Harrison & Treagust, 1993).

Additionally, teachers usually select analogies that are part of the students' world to explain science concepts. In the Harrison and Treagust study (1993), the teacher uses the wheels analogy to illustrate and explain refraction of light because of a change in medium. (See Figure 7-3.)

When analogies are used in teaching science, both the students and the teacher are engaged in analogical reasoning. Comparing similarities between the students' real world and science concepts increases students' motivation (Duit, 1991).

FIGURE 7-3
Refraction of light (NOTE: From "Teaching with Analogies: A Case Study in Grade-10 Optics," by A. G. Harrison and D. F. Treagust, 1993, *Journal of Research in Science Teaching, 30,* p. 1295. Copyright 1993 by John Wiley & Sons. Reprinted with permission.)

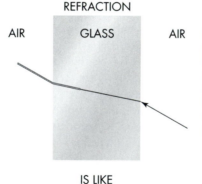

REFRACTION

AIR   GLASS   AIR   Refraction of light as it passes obliquely from a less dense medium such as air into a more dense medium such as glass is like a pair of wheels rolling obliquely from paper onto carpet.

IS LIKE

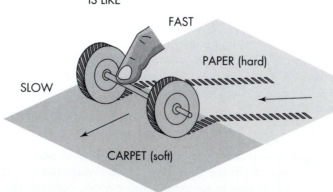

FAST

PAPER (hard)

SLOW

CARPET (soft)

Consider some of the cautions outlined by Treagust (1993, p. 296) in the use of analogies:

- Students may take the analogy too far and may be unable to separate it from the content being learned.
- Students may remember only the analogy and not the concept under study.
- Uncritical use of analogies may generate alternative conceptions when unshared attributes are treated as valid or where the learners are unfamiliar with the analogy.

TEACHER PRACTICE

Constructing Analogy Maps

Select an analogy from a student science textbook. Using the FAR guide for analogical reasoning, construct an analogy map.

The following is an analogy that can be used in tenth-grade science and eleventh-grade chemistry classes when introducing kinetic molecular theory. Prepare an analogy map using the FAR guide.

> The analogy of a popcorn machine can be used to represent the movement of particles in three states of matter: solids, liquids, and gases. In the initial stage, when the machine starts, the movement is restricted to rotation of corn kernels only (this is the solid state). Once the machine starts to blow warmer air, the movement of the corn kernels starts to increase and some corn starts popping (this is the liquid state). When the machine reaches its maximum strength in blowing warm air, the corn kernels start to move much faster, with greater distance between them. This is the stage where the actual popcorn kernels are popped (this is the gaseous state).

HUMANIZING SCIENCE CONCEPTS THROUGH DRAMA AND ROLE PLAY

Drama involves reading, writing, experimenting, demonstrating, cooperating, improvising, expressing, communicating, and analyzing. Drama creates an environment where students are free to explore ideas. It provokes thought and allows freedom of imagination and expression. Creating meaningful life experiences for the students through role playing deepens their understanding and connects real feelings and actions to historical and biographical facts as well as science inventions and discoveries. It can also allow students to play out the feasibility of a scientific idea or debate a controversial science topic. For example, in a tenth-grade science class, a night club scene can be created by letting students represent the elements in the periodic table. One student can become a chlorine atom (a very reactive element) and several other students can represent various other atoms in the periodic table. The goal is to promote the idea of how the chlorine

The idea behind role playing in science class is to let students personify science in a way that makes the concepts more concrete. It is also a way of exploring students' ideas and concepts.

atom reacts with other elements and to talk about the reasons for the reactions that take place between the elements.

The teacher may initiate a role-play situation by creating a problematic scenario that will challenge students. For example, the teacher initiates a scenario in which someone has forged a check and asks how one might find the culprit. This involves activities such as fingerprinting and paper chromatography at the scientific level. The students act as co-workers, lab assistants, or colleagues working in a technological field. The teacher may serve as the main character throughout this activity, modeling scientific thinking processes and behaviors for the students. The teacher becomes a collaborative research partner in this activity. Role playing motivates and inspires the students because the role that the teacher plays is that of a scientist with a problem that needs solving. The students take on the role of fellow scientists who share common goals, commitments, and concerns in

 TEACHER PRACTICE

Ideas for Role Playing

List science topics that lend themselves to role playing. Suggest examples for each topic. Try out some of the role playing.

Here are three examples:
- chemical versus nuclear reactions
- an electrical circuit including a battery and at least one light bulb
- "The Party of Atoms": Yes, the atoms are having a party, and you, an oxygen atom, are invited to attend. The food is free and the music is booming. After a while of partying, you notice that a new relationship begins to develop. Two of the guests, sodium and chlorine, have been looking at each other (across a crowded room) all evening, and now they are moving closer together. It looks like the beginning of a special relationship!
  - Describe what you observe, the exchanges that occur, and the manner in which the relationship appears to develop!
  - Is it a lasting friendship, or does it dissolve with no happy solution?
  - Include the following terms in your description: ions, action, anion, positive charge, negative charge, electrons, bonding, and shells.
- *Scene Two:*
  While all this is happening, you are being drawn into a strange relationship yourself. As one of the few oxygen atoms at the party, you find yourself the topic of conversation among a nearby group of happy hydrogen atoms. Suddenly, two of the hydrogen atoms move away from their group and approach you. The music continues to fill the room.
  - What happens to you during the rest of the evening? What type of relationship are you drawn into? Is this the beginning of a watery affair?
  - Include the following terms in your description: covalent, electrons, shells, and sharing.

The "Party of Atoms" activity first appeared in the *McClintock Memos*, Volume 8, December, 1987, The atoms party by Liz James. It was reprinted with permission by the *The Australian Science Teachers Journal*, August 1989, Vol 35, No 3, p. 72. It is a creative writing activity suitable for chemistry students.

P-STAR CONFERENCE PAPER (7-2)

Using Role Play

Tamara Kosteki

The grade 7 students are studying a unit on matter and I decided to have students do some role playing. They have learned that solids, liquids, and gases are made up of small particles called molecules arranged in different patterns. We reviewed what we know about matter. The molecules in solids are good neighbors and live very close together; in liquids, the molecules like their space and live farther apart; in gases, the molecules don't like each other at all and try to stay as far away as possible. The students then practiced standing as solids (close together), liquids (at arm's length), and gases (as far away as possible). Once students understood the instructions, I called out a state of matter and the students had to arrange themselves correctly. Then I called out an object such as wood, milk, air, and so on to test understanding.

Students' Work

They responded enthusiastically.

To check their understanding of the concept I had them place the arrangement of the molecules on a sheet.

Personal Reflections

The activity was very well received by both the students and my cooperating teacher. I felt this activity helped reinforce the molecular arrangement of the different forms of matter.

Considerations

The space for playing this game is important. Students need a space with boundaries and with no chairs or equipment they may run into. A gymnasium is probably the best place.

the research endeavor. On the other hand, the teacher may play the role of the expert scientist and the students may play the role of becoming experts in the field by being guided and tutored by the expert (as in a scientist–graduate student relationship).

Students can put on plays about historical events or characters using their understanding of concepts.

Preservice teachers should research scientific ideas and the history of the scientist being studied before writing dramatizations.

⊠ CUBING

Cubing encourages students to consider a topic from six dimensions (Tompkins & Hoskisson, 1991, p. 214). These dimensions are:

Describing: What are the characteristics?
Comparing: What is it similar to or different from?
Associating: What does it make you think of?
Analyzing: How is it made or what is it composed of?
Translating: What can you do with it? How is it used?
Arguing: Take a stand and list reasons for supporting it. (Tompkins and Hoskisson, 1991, p. 214)

An example of these dimensions is illustrated on the faces of a cube in Figure 7-4.

The categories of the cubing model guide student exploration of a science topic from different angles, thereby gaining a more complete understanding of the topic. Moreover, cubing "encourages students to become more flexible in their thinking" (Tompkins & Hoskisson, 1991, p. 215). The teacher can also provide a set of questions specific to the topic under consideration, based on the six sides of the cube (Tompkins & Hoskisson, 1991, pp. 214–217).

Describing: Chloroplasts contain chlorophyll.
Comparing: Similar in appearance to mitochondria but different in functions
Associating: Food making
Analyzing: Consists of disclike cases known an thykaloids; the space within the structure is known as the stoma.

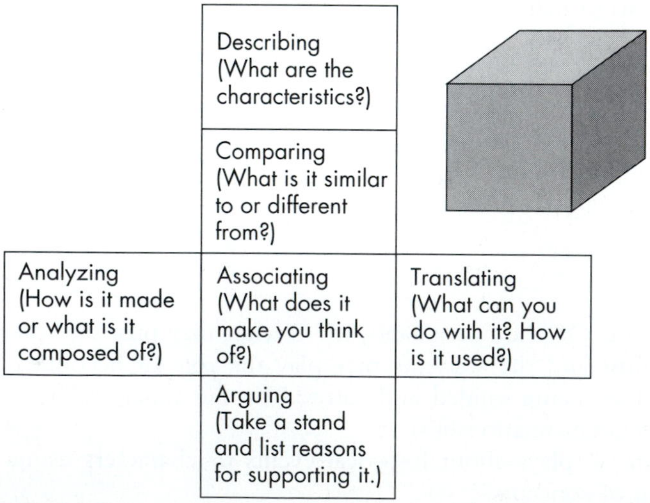

FIGURE 7-4
A model of a cube with six dimensions (*NOTE:* From *Language Arts: Content and Teaching Strategies,* 2nd ed., by G. Tompkins and K. Hoskisson, ©1991. Adapted by permission of Prentice-Hall, Inc., Upper Saddle River, NJ.)

Translating: The light energy is captured and used to split water, which gives off energy, which in turns makes ATP.

Arguing: Without chloroplasts, there would be no life on this planet.

1. What does the chloroplast consist of?
2. How are chloroplasts and mitochondria similar and how are they different?
3. What is the significance of chloroplasts for life on this planet?
4. Explain why chloroplasts are called the powerhouse of plants.

 TEACHER PRACTICE

Cubing

Examine a science concept from all six angles, as indicated on the cube.

LETTER WRITING

Adolescents find pleasure in writing letters to their friends and penpals. With e-mail and the Internet, students can actually communicate with worldwide peers very effectively and quickly.

 TEACHER PRACTICE

Letter Writing

Imagine that a friend was away from your science class. Write a letter to this friend explaining to her or him some of the important ideas you learned in science.

"Write a letter to a person who fears fire from a Bunsen burner's point of view" (McClintock Collective, 1989, p. 72).

"Write a letter to your ten-year-old cousin, telling her what you think she ought to know before she has her first period" (McClintock Collective, 1989, p. 72).

"You are a photon of light emitted from a tungsten filament. Write a letter home describing your travels" (McClintock Collective, 1989, p. 72).

CONCEPT STORIES

Concept stories are science concepts narrated (written) in a story form. Concept stories provide insight into the meaning students attach to concepts. The story line can be developed around a sequence of events in a science phenomenon. Concept stories help students develop an

P-STAR CONFERENCE PAPER (7-3)

Science Letters for Assessment

Lucia Luz

Our class has been studying the water cycle. In order to assess their under-standing of it, I decided to have my students write a letter explaining the water cycle. I chose this form of assessment because it allowed my students to include any concept that they felt was relevant to their particular ideas in their letter. They were to pretend that they were aliens that had recently visited Earth. They were to write a letter back home to their fellow aliens (who knew nothing of the water cycle), and explain the water cycle. After this was completed, they were to give this letter to a classmate to read for feedback. (See Figure 7-5 for a student's science letter.)

Surprises!

Creativity:

What surprised me about this project was the amount of creativity that some of my students put into their letters. The purpose of this assignment was to test their knowledge of the concepts involved in the water cycle. Although the students were aware of this, some students were so focused on the creative aspects of the letter, they forgot about the scientific aspects. For example, many of my students forgot such terms as evaporation, energy, water vapor, dew point, condensation, or precipitation. By not writing the main concepts on the board, and by not telling my students which concepts to include, I was able to assess my students' knowledge and understanding of the water cycle. I was able to see if they remembered all of the important concepts and terms, and whether they could explain them in a comprehensive manner.

Criteria for Marking: Creativity and/or Content?

At first, I was unsure of how to mark this assignment—should I just mark the inclusion of specific concepts that relate to the water cycle (content), or should I also be marking their creativity? This was a difficult decision to make in that some letters were very creative, but lacked specific concepts, while others knew the concepts, but did not express this knowledge very creatively. I decided to do both. I looked at how well the students were able to explain the various concepts. I also checked to make sure that they had included all of the concepts and main terms. Some students chose to include diagrams in their letter to further illustrate their understanding of the concepts.

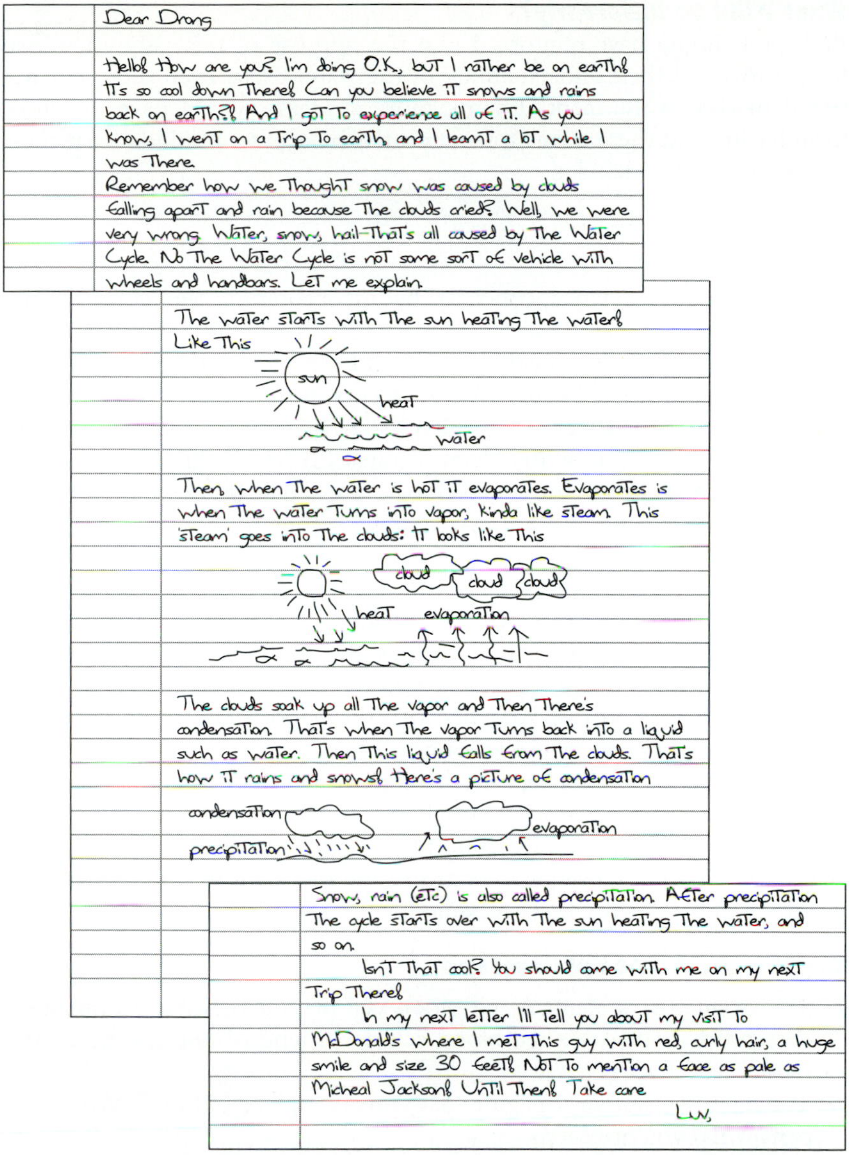

FIGURE 7-5
A student's science letter

Dear Drang

Hello! How are you? I'm doing O.K, but I rather be on earth! It's so cool down there! Can you believe it snows and rains back on earth?! And I got to experience all of it. As you know, I went on a trip to earth and I learnt a lot while I was there.
Remember how we thought snow was caused by clouds falling apart and rain because the clouds cried? Well, we were very wrong. Water, snow, hail—That's all caused by the Water Cycle. No the Water Cycle is not some sort of vehicle with wheels and handbars. Let me explain.

The water starts with the sun heating the water! Like this

[drawing: sun, heat, water]

Then when the water is hot it evaporates. Evaporates is when the water turns into vapor, kinda like steam. This 'steam' goes into the clouds; it looks like this

[drawing: sun, cloud, cloud, cloud, heat, evaporation, water]

The clouds soak up all the vapor and then there's condensation. That's when the vapor turns back into a liquid such as water. Then this liquid falls from the clouds. That's how it rains and snows! Here's a picture of condensation

[drawing: condensation, precipitation, evaporation]

Snow, rain (etc) is also called precipitation. After precipitation the cycle starts over with the sun heating the water, and so on.
   Isn't that cool? You should come with me on my next trip there!
   In my next letter I'll tell you about my visit to McDonald's where I met this guy with red, curly hair, a huge smile and size 30 feet! Not to mention a face as pale as Micheal Jackson! Until then! Take care
                                                                 Luv,

Students Respond Differently:

It was also surprising to find out how often students forgot to include specific concepts within their letter. I found out that many of my students were more relaxed during this assessment process than if they were having a test or quiz. Some students were unsure of how to begin their letters, but once they started writing, there seemed to be a flow in their writing. Many even seemed to enjoy this assessment! This was the first time that I had used this type of assessment and I really enjoyed it.

What Will I Do Differently?

Perhaps I should have reinforced that the purpose of this assignment was for me to assess their understanding of the water cycle, even though it was stated in their assignment. I think more students would have benefited from having had these terms written on the board as a reminder that these terms were to be included.

understanding of science concepts by incorporating the concept into real-life situations.

Concept stories will illustrate a student's understanding of a science concept. Students may be given key concepts from a science topic to assist them in writing their story, or students may brainstorm the key concepts and write a story. The writer demonstrates his or her knowledge of the concept by how he or she connects the concepts. Students reformulate and apply content information in a creative manner.

Since the assignment discourages a mere regurgitation of text or class notes, students are forced to review the content material. Students will be more likely to identify areas of difficulty and, as a result, develop a better understanding of the content. The stories give students the opportunity to use their imagination and express themselves in a creative manner.

Concept stories provide students with the opportunity to practice their writing skills as well as to use writing to learn.

While students use concept stories to demonstrate their understanding of a particular science concept, teachers use them as a form of assessing student knowledge of science concepts. Concept stories are most beneficial to the student and the teacher at the end of a unit, where teachers may use them as part of the unit assessment.

Topics for Concept Stories

1. The circulatory system: A red blood cell plays a vital role in our lives. Pretend that you are a red blood cell or a friend of one and describe a typical day.
2. The digestive system: Imagine that you are a piece of bread. What happens when you are eaten?
3. The development and spread of cancer at the cellular level.
4. Heart attacks.

Teaching Concept Stories

1. Conduct a series of lessons on a unit topic. Students can also do research on their own.
2. Read samples of concept stories to show different ways that the concepts of a science topic could be written as a story.
3. Organize students into groups of four to brainstorm story ideas. Each student in the group will record the ideas.

4. Have a student in each group read the ideas for teacher and peer feedback.
5. Individually, students choose an idea from the list and elaborate on this one point for more ideas to use in their story (characters, main events, solutions to problems).
6. Students complete a rough draft of their story.
7. Students peer-edit their stories in dyads, making constructive suggestions.
8. The teacher edits the stories after student editing.
9. Students write a good copy and plan for illustrations.
10. Students illustrate their stories.
11. Students read their stories.
12. Students write a journal entry responding to the following question: Did writing a story help you think about the concept? Why or why not? What did you think about while you were writing?

Considerations for Assessment

Consider different aspects of the story-writing activity:

1. *Participation*—group work skills—such as cooperation, respectful attitudes, listening to sample stories, and making useful comments.
2. *Content*—originality, deep understanding of the concepts, critical thinking, written presentation, and illustration.

TEACHER PRACTICE

Writing Creative Concept Stories

Choose a topic from the following list and write a two-page double-spaced concept story. Use scientific concepts in your story. The story line is fictional. Be creative. Give characters names and personalities. Illustrate with drawings where possible. Read this story to your peer group in your class.

1. What happens to an amino acid that starts in a Big Mac and ends up in one of your leg muscles?
2. Tell the life story of a sperm from the time it forms to the time it fertilizes an egg.
3. Tell the story of an oxygen atom as it travels from the air into a muscle in the leg, back into the air as CO_2, and ending up as part of a sugar molecule in an apple.
4. In the year 2090 the ozone layer is almost gone. Describe life on Earth.
5. You travel back in time to the year 1990. Describe what you would do to save the ozone layer and thus change the course of history.
6. You are a water molecule. What has been happening to you in the last month?
7. You are a large granite rock. Talk about yourself.

The first three examples are from Williams (1991).

The last seven examples are from McClintock Collective (1989).

8. You are a pendulum in a grandmother clock. Talk to the minute hand and compare notes about your respective energy changes (kinetic, potential, and so on).
9. You are a football. Talk with the goalpost about the forces you both experience.
10. Irene Ice Cube meets Brenda Bunsen Burner. Include words such as *atom, solid, liquid, gas, particle, melting, freezing, steam, evaporate, free to move,* and *hold tightly,* to name a few.

POETRY

Poetry is the language of the imagination or emotions expressed through writing. Poetry enables students to creatively express their experiences (thoughts, feelings, and opinions) and hence may be a unique and interesting way to reach teenage students in a science class. Students have the opportunity to explore science concepts and present them artistically. Poetry might give a different perspective in learning science. Students can write poems before and after learning a science concept or theme. Students can assess their poems to see how they have changed their ideas. Students may choose to write their own type of poem, although some find it easier to follow a prescribed format when they begin to express their learning through poems. Students may compose poems to describe a topic, explain a phenomenon, describe the result of an investigation, or interpret an observation. The following example shows how one teenager used a rhyming format to express his ideas learned from a unit on weather (contributed by Sharon Mohammed, a preservice teacher).

The sun has heated the earth,
For all time, even since my birth.
Dark objects heat up fast,
While light colored ones are last.
Dew drops condense on cold objects I think,
Like those droplets on a cold canned drink.
Clouds form when air cools down to dew point and water vapor condenses in mid-air,
Cumulus clouds are one type that form which usually signal weather that's fair.
Layered clouds are called Stratus,
Curled wispy clouds are called Cirrus.
There are many other things in this unit of study,
But it's warm out and I'm going to play with my buddy.

Some of the things that this student shows understanding of are:

1. The sun heats the earth.
2. Dark objects heat up faster than light-colored ones.
3. Condensation.
4. How clouds form.
5. Different types of clouds.

Following is a poem entitled "Change in Phase," composed by Shelby Primmett, a chemistry preservice teacher.

Shelby presented this poem at the 1998 Chemistry P-STAR conference.

CHANGE IN PHASE

When I first met him my heart melted
I could feel my bonds getting weak
So quickly he changed my state
Of mind with just one kiss on my cheek.

I once was hard, rigid and cold
But he transfers to me all the energy I need and more
To break from these hydrogen chains
And flow, ebb, oscillate like never before.

With him I easily took the shape of my environment
My cohesive power was discrepant to see
And then he would transfer more energy and
Oh that could only mean vaporization for me!

But then there was the inevitable collision
Of two in a straight path, pressure, space
He was not lost to the world, but from me he was transferred
And I became alone, condensing tear falling down the face.

For he was heat
And I am mere matter
Waiting, waiting,
Waiting for nature to grant me one last change in phase
Waiting, waiting.

Teaching Poetry in a Science Setting

1. Select a topic that interests students.
2. Do some research to find suitable poems.
3. Expose students to written poetry through reading.
4. Analyze several formats: formula poems (recipe-like, providing a "skeleton"), free-form poems (expression of a thought with no concern for rhyme or other arrangements), syllable- and word-count poems (structured poems to help students succeed in writing, such as haiku, tanka, cinquains, diamantes), rhymed poems (rhymed verse form—limericks, clerihews).
5. Brainstorm key science concepts, principles, and theories of a life, earth, physical, or environmental science topic.
6. Teach students how to use the brainstormed ideas to compose a poem.
7. Encourage students to write poems individually or collaboratively.
8. Give students opportunity to share their poems.
9. Display students' poems on a bulletin board or in the hallway.

Tips for Reading Poetry to Students

1. Familiarize yourself with the poem before reading it to your students to get the feel of the words and the rhythm. Mark the phrases you wish to emphasize.

2. Follow the rhythm of the poem, reading it naturally.
3. Make pauses at appropriate places. This can be very effective if done properly.
4. Read the poem in a natural voice.
5. After reading a poem, help students reflect.

This section illustrates linking the expression of experiences, feelings, and understanding.

P-STAR CONFERENCE PAPER (7-4)

Poetry in Science Education

Chris Roe

Why Science and Poetry?

During the first term I worked at creating visual poetry with grade 8 students on the theme of experiences of peace. What I found was that over 75 percent of the poetry created had links to the students' experiences in natural settings. Many of the poems had powerful messages of conservation and/or the student's affective connection to, and understanding of, living things. Given my background in outdoor education, I found the power of the students' poetic responses to be quite natural. Moreover, I began to think of the motivational and personal benefits for students to harness this affective/experiential energy, with the conceptual needs of science education.

As I looked into the existing science-poetry connections, I found I could make two general categories:

1. *Factual poetry*—classroom poetry designed as a study tool, as a way to reinforce the vocabulary of specific concepts, or to record descriptions of scientific events and topics.
2. *Experiential poetry*—essentially an expression of feelings and free-flowing sensory experiences in an outdoor setting.

Consequently, my aim is twofold: (1) to present a poetic model using these two categories and add a third category, which combines both to create poetry that is effectively expressive, scientifically informative, and above all poetic; and (2) to present other models and possibilities for science and poetry.

Factual Poetry

Objective:

To reinforce factual knowledge through the use of vocabulary.

Procedure:

As in acrostic poems, students list the letters of the topic they are studying vertically. Students must list one fact on each line and use scientific
vocabulary.

> **B**eavers of genus *Castor*
> **E**at only plants and trees, especially birch, which makes them herbivores,
> **A**nd use trees to build dams which protect their lodges, while . . .
> **V**ery busy all year, beavers hibernate in winter,
> **E**at with chisel-like teeth, which they use to gnaw vegetation; are
> **R**odents belonging to the same group as mice,
> **S**lide through the water with a rudder for a tail and paddles as feet.

Experiential Poetry

Objective:

To reflect on and express the sensory or affective experience of seeing,
hearing, or otherwise observing a beaver (live, on film, in photographs).

Procedure:

Students list images or mind pictures that they associate with beavers and
their environment, under the sensory headings of "What I *see, hear, touch,
taste,* and *smell.*"

- Students choose the words they like best in each category.
- Underline the nouns and create adjectives.
- Circle the verbs and create adverbs.
- Choose from this word bank to create an acrostic poem.

> **B**eaver, the great silver-backed *Castor*
> **E**ndeavor to swim into the current of the mighty rapid.
> **A**ll over you slip under the roar and splash of the wave,
> **V**enting your strength you churn to the top, standing on your rock podium.
> **E**erie is the dark look of your lodge kingdom,
> **R**ank and musty is the smell of your pond.
> **S**tartled, you see me and for an instant hiss, "Trespasser," while you slip away.

Factual and Experiential Poetry

Objective:

To combine the best of factual and experiential poetry.

Procedure:

Students both reflect on an experience and gather sensory information as
in experiential poetry, but also need formal research time as in factual
poetry. If the students go into the outdoors having done research or
reflected on prior knowledge, they have the advantage of an outlook into
the natural setting—essentially a conceptual base from which to interpret
the world around them (Van Matre, 1990, p. 33).

- When getting down to writing, students may need to have had some practice in factual and experiential poetry, depending on their strengths.
- Set a requisite list of science vocabulary and sensory words that the students must include in each line.
- Students need to set a frame of reference, such as a story or conversation with an animal.
- It is the outlet of a student's experience and subsequent interest that makes the poem meaningful.

Beaver the Castor, king of the rodents,
Eating trees on land, at home in the water, the amphibious herbivore.
Answer me, how can one so small swim the mighty rapid and fell a tree so tall?
"Very simple," hissed the Beaver, "with my feet I churn and paddle into the fray,
Easily I steer with my rudder tail around the froth,
Razor sharp I wield my gnawing front teeth,
So skilled I take down the birch to build my fortress dam and lodge castle."

Tanka (Japanese)

Objective:
To write a poem in the tanka format.

Procedure:
Very similar to haiku, only tanka involves five lines of unrhymed verse instead of three, with a syllable count of 5,7,5,7,7. You can also present students with a haiku and ask them to create two more lines, thus creating a tanka.

This is an experiential poem.

Glimmering landscape
Black tree trunks. Crimson-red sun.
Streaks of dying day
Crows winging their way homewards.
Smoke rising from evening fires.
(Unknown)

Habitat Diamantes (Maxwell, 1996)

Objective:
To write a poem in diamante format.

Procedure:
After a period of writing and research about a specific animal, students follow these steps:

1. Pick a word that best reflects their topic for line 1.
2. Choose two words for the appearance of the animal for line 2.
3. Line 3 is three words describing the animal's specific habitat and movement.

4. Line 4 is two words that reflect the animal's niche in the ecosystem.
5. Line 5 is the name of the animal.

Canis
Snowy fur
Prowl, stalking, dens
Carnivore, hunter
Wolf

This is a factual poem.

In these last two models (tanka and diamantes), students may add a visual (picture, photo, or drawing) for effect.

Visual or Concrete Poetry

Objective:
To use words to create images or shapes, as in a drawing or painting.

Procedure:
Students collect words for experiential, factual, or combination poems, using the words to create images or shapes. Students can outline an object or fill in an object with words. As well, the shape of the words can be bent or spaced to reflect the visual shape the word represents. For example, a specific factual connection may be created by drawing crystals with words from the formal observation of the crystal-growing experiment. Finally, there are all kinds of art connections that one can blend into the use of the word shapes.

Reflection
In my experiences with both visual poetry and poetry in the outdoors, I've found that it is possible for students of all ability levels to succeed if they make a personal connection between the poetry and their experiences. Science poetry is an excellent vehicle for this because it combines the powerful affective/sensory domains with the cognitive experience. Finally, when you allow for multiple intelligences and integration in any activity such as science poetry, you cast a wide net of success for students.

Sites for student's (K-12) science poetry readings and contributions can be found at http://archives.gsn.org/may96/0015.html.

 TEACHER PRACTICE

Writing Poetry
Follow one or more of Chris's poetry models to write a poem about a science concept. Read this poem to your class. Following is a list of topics:

- the beneficial and harmful effects of microorganisms in food
- the role of genes in heredity
- intramolecular and intermolecular forces in ionic, covalent, and metallic substances
- simple machines in everyday life
- simple chemical changes

⌖ CARTOONS AND COMICS

Cartoons and comic strips are a form of creative expression that is often overlooked as a teaching tool in a science class because they are an art form. However, their place in popular culture is a reason to incorporate them into science class. Many teachers use professional comic strips in the classroom as an incidental learning experience—for example, to address some point of interest; essentially, they add humor to the lesson but are rarely used as tools to help make connections between concepts or ideas.

Cartoons and comics are ways to express knowledge, thoughts, and ideas on a given subject with words or limited dialogue and pictures. There are cartoons on paper as well as animated cartoons (Lenburg, 1991). The film *S.P.L.A.S.H.* by the National Film Board of Canada (Hopkins, Legros, & Mills, 1991) is an example of an animated cartoon that teaches the hydrological cycle and raises certain environmental issues regarding pollution.

Cartoons have only one panel, whereas comics consist of several panels. Comics have a distinct sequence with a beginning, middle, and an end just like stories. Events are depicted sequentially in each successive panel of the comic strip.

Comic strips can be incorporated into science lessons for a variety of reasons:

- to explore the world
- to record ideas and experiences
- to determine prior conceptions
- to teach new concepts
- to reinforce concepts
- to monitor students' understanding
- to assess students' learning

Exploring through cartoons might bring students to the depths of the ocean or to the mysteries of outer space. Comic strips encourage students to be active thinkers about what they are learning. Comic strips can convey what students have learned, indicate areas requiring further clarification, reveal the level of student understanding, and reveal the progress of the student. Although not a traditional method of science teaching, using this strategy as either a teaching or assessment tool has important benefits:

- Comic strips are a familiar form of expression.
- Comic strips are an excellent motivational tool for learning.
- Comic strip writing appeals to a wide range of learning styles.
- Comic strips provide an alternative method for students to demonstrate their understanding by expressing a variety of concepts or scientific relationships.
- Comic strips convey messages for the reader from the author's viewpoint.

Teaching Students How to Make Comic Strips

Students need to be reminded of or taught the principles of writing comic strips:

- Have students bring a comic book from home or the library, or you can provide a comic; newspapers have comics too.
- In small groups, have students analyze comics and collaborate to develop some ideas about the characteristics of a comic strip.
- Do a comic strip on a simple science topic—for example, "What are rocks used for?"
- Separate into small groups and discuss the usefulness of rocks.
- Bring students together and write their ideas about the usefulness of rocks on the chalkboard or chart paper.
- With these ideas, have students write a comic strip individually or in small groups.
  - Draw discrete boxes.
  - Devise a script for the "speech bubble" used by comic strip characters.
  - Inside each box, make a sketch that illustrates one idea.
  - Demonstrate a progression of ideas when each box is linked in a series.
- Have students share their comics with another person (a critical friend) or another group.
- Have the "critical friend(s)" critique the comic strip on the content, grammar, spelling, and punctuation.
- Comics may be photocopied and organized into a comic book.

Tips for Using Comic Strips

When using comic strips, teachers should keep in mind some or all of the following tips and considerations:

- Decide on the purpose for using comics ahead of time. Will it be used for teaching and learning or assessment?
- If students are not familiar with cartooning in science, take time to teach how to cartoon and prepare comic strips. Show examples of cartoons that illustrate science concepts and fictions. This would give students ideas for their own cartooning.
- Have students work in groups so that they can make decisions together.
- Decide how you will structure the comic strip. Will there be a minimum number of boxes required? The number of boxes depends upon the illustration of the idea.
- Emphasize the importance of incorporating the concepts they have learned in class into the comic strip, so that you can assess student understanding and interpretations.
- Decide on the content you will require. What guidelines will you give your students regarding the content? For example, will you expect

Students should focus on their ideas within the comics rather than appearance. Fun and amusement should be secondary.

the students to include X number of terms to demonstrate their understanding of concept Y?

- Decide how you will evaluate the comic strips (if at all). Will the students be assigned grades, or will written feedback suffice?

P-STAR CONFERENCE PAPER (7-5)

Using Comics or Cartoons for Science Teaching

Marcia Loewen

Using comic strips as a teaching or assessment tool in science teaching was not new to me as a preservice teacher. In fact, I used comic strips in my grade 8 cell unit during my student teaching block in the first term. My decision to use comic strips as a teaching tool was based on the information I had previously gathered from my students. I noticed that while most students were familiar with the different structures and functions of the cell, many were having difficulty making connections between the individual parts. They did not see the cell as a whole made up of these individual parts. This presented a challenge to me as a teacher. How could I get my students to see the relationships and connections between the individual parts?

Knowing that this particular class was familiar with the construction of comic strips, I decided that a comic strip would not only be an ideal way to reinforce the science concepts they already knew, but would also provide a framework for the connections that I wanted them to make. I believed that the construction of the comic strip, in that it tells a story in parts, would provide the students with a solid foundation upon which to build their connections (that is, the students had the parts; they now needed to arrange them into a story that made sense scientifically).

Once I had decided upon my plan of action, I was surprised to discover the motivation this activity provided. I was careful to be very specific in my expectations. I emphasized that specific terms and explanations were required in order for the assignment to be considered complete. Otherwise, the students had creative license. Anything they could dream up was valid, as long as it was scientifically sound.

One of the key components to the success of this learning experience was that we, as a class, had a number of discussions about the relationships among the different parts of the cell prior to this activity. Creating the comic strip was not to test the students on how they could make connections, but rather on their understandings of the connections they had discovered and discussed over the previous classes. I think it was the advance preparation that gave the students confidence to tackle this assignment with enthusiasm. One drawback, however, was that many of the comics were similar to the situation we had discussed as a class

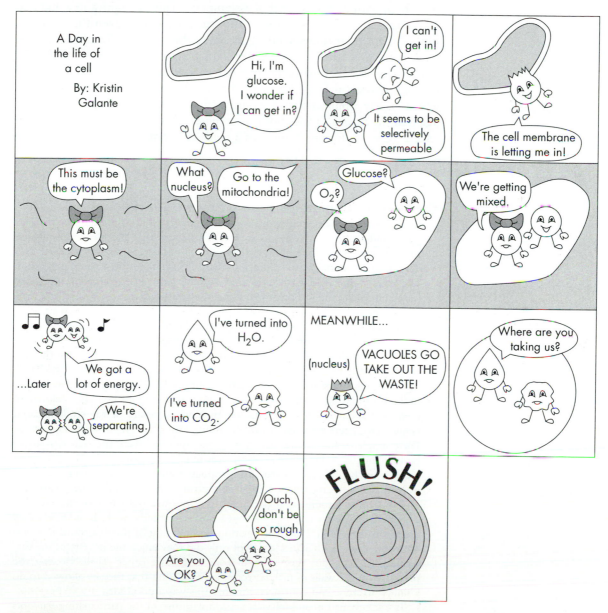

FIGURE 7-6
A day in the life of a cell

(putting ourselves in the position of a glucose molecule). Many students had similar comics because they had to display content knowledge and understanding.

Using comic strips as a teaching tool was a great experience for me. I found that the students who excelled at art but not necessarily at writing were not as restricted in demonstrating their knowledge as they might have been with a strictly written assignment. This brought a new light to the subject of science for some of the students. When given the opportunity to share their understanding in a way that was comfortable, the students somehow felt that they had a solid grasp on the concept of the different parts of a cell working together as a whole. The appeal to diverse learning styles was indeed evident through the use of this teaching strategy. It is my opinion that I would definitely use this teaching strategy again in the future. It met both my expectations and that of the students. (See Figure 7-6 for an example of a student's comic strip.)

Cartooning: Comments from a Science Teacher

Certain science ideas can be difficult for students to grasp because of the language and number of concepts involved. I believe that the life cycles of high and low mass stars is one of these. Therefore, I decided to ask my Science 9 students if they would like to summarize these life cycles in the form of a cartoon. They were instructed to use as much of the new vocabulary that they had learned in their study of this topic using the new grade nine *Science Probe* textbook as possible. At first they were surprised by the novelty of this suggestion but I assured them that they could have a week to complete the task.

My students almost immediately were engaged in the task. They were buzzing with ideas. I allowed them about ten minutes of work time for the cartooning at the beginning of each class. They were most enthusiastic, exchanging ideas, and pursuing a large variety of approaches. Judging from the quality of work submitted at the end of the week it was obvious that the majority of them had spent much extra time on their work. Some of the students used familiar characters while many others invented their own themes and characters. For example, some themes which were incorporated were the star as a stockbroker, the star's life as that of an individual in a family, and a soap opera account of the life cycle. Their final products were of poster dimensions. They were attached to construction paper and posted on the walls of the classroom.

I was quite astounded at the number of positive outcomes of the exercise. The students were eager to view and read each other's work. In addition they seemed to have no difficulty in relating the meaning of their cartoons in terms of the life cycle of an actual star. Not only did they enjoy the novelty of the cartooning exercise but they learned from it. In fact other classes viewing the products on the walls of my classroom kept insisting that they be allowed to do a similar exercise and convinced me that this was a good idea.

It was revealed in an interview session with five of the participating students that they considered this teaching strategy a good one. They said that they were able to express the life cycle of a star in their own way—a way that was creative and one that engaged their own thinking about the topic using an imaginative format.

Cartooning, I have found, adds interest to science teaching. The students enjoy it and learn from it. Why not try it for yourself and see what happens.

TEACHER PRACTICE

Cartooning

In a small group, devise a comic strip for a science concept. Follow the sequence in the section titled "Teaching Students How to Make Comic Strips."

⚛ BROCHURES

What Are Brochures?

Brochures are compact, brief booklets or pamphlets that are used to describe and illustrate a specific topic. They are often made by folding a large piece of paper lengthwise a number of times (usually two or three), forming a small booklet in which each page is separated from the others by a fold. The front of the brochure is used as a title page and identifies the information that will be found inside. Commonly, this information is separated into different subtopics, which are preceded by headings and illustrated with appropriate pictures and diagrams. The content of the brochure might include concerns, problems, questions, and solutions of current events and issues; facts and statistics with charts and graphs; and resources.

> A brochure is a passive medium which must draw the potential reader to pick it up. People will pick up a brochure if it is colorful, has a good design, is easy to read, and is well organized. It must also have a convincing message.

Why Are Brochures Used in the Real World?

The main intent of brochures is to inform and provide a brief snapshot of information about a person, place, object, animal, organization, school, or other subject. Brochures impart information in a reader-friendly fashion, accurately, and succinctly. Some brochures, such as advertisement brochures, may provide information with the intent to persuade.

Why Are Brochures Used in the Classroom?

Brochures used in the classroom transfer methods used effectively by the business community, such as corporations and foundations, to express their ideas to the public. Brochures are a motivational tool that can be used to summarize students' learning and understanding about a specific topic. Using brochures in the classroom broadens the appeal of learning to include students who may not learn by traditional methods. The additional benefits of a hard-copy brochure are portability and permanent availability for further study or reflection. A brochure that puts the main concept before the student is easy to read and remember, while providing sufficient detail to encourage understanding beyond the main concept. Brochures would be an excellent quick reference and study guide.

Using a basic template and their own experience with brochures, students focus on the main concept and provide explanations and examples from their own experience that have meaning for them. Such an exercise is helpful as review, provides assessment of the students' knowledge, and is more enjoyable than writing notes or reading to memorize. Further, the integration of writing scientific terminology combined with everyday language enriches the learning experience and is helpful in the transfer of knowledge to long-term memory. A unit with many related subtopics is ideal for writing brochures. A good example is simple machines, a range of individual machines within one major concept. Another good example would be energy, using brochures to describe the different forms of energy. Both examples have a wealth of highly visible, everyday examples for students to draw upon.

A brochure in the classroom can serve as a bridge between the students, their everyday lives, and the teacher. A teacher's goal is (1) to develop the students' ability to learn independently, and (2) to seek out information in whatever format is appropriate to the student and his or her learning style.

How Do You Begin a Lesson on Brochures?

1. Provide students with sample brochures.
2. Have students determine the various components of a brochure by looking at the consistent patterns of brochures. Have students observe the language used.
3. List their observations and questions on the board.
4. Develop an outline for the students to follow. This should include:
   • types of questions
   • guidelines
   • what they must include
5. Discuss what makes a brochure appealing and interesting to read.
6. Have students choose a topic to research (for example, animal adaptation).
7. Students research their topic.
   • summarize findings
   • develop a method of organization
   • create or find visuals
   • put the brochure together
8. Students present their brochures to the class.

How Do You Assess a Student's Brochure?

Before students begin, they will receive a checklist they must follow in order to earn full points.

Types of research include the following:
• Library research: Books, encyclopedias, magazines, the Internet, etc.
• Businesses/foundations/charities: Information should be collected from organizations that deal with the brochure topic
• Interviews: Topics should be supported using others' opinions and ideas
• Surveys: Information presented should represent a large part of the population

A variety of skills are involved when students create brochures. They include:
• organization skills
• summarizing skills
• research skills
• interpretation skills
• writing skills

Brochures are also an excellent interdisciplinary activity. They can be used to link science with social studies, art, health, and language arts.

5 marks	1.	Research information: five facts, five questions, or five problems must be developed and summarized.
5 marks	2.	Organization: cover, introduction, body, closing, resources; problem/solution style; question/answer style
5 marks	3.	Visuals: brochure must include at least one picture, graph, chart, diagram, or map
5 marks	4.	Spelling, grammar, punctuation
5 marks	5.	Completeness and neatness
5 marks	6.	Resources: brochure must use two or more resources

Total 30 marks.

Organization

1. Ask students to work individually or as partners.
2. Bring resources into the classroom so students can do research to extract information and put together their ideas.
3. Have students make a rough copy before starting on their good copy.
4. Give students an opportunity to confer in small groups for peer feedback.
5. Set students' brochures on display. If professional brochures on the topic are available, add them to the student display.

Here are three ways a preservice teacher, Lorinda Hubert, plans to use brochures in her classroom:

Endangered Species Brochures: The students will research one particular endangered animal. Students will examine literature on the animal's habitat and why the animal has become endangered. Then they will problem-solve to think of ways that the animal could be protected. The research is presented in the form of an illustrated and informative brochure with a title page and headings titled with the name of the endangered animal, "Where does [my animal] live?," "Why is [my animal] endangered?," and "What can be done so that [my animal] doesn't become extinct?" The completed brochures are displayed both in the classroom and in the library for other students to read.

Tourist Brochures: Students study a region by taking weekly field trips. Students explore and gather information to help them understand their region. To apply the information that they learned concerning the wildlife, marine life, and plant life in the area, students will create tourist brochures. These pamphlets will include students' illustrations, personal comments about the region, and guidelines for protecting the natural features and attractions. With the help of tourism and conservation organizations, students' brochures can be printed and distributed. This process will give students and their community a sense of pride, both about themselves and about the unique region in which they live.

Travel Brochures: Students design travel brochures for specific planets. Students will research information concerning the formation, position, physical characteristics, and other interesting facts about their planet. Upon completion of the brochures, students will persuade classmates to travel to their planet.

P-STAR CONFERENCE PAPER (7-6)

Brochures in the Science Classroom

Deanna Shanks

Booklets of information were provided for the students and they were required to research a planet or other celestial body and create an illustrated travel brochure. The students had to do a rough draft that was approved by the teacher before they moved on to complete the good copy. They had to include the following in their brochure:

1. Name of the planet or celestial body.
2. Description (color, size, texture, temperature, etc.).
3. Location/distance from the sun.
4. Origin of the planet or celestial body.
5. Special features (revolutions around the sun, rotation, rings, spots, craters, etc.).
6. Visuals: Diagrams of the planet or celestial body with its dimensions labeled and pictures of the planet's or celestial body's attractions.
7. Travel information that makes your tourist location sound as inviting as possible. The following questions should help you get started:
   • Why should people visit?
   • How long is the voyage from Earth and when are flights available?
   • What is the cost of a vacation package?

I was impressed with how motivated the students were when this activity was introduced. They were eager to read through the booklets to find information for their brochures. They were discussing interesting facts with their peers and using their imaginations to come up with novel ideas to lure tourists to their planet.

This activity helped the students learn how to pick and choose relevant information because there was not enough room to include everything in their brochures. It was a good opportunity for the students to practice note taking and summarizing.

In the future I might have students create their brochures using the computer. I was unable to use the computers for this purpose because the students had just been introduced to using graphics in computer class. If I had waited a month this activity would have been a nice culminating activity for both computer class and science class.

Both students with exceptional writing abilities and students with an aptitude for artistic design are able to display their abilities. Developing brochures gives students a sense of purpose in their work, because in a sense they are taking on the role of a teacher; they are trying to inform people through their brochures.

 TEACHER PRACTICE

Brochures

List topics for brochures. Create at least one brochure.

⚙ CHAPTER REVIEW

We began this chapter by helping you understand how secondary students may learn science through analogical mapping using the FAR guide. This chapter then introduced to you some uncommon strategies (humanizing science, cubing, letter writing, concept stories, poetry, cartoons, brochures) that can be successfully used in teaching science. These strategies might sound very language "artsy"; however, our preservice teachers have used these strategies with much success in their practicum.

This chapter also highlighted the experience of a teacher experimenting with cartooning in his science class. Both preservice and practicing teachers have testified that they were able to reach most of the students in science class using novel strategies of learning. This chapter reiterates the concept of science for all students and the importance of providing activities that address a number of different intelligences.

PROBES

1. Select a science unit topic. After reviewing the various writing strategies in this chapter, suggest where and how they might be used in your unit. Practice a writing strategy with your peers or a group of students.
2. Try at least one of the teaching and learning strategies described in this chapter in your practicum classroom.

CHAPTER 8

Explanation, Evidence, Relevance

STUDY QUESTIONS

1. What are the different ways of organizing science knowledge structures?

2. How would you teach students concept mapping?

3. What are some of the reasons for using a Vee diagram to write your science activity?

4. What are the advantages of meaningful learning over rote learning?

5. What is the psychological learning theory behind concept mapping and Vee diagramming?

Reflective Inquiry

KATHLEEN'S VOICE

It is early in the year and the Vee diagram is a new tool to learn. I'm sure I will get the hang of it. I like the areas for recording observations and for naming concepts. However, I am having some trouble with keeping the knowledge claims broad. I think my value claims will develop as well. Are these to be like the rationale for doing the activity? Is this where I as the teacher make a statement that accounts for the usefulness of the activity? Practice will increase my comfort with and understanding of Vee diagrams.

I've used concept webs for my research papers and creative writing and feel comfortable with the concept. I am nervous about my own knowledge of scientific concepts and that I may have big holes in my planning. I suppose when new information is acquired, the concept map can easily be expanded.

I have been working on a map for my science activity and struggling a bit. I have some books from the library, but I think your walk through a map with our group in class has cleared up some of my questions.

I can see their use in planning and assessing lessons. Taking time to prepare and research a topic is as important as reflecting on one's presentation to see what worked, what needs to be reworked, and what aspects were confusing. I like the ideas of both the Vee diagram and the concept mapping as planning tools because of the structure they provide. I have produced some lengthy lesson plans these past years and I need something to help me be more concise. They'll take practice.

I found the process of arranging (or trying to arrange) the concepts especially helpful in developing my understanding. Sometimes talking to other people also helped make things clearer.

JOURNAL ACTIVITY

Organization of a Science Activity
What are the different methods you have employed in the past to structure reading material?
Think back to your school days. How have you reported on a science activity?

⊠ LEARNING TOOLS

In this chapter, you will learn to construct concept maps and Vee diagrams of science topics. You will also learn how to teach your students concept mapping and Vee diagramming. The efficacy of these learning tools will be shown through examples. Finally, you will study Ausubel's theory of meaningful learning, which underpins these two learning tools.

Concept mapping and Vee diagramming are two powerful learning tools. These knowledge-producing tools originated in the late 1970s when Joseph Novak of Cornell University proposed an alternative to Piagetian psychology for science teaching and learning (Novak, 1977, 1985, 1988). These learning tools are based on Ausubel's learning theory of **meaningful learning** (Ausubel, Novak, & Hanesian, 1978).

Meaningful learning is making a conscious effort or commitment to relate new learning to prior concepts in the cognitive structure in a higher order.

In recent times, science education journals have reported concept mapping and Vee diagramming in the school classroom (Ebenezer, 1992; Roth, 1990; Roth & Verachaka, 1993). These tools have been successfully used to explore and assess students' ideas for lesson planning as well as to "construct new and more powerful meanings" during a unit of study (Novak, 1991; Novak & Gowin, 1984).

⊠ CONCEPT MAPPING

What Is a Concept?

Novak and Gowin (1984) explain the term *concept* as a "perceived regularity in events or objects." A concept is given a label. For example, a chair is called a *chair* because it exhibits a perceived regularity—it has four legs, a seat, and a back. Consider an example in science. The concept label *force* is given to an object in motion because force is determined by the mass of the object and the acceleration (speed and direction) with which it moves.

What Is a Concept Map?

Concept mapping can be described as "a way of graphically displaying concepts and relationships between or among concepts" (West, Farmer, & Wolff, 1991). A concept map is a structural respresentation consisting of *nodes* and *labeled lines*. The nodes correspond to important terms that are used broadly as concepts. The line denotes a relation between a pair of concepts (nodes), and the labeled line is called a *proposition*. Concept maps represent some important aspects of a student's structural knowledge in content domains, such as physics, chemistry, and biology.

Concept maps were originally perceived to be hierarchical (Novak & Gowin, 1984). The latest research has shown that imposing a hierarchical structure, regardless of content domain, is unnecessary (Ruiz-Primo & Shavelson, 1996; Ruiz-Primo, Shavelson, & Schultz, 1997; White & Gunstone, 1992), because not all concept domains are hierarchical and an accurate concept-map representation of a hierarchical domain will be hierarchical itself. Jones, Palinscar, Ogle, and Carr (1987) identify three types of concept maps:

See http://www.cotf.edu/ETE/ concept.html, a site for concept maps.

- Hierarchical concept maps
- Cluster maps
- Chain maps

There probably is not only one correct way to construct a concept map. The hierarchical concept map is very close in nature to an outline form, and the cluster concept map is similar to a hierarchical map; it is just spatially arranged differently.

Hierarchical Concept Maps

Hierarchical concept maps show relationships among concepts in a hierarchical fashion: the most general concept is placed at the top, more specific concepts are placed below the more general concepts, and specific examples are usually placed at the bottom. Figure 8-1 gives an example of a hierarchical map.

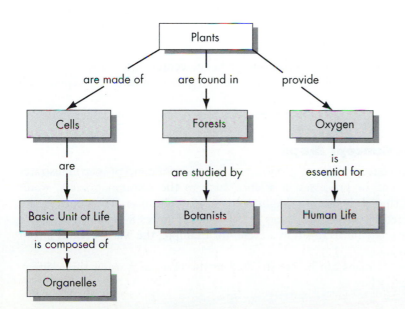

FIGURE 8-1
A hierarchical concept map of plants

FIGURE 8-2

A cluster concept map of current and electricity (*NOTE:* From Manitoba Education and Training, *Senior Years Science Teachers' Handbook: A Teaching Resource.* Winnipeg, MB: Manitoba Education and Training, 1997, p. 11.13. Reproduced with permission. Lynda Matchullis, a Senior Years science teacher, developed this figure for Manitoba Education and Training.)

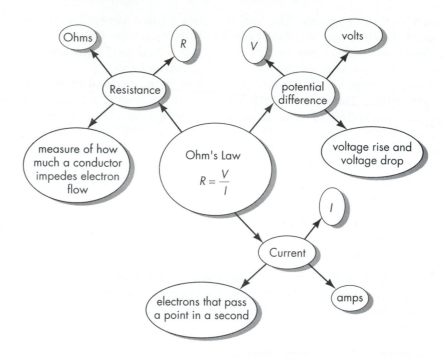

Cluster Concept Maps

A cluster concept map (also called a *category* or *thematic* concept map) presents a theme such as chemical reactions (single displacement, double displacement, addition, substitution) and forms of energy (mechanical, chemical, electrical, radiant). See Figure 8-2 for a cluster map showing the relationships of current, resistance, and voltage in Ohm's law.

To create a cluster map:

1. Place the main or general concept in the center of the map.
2. Connect the main concept to the categories (specific concepts) with lines and arrows.
3. Connect the categories to subcategories (more specific concepts).

Chain Concept Maps

A chain concept map (also known as a *sequential* concept map) illustrates phenomena or processes in science such as the solution process, water cycle, osmosis, behavior of light, and DNA replication. The concepts are connected by arrows in a series of boxes (see Figures 8-3a and 8-3b). The concepts may be arranged in a cycle; for example, the water cycle is linked in a circle.

Concept maps can be constructed in the classroom using three different approaches:

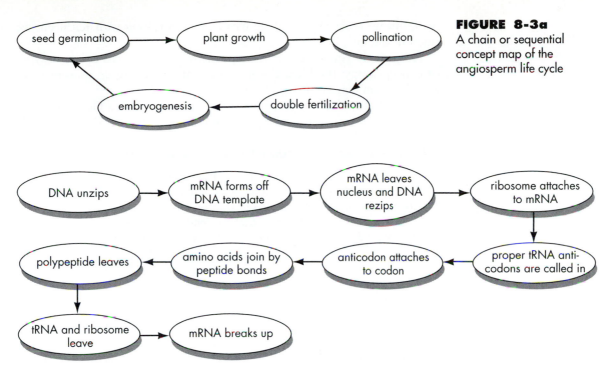

FIGURE 8-3a
A chain or sequential concept map of the angiosperm life cycle

FIGURE 8-3b
A chain concept map of protein synthesis (*NOTE:* Figures 8-3a and 8-3b are from Manitoba Education and Training, *Senior Years Science Teachers' Handbook: A Teaching Resource.* Winnipeg, MB: Manitoba Education and Training, 1997, p. 11.15. Reproduced with permission. Lynda Matchullis, a Senior Years science teacher, developed these figures for Manitoba Education and Training.)

- Students construct the maps using concept words supplied by the teacher.
- Students construct the maps by identifying the concepts from an information source.
- Students construct the maps from their own personal knowledge.

Learning to Construct Concept Maps

You should learn how to construct proper concept maps so that you can use this learning tool for planning and assessing lessons. You will be able to confidently teach students how to create them. Students will use concept maps for revealing, clarifying, and elaborating their own conceptions and understandings, as well as organizing and learning textual materials. When we construct a concept map, we have visually displayed the concepts that we know about a topic, as well as adding more concepts to our original map from purposive reading. It takes time to construct a concept map, but we remember what we have drawn. So along with Kathleen, we suggest you give it a try!

How would you construct concept maps? We will focus on three types of concept maps: the hierarchical concept map, the cluster concept map, and the chain concept map.

Figure 8-4 is a concept mapping sequence that shows a hierarchy. Each step is subsequently outlined with examples (see Figure 8-5).

Step 1: Choose a passage from a science book.

A Summary: Plant Roots

From each seed, a tiny root pushes down into the earth and spreads out in the ground. The root can be either a taproot or a fibrous root.

Taproots have one large vertically extending root known as the primary root. Secondary roots grow off the primary root. Each root has a root cap,

FIGURE 8-4

Sequential steps for creating a hierarchical concept map

Alternative idea: If you are not constructing a hierarchical concept map, arrange the concepts in a way that makes sense to you. Concepts you see as related should be kept fairly close together, but leave space between even the closest concepts. When you are satisfied with your arrangments of the concepts, stick them on a sheet of paper.

1. Choose a passage from a science book related to your selected topic (for example, reproduction).
2. Circle or underline the main concepts in this passage. *Or* omit steps 1 and 2; a group or a class of students can brainstorm for concepts (objects and events) and write them on paper. Alternately, the teacher can provide students with concepts.
3. Write or print the concepts on index cards, Post-it notes, or something similar so that the concepts can be moved around. A computer program such as Inspiration (http://www.inspiration.com) may be used to design a map. (In our example, concepts might include reproduction, zygote, sexual, mitosis, meiosis I, asexual, zygote, meiosis II, male gamete, female gamete, fertilized egg, fusion, 46 chromosomes, 2 cells (half-complement, double-stranded), 4 cells (half-complement, single-stranded, complete individual).
4. Rank the list of concepts from the superordinate (most concrete, inclusive, most general—for example, reproduction) to the subordinate (most abstract and exclusive, most specific—for example, chromosome). Place the most general concept right on top.
5. Arrange the subsuming and more inclusive concepts from top to bottom (most general to most specific) to indicate a hierarchy. In the construction of this hierarchy, place concepts next to each other horizontally if they function at a similar level of abstraction (for example, sexual/asexual) or interrelate closely (for example, fertilized egg, zygote, chromosome).
6. Link related concepts with lines (cross-links) and label each line in propositional or prepositional form. Each linkage should read as a meaningful phrase (for example, fertilized egg *is called* zygote). Mark the cross-links with arrows to indicate direction. Support the concepts with examples below each concept. Alternatively, it can help to put an arrowhead on the line to show how to read the relation.
7. Have the group critically analyze the concept map to improve upon and extend your ideas further.

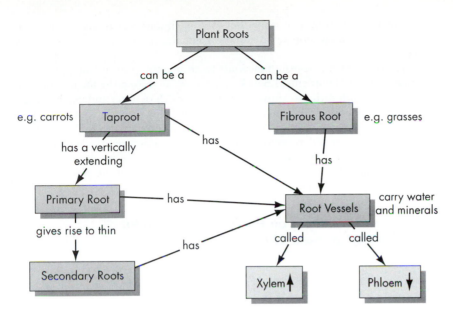

FIGURE 8-5
Description of concept mapping sequence

which protects the root tip as it grows and pushes through the soil. Examples of taproots are beets, carrots, radishes, and turnips. There is food stored in the roots that are listed as examples.

Fibrous roots consist of many thin root extensions that usually grow in all directions in a more horizontal fashion. Examples of fibrous roots are grasses and rye.

The roots have two main functions: to anchor the plant in the soil and to absorb water and nutrients. Roots keep growing all during the life of a healthy plant. They push their way through the soil in search of water and minerals such as copper and iron. These functions are carried out through root caps, root hairs, and root tubes or vessels called xylem and phloem. Roots act like sponges that soak up water and minerals. Root hairs are an advantageous adaptation that allow the root greater access to food and water by expanding the surface area of epidermal cells. The xylem carries food up the plant and the phloem carries food down into the roots.

Step 2: Circle or underline the main concepts in this passage.

The major concepts are underlined.

A Summary: Plant Roots

From each seed, a tiny root pushes down into the earth and spreads out in the ground. The root can be either a <u>taproot</u> or a <u>fibrous root.</u>

<u>Taproots</u> have one large vertically extending root known as the <u>primary root.</u> <u>Secondary roots</u> grow off the primary root. Each root has a <u>root cap</u>, which protects the <u>root tip</u> as it grows and pushes through the soil. Examples of taproots are beets, carrots, radishes, and turnips. There is food stored in the roots that are listed as examples.

Fibrous roots consist of many thin root extensions that usually grow in all directions in a more horizontal fashion. Examples of fibrous roots are grasses and rye.

The roots have two main functions: to anchor the plant in the soil and to absorb water and nutrients. Roots keep growing all during the life of a healthy plant. They push their way through the soil in search of water and minerals such as copper and iron. These functions are carried out through root caps, <u>root hairs</u>, and <u>root tubes</u> or vessels called <u>xylem</u> and <u>phloem</u>. Roots act like sponges that soak up water and minerals. <u>Root hairs</u> are an advantageous adaptation that allow the root greater access to food and water by expanding the surface area of <u>epidermal cells</u>. The xylem carries food up the plant and the phloem carries food down into the roots.

Step 3: Print concepts on flash cards or Post-it notes for appropriate placement.

plant roots
taproot—beets and carrots
fibrous root—grasses and rye
primary root
secondary roots
root cap
root tip
root hairs
root tubes
root vessels
xylem
phloem
epidermal cells

Step 4: Place the most general concept on top.
Alternatively, arrange the concepts in a way that you see how they relate. Keep the related concepts close together.

Plant roots

Step 5: Arrange the subsuming and more inclusive concepts from top to bottom, thus showing a hierarchy of concepts.
Alternatively, stick concepts on a sheet of paper the way you see fit.

general characteristics   Plant roots

Taproot   Fibrous root

Primary root   Secondary root

Root vessels

specific characteristics   Xylem   Phloem

Step 6: Relate all the concepts with propositions or connecting words.

Also, provide examples wherever appropriate.

Teaching Students to Construct Concept Maps

You can help students relate the concepts that they bring to or learn in the classroom by asking them to construct concept maps. Students may know isolated concepts but they may not know how the concepts relate to each other. Students may write paragraphs about the concepts involved in a topic but still not show that they understand how the concepts are inter-related.

How do you teach students how to construct concept maps? You engage your students in individual as well as collaborative learning, just like Kathleen suggested, when you teach them how to draw concept maps. The method is outlined in Figure 8-6.

Concept mapping takes regular practice and feedback. Take time to teach students how to construct concept maps and to learn how to criticize them constructively.

Creating concept maps with computer programs is explored in Chapter 10.

Uses of Concept Mapping

You may use concept mapping in the following ways while planning for and teaching a unit of study (Ebenezer, 1992).

In their book *Probing Understanding*, White and Gunstone (1992, pp. 30–42) discuss other uses of concept mapping.

1. *Preparing concept cards.* Prepare a set of concept cards for each small group of students in your class.
2. *Arranging concept cards in sequence.* Give each group a piece of paper on which to arrange the cards. Ask the students to sort through the concept cards, tentatively placing them on the sheet in the way they believe the cards are related.
3. *Negotiating to reach agreed-upon meanings.* Engage students to discuss their arrangements in their small groups with peers. Encourage students in each group to come to a consensus.
4. *Drawing relationships between and among concepts.* Ask students to write words on the lines between the concepts to show how they are related. Remind students that the words on the lines should be connecting words or phrases that have verbs in them so that the conceptual links can be read as sentences down and across.
5. *Justifying the position of concept cards.* Ask each group to show and explain its map and justify the positions of the concept cards and the interconnecting sentences.

FIGURE 8-6
Teaching students to construct concept maps

A Big-Picture Look at a Science Unit

In the preparation of a unit, you may construct a concept map to get an integrated understanding of the concepts involved. You may also use a concept map as an advanced organizer to present students with a big picture of a unit (see Figure 8-7). The students will then view knowledge not as bits and pieces of information; rather, they will see each topic or lesson as integrated rather than isolated. After introducing a unit of study in this manner, draw back from the larger picture and focus students' attention on the details of a smaller segment of the unit.

The Revealing of Prior Conceptions

Students can construct concept maps before a unit begins. For example: (a) demonstrate an experiment and ask students to think of all the concepts that pertain or relate to this activity, (b) give students a list of concepts and have students link them, or (c) give students a topic and ask them to identify the concepts and to state the relationships among the concepts.

FIGURE 8-7

A concept map—an advance organizer of a unit on water cycle

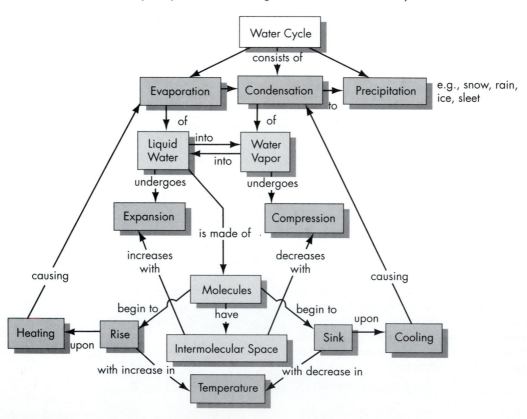

   The maps will not only identify the range of concepts and ideas that the students use but will also reveal students' conceptions that should be explored further. You, therefore, have an opportunity to become aware of students' conceptions of the topic under study. As well, students can be made aware of their own understanding of the topic with their own concept maps. It then becomes easier to plan activities either to clarify students' thinking or to elaborate upon their ideas. In addition, motivation, attitude, and interest will improve when students recognize that they already know something about the new lesson or a new topic of study when they construct a concept map. Then ask them to connect the concepts giving examples of concepts in meaningful ways.

The Opportunity for Students to Make Revisions

During the course of the unit, or as learning progresses, students can be given opportunities to review their concept maps several times. The students will no doubt evaluate their map in light of what they have been learning. With your help or even in conversation with their peers, the students will be able to spot the different relationships among concepts. In addition, more concepts and examples might be evident in students' subsequent maps. Figures 8-8a, 8-8b, and 8-8c give examples of progressive maps a group of students made during a unit of study.

Development of Collaborative Relationships

You can develop a better relationship between you and your students when they share the progression of ideas in science in conversation through the exposition of concept maps. A recent study has traced the

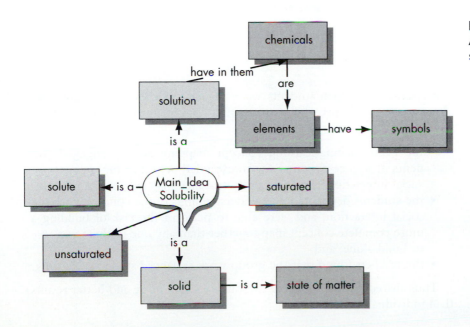

FIGURE 8-8a
A concept map of solubility—map 1

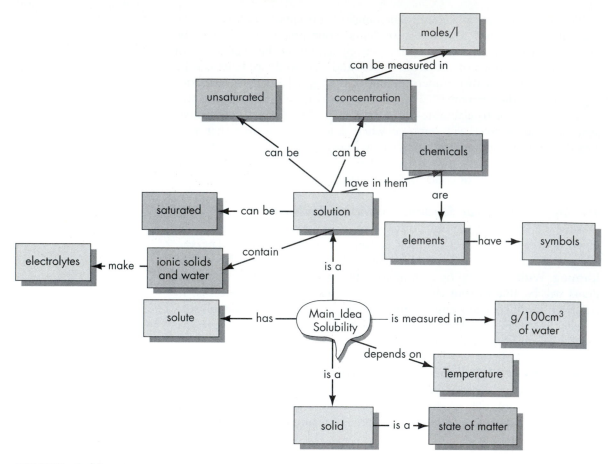

FIGURE 8-8b
A concept map of solubility—map 2

conversations in which students were engaged as they were negotiating about science concepts while constructing concept maps (Briscoe, 1993). This study concluded that:

- the peer teaching-learning concept mapping activity engaged students in science discourse for an extended period of time;
- social interactions involving peer assistance may enhance learning;
- the students negotiated new understandings of the concepts through social interaction, and were able to perform the task of building a more complete concept map together than any one of them was able to build alone; and
- the teachers found that the group work enhanced students' learning.

Thus shared meaning-making can only result in more and better results than individual work.

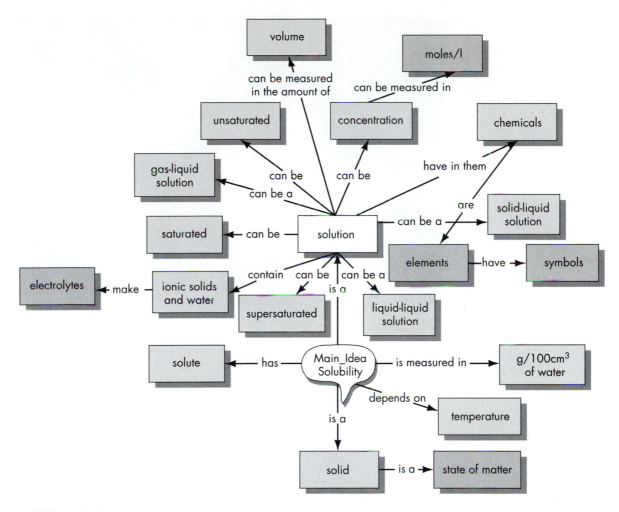

FIGURE 8-8c
A concept map of solubility—map 3

Assessment of Students' Understanding

At the end of the unit, students can refine or correct their "*n*th" concept map. To assess students' understanding in a science unit, you may have students present a portion of their concept maps to the rest of the class or have students explain their maps to you individually. Students should map their concepts without reference to their textbooks at this point. The intention is to clearly reveal students' thinking, allowing you to assess and score students' learning (see Chapter 13 for criteria for scoring a concept map). In this manner, concept mapping can be effectively used as a learning strategy that enables students to actively create content knowledge of science.

⊗ VEE DIAGRAMMING

The knowledge Vee developed by Bob Gowin in 1977 is a simple heuristic device. It illustrates key ideas regarding the nature of knowledge and the process by which new knowledge is constructed in science investigations (Novak & Gowin, 1984). Vee diagramming helps people learn how knowledge is constructed and reconstructed by allowing students to consider their own conceptions of the natural phenomenon under study. The Vee diagram also helps an individual to develop questions, plan, design, and conduct an activity, as well as interpret the results. In this manner, students can construct new meanings based on their own current meanings. Finally, a Vee diagram helps students link science to personal needs.

Learning to Construct a Vee Diagram

My Understanding and My Doing
A Vee diagram consists of two sides. The left side is called "My Understanding" of scientists' key ideas (the conceptual side). The right side is called "My Doing" (the methodological side)—and contains observations and statements of conclusions (see Figure 8-9a).

Event
The point at which the My Understanding side and the My Doing side intersect (the tip of the Vee) is the event that you will be studying or investigating. The event is the problem task. Everything revolves around it (see Figure 8-9b).

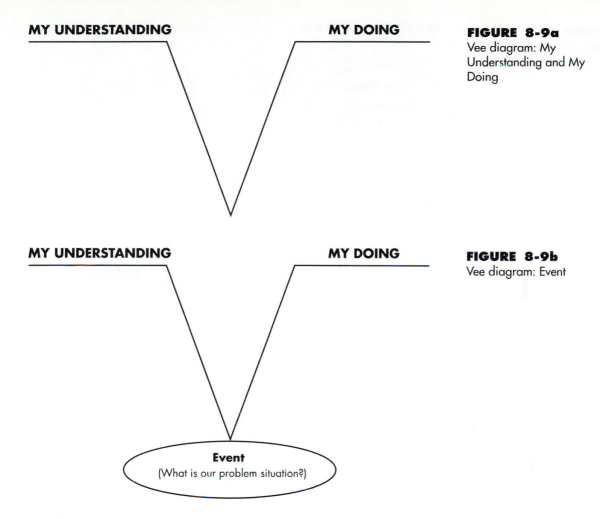

FIGURE 8-9a
Vee diagram: My Understanding and My Doing

FIGURE 8-9b
Vee diagram: Event

Key Ideas

When observing the event, you should ask yourself, "What do I know about this event?" and "What do scientists or experts say about this particular event?" In other words, "What are the major ideas?" The label "Key Ideas" comes just below My Understanding, because these ideas will guide your study of the event (see Figure 8-9c).

Concept Labels

When observing the event, you should ask yourself, "What concept labels can I attach to this event?" and "What concept labels have scientists or experts given to this particular event?" In other words, "What are the concept labels?" The label "Concepts" is placed on the My Understanding side, just below Key Ideas (Figure 8-9d).

FIGURE 8-9c
Vee diagram: Key ideas

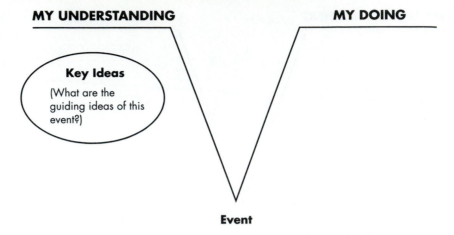

FIGURE 8-9d
Vee diagram: Concepts

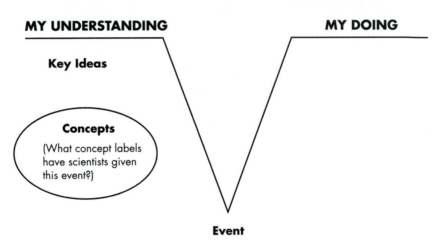

Focus Question

Knowing the key ideas and concept labels for the event, you will now ask a question that focuses on the event. This question, called the "Focus Question," is stated in the open mouth of the Vee (see Figure 8-9e).

Records

Set up procedures and conduct the investigation. You may observe the results of the investigation. Then you will systematically record the observations on the My Doing side, directly above the event. This is because observations are what you actually saw during the event. This is called "Records" (see Figure 8-9f).

Transformation of Data

Your observations in some investigations can easily be organized into a chart or a graph. This is called "Transformation of Data," which is written

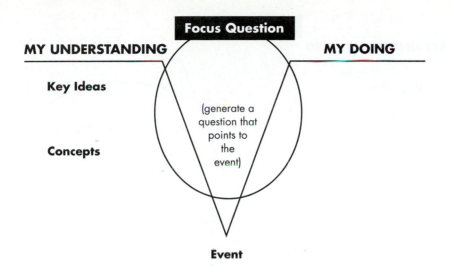

FIGURE 8-9e
Vee diagram: Focus
question

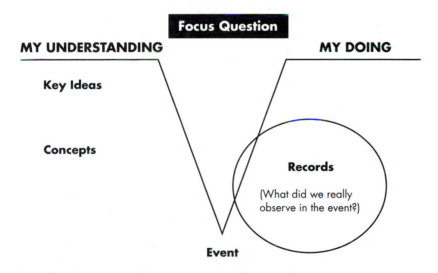

FIGURE 8-9f
Vee diagram: Records

directly above Records because we are reducing our observations for communication purposes into a simple form (see Figure 8-9g).

Knowledge Claims

What general conclusions can you make about your observations? The term used for conclusions is "Knowledge Claims," because you have indeed generated knowledge that must match the experts' key ideas on the left side of the Vee. However, write these knowledge claims in your own words. Knowledge claims are yours. Actually, the key ideas explain your knowledge claims in scientific language. State your knowledge claims above Transformation of Data on the right side of the Vee (see Figure 8-9h).

FIGURE 8-9g
Vee diagram:
Transformation of data

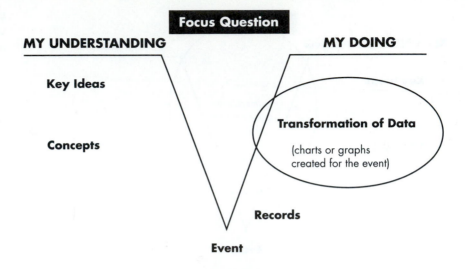

FIGURE 8-9h
Vee diagram:
Knowledge claims

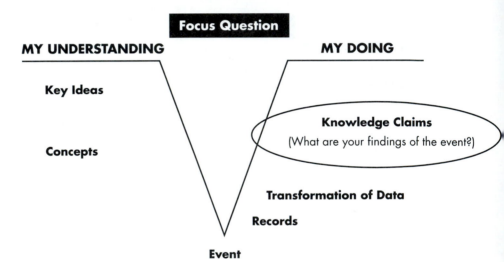

Value Claims

What are the values of this investigation—for you, for your students? The term "Value Claims" is stated above the Knowledge Claims on the right side of the Vee (see Figure 8-9i).

Putting Together All the Knowledge Elements of the Vee

All the knowledge elements or components of the knowledge Vee have been described (see Figure 8-9j). All the knowledge elements must relate to one another and to the event and focus question. Make sure you have actually answered the focus question on the Vee.

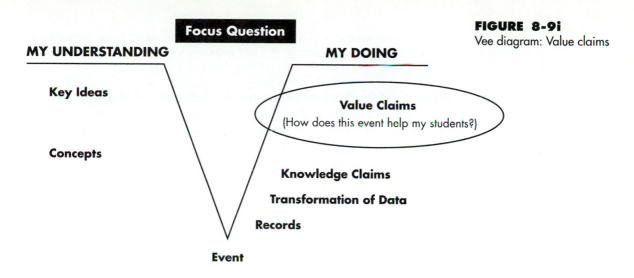

FIGURE 8-9i
Vee diagram: Value claims

FIGURE 8-9j
Vee diagram: Knowledge elements

Steps to Create a Vee Diagram

Next, you will learn how to create a Vee diagram using a particular event.

Step 1: Choose an event or a problem context.

In this case, the event is "inducing voltage with a magnet."

Step 2: Write the procedures for the investigation under the event.

You may develop your own or borrow from a science activity book. Write the procedures under the heading "Event."

Event

Move a bar magnet into and out of a coil of wire whose ends are connected to the terminals of a galvanometer. Then move the coil over the magnet. Observe both times.

Step 3: Write the key ideas on the left side of the Vee.

What do you know about electromagnetic induction? Consult a secondary- or university-level science text. What information is key to the event? Summarize the information and write it under the heading "Key Ideas" on the left side of the Vee.

Key Ideas

When the magnet is plunged into a coil of wire, a voltage can be induced. Electric current can be made to flow in a wire by simply moving a magnet into or out of a coil of wire. This phenomenon is called electromagnetic induction.

Step 4: Write all the concept labels under the heading "Concepts" on the left side of Vee just below "Key Ideas."

What concept labels do you know about electromagnetic induction? What concept labels can you pick up from reading about electromagnetic induction? What are the key concepts that give meaning to the event?

Concepts

current, induction, galvanometer, electric current, electric charge, magnetism, field, proximity

Step 5: Construct a concept map.

Since concepts are part of your Vee, construct a concept map with the concepts you have listed on another sheet of paper. Follow the instructions for creating a concept map if you are unsure of how to construct one. For a concept map on electromagnetic induction, see Figure 8-10.

Step 6: Write the focus question.

Based on your knowledge of the key ideas as well as the concepts of electromagnetic induction (the event), what question will you ask to carry out the investigation or study the event? Write this question under the heading "Focus Question" on your Vee.

Focus Question

How does a magnet induce electric current?

Step 7: Write your observations.

What did you observe when you conducted the investigation on electromagnetic induction? State it in your own words under "Records." Observations should cover each specific situation described.

Records
Movement of magnet and coil
(see table in Fig. 8-11)

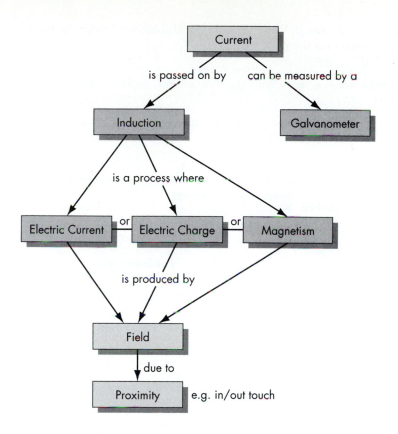

FIGURE 8-10
A concept map of
electromagnetic induction

Step 8: Transform your data.

Can you reduce your records? This is called *transformation of data*. Transformation of data should be more general.

Transformation of Data

The motion of the magnet produced a current, which was detected by the galvanometer. Similarly, the motion of the coil produced a current.

Step 9: Write your knowledge claims.

What general conclusions can you make about this investigation on electromagnetic induction? Write your conclusions under the heading "Knowledge Claims" on the right side of the Vee.

Knowledge Claims

Moving a magnet through a coil or moving the coil over the magnet produces a current.

Step 10: Write your value claims.

Is there a value for doing this activity on electromagnetic induction—for yourself or for your students? The value claim statement should be written as a student would write it. Write the value of this activity under the heading "Value Claims" on the right side of the Vee.

Value Claims

This activity teaches me about the relationship between electricity and magnetism.

How does your knowledge Vee look after you have put all of its elements together (see Figure 8-11)?

FIGURE 8-11
Knowledge Vee of
electromagnetic induction

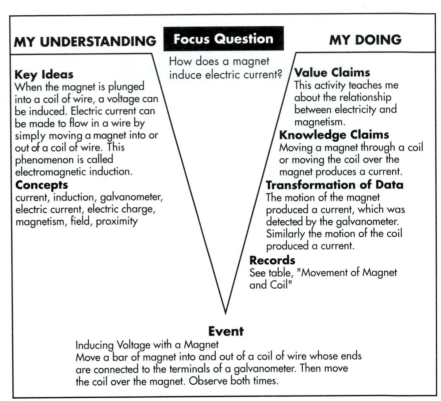

MY UNDERSTANDING   **Focus Question**   **MY DOING**

How does a magnet
induce electric current?

Key Ideas
When the magnet is plunged
into a coil of wire, a voltage can
be induced. Electric current can
be made to flow in a wire by
simply moving a magnet into or
out of a coil of wire. This
phenomenon is called
electromagnetic induction.

Value Claims
This activity teaches me
about the relationship
between electricity and
magnetism.

Knowledge Claims
Moving a magnet through a coil
or moving the coil over the
magnet produces a current.

Concepts
current, induction, galvanometer,
electric current, electric charge,
magnetism, field, proximity

Transformation of Data
The motion of the magnet
produced a current, which was
detected by the galvanometer.
Similarly the motion of the coil
produced a current.

Records
See table, "Movement of Magnet
and Coil"

Event
Inducing Voltage with a Magnet
Move a bar of magnet into and out of a coil of wire whose ends
are connected to the terminals of a galvanometer. Then move
the coil over the magnet. Observe both times.

Transformation of Data: Movement of Magnet and Coil

Position	Current
Single wire	No current
Coil connected to galvanometer	No current
Coil connected and bar moved through coil	Current produced
Coil connected and moved across magnet	Current produced
Coil connected, bar moved through coil and left there	Current initially produced, but stopped
Coil connected, coil moved over magnet and left there	Current initially produced, but stopped

You have learned a new way of representing knowledge. You have also learned how to construct knowledge by observing events and objects and answering the questions in science teaching—"How"? (principles) and "Why?" (theory). In asking and answering these crucial questions, you have probed the conceptual systems that scientists have constructed about the nature of physical systems, represented on the left side of the Vee diagram. In turn, the principles and theories were connected to the right side of the Vee diagram, which consists of the methodological elements of knowledge making.

You must stress the active interplay between what students observe or do in science and the evolving concepts, principles, and theories that guide scientific inquiry. The knowledge Vee is a simple and yet powerful heuristic that can accomplish this purpose. Visually, the Vee highlights the interplay between the My Understanding and My Doing sides by directing attention to and explaining the event, the point at which theory and practice coincide.

 TEACHER PRACTICE

Concept Mapping and Vee Diagramming
  Method: Paired activity
  Expectation: At the end of class, submit a Vee diagram–concept map
    combination and reflections on the activity.
  Lesson Foci:
  • To see the explanation-evidence-relevance connection in science
  • To understand major science ideas and the relationships of these ideas
  • To identify relationships of the core concepts and subconcepts of a sci-
    ence topic
  • To structure and organize disciplinary knowledge
  Events:
  • In groups of two, select a science activity.
  • Bring materials to class to conduct this activity. (This depends on the lab
    facilities.)
  • Read the background material or subject content of this activity at home
    and bring the reference book you are using to class.
  • Conduct the activity in class.
  • Draw a Vee diagram and concept map.
  • Submit your Vee diagram, concept map, and reflections on this activity.

You have practiced constructing concept maps and Vee diagrams. What is the theory behind concept mapping and Vee diagramming? Psychologist David Ausubel contrasted meaningful learning with rote learning.

⚅ MEANINGFUL LEARNING

Ausubel's dictum reads: "[T]he most important single factor influencing learning is what the learner already knows. Ascertain this, and teach him [or her] accordingly" (Ausubel, 1968, p. vi). Based on this assumption of learning, Novak (1978) argued that the quality and quantity of relevant concepts and prepositional frameworks are the primary factors in new learning; these are age-related primarily in an experiential rather than developmental manner.

Superordinate refers to a general, inclusive concept.

Subordinate refers to a specific, exclusive concept.

Meaningful learning occurs through a process of assimilation and accommodation, as discussed in Chapter 3 with respect to Piaget's view on human development. Meaningful learning depends upon the availability of **superordinate** and **subordinate** concepts in the learner's cognitive structure. New information may be linked to a superordinate idea. This would then represent another example of that idea or an extension of it. The critical attributes of the concept are not changed, but new examples are recognized as relevant. New information may also be linked to a superordinate idea so that it becomes a modification of that idea. The critical attributes of meaningful learning are that the concept may be extended or modified.

An **advance organizer** enables the learner to mentally prepare for what is to come.

To help link prior ideas with new information, Ausubel has proposed a three-stage model: presentation of an **advance organizer,** logical presentation of the new learning, and strengthening cognitive organization by relating the current information.

Advance Organizer

The *first phase* is the presentation of the advance organizer. The teacher can present the advance organizer in written, oral, graphic, and pictorial form. For instance, if the topic is electromagnetic induction, the graphic advance organizer can be the left side of the Vee diagram (the key ideas and concept labels) or the concept map of the topic. The advance organizer can also be a pictorial representation of real transformers, generators, telephones, cassette tapes, computer discs, and television sets—because all of these use the principle of electromagnetic induction. For example, students may be shown a visual of how a transformer works using an animation on a computer. An advance organizer presents the purpose of the lesson, which, together with Vee diagrams and concept maps, may make students mentally ready for new learning. Slavin (1988) states that the advance organizer performs "mental scaffolding" by linking new knowledge to prior learning. Learning, according to Ausubel, takes place deductively; the advance organizer is the prior framework. In a Vee diagram, the left side is indeed the deductive framework for your empirical inquiry, which is represented by the right side of the Vee. A concept map on electromagnetic induction could be the advance organizer for in-depth meaningful learning on magnetism and electric current.

Logical Presentation

The *second phase* of Ausubel's learning theory is the explicit or logical presentation of the new learning task. The right side of the Vee diagram is a logical presentation of how scientific inquiry is conducted and how knowledge is generated. Students can study electromagnetic induction by moving a bar magnet into and out of a coil of wire whose ends are connected to the terminals of the galvanometer. They may then present transformation of data and make knowledge and value claims.

Similarly, in concept mapping, there is a logical hierarchical (general to specific) relationship among concepts. Core concepts are logically linked to subconcepts. You can also show students how a transformer works by showing a video sequence.

Strengthening Cognitive Organization

In the *third phase*, cognitive organization is strengthened by relating the current information to the advance organizer. How the current or magnetic field is produced can be connected to the advance organizer, the left side of the Vee diagram. According to Ausubel, this promotes active reception learning. During this phase, the concept map on electromagnetic induction may represent a stronger cognitive organization.

According to Ausubel, the three phases of this theory constitute meaningful learning. Ausubel contrasts meaningful learning with rote learning (Novak, 1985, p. 190). Meaningful learning is non-arbitrary, substantive, and nonverbatim, whereas rote learning is the arbitrary, nonsubstantive, verbatim incorporation of new knowledge into cognitive structure.

Critical Attributes of Meaningful Learning

The critical attributes of meaningful learning are illustrated by concepts taken from a unit on electromagnetism (see Figure 8-12).

Non-Arbitrary

Non-arbitrary means that a learner must choose to fit or relate new knowledge into the existing cognitive structure. If a student is learning what electromagnetism is, he or she should choose to relate this knowledge purposefully, not arbitrarily, to what he or she already knows, such as associating the term *electromagnetism* with electricity and magnetism.

Substantive

Substantive learning occurs when the learner makes a conscious effort to identify the key concepts in the new knowledge—What are the key ideas of electromagnetism? Electric charges move, and these moving charges generate magnetism. Hence, we can produce magnetic fields. For instance, attach a long piece of wire to the terminals of a battery through a switch. With the switch open, place the wire over a compass so that the compass needle is parallel to the wire. Close the switch. Observe. If the current in

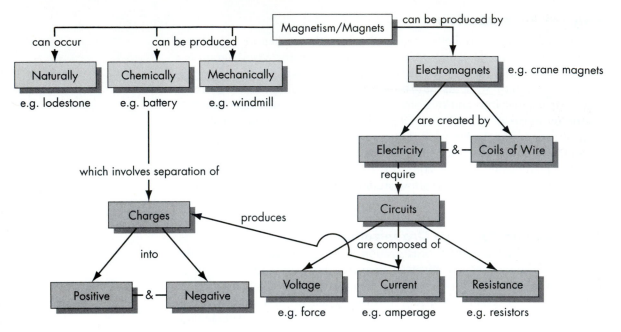

FIGURE 8-12
Concept map of a unit on electromagnetism

the wire is sufficiently strong, the compass needle will be deflected across the wire. This confirms that electric currents can produce magnetic fields in the surrounding area. Do you see the relationship between electric currents and magnetic fields? See Figure 8-13.

Both non-arbitrary and substantive learning, therefore, require a conscious effort on the part of the learner.

Non-Verbatim

Verbatim learning occurs when definitions are memorized, without stopping to consider the individual or combined meaning of each word in the definition. *Non-verbatim* learning is the product of non-arbitrary and substantive learning. If you write or dictate the definition of electromagnetism and the students memorize this definition without putting forth any effort in thinking about what the concepts mean, students are engaged in verbatim learning. At the end of the lesson on electromagnetism, most students will be able to define correctly what electromagnetism is, causing you to happily assume that students have mastered the concept. However, within two or three days, students are likely to have forgotten these rote-memorized definition for electromagnetism.

Rote/Meaningful

Rote learning is the opposite of *meaningful learning*. Ausubel stresses that the rote/meaningful distinction is not a dichotomy, but a continuum. For

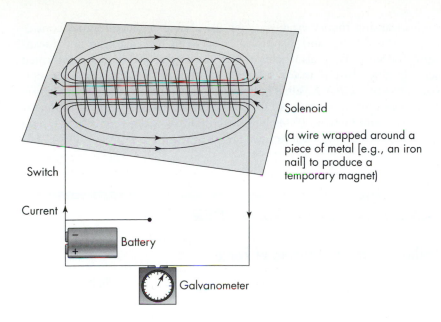

FIGURE 8-13
Relationship between
electric current and
magnetic fields

Solenoid

(a wire wrapped around a
piece of metal [e.g., an iron
nail] to produce a
temporary magnet)

Switch

Current

Battery

Galvanometer

example, a student might say, "Electromagnetism is electricity and magnetism," denoting separate phenomena. It can be said that the student is
on the continuum from rote learning to meaningful learning. But as a student's ideas progress and as the student learns the language of science, he
or she will progressively advance a substantively similar explanation to
those that are widely accepted. For example, the student should see the
relationship between magnetism and electric current.

Subsumption

Subsumption is described as the idiosyncratic nature of meaningful learning. New knowledge is usually incorporated (subsumed or anchored) into
more general concepts. Most students, for example, will have the notion
that electromagnetism consists of electricity and magnetism because the
main concept of electromagnetism gives a clue to the subconcepts: electricity and magnetism. Very few students will know the nature of electricity and magnetism: Electrons make the force called electricity. While the
protons and neutrons stick to their atoms, the electrons move quite easily
from one atom to the next. When an extra electron pushes one electron
from the first atom, the pushed-off electron jumps to the second atom.
This jumping of electrons from one atom to the next is what we call electricity. Magnetism, a property of matter, is caused by the spinning of the
outer electrons around the nucleus in the same direction. As they spin, the
electrons produce a magnetic field, giving the metal its magnetic properties. A magnetic field is a series of imaginary circular lines that surround a
magnet. The magnetic field has a pulling or pushing force on certain elements. When a student considers the relationship between the moving
electric charges and the magnetic field, he or she is said to have subsumed
this knowledge into a more general concept of electromagnetism.

This learning theory established by Ausubel and his colleagues considers prior knowledge and distinguishes between rote learning and meaningful learning. They also believe that knowledge structures are formed hierarchically, with a major concept subsuming a subsidiary concept. Novak has translated Ausubel's theory of learning into science education theories and practices (Novak, 1977). Based on Ausubel's theory of learning, Novak and Gowin (1984) have invented two tools—concept mapping and Vee diagramming—for knowledge production.

P-STAR CONFERENCE PAPER (8-1)

Teaching Concept Mapping of Force

Kathryn Slovinsky

I elected to introduce concept mapping in this unit for two primary reasons: (1) the students had studied force the year before and would therefore be less anxious about beginning a new topic with an entirely new strategy, and and (2) the concept of force extends into so many other areas in science that I felt I needed to give my students the best chance possible for engaging in and understanding this fundamental concept.

In order to introduce the idea of a concept map, I asked the students to define a concept (which we agreed was a big idea that contained a lot of other ideas that fit together). As an example, one of the students suggested the term *racism*. So I asked the class to tell me what they knew about the concept of racism. I wrote the terms *racism, causes, effects,* and *forms* on the board in hierarchical order. Then we proceeded to fill in additional information. I showed them how to connect ideas with labeled lines, and indicated that each connection must form all or part of a sentence.

At this point I introduced the topic of force. Just as I had with racism, I asked the students to tell me what they knew about force. It was not a surprise to me that the limit of their knowledge seemed to be that force was a push or pull, as I had discovered this through probing their conceptions earlier. I placed this information on the board in the proper order. Then I showed them how seeing what they know can lead to questioning what they don't yet know. One of the questions they came up with was, "So what does that (force) do?" I rewrote the question using more scientific terms to read, "What effect does force have on objects?" I felt it was important to have the students understand in their own terms what we were doing, but it was equally important to begin to use scientific language to express ourselves.

On a web we brainstormed the idea of what effects force has. The students came up with many suggestions, which we categorized into setting in motion, stopping, accelerating, changing direction, decelerating, or changing shape. These effects were then added to the concept map as nodes. I became aware of the students' limitations in their understanding of the concept map when they were unable to tell me where these new nodes should go and how to connect them. As a result, I demonstrated this for them.

In this situation, I needed to assess two separate concepts: the students' understanding of force and its effects on objects (the primary focus); and their understanding of how a concept map works. In order to assess their understanding of the first, I asked each student to draw a set of pictures illustrating each effect (see Figure 8-14). From these illustrations I was able to determine that a large number of students tended to use mechanical means to illustrate some of the effects. Many students used a car braking to show either deceleration or stopping. The next several classes revolved around demonstration of the effects of force (see Figure 8-15).

The assessment of their understanding of concept mapping was a little more difficult as this was their first introduction to the strategy (see Figure 8-16). Through conversation, I found that they appreciated how concept maps work—they used them later as a study tool, but at the time they were having difficulty understanding where the nodes belonged. I feel that the idea of hierarchy was a little too much for them to understand at this level. In the future, when teaching this strategy at this level again, I will let the students concentrate on getting their ideas down on paper and connected; the hierarchical placement will not be my concern until they are more familiar with the usage (see Figure 8-17).

1. Set in motion

2. Stop

3. Accelerate

4. Change direction

5. Decelerate

6. Change shape

FIGURE 8-14
A student's illustrations of force

FORCE

PUSH   PULL

SET IN MOTION   CHANGE DIRECTION   SLOW DOWN

FIGURE 8-15
Kathryn's illustrations of force

FIGURE 8-16
A student's concept map of force

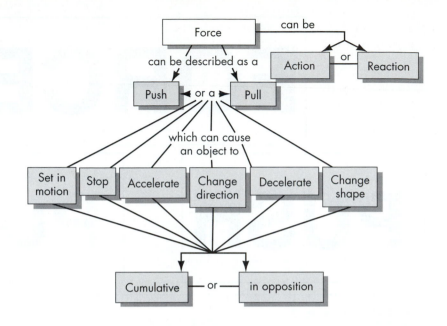

FIGURE 8-17
Kathryn's concept map of force

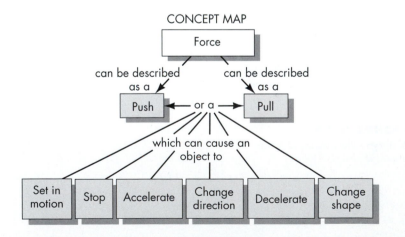

P-STAR CONFERENCE PAPER (8-2)

Vee Diagramming with Students

Corinna Turzak

Lesson: The Cell

I structured my lesson around a concept of the cell, specifically comparing plant and animal cells. When I originally taught this lesson, I had my students prepare their own onion cell wet mounts. From here the students were responsible for observing the wet mounts under the microscopes, recording their observations by drawing and labeling diagrams, and then completing a question sheet pertaining to this activity. This procedure was effective in getting the students to learn the content material.

Step 1: Students learn the plant cell by preparing their own wet mounts of onion cells and answering a teacher-made questionnaire.

I began by reviewing all the content knowledge with my students. We discussed what structures are found in plant cells and animal cells, and the functions these structures served. We then made comparisons between plant and animal cells, keeping note of the differences that existed between the two. When I felt that my students had a firm grasp on the material, I introduced the Vee diagram to them.

Step 2: Corinna discusses the difference between plant cells and animal cells. What step did Corinna miss?

I explained to the students that the Vee diagram was a learning tool in which they had an opportunity to examine the *information* they knew about plant and animal cell and conclude what new knowledge they acquired after doing an *experiment* or demonstration. I went through the "Event," "Focus Question," "Key Ideas," and "Concepts" and the students recorded their responses for these knowledge elements. At the completion of this part of the lesson, I had the students observe three wet mounts (human cheek cell, onion cell, Elodea plant cell) that I had prepared ahead of time. After the observations had taken place, I then returned the students' focus back to the Vee diagram. This time attention was placed on the "My Doing" side of the Vee diagram, where we discussed our "Records," "Knowledge Claims," and "Value Claims." (See Figure 8-18 for the Vee diagram that Corinna and her students constructed together.) After they completed filling out their information on the Vee diagram, Corinna took the opportunity to discuss with the students what they thought of using the Vee diagram.

Corinna is linking theory (information) with evidence (experiment).

Corinna starts with the event and the focus question and then focuses her students' attention on the left side ("My Understanding," or the theoretical side) of the Vee diagram.

Students observe the cells (look for evidence) and do the right side ("My Doing," or the methodological side) of the Vee diagram.

Students' Feelings

At first, my students thought that the Vee diagram was just going to be another useless assignment. However, after completing the Vee diagram the students began to see the benefits of using the Vee diagram. Overall, the general impression the students had toward Vee diagramming was that they found it to be conclusive. Students decided that it was a very useful

The Vee diagram is perceived by students as a tool for evaluation and organization of knowledge. What is more important for students to realize? How can you help students understand the nature of scientific inquiry with Vee diagramming?

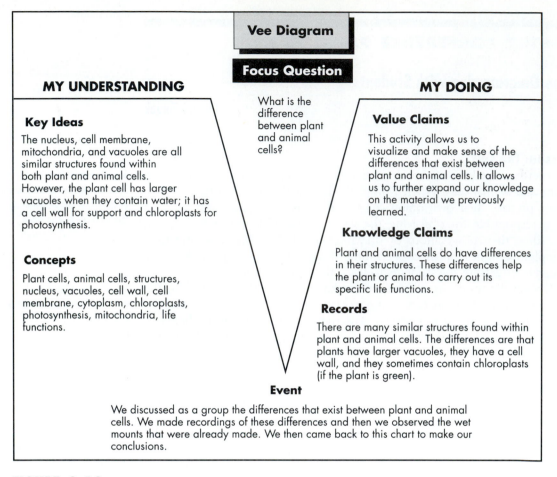

FIGURE 8-18

A Vee diagram of the difference between plant and animal cells

tool in concluding an experiment or demonstration in that it allowed them to evaluate what they knew about plant and animal cells, and it assisted in organizing what new knowledge they possessed from doing the microscope observations. As a whole, it allowed them to organize their data and to structure their final conclusions about plant and animal cells.

Personal Reflections

Worry!

When I first introduced the Vee diagram to the students I was very unsure as to how they would react to it. I had a strong feeling that this would be the first time they had seen a Vee diagram and I was worried that this might threaten them. However, to my surprise the students were not threatened by this at all.

An easy procedure

In fact, students found the Vee diagram an easy procedure to follow. They found it very straightforward and a simple way for them to organize their knowledge. From this I learned that one important thing that students need is organized structure. One thing they liked very much was the fact that the Vee diagram contained headings. I feel this is what made the procedure seem simple and nonthreatening to them.

Will it work at all middle grade levels?

Although this teaching strategy worked very well with these grade 8 students, I do not feel that it would work well with all middle grade levels. Grade 8 students are at a stage where they begin to ask questions about what they are doing and why. They begin to take notice and understand the methods to their learning. Therefore, this strategy of using Vee diagrams is very effective at this age level. I feel that if you were to try using this activity with a grade 5 class, they might find it too complex. Chances are they would not understand the reasoning for using this method, and they might also find it too difficult to organize their thoughts in such a manner.

What are your reactions to Corinna's comments about the nature of grade 8 students?

What methods will you adopt to teach Vee diagramming to middle school students?

Recommendations

One thing I would recommend to someone who wishes to use Vee diagramming as a strategy for teaching is that they need to make sure that the students are familiar with the content knowledge prior to presenting the Vee diagram to them. I feel that if the students do not have a good grasp on the material prior to using the Vee diagram, they may find it difficult to discuss their understanding or their doing throughout the lesson. This is why I feel that Vee diagramming is more effective when used at the completion of an experiment, demonstration, or unit.

What are your reactions to Corinna's statement about knowing the content (the expert, theoretical, or left side of Vee knowledge) before doing the Vee?

Corinna has given her reason why the content knowledge is important before doing a Vee diagram. Do you agree with her reasoning? Explain.

I found Vee diagramming an excellent way of explaining an experiment. It allows us to formulate ideas before performing the experiment, to describe the process in which the experiment is carried out, and, finally, to conclude our results at the completion of the experiment. I also feel that working on Vee diagramming together in groups is very useful—discussing the experiment, concepts, and results with others helps us make sense of and organize the information in our own heads.

Another important insight I would like to make regarding Vee diagrams is that they are not just an excellent tool for using in class, but they are an excellent tool for preparing a class lesson. They not only allow the teacher to focus on the material, but they also allow us to organize ourselves as teachers by clarifying our own objectives for the class and what we expect our students to learn throughout the lesson.

Corinna finds Vee diagrams a useful tool for lesson planning. Based on your knowledge about the nature of scientific inquiry, why would you consider a Vee diagram a good tool for lesson planning?

PEER TALK

Technical Concerns

Whereas many claims are made for the efficacy of concept mapping and Vee diagramming, some researchers and teachers using these pedagogical strategies have stated some technical concerns (Ebenezer, 1992).

What problems do you recognize in Vee diagramming?
What are the problems with concept mapping?

⊠ CHAPTER REVIEW

Pedagogy that is built on adequate theoretical perspectives, such as Ausubel's learning theory (1968), can provide a sound foundation for learning science. Concept maps and Vee diagrams can help you explore students' prior knowledge, plan a large mental map of how the unit should be carried out in order to link students' ideas with school science, develop collaborative social skills, clarify students' meanings, and assess students' understandings.

PROBES

1. Carry out concept mapping in your practicum class or with a group of students.
2. Conduct an investigation and have a group of students draw a Vee diagram.
3. Choose a topic of study from the following list:
   • Structure and properties of matter
   • Chemical reactions
   • Motion and forces
   • Conservation of energy
   • Behavior of an organism
   • Interdependence of organisms

Carry out a number of exploration activities connected with such a study and create a number of Vee diagrams and concept maps for your teaching resource files.

PART THREE

SCIENCE CURRICULAR CONTENT, ISSUES, AND TRENDS

In Part Two we focused on a number of diverse teaching strategies that help make science learning and understanding more accessible to diverse learners. In this Part we look at broader considerations—issues and trends that influence modern science curricula and science teaching.

Chapter 9 introduces the large context problem approach, a model developed by Art Stinner. In this approach, science topics are embedded in a current or historical context to make the topic more socially relevant and to facilitate learning.

Computer technology is the focus of Chapter 10. Surfing the Internet and using computers to structure knowledge are both examined.

In Chapter 11 we turn to one of the major foci for many modern science programs—science, technology, society, and the environment. Design technology and sustainable development are also considered.

Chapter 12 focuses on the diversity we find among students in modern classrooms—multicultural learners and learners with special needs.

A critical issue, as we approach the twenty-first century, is that of assessment, the subject of Chapter 13. In the final chapter of Part Three we consider various forms of assessment and assessment strategies, including writing test items, the use of rubrics, standardized tests, and authentic assessment.

CHAPTER 9

Contextual Science from a Historical Perspective

STUDY QUESTIONS

1. What are the crucial elements in designing a large context problem?

2. Design a large context problem from a historical approach to study science.

3. Name some topics that can easily incorporate large context problems.

Reflective Inquiry

Barbara's Voice

There are many contexts through which students can be brought into contact with the content and methods of science. Until I registered for a course with Arthur Stinner in the history of science and science teaching, I had never considered using the historical development of scientific thinking in my teaching. The reason, I believe, was my almost complete lack of knowledge in this area. I had completed undergraduate and graduate degrees in a science faculty, but knew little of the men and women who had contributed to the knowledge I had learned and used in my own research. Of course everyone who studied genetics, for instance, knew the names Lamarck, Darwin, Pasteur, Mendel, Watson and Crick, and Meselson and Stahl, and many of us could recount the results of the research with which each specific name was associated. But I could not—and I would venture to guess that few if any of my classmates could—place these men on a timeline, discuss the sociocultural context in which they lived and worked, and describe the studies and research programs that led to their discoveries and theoretical models. At the time, this kind of information was believed to be extraneous. It took precious time away from the material we really needed to become familiar with and know.

As a result, I began Dr. Stinner's course with skepticism. Ann Walker, with whom I worked on three curriculum assignments, and I struggled with the first large context problem we designed using the LEP model and a historical context. We chose to develop a middle-years unit based upon Aristotle's notion of matter, but paid more attention to the psychological plane (what the students currently believed) and the logical plane (what Aristotle thought) than the evidential plane (why Aristotle came to believe that fire, air, earth, and water were the components of all earthly materials).

Our second attempt was the unit on Newton's studies of light and color. I think you will have no difficulty finding the links we developed between the life experiences children will have had with the refraction of light, the progression of work in which Newton was engaged in his attempts to understand the relationship between color and white light, and the conclusions he was able to construct as a consequence. They are certainly more obvious and

continued

less contrived than many we chose not to include. Our final attempt, Darwin's theory of evolution, was even more successful. At this point in the course, Ann and I were more comfortable designing large context problems based upon the LEP model, and the resources that we needed to reconstruct Darwin's life and work are plentiful and a pleasure to read.

Units of this kind take a lot of work to develop well, but I believe they are worth the time and effort spent. They are respectful of children's ideas, build upon their past experiences, and help them to see the world in a different, but hopefully more generative, way. Their attention to the history of science provides children with a glimpse of the physical and mental work that goes into the construction of scientific knowledge at specific times in history. They may walk away from these lessons and activities with a more thorough understanding of the nature of science. Finally, research suggests that many of the explanations that children give for events and phenomena in their environment were at one time similar to the explanations scientists would have presented. Looking at the research evidence and thinking that helped to revise or overturn these scientific explanations helps children to question and perhaps begin to reconstruct their own beliefs.

JOURNAL ACTIVITY

Science in Everyday Experiences

What are some of the science concept–related events you experience in the world (for example, rainbows)? List these events. What science concepts are embedded in these events?

⊠ LARGE CONTEXT PROBLEMS

Art Stinner, a science educator in Canada, has developed the large context problem (LCP) approach to teaching science in responding to the notion that "learning in physics could be well motivated by a context with one unifying central idea capable of capturing the imagination of the students" (Stinner, 1994, p. 45). His first attempt to design an LCP was based on a detailed report by *Time* (*Time,* May 18, 1970) on the construction of the giant solar furnace in the Pyrenees. Stinner argues that context-generated questions and problems are more interesting and motivating than similar problems presented in textbooks. Each LCP is designed so that science-related ideas for a particular topic are used for the successful completion of the problems suggested by the context. The context automatically generates questions and problems that lead to the inclusion of *out-of-context* (contrived) problems in textbooks. The context enables the teacher and students to work as cohorts or associates in an ongoing research program, because many of the questions and problems generated do not have obvious answers for the involved researchers (teacher and students). An approach of this nature develops the learners' ability to answer questions and solve problems. Usually, in designing, developing, and solving large context problems, students traverse "the path from romance to precision to generalization" (Whitehead, 1967). For instance, technological designs with Tinkertoys and Lego sets by elementary children may be the "romance stage" of large context problems. The romance stage provides the setting for problem solving or the stage of precision that involves the systematic organization of children's experiences, thus relating a coherent science story with a beginning, a middle, and a provisional end (Kenealy, 1989).

Guidelines for the Design of Large Context Problems

1. Map out a context with one unifying central idea that is considered important in science and is likely to capture the imagination of students.
2. Provide students with experiences that can be related to their everyday world.
3. Invent a "story line" that will dramatize and highlight the main idea.
4. Ensure that the major ideas, concepts, and problems of the topic are generated naturally by the context—that it will include those things students would learn piecemeal in a conventional textbook approach.
5. Secure the path from romance to precision to generalization. This is best accomplished by showing the student that:
   a. problem situations come out of the context and are interesting;
   b. concepts are diversely connected, within the setting of the story as well as with present-day science and technology; and
   c. there is room for individual extension and generalization of ideas, problems, and conclusions.
6. Ideally, the context should be designed by the teacher, in cooperation with students, where the teacher assumes the role of the research leader and the student becomes part of an ongoing research program. (Stinner, 1993, p. 21)

Figure 9-1 is an outline of contextual science teaching from early years to senior years (Stinner, 1993, p. 26).

Stinner suggests that teachers use the LEP model while doing a large context problem.

FIGURE 9-1

Contextual science teaching: From early-years to senior-years teaching in physics (*NOTE:* From "Contextual Teaching in Physics: From Science Stories to Large-Context Problems," by A. Stinner, 1993, *Alberta Science Education Journal, 26*(1), p. 26. Copyright 1993 by the Alberta Teachers' Association. Adapted with permission.)

Contextual Science Teaching: From Early to Senior Years

Early Years (6–10)	Middle Years (11–14)	Senior Years (15–18)
1. Science stories (based on the imagination)	1. Science stories (based on history)	1. Large-context problems
2. Science stories (based on history)	2. Contextual setting (based on student experience)	2. Thematic problems
3. Contextual settings (based on student experience)	3. Contextual setting (based on contemporary issues of interest)	3. Popular science literature
Examples:		Examples:
1. *Star Trek* stories involving space travel	Examples:	1. Physics and the Bionic Man
2. Archimedes' adventures	1. Torricelli and the weight of the atmosphere	2. *The Story of Force*
3. *Ontario Science Centre Book of Experiments:*	2. Electricity in the home	3. Stephen Hawking's *A Brief History of Time*
Ice fishing	3. Safety in nuclear power plants	
Inertia trick		
Earth speedometer		
Solar cooker		

Embedded in a Program of Activities and Guided by the Requirements of the LEP Conceptual Model Involving:		Embedded in the Contexts of Inquiry
1. air tables to study motion qualitatively	1. discrepant events	1. presuppositions
2. watching and discussing things fall in air, in a vacuum	2. group discussions	2. questions
3. learning that words can have different meaning in a different context	3. using bridging analogies	3. problems
4. discussing images from science fiction	4. providing alternate theories (hypotheses) to fit evidence	4. experiments
5. discussing the need for definitions in science—children make up their own	5. computer-based programs	5. new questions
	6. multimedia programs	

Considerations for Carrying Out LCPs

A contextual approach to science teaching is more time-consuming than the conventional book approach. At the initial stages, the teacher designs the LCPs. When students are more comfortable, both the teacher and students can cooperatively design the LCPs. This gives students the status of participating in an ongoing research program with the expert teacher-researcher.

The LCP can be an extension to a unit of study or an enrichment activity. An LCP can also serve as the central activity and be related to the contexts of inquiry in physics. The second option liberates a teacher from the grip of a textbook. In addition, the contexts of inquiry in LCP will place the study of physics historically and will encourage "teachers and students to engage in an inquiry process that clearly states what the presuppositions, major questions, and central experiments of a science are and what new questions the science generates" (Stinner, 1993, p. 22).

Designing suitable LCP activities and sequencing them appropriately requires self-confidence and time. Hence, the number of LCPs a teacher wishes to do must be his or her choice.

TEACHER PRACTICE

Designing Large Context Problems

In small groups of three, design a large context problem of your choice following Stinner's guidelines, described earlier. You may select the LCP topics from Figure 9-1.

- Identify core questions and problems for the LCP.
- Write the science ideas that respond to the core questions and problems of the LCP.
- Present your LCP questions.
- Discuss the problems the context generated.
- Describe the experiments that can be performed.

NEWTON'S OPTICAL EXPERIMENTS

The following sample unit sets the large context problem within a historical context and also relates it to students' interest and their experiences. The teacher involves students in generating questions and problems and proposes simple experiments. Developing appropriate science this way would relate to students' interests as well as allow them to translate science theory to context.

Topic: Colors of Light
Personal Context: Experiencing Rainbows
Historical Context: Newton's Optical Experiments
Authors: Barbara McMillan and Ann Walker (1992)
Grade: Middle School/Junior High
Teaching Approach: Large Context Problem Approach

Context of Inquiry

You've probably seen lots of rainbows. But have you ever wondered what a rainbow really is and what causes one? This problem puzzled people for thousands of years. Then, in 1672, an Englishman named Isaac Newton showed people how the colors of the rainbow are formed from light.

Pedagogical Question

How will you make a rainbow in the classroom or at home?

Teacher-Students' Investigations

1. Place a beaker or clear glass container of water on the sill of a window in bright sunlight, so that it sits half on and half off the sill. Hold a piece of white paper in front of and slightly below the beaker and watch the colors

appear on the surface of the paper. What colors can you see? Do you see any colors in the water? What happens when you move the beaker out of the sunshine and into the shade?

2. Notice the glass hanging ornaments in the window (maybe you have some in your home). As they move, you can often see specks of light dancing around the room. Follow one of the specks of light and try to catch it on a piece of white paper. Can you see any colors? What colors are they?

3. Try moving one of the crystal animals in the sunlight so that the crystal catches the light. Try catching the reflected light on a piece of white paper. What colors can you see? Can you see any colors in the crystal itself? What happens when you move the crystal from the sunshine into the shade?

Did you see the same colors in the rainbows you made with the sunlight shining through the water-filled beaker, the glass ornaments, and the crystal animals? Do these colors always appear in the same order? If so, what is the order you noticed?

Match your answer to the photograph of the rainbow on the wall of the classroom. Are your homemade rainbows similar to this picture of a rainbow in the sky?

Placing the LCP within a Historical Perspective: Replications of Newton's Experiments

When Isaac Newton was a boy, people had noticed the colors of the rainbow and knew that they could make homemade rainbows too. They used triangular pieces of glass called *prisms* to make rainbows. There are some prisms at the front of the classroom. Take a look at them. See if you can make a rainbow with them using sunlight. Then try using a smaller, more concentrated source of light, such as a light box.

Isaac Newton became interested in rainbows when he was making telescopes. At times, when he was looking through his telescope, he saw a mix of blurred color at the edges. This annoyed him, as he wanted to get a clear image. He began wondering how this effect, called *chromatic aberration,* was produced. A telescope contains circular pieces of glass called *lenses.* Look through the telescope set up in the classroom. Can you see any chromatic aberrations?

At that time there were several different theories of color. Most people thought that white light from the sun was colored in some way, but they did not know how. Others believed that the glass of the prism was responsible.

- White light passing through the thin edge of the glass prism was darkened a little, to red.
- White light passing through a thicker part of the glass prism was darkened a little more, to green.
- White light passing through the thickest part of the glass prism was darkened a lot, to blue.

Does this agree with what you observed? Do you feel that this idea does a good job of explaining what is happening when light strikes a prism?

Newton was not satisfied with this "darkening" explanation. He decided to look at the problem himself while he was studying at Cambridge University in England. In those days there was no electricity, and he used the sun as a source of light for his investigation. However, to see the rainbow clearly, he closed the window shutters, until just a crack remained. This crack let in a narrow beam of

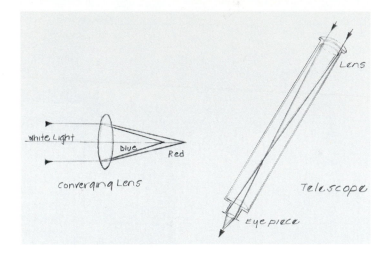

light which he used for his experiments. You will be repeating his experiments. But your light source will be a light box instead of the sun, and you will use metal blocks to make a slit.

Start by placing a slit near the light source, so that you get a narrow beam. Can you make a rainbow on the screen? (Newton used the wall instead of a screen.) What shape is the beam just before it enters the prism? What happened to the direction of the beam as it passed through the prism? What shape is the rainbow? What has happened to the shape of the beam as it passed through the prism?

Remember that at the time Newton was doing his experiments, most people thought that the light was being darkened by the prism. This suggests that red light (white light that has been darkened a little) can be changed to green light or blue light (white light that has been darkened a lot) by a second prism. See if you can change red light coming out of the prism to blue light with the use of a second prism. This is tricky, so you will have to work carefully. Take one of the cards at the front of the classroom in which a hole has been punched. Put this card in the path of the rainbow. With a little care, you should be able to position the card so that the red part of the rainbow passes through the hole.

Now that you have the red part of the rainbow passing through the hole in the card, try to change it to blue light. Rotate the second prism in the beam of red light. What happens? Does the second prism change the color of the red light?

Try passing the red light through a blue filter or piece of blue cellophane. If you hold the blue filter up to your eyes in a well-lit room, everything looks blue. Can you change red light to blue light by placing this filter in the path of the red light?

Now try to obtain a ray of blue light through the hole in the card. Can you change blue light into red light using the prisms? What happens to the blue light when you place a blue filter or a red filter in its path?

Newton guessed (or hypothesized) that white light is made up of all the colors of the rainbow. Then, when white light passes through a prism, the colors are split up. What evidence do you have to show he was right (what evidence do you have to support Newton's hypothesis)?

Can you think of a final experiment that you could do to finish off the story to show that Newton was right? Try your experiment to see if it works!

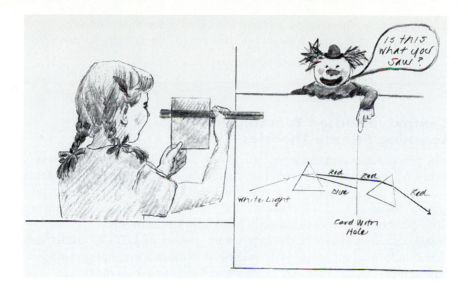

Theoretical Structures (Science Ideas)

Today you have made homemade rainbows. The scientific word for a homemade rainbow is *spectrum*. A spectrum can be made by splitting up white light into its component colors. A real rainbow is a spectrum that appears when the sun is behind the observer and low in the sky, and falling water is in front. You made spectra using a glass prism. As the light entered and passed through the prism, its path was bent. This effect is called *refraction*. Orange light is refracted more by a glass prism than red light. Yellow light is refracted more than orange light. Green light is refracted more than yellow light. And so on through the spectral colors. What do you think refracts the sunlight to cause a real rainbow in the sky?

Contextual-Based Teaching for Learning Science Theories

The preceding contextual-based teaching is set within the past (Newton's study of light) and the present (children's life experiences). Students study the properties of light (the theoretical structure) by conducting simple "pedagogical" experiments and, at the same time, by studying how Newton conceptualized light (the historical context). Contextual-based teaching consists of the appropriate placing of LCPs to attract students' individual interests, while making provisions for continued student engagement in questioning, problem solving, and experimenting. The theoretical structure, on the other hand, can be thought of as a pedagogical scaffolding that illuminates the status of theory, establishes what counts as evidence, clarifies the relationship between experiment and explanation, and makes connections to the history of science. Such a theoretical structure then guides the organization and the presentation of science.

⚛ HISTORY OF SCIENCE IN THE SCIENCE CURRICULUM

The integration of the history of science in the science curriculum provides an excellent means to promote the nature of science and scientific ideas. It is not possible to re-enact the trials of history, but students should be given an opportunity to encounter the same conceptual difficulties, and their mediation, that confronted the great scientists of history. Unfortunately, the introduction of history in the science texts of today is reduced to historical vignettes, sidebars, and photographs of scientists. An example from curriculum that outlines a historical perspective is the development of a model of electricity.

Developing a Model of Electricity

Don Metz is a physics teacher at the secondary level who not only believes that the history and the philosophy of science should be integrated in science curriculum, but also teaches physics from a historical perspective. Hear what Don has to say about teaching electricity using historical ideas (Don Metz, personal communication, 1998).

A principle of a constructivist model of learning advocates that students must be active participants in their own construction of knowledge. However, in a typical textbook electricity is introduced with natural phenomena like lightning, and almost immediately the atomic model (electrons) is used to describe electrostatics. Diagrams depicting charge provide the evidential basis for the nature of electrostatics, and students have no chance to challenge the model. There is no logical progression in the development of the model; it is given as a statement of fact.

Early models of electricity were often associated with heat; Plutarch (100 A.D.) suggested that the air around some amber charged by friction was heated and moved away from the amber. The air would swirl around a nearby object, pushing it back to the amber. Gilbert (1600 A.D.), in his treatise *De Magnete*, described an effluvium that emanated from a charged rod. Students need to be challenged with such early tentative models and should examine the plausibility of the model and develop their own tests for the model. Students will readily suggest tests in a vacuum or the introduction of materials between objects and should be encouraged to conduct these tests, if possible. It also becomes apparent why so few significant developments occurred between Plutarch's and Gilbert's times (when was the vacuum pump invented?).

In the seventeenth century and those that followed, scientists presented three successful models of electricity: the one-fluid model, the two fluid model, and the particle model. Students should be given the opportunity to become fluidists and debate the merits of one model versus the other. The two-fluid model adequately explains electrostatic phenomena, and we accept the particle model because of evidence such as Rutherford's gold foil experiments for the nature of the atom. The tenets of the particle model now seem plausible for the novice and can be used to direct a useful research program. Students now should use the model to make predictions about electrostatic phenomena and test these predictions with hands-on activities.

Many other examples of the utility of historical perspective can be found (see Stinner's "The Story of Force" [1990]) and used directly in the classroom to challenge student ideas and demonstrate that some of the most famous scientists of all time held views of nature similar to those of our students. These methods help promote the nature of science as tentative and suggest a means to develop deductive thinking skills. The lessons presented by the study of the historical developments of scientific theories can provide guidance and ideas to develop these theories logically in a classroom setting; they provide interesting and often intriguing stories that develop a conceptual base and promote positive attitudes in science education. (Don Metz, personal communication, 1998)

Reading about historical accounts is important. You may find sources in Conant's case histories in science. Also, Harvard Project Physics has readings about historical events in science. Piaget also co-authored a book with Rolando Garcia in the 1980s about the development of science and how it parallels the development of logical reasoning (Piaget & Garcia, 1989).

⚙ CHAPTER REVIEW

The history of science can provide some important insights into the nature of science. This chapter is a start in helping science teachers use the history of science. We have presented arguments and Newton's optical experiments as a means to consider the scientific enterprise as more philosophical, social, and human. The teaching of science that is grounded in contextual activities must be connected to a theoretical structure that guides the organization as well as the presentation of concepts and ideas. LCP case studies partially free the teacher and students from textbooks. Outlining a theoretical structure in LCP case studies places the study of science historically as well as introducing contemporary science. LCP case studies enable student researchers to state presuppositions, major questions, central problems, and key experiments of a science as well as the new questions science generates.

PROBES

1. Identify an LCP. Relate this to the historical figures in science and the evolution of their ideas.
2. What are some problems you might anticipate when you model an LCP approach?
3. This chapter is a start in helping you use the history of science. Develop other techniques of teaching the history of science to students. *Note:* Reading historical accounts could be one way of learning science. For example, Harvard Project Physics has readings about historical events in science.

CHAPTER 10

Interactive Learning with Computer Technology

STUDY QUESTIONS

1. How can the Internet be used to enrich your science teaching?

2. What are the special features of hypermedia?

3. How can science teachers use hypermedia programs in their classrooms?

4. How can teachers and students use hypermedia for conceptual change?

5. What are computer microworlds? Why does a teacher use a microworld?

6. What are the advantages of the electronic laboratories used in science?

7. What are the special features of computer-based semantics?

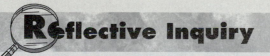

Reflective Inquiry

GORDON'S VOICE

The students were able to use the multimedia system for themselves and it became more meaningful in less time. That is not to say I did not help them . . . I did, and that should be a vital part of the learning system. The computer is not intended to be a one-way street, nor should it be. It still requires the added touch of the classroom teacher to make lessons come to life. Both are the essence of good teaching, just as a variety of teaching tools and methods of presenting is vital. The multimedia will not replace the teacher's lesson.

JOURNAL ACTIVITY

Computer Technology in Science Education

How have you used computer technology in science? Identify the various ways teachers use computers for teaching science.

⚛ THE INTERNET FOR INTERACTIVE LEARNING

In this chapter we will use several examples to discuss how computer technologies are used in secondary science classrooms. We will not go into technical details of computer technology, but will leave this to teachers of computer application courses.

Interactive science programs and lessons can be developed with modern computer technologies. One only needs to surf the Internet to experience the interactive nature of information. The click of a mouse on a *hot link* can lead you down many different paths. For example, the Web site at http://www.yahoo.com/Science/Education/K_12/Activities/ shows hundreds of interactive, hierarchical sites in science. Because of the multiple paths and the combination of textual material, graphics, sounds, videos, photographs, images, animation, and 3-D models available, the Internet can be considered interactive. But can computer learning be interactive?

For interactive learning to occur, a learner must *think* about what he or she is learning, regardless of the medium in which knowledge is presented. Because computers have the added power of providing attractively interactive presentations, students may become motivated to learn. Computer technologies are therefore prime potential media for interactive learning. For example, students can currently use a Web browser to collect *gifs* (picture files) and construct links to interesting sites on their personal Web pages. They can also create bookmark folders and add *bookmarks* (links to favorite Web sites they have visited). It is easy to see how a science teacher could use these Internet tools for interactive learning.

How Do Teachers Use the Internet?

Joel Bass, a science teacher educator at Sam Houston University, uses the Internet to help his students collect real-time data. Marlene Kroeker, a secondary science teacher, uses the Internet for planning science fairs. Mark

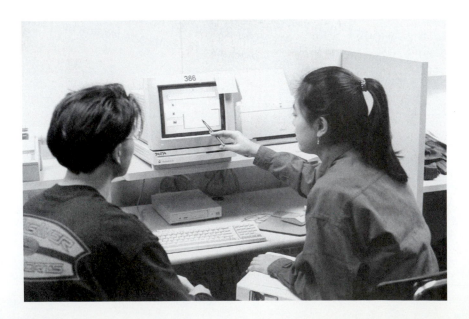

Huebert, a secondary science preservice teacher, uses the Internet for research. These teachers' experiences with the Internet are described in this section.

Collecting Real-Time Data (Joel Bass)

I am currently doing a lab which requires the use of real-time tide data from NOAA. Students have to go to San Francisco and other sites to collect data throughout the day. This data is submitted to an online database on my machine, from which they retrieve data and develop charts and graphs. This type of activity uses the power of the Internet. (J. Bass, personal communications, November 1997)

The Internet has been an important means for scientists at multiple sites to collaborate in research projects. Just as the Internet has been productive in scientific research, it can be an excellent tool in the science classroom in promoting a constructivist approach to interactive exploration and learning. By bringing interesting and significant information into the classroom, technology can provide effective enrichments that might not be possible otherwise.

The New Jersey Networking Infrastructure in Education (NJNIE). The NJNIE project has taken a lead in developing online activities for students (Friedman, Baron, & Addison, 1996). In NJNIE Internet activities, the focus is on analysis of quantitative data that is emerging from current sources. Through working with data from the Internet, students not only deepen their knowledge of science, but also increase their mathematical skills as they encounter the precise order, regularity, and predictability that is inherent in the natural world. NJNIE has done valuable preliminary work in designing activities that suggest how Internet data sources might be used in science classes. Consider the NJNIE activity "The Stowaway Adventure" as an example. If you have Internet access, you might wish to examine the site at njnie.dl.stevens-tech.edu/curriculum/oceans/stowaway.html.

Hundreds of ships in the world's oceans regularly report their precise locations along with basic information about weather and water conditions. Oceanweather, Inc. maintains a database on this information, updating it several times each day. Ships are designated by IDs; locations of each ship are given by latitude and longitude and can also be seen on an ocean graphic map. The sheer volume of data can be overwhelming, but it becomes manageable within the context of engaging students in problems related to vicarious travel. In "The Stowaway Adventure," students pretend they are stowaways on a ship with a given ID. The stowaways wonder where they are going and when they will arrive. Somehow they obtain access to the Internet; then, referring to sequential reports of their ship's location given on the Internet, students map their trip and try to predict the location of the port to which the ship is bound. Internet sources linked to the site can also be used to determine how far the ship has traveled between two specific locations. Using the distance information and time data drawn from the ship's reports, students can calculate the ship's rate of speed. With this information, and calculations of the distance from their current location to the destination port, students can estimate their time of arrival. The whole scenario is presented as a problem, with students having to determine which concepts are relevant and how the concepts are to be used.

WhaleNet Web Site. Activities somewhat similar to NJNIE's "Stowaway Adventure" can be carried out with data on the locations of whales given on the WhaleNet Web site at http://whale.wheelock.edu/.

Similar to the Oceanweather database, WhaleNet provides information on the date and location (latitude and longitude) for each sighting of a right whale named Rat. A black-and-white map of the ocean is provided for mapping data on Rat's movements. Students can enter the latitude and longitude data for two points on the map into a "Distance Generator," which is provided at a site linked to WhaleNet, and determine how far apart the points are. In an inservice project for middle school math and science teachers, participants were encouraged to formulate and address different questions about Rat's movement. Some questions addressed by the teachers were: What was the maximum distance Rat traveled in one day? What was his maximum speed? Are weather and water conditions related to the fact that Rat seems to linger near particular locations? The teachers worked to answer the questions through analysis of the data available on the Internet.

The Internet facilitates new types of interesting, intellectually significant educational tasks that are not likely to reach learners via other methods. Through database Internet activities, students at all levels can engage in the constructive types of explorations that are common among scientists.

Planning Science Fairs (Marlene Kroeker)

Do the words "Science Fair" fill you with dread and anxiety? Do you wish for a plan that could eliminate science fair stress? For many elementary school educators science fair time is just one big headache. My first rounds at science fairs were not a good experience . . . for me (my students seemed to enjoy themselves). Until one year I spent some time to develop an eight-week science fair "game plan" . . . How do I begin science fair projects in my class? How do I use the Internet activities for science fair? I take an eight-week block to help my students with science fair projects during science and language arts classes. (Kroeker, 1997)

Getting Started

Science World
http://golfball.scienceworld.bc.ca:457/SCIENCEFAIRS/SFLinks.
    html
An encouraging home page that answers the question, "How can science fairs provide great learning opportunities?"

The Teacherlounge
http://golfball.scienceworld.bc.ca:457/SCIENCEFAIRS/
  SFTeacherLounge.html
This site suggests advice for organizing the actual science fair and some
  project ideas.

Science Project
http://golfball.scienceworld.bc.ca:457/SCIENCEFAIRS/
  SFProject.html
This site gets you started with science fairs.

How To Do a Science Fair Project.
http://www.superscience.com/HOWtoSciFair.html
As a class, my students and I visited this site, which was very eye-
  catching and gave simple, well-detailed information for every step of
  the project. Unfortunately, web sites are often temporary as was this
  one. Conduct a search for other sites that will give you ideas about
  science fair projects.

The Nature of the Science Fair Project
http://golfball.scienceworld.bc.ca:457/SCIENCEFAIRS/
  SFNature.html

A Student Checklist
http://golfball.scienceworld.bc.ca:457/SCIENCEFAIRS/
  SFStudentLounge.html
This site provides a working outline.

The Mad Scientist: Why Scientists Need to Keep Notes
http://oakview.fcps.edu/~glazewsk/96-97/scientist/why-write.html
A short discussion of why it is important to maintain journal accounts
  of daily experimental work.

The Mad Scientist: The Scientific Method
http://oakview.fcps.edu/~glazewsk/96-97/scientist/method.html
An outline of the scientific method that students can follow.

The Mad Scientist: Small Things Glossary
http://oakview.fcps.edu/~glazewsk/96-97/scientist/glossary.html
A useful glossary of science terms.

The Mad Scientist: The Experiments
http://oakview.fcps.edu/~glazewsk/96-97/scientist/experiments.html
Simple experiments.

Oak View Elementary: Lesson Plans and Curriculum Materials
http://oakview.fcps.edu/teachers/
This site provides a variety of project ideas.

Possible Science Fair Projects
http://www.scri.fsu.edu/~dennisl/special/sf_projects.html
Simple science activities that can be changed into science fair projects.

Showboard
http://www.showboard.com/science/scibk.htm
A list of inexpensive science fair project books.

Making a Problem Statement. Students have now identified project ideas. They are ready to make a problem statement, which is written in the form of a question in their journal. A sample experiment is available at the following site:

The Mad Scientists Pendulums: Does Amplitude Affect Frequency?
http://oakview.fcps.edu:80/~glazewsk/96-97/scientist/
    pendulum/amp/

Visit Completed Science Fairs on the Internet. It is important that students read other students' work as they continue to do their own projects. See the following site:

Grade 8 Science Fair
http://www2.excite.sfu.ca/pgm/scifair/pgmsci.html
Three completed projects using the scientific method.

Statement of Hypothesis. Students should be reading, surfing the Internet, interviewing experts, and doing other research about their topic to formulate a hypothesis and reasons for their hypothesis.

Hypothesis
http://oakview.fcps.edu/~ glazewsk/96-97/scientist/glossary.
    html# hypothesis
A definition.

Experimental Organization. Students should organize the material for their experiments, write up the method, and identify the independent and controlled variables. See the following two sites:

Showboard
http://www.showboard.com/science/science.htm
A science fair demonstration kit that can give students ideas for their
    experiment and finished product.

Science Fairs and Students
http://golfball.scienceworld.bc.ca:457/SCIENCEFAIRS/
    SFStudentLounge.html

Experimentation and Observation. Students do the experiments and conduct fair tests for comparing results. They make careful observations and record their observations in a chart or graph. Then they write conclusions to the problem. Was their hypothesis confirmed?

Finding Judges and Awards

Ribbons, Certificates, and Buttons
http://www.showboard.com/science/science.htm

MARK'S VOICE

Some of the students initially needed further assistance in finding the Internet browser or entering URLs. Some students wanted more clarification on what was expected of them. However, most students had little difficulty in satisfactorily completing the assignment by the end of the period. The majority of the students stayed on task for most of the period, working hard at completing the assignment. They appeared to enjoy working in pairs, and quietly conversed with one another while searching the web pages for pertinent information and writing their reports. The change in the learning environment from a regular classroom to the computer lab also seemed to be to the liking of the students.

Mark used the Internet for research purposes in his practicum. He had his biology students research diseases of the digestive system. His lesson plan follows.

Lesson Plan 10-1: Diseases of the Digestive System

Objectives:

- To learn about some of the major diseases/disorders of the digestive system.
- To become aware of the role society plays in encouraging eating disorders.
- To practice using the Internet as a resource for research.

Prerequisite Skills:

Some basic Windows and Internet skills

Skills Students Will Develop:

- Using a Web browser
- Opening Web sites by typing in specific URLs given by the teacher
- Retrieving information about disorders and diseases of the digestive system from Web sites

- Making a brief about four disorders/diseases of the digestive system using this information

Materials Needed:

IBM-compatible PC, 486 processor or higher (Pentium preferable), Windows 3.1 or higher, 8 or more MB RAM

Web browser (for example, Netscape Navigator or Microsoft Internet Explorer)

Modem (14400 bps or higher preferable)

Handout with questions to answer in report, other instructions, and URLs

Procedure:

1. Give students the handout (text follows) and instruct them to research any four diseases or disorders of the digestive system using the URLs provided, with one of their choices being either bulimia or anorexia.

   Handout Given to Students:

   Internet Sites about Disorders and Diseases of the Digestive System
       Your job is to pick four of the disorders/diseases below and write a brief report.

   Hepatitis, cirrhosis, Crohn's disease, gallstones, heartburn, hemorrhoids, lactose intolerance, ulcers, colitis, irritable bowel syndrome
   http://www.niddk.nih.gov/health/digest/digest.htm
   Food poisoning
   http://www.columbia.edu/cu/healthwise/0641.html
   http://www.altabates.com/housecalls/FoodPoisoning.html
   Lactose intolerance
   http://www.niddk.nih.gov/health/digest/pubs/lactose/lactose.htm
   http://www.adelaide.net.au/~ndk/no_milk.htm
   Eating disorders (anorexia and bulimia)
   http://members.aol.com/amanbu/index.html
   http://www.nimh.nih.gov/publicat/eatdis.htm
   Diabetes
   http://www.niddk.nih.gov/health/diabetes/diabetes.htm
   http://www.diabetes.com/L3TABLES/L3T100117.htm
   Cholera
   http://www-leland.stanford.edu/~moore/Cholera.html
   http://www.cdc.gov/travel/cholera.htm

2. Give a brief overview of how to enter in the URLs.
3. Have students work alone or in pairs, but ask every student to hand in his or her individual work at the end of the period.
4. Have students share their findings with the class in the next period.
5. Discuss the role of today's society in increasing the incidence of anorexia and bulimia in Western countries.

Assessment:

Assessment will be based on students' effort during Internet research and their final oral and written reports about one of the diseases.

Reflection:

In this lesson students will direct their own learning, with the teacher being the guide and resource person. The computer lab setting allows the teacher to monitor and interact with individual students with relative ease.

 TEACHER PRACTICE

Selecting Net-Worthy Sites
Find at least ten Internet sites that will be useful for your science teaching. Annotate your list in terms of content, grade level, teaching and learning approaches, real-time data, problem solving, etc. Share your ratings with your peers.

WHAT IS HYPERMEDIA?

Information and resource materials on the Internet are presented using the principles and features of *hypermedia*. Hypermedia consists of *multimedia* and *hypertext* (Jonassen, 1996).

Multimedia

Current computer-based multimedia integrates text, graphics, animation, video, and images. "High-resolution monitors, sound and video compression cards, and high RAM and processing speed" are required to develop and run sophisticated multimedia programs (Jonassen, 1996, p. 185). A multimedia programmer needs to learn how to capture sound and video, how to synthesize sound and video to get special effects, how to import graphics or draw freehand, and how to combine the desired graphics by using *scripts* to produce animation.

"Salt Dissolving" (Ebenezer, 1996) is a hypermedia presentation created with Macromedia Director. This presentation outlines students' conceptions of dissolving and enables students to go through a series of progressive lessons based on chemists' theoretical ideas. It presents text as well as video sequences of teacher demonstrations and explanations of key concepts in solution chemistry. For example, the polarity of water is illustrated through text and video clips. Also, the separation of table salt into sodium ions and chloride ions, and hydration of these ions are graphically represented through animations (see Figure 10-1). This presentation is also

HyperCard and HyperStudio are two very user friendly hypermedia programs that teachers and students can use to develop science activities. Students really enjoy using these hypermedia programs to author simple activities. Because of the multimedia capabilities and multisensory modalities of learning, hypermedia programs are useful as thinking and negotiating environments. They allow students to be active constructors rather than passive receivers of knowledge (Gabel, 1994).

Script is a language that the computer can understand

Macromedia Director is an advanced hypermedia system for the Macintosh. It has very powerful animation capabilities and high interactivity and plays QuickTime movies.

We discuss "Salt Dissolving" in more detail here because later in this chapter we use it as an example for conceptual-change teaching.

FIGURE 10-1
Separation and solvation of sodium and chloride ions

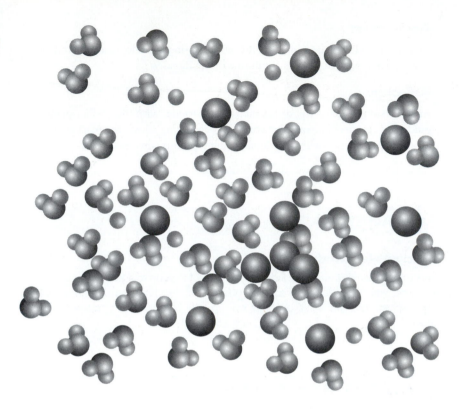

linked to a drawing program so that students can depict their conceptions. In this program students can engage in a meaningful conversation with peers and the teacher via Internet Relay Chat (IRC).

Hypertext

Hypertext provides a nonsequential way of arranging and displaying text. What makes this nonlinear arrangement of different media possible? The fundamental storage unit of hypertext is called a *node*. Metaphorically, it can be referred to as a "card" that can contain a piece of text. Because each node consists of links to other related nodes (depending on the author's wish and the various types of knowledge in a domain of science), the learner may access any other nodes while reading the text on one node. For instance, a description of what is meant by solubility may be on one node. On the same node, links may be available to other nodes such as (a) instructions for how to determine the solubility of salt, (b) a data chart to record the results, (c) a graph sheet on which a graph can be drawn, and (d) solubility problems. Hence, while you have one node open you can also access other nodes through transparent or hidden buttons, or even highlighted words. This is possible only because links and interlinks are made to nodes through a scripting language, making hypertext dynamic.

Thus, hypertext uses random access to information, enabling the learner to take control of and explore knowledge in a nonlinear fashion (Marsh & Kumar, 1992). Although with hypertext the student does not have to read from one end to the other, sequential learning is important for understanding the hierarchy of knowledge in science. For example, it is important that students learn the three levels of chemical knowledge (Johnstone, 1991): the *macroscopic* aspects (table salt dissolving in water); the *sub-microscopic*, theoretical constructs and models (the chemical structure of sodium chloride and water, and the dissolution process at the particulate level); and the *symbolic* system ($NaCl(s) + H_2O \rightarrow Na^+(aq) + Cl^-(aq)$).

For science classroom use, a multimedia presentation with a few hypertexts can be made so that the learner can learn the key processes in science *from* the hypertext. This initial step is essential so that students do not become disoriented with millions of hypertexts, such as in Netscape. Students can create their own hypertexts to reveal their personal or collective understanding. Hence, students have the opportunity not only to learn *from* the hypertext but also to learn *with* the hypertext, that is, to create their personal nodes (Salomon, Perkins, & Globerson, 1991). This *process* of creating interrelationships helps students to be better learners rather than producers of advanced systems of hypertexts. Indeed, students may be asked to interconnect the multiple representations of knowledge in science—namely, strings, propositions, images, episodes, intellectual skills, motor skills, and cognitive strategies (White, 1988)—or to integrate Gardner's (1991) three knowledge domains or critical forms of knowing: notational conventions, epistemic rules, and conceptual understandings. When a teacher demonstrates the efficacy of hypertexts, students will see the power that hypertext can have in their learning. However, this becomes a reality only when schools or homes are electronically rich.

In summary, the primary feature of the hypermedia environment is the combination of multimedia and hypertext. Each node can contain a particular medium or a combination of appropriate media. Hence a node may consist of text, graphics, photographic images, animations, sounds, audio, and video sequences. Instead of reading about the solution process, students can actually see the solution process through animation. Ionic equations have special meaning because students can now visualize the solution process. Hypermedia thus provides students with visual experience of chemical processes.

Hypermedia offers much promise because it fosters "flexibility in the structuring of knowledge" (Gabel, 1994) to help students negotiate scientific concepts. Christopher Dede, a professor of information technology, argues that new technologies can help transform schools if they are used to support new models of teaching and learning—models that characterize sustained community-centered constructivist classrooms for learner investigation, collaboration, and construction (O'Neil, 1995).

> While ideally there is nonsequentiality to multimedia and information can be accessed randomly, a chemistry lesson sequence should progress from simple to complex, so that chemistry students can understand the hierarchy of knowledge.

TEACHER PRACTICE

Simulating a Physical Process

Some preservice teachers have developed simple hypermedia activities in science as part of their methods course. Use a hypermedia program such as HyperStudio to simulate a physical process.

COMPUTER MICROWORLDS FOR SIMULATING REALITIES

Computer microworlds are simulations or replications of real-world phenomena in electronic media. Computer simulations are developed using the features of hypermedia: graphics, animations, buttons, videos, and sound. The purpose of computer microworlds is to construct artificial mirrors of realities that can be manipulated by students in their explorations. They are controlled learning environments that have electronic tools such as the mouse and an on-screen video recorder for exploration (observation and manipulation). Computer microworlds thus enable students to speculate and test their hypotheses.

Complex natural phenomena are learned through simple problem-solving activities based on knowledge, skills, and attitudes. Hence, computer microworlds are not used for knowledge representation; rather, they are used for testing knowledge. Computer microworlds are based on learners' experiences and interests and students learn how to use microworlds by actually doing so. Therefore, students regulate their own learning and are responsible for determining and achieving their objectives in the computer microworld environment.

Computer microworlds give a more holistic view of the subject material and are often closer to real life than a textbook version would be. Microworlds enable students to think. Concepts are built in implicitly rather than merely representing them in the form of knowledge. Examples of computer microworlds are Stella (Steed, 1992) and ThinkerTools (White, 1993).

Interactive Physics is a computer microworld environment for exploring topics in Newtonian mechanics, such as momentum, force, and acceleration. It consists of a number of demonstrations (Car Crash, Falling Object, Projectile Motion) and experiments (Equilibrium, Motion in a Plane). Interactive Physics provides objects and tools that enable learners to design their own experiments to model Newtonian phenomena. It allows learners to manipulate attributes of the world, such as gravity, air resistance, and elasticity of bodies. They can also choose aspects of the microworld they want to attend by showing grids, rulers, vectors, axes, and centers of mass. Interactive Physics develops *critical-thinking skills, creative-thinking skills,* and *complex-thinking skills;* computer microworlds in general promote self-regulated learning, self-directed problem-solving practice, incidental learning, experiential learning, teacher modeling and coaching, and collaborative learning (Jonassen, 1996).

A Physics Teacher's Simulations and Animations

Don Metz, a physics teacher, uses animations to make physics concepts come alive. In the photoelectric animation (see Figure 10-2), the predictions of the wave model (the wrong model) help demonstrate that electrons would be liberated at any frequency, contrary to the observations recorded by experiment. In the ball toss animation (Figure 10-3), energy bars are used simultaneously to describe the changes in energy throughout the motion of the ball. By moving the energy bar horizontally, students can draw a graph of energy versus time to make a connection between energy concepts and mathematical displays. In all of these simulated activities, the analysis by students is still required as in the traditional lab; the computer is used only for animation and is not intended to do the work of the student.

Many scientific phenomena occur too fast, too slow, too close, or too far away for students to be able to observe them. Animated simulations can be used to examine corresponding scientific explanations and can be zoomed, slowed, stopped, or repeated as needed. Animation also permits

Evaluating, analyzing, and connecting are critical-thinking skills.

Elaborating, synthesizing, and imagining are creative-thinking skills.

Designing, problem solving, and decision making are complex-thinking skills.

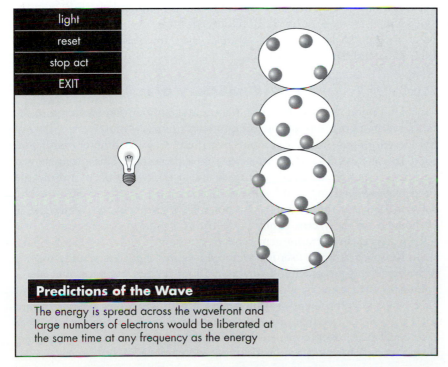

Predictions of the Wave

The energy is spread across the wavefront and large numbers of electrons would be liberated at the same time at any frequency as the energy

FIGURE 10-2
Predictions of the wave

FIGURE 10-3
Ball toss

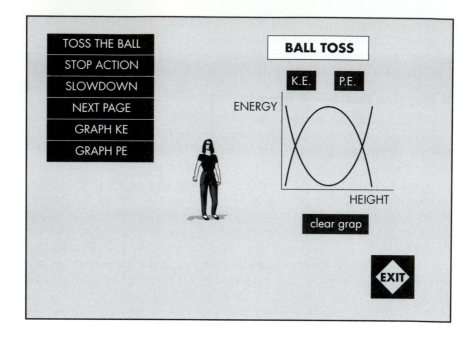

related events to be played concurrently. Computer animations enable teachers to use their own ideas and skills to represent and clarify a concept. With readily available software development tools, even those with little or no computer background can produce their own animations to reflect their ideas and teaching strategies.

Students Program the Trajectory of a Projectile

Gary DeBlunde teaches physics and computer programming; therefore, he takes every opportunity to integrate physics in his computer class. Two of his eleventh-grade physics students who also study computers with him used Pascal to program the trajectory of a projectile. This program was designed to aid physics students in visualizing the trajectory of a projectile fired at a specified angle and velocity. It is especially useful in showing the relation between the x- and y-components of the velocity. While the y-component of the vector conforms to the acceleration due to gravity of a falling object, the x-component remains constant.

In this program, the user is prompted to enter the velocity and angle of a projectile and the gravitational acceleration. It then accurately calculates values for maximum height, range, time, the x-velocity component, and the y-velocity component as it plots the path of the projectile (see Figure 10-4). Gary believes that using an accurate visual representation of a projectile makes it possible for students to learn this concept quickly and easily without performing time-consuming calculations.

Pascal is a high-level computer programming language widely accepted as a teaching tool for programming concepts and for use in industry. Because it is a highly structured language, it lends itself well to modern programming techniques. Its simplicity and readability make it one of the best languages for teaching the concepts of programming.

 TEACHER PRACTICE

Computer Microworlds on the Internet

Search for microworlds on the Internet that facilitate scientific inquiry. Collect real-time data and share this information with your peers.

Computer Simulations for Conceptual Change

Researchers such as diSessa (1987), Hennessy et al. (1995a, 1995b), Twigger et al. (1991), Twigger et al. (1994), White and Horwitz (1988), and Zietsman and Hewson (1986) have developed computer simulations in physics to explore and incorporate students' ideas in science instruction. For example, a recent study on students' conceptions of light propagation and visual patterns (Langley, Ronen, & Eylon, 1997) has advocated the use of computer technology. The RAY optics simulation software (Ronen et al., 1993; Ronen & Rivlin, 1995) and the Visual Physics Optics Simulation (Tek, 1994) are instructional environments. Physics education researchers see the computer as providing a context in which students' conceptions may be explored and negotiated through simulations. Let us examine an example of a computer simulation in mechanics in detail.

Hennessy et al. (1995a) present a teaching sequence of mechanics simulations: Rocket Skater, Cardboard Box, Speedboat, and Parachutist. Each

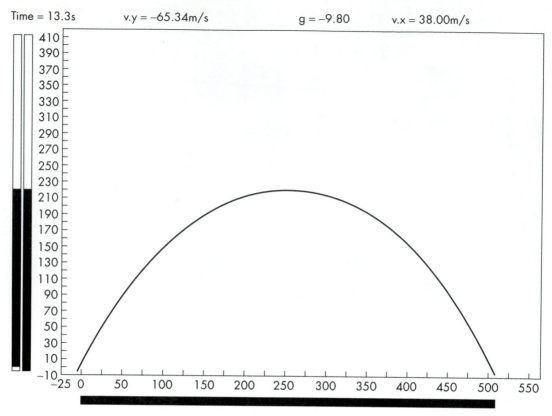

FIGURE 10-4
The path of a projectile fired at a specified angle and velocity

Students' prior conceptions were obtained from a previous study (Twigger et al., 1994) and refined for Hennessy et al.'s (1995a, 1995b) classroom-based study.

Hennessy et al. use the term *conception networks* because they believe that experts' and children's conceptions are components of their respective interrelated networks. Therefore, children's conceptions cannot be mapped out showing one-to-one relationship with the goal conceptions.

of the simulations addresses particular aspects of students' conceptions and develops specific aspects of Newtonian theory. The Rocket Skater simulates a frictionless environment in which a skater figure provides either impulsive or continuous horizontal forces. The Cardboard Box simulates horizontal motion in which friction is a force that opposes motion. The Speedboat simulates speed-dependent resistance; that is, resistive force is offered by the fluid. The fluid resistance increases with the speed of the boat, thus reaching a terminal velocity. The Parachutist develops the idea of vertical motion under gravity. Air resistance is involved. See Figure 10-5 for a sample screen representation of the Rocket Skater computer simulation.

These computer simulations were created based on students' prior conceptions and goal conceptions (see Table 10-1). The pedagogic aim was to help students change from their prior conceptions network to the goal conceptions network (Newtonian theory) using computer simulations. The students progressed from simple to complex qualitative reasoning.

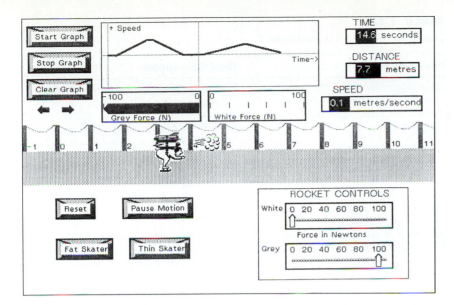

FIGURE 10-5
Rocket skater (with continuous rocket forces and mass variation) (*NOTE:* From "Design of a Computer-Augmented Curriculum for Mechanics," by S. Hennessy et al., 1995, *International Journal of Science Education, 17*(1), p. 81. Copyright 1995 by Taylor & Francis Group. Reprinted with permission.)

 TEACHER PRACTICE

Computer Simulations for Conceptual Change

Identify students' conceptions from the literature on a topic that you like. Search for simulations on the Internet that can be used to revise students' conceptions to goal conceptions. Or, use a hypermedia program that you are comfortable with to develop a computer simulation that can help students revise their conceptions.

Animations of Chemical Processes for Conceptual Change

Chemistry education researchers have focused on computer animations for addressing students' conceptions of chemical processes. For example, Williamson and Abraham (1995) studied the effect of computer animations depicting the particulate nature of matter on college chemistry students' mental models of chemical phenomena such as phase transitions, intermolecular forces, solution, ionic solution, precipitation, and temperature effects on dissolving. These authors reported that their treatment groups received significantly higher conceptual understanding scores on an evaluation test on the particulate nature of matter.

Sanger and Greenbowe (1997a) have identified college students' conceptions in electrochemistry. One of the common conceptions was that electrons flow through the salt bridge and electrolyte solutions to complete the circuit. Sanger and Greenbowe (1997b) suggested that using

TABLE 10-1
Conception Networks in Mechanics

Prior Conception	Goal Conception
A moving object has a "force of motion" in it. The object stops when this force "runs out."	Force opposing motion slows things down.
In space an object "drifts about."	Objects continue at a constant speed in a straight line when no force acts on them.
Friction is not identified as a force.	Friction is a force that acts in a direction opposing motion.
Driving force must be greater than resistance for an object to move at a constant speed.	Driving force equals resistive force when an object moves at a constant speed.
An object moves in the direction of the applied force.	An object accelerates in the direction of the net force. If this opposes motion, then the effect is that the object keeps traveling in the opposite direction to the force, but slows down.
Heavier things are harder to get going, are harder to keep going, and stop more quickly.	More massive things are harder to get going and to stop. Where gravity and friction act, the increased mass gives increased weight and increased friction, which combines with the increased mass effect to make acceleration harder, but on deceleration, the increased mass counterbalances the effect of the increased frictional force.
Heavier objects fall faster than lighter objects.	Objects of different weights fall with the same acceleration (ignoring air resistance).

NOTE: From "Design of a Computer-Augmented Curriculum for Mechanics," by S. Hennessy et al., 1995, *International Journal of Science Education, 17*(1), p. 85. Copyright 1995 by Taylor & Francis Group. Adapted with permission.

computer animations depicting chemical reactions on the molecular level and a teaching approach that confronted student conceptions dramatically decreased the proportion of students who consistently demonstrated their personal conception that electrons can travel through aqueous solutions.

Greenbowe (1994) has developed computer animations that illustrate the migration of cations and anions in the salt bridge of an electrochemical cell. Sanger and Greenbowe's study (1997a), which examined the effects of these computer animations and the conceptual change approach on student understanding, suggests that the conceptual change approach is generally effective at preventing or dispelling the student misconception that electrons flow in aqueous solutions. Additionally, these authors report that animations appear to be helpful when the questions require students to visualize chemical processes on the molecular level.

Cards 38–42 in animation.
Card 42.

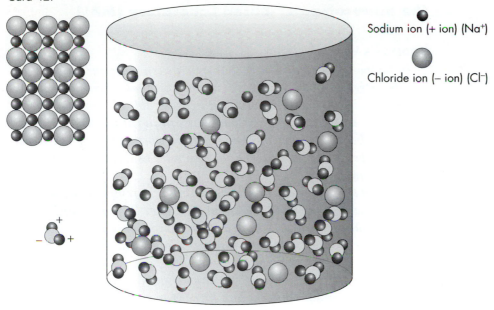

Sodium ion (+ ion) (Na⁺)

Chloride ion (– ion) (Cl⁻)

FIGURE 10-6
Salt dissolving in water (*NOTE:* Ebenezer, J.V. (1996). Salt dissolving hypermedia program with Macromedia Director 4.0. Winnipeg, Canada: University of Manitoba.)

   Jazlin Ebenezer has used a hypermedia environment to explore a group of eleventh-grade chemistry students' conceptions of table salt dissolving in water (see Figure 10-6). Hypermedia was used to negotiate two conceptions students had about the process of dissolving table salt in water: (a) the transformation of solid to liquid, and (b) the chemical combination of solute and solvent. The findings of this study indicate that a hypermedia environment can be used to explore, negotiate, and assess students' understandings of the submicroscopic aspects of solution chemistry.

 PEER TALK

Hypermedia for Conceptual Change

Several articles in the reference section for this chapter discuss the use of hypermedia for conceptual change (Hameed, Hackling, & Garnett, 1993; Hennessy et al. 1995a & b; Perkins, 1991; Sanger & Greenbowe, 1997a & b; White & Horowitz, 1988; Williamson & Abraham, 1995; Zietsman & Hewson, 1986). Read one of these articles. Discuss the salient points the author(s) brings out in this article and share your views on using hypermedia for conceptual change with your peers.

⊠ ELECTRONIC LABORATORIES

The Microcomputer-Based Laboratory (MBL)

RODELYN'S VOICE

In my own classroom, I have found that science becomes truly interactive with the use of MBL in the sense that learning became more concrete and more connected to observable phenomena. For example, students had a better understanding of what was meant by endothermic and exothermic reactions when they observed what was happening graphically on the computer as the reaction was taking place.

Using the traditional method of taking the temperature using a thermometer every 30 seconds would not have been as meaningful for the students since the analysis of the data would have taken place after the experiment and not during. Also, seeing the graph of the reaction as it was occurring provided an opportunity for students to share their ideas about what was happening and why. As I circulated around the room and listened to students discussing their observations and ideas, it was clear to me that students were learning about the concepts, using their own language and analogies.

MBLs also allow students to develop and test out their own hypotheses. For example, in my physics class, students created their own experiments to see what happened to a graph when an object approached a motion detector at different speeds and from different distances. They also tried to emulate a given graph using the probe and the object. Students found these activities motivating and interesting and could see immediately the effects of their actions on the graph. Because of the ease of the equipment, students could perform the experiments several times, testing out their different ideas.

The measurements are taken by the probe and are displayed directly on the computer in real time. These measurements can then be saved, further analyzed in diverse ways, or printed out.

An MBL is a technological system based on the principle of interfacing microcomputers with probes and laboratory equipment. This computer system collects and graphically displays quantitative measurements such as temperature, light and sound intensities, pH, and relative velocity against real time. A promising feature of MBLs is that experimentation and experimental analysis occur simultaneously, thus minimizing laborious data collection efforts and providing more time for data analysis. Some science teachers use MBLs in their research as an instructional mode to enhance scientific attitudes in students.

According to Krajcik and Layman (1993), the MBL provides opportunities for asking and refining questions, making predictions, designing plans and/or experiments, collecting and analyzing data, debating ideas, communicating ideas and findings with others, drawing conclusions, and asking new questions. All of these attributes point to a constructivist approach to teaching and learning science. However, probes do not help students construct understanding about scientific concepts—a teacher must do that. For example, if students use an MBL to monitor the temperature of physical systems, the teacher must help students analyze the MBL-produced graphs and science concepts involved in the activity.

Despite all the nice features of the MBL, a teacher must make a conscious effort to incorporate his or her knowledge of MBLs with students' conceptions. Before students can plan and design experiments, common knowledge between the teacher and the students must be achieved; *then* the information on the graph becomes clear. The tool only puts out graphs and information quickly; the interpretation of these belongs to the experimenter—the student. Nachmias and Linn (1987) show that without adequate theoretical reasoning, students usually tend to perceptually view and interpret the graphs they were able to produce by manipulating variables. The science process skills that enable problem solving may be enhanced as a result of MBLs (Friedler, Nachmias, & Linn, 1990). But the learning of science concepts depends on students' conceptual ecology and the teacher's teaching ecology. The overall effectiveness of MBLs depends on the teacher's understanding of how to use the new technology, personal knowledge of the concepts involved, and knowledge of how to help students link their MBL experiences with science concepts.

The MBL-Based Computer as Learning Partner (CLP) Project

The MBL-based *Computer as Learning Partner (CLP) Project* is an ongoing educational research effort at the School of Education at the University of California at Berkeley. The CLP research has created and refined a semester-long middle school curriculum on thermodynamics, light, and sound for achieving integrated science understanding that involves the innovative use of computers in the classroom. The Cokes and Potatoes lab is an example of a CLP activity.

Electronic Laboratory Notebook

E-LabBook is an *electronic laboratory notebook*. It is a piece of software (actually several HyperCard stacks) that has been developed for use in an eighth-grade physical science classroom as part of the CLP project.

E-LabBook serves as simulation software, real-time data collection software, and networked database software. The structure of the notebook and the activities incorporated in the notebook reflect the goals of the CLP project. It is important to understand that the software is not stand-alone self-paced software—it is designed to work in partnership

Computer as Learning Partner
http://www.clp.berkeley.edu/

Knowledge Integration Environment
http://www.kie.berkeley.edu/KIE.html

Center for Innovative Learning Technologies
http://www.CILT.LTC.Vanderbilt.edu/

Instructional Technology Program
http://www.itp.berkeley.edu/

You can download .pdf files with complete descriptions of CLP activities at the CLP site; you'll need Adobe Acrobat Reader to view these files.

ACTIVITY 10-1

COKE AND POTATOES LAB ("SODA AND SPUDS")
SIMULATED LABS: 6-7 DAYS

Description:

The students investigate how different wrapping materials affect the rate at which a hot potato cools and the rate at which a cold Coke warms up.

Cognitive Goals:

Students bring a variety of naïve conceptions about thermal insulators into science. We have found the following conceptions:

- Aluminum is a good insulator because everybody uses it to wrap Cokes with.
- When wool is used as a wrap, it will heat up whatever it is wrapping.
- Heat flows through the holes in a material, so aluminum is a good insulator because it is airtight.
- Cold energy flows from cold objects to hot objects.
- Heat energy always flows outward from an object *or* heat always flows up.
- Metals like aluminum attract cold.
- Insulating properties of wraps depend on whether the wrap is wrapping something hot or cold.
- Heat energy flows more or less easily through different materials. The rate at which heat energy flows affects the rate at which objects heat up or cool down.
- Any given material may be placed along a continuum from "poor conductor" to "good conductor." Insulation and conduction are related to each other and to the rate at which heat flows through a material. (The terms *insulation* and *conduction* will be new to many students.)

Related concepts to be developed in class discussion and interpretation of the data are as follows:

- Objects tend to heat up or cool down to room temperature.
- Heat energy flows from objects at higher temperatures to objects at lower temperatures.
- Heat energy flowing out of an object causes the object's temperature to decrease.
- When two objects are in contact, the difference in temperature between them affects the rate of heat energy flow.

Classroom Environment:

The Computer as Learning Partner classroom/laboratory has 16 student stations, each with a Macintosh LC II and a Universal Lab Interface from Vernier Software. The computers are connected by an Ethernet network to a Macintosh Centris 650 server. In our situation, randomly selected groups of two have proven most effective in terms of both time on task and constructive discussions between partners.

Themes: Energy Systems and Interactions
Physical Science Content Areas: Energy: Heat. "What is heat energy? Where does it come from, and what are its properties?" "How do we use heat energy?"

The CLP curriculum is designed to move the students toward a heat-flow model.

Materials List:

printer paper
graphs of previous students' results
    for the lab

Period 1—Potatoes Lab: Design, Prediction, Data, Notes

ACTIVITY PLAN

- Introduce the activity. Doug tells a story of baking potatoes for a party and needing to keep them warm for an hour and a half. What is the best thing to wrap them in? He has available paper towels, thin polystyrene insulation, a wool scarf, aluminum foil, and Saran Wrap.
- As part of the introduction, he also discusses why a potato in the oven will not reach 100°C. (Potato temperature is about 95°C.) This information is needed when the students select their initial temperature for the potato.
- Mr. K. discusses simulation. Eileen did several trials of each wrap, then averaged them and came up with a mathematical equation so the computer can run the calculations. The graph is the "average curve for the condition you set."
- The students start the lab. Mr. K carries a thermometer and has students individually read it when they ask about what to put for room temperature.
- Students sometimes are unsure about what to put for the limits on the axes of their graphs. They ask questions such as, "What's the highest temperature the potato will be?" and "How long do you think it will take for the potato to cool down?"
- Students work on the lab.

EXPECTATIONS

- Students should finish taking data.

Period 2—Potatoes Lab: Notes, Design Coke Lab

ACTIVITY PLAN

- Mr K. stresses the "heat-flow analysis note." He asks the students to think about heat flow during the entire time period of the graph, beginning to end, and when on the graph does heat flow the fastest.
- Finish the potatoes lab. (30 minutes)

EXPECTATIONS

- Students will print out and store their potatoes labs.

Period 3—Cokes Lab: Prediction, Data, Notes, Network Data Exchange

ACTIVITY PLAN

- Continue with the lab for about 40 minutes.
- Introduce "network poll" and "network request" by starting the poll: "What wraps did you use?" This information is needed for the worksheet. Mr. K. also steps through the procedures for the network request. (20 minutes)

EXPECTATIONS

- Students will start their worksheets.

Period 4—Cokes Lab: Exchange Data Worksheet, Notes

ACTIVITY PLAN

- Continue to work on labs. Some students will be close to finishing.
- Students are generally unfamiliar with the term *conductor*. It is useful to have a short discussion

of this before the last part of the worksheet and the principle notes.

EXPECTATIONS
- Students will be working on their principle notes.

Period 5—Finish Cokes Lab

ACTIVITY PLAN
- Continue to work on labs. Most students will finish. Print out labs.

EXPECTATIONS
- Students will turn in potatoes and Cokes labs stapled together.

Period 6—Stragglers and Post-Lab Discussion

ACTIVITY PLAN
- Some students finish lab.
- Discuss issues such as why wool won't heat up the Cokes.

EXPECTATIONS
- Students will turn in potatoes and Cokes labs stapled together.

---

with a teacher who understands its goals, its metaphors, and the way it works.

The goals of the CLP project have been to create a tool that can be used in the classroom as an application of the CLP teaching approach. The researchers of the CLP project are continually making changes to the software; it is still in the beta-testing stage.

Approximately 180 students each semester use E-LabBook for a period of about fourteen weeks in units covering light, heat and temperature, and sound. With E-LabBook, they design an experiment by setting values for various variables, predict the results of the experiment, run the experiment—either by actually collecting data using temperature-sensitive probes connected to the computer or by running a simulation—and, finally, prepare a report. Interspersed throughout these core activities are a variety of other activities designed to encourage reflection about the science involved with the experiment. Most of these additional activities consist of prompted writing tasks, as shown in Figure 10-7.

The system is designed to run over on Ethernet network, enabling students to share their work much as real scientists would. (The network also enables them to quickly and easily update the software as they think of new features or discover new bugs.)

The Personal Science Laboratory (PSL)

See http://www.teamlabs.com/ psldesc.html for a description of PSL.

Personal Science Laboratory (PSL) Explorer is an IBM-based MBL program. PSL is a laboratory-grade scientific instrument designed to do real science; it encourages hands-on investigations, scientific inquiry, and collaborative learning. PSL runs experiments using a variety of probes, such as temperature, light, pH, and motion probes. A computer is used to capture and graph the data. Students focus on scientific inquiry and problem-solving skills such as examining data, doing analysis, and graphing results.

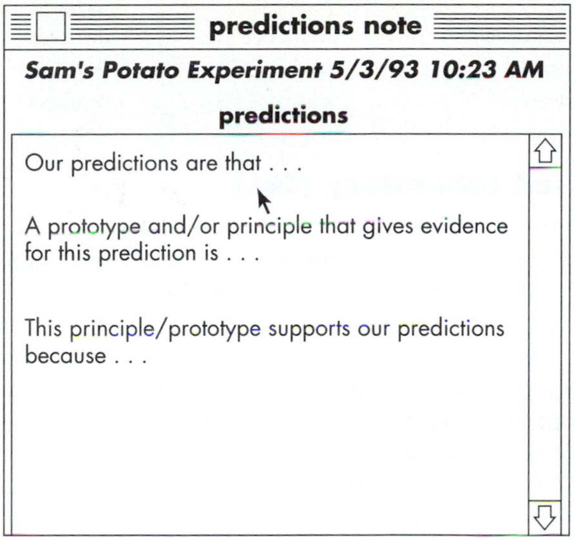

FIGURE 10-7
Prompted writing in
E-LabBook

PSL is applicable from third-grade to college levels in physical science, earth science, life science, math, physics, chemistry, biology, and technology; its grade-specific probeware, software, and curriculum is in line with the National Science Education Standards.

There are six important steps to follow to set up and run an experiment with PSL:

1. Set up the PSL equipment. Connect the PSL base unit to the correct communication port.
2. Start the PSL Explorer program. Choose the experiment you want on the "Select Experiment" menu. For example, select the experiment "Endothermic and Exothermic Reactions." Then select "One Temperature vs. Time."
3. Use the "Reset Parameters" option to set the range and duration values. For endothermic and exothermic reactions, enter the following values in the table for range and duration:

RANGE   *DURATION*
y-min 10 degrees C   40 seconds
y-max 30 degrees C

4. Select "Run Experiment."
5. Select "Calibrate" and enter the calibration values for the probes you are using. In the case of endothermic and exothermic reactions, you will use the temperature probes.
6. Observe probe readings to make sure they are consistent.

Take temperature reading for other chemicals such as sodium hydroxide, sodium thiosulfate, and sodium acetate. Check for consistency in the probe's configuration. Change the configuration, if necessary.

http://www.vernier.com/cbl/cbl.html
http://www.vernier.com/probes/probes.html

Activity workbooks for CBL include *Explorations in Biology, Chemistry with Computers,* and *CBL Activities for Physics.* Workbooks at http://www.vernier.com/cmat/cmat.html

Ordering:
Vernier Software
8565 SW Beaverton-Hillsdale Hwy.
Portland, OR 97225-2429
Phone (503) 297-5317
Fax (503) 297-1760
Orders can be sent via email to orders@vernier.com

Selected CBL/MBL Sites
http://www.phy.nau.edu/~danmac/whyMBL.html
http://www2.ncsu.edu/sciencejunction/terminal/imse/lowres/3/cblmbl.htm

CHEMICAL	T_1	T_2	delta T
NaCl	degrees C	degrees C	degrees C
$CaCl_2$	degrees C	degrees C	degrees C
KCl	degrees C	degrees C	degrees C
$C_{12}H_{22}O_{11}$	degrees C	degrees C	degrees C

The Calculator-Based Laboratory (CBL)

CBL is a portable and versatile data collection device. The CBL System package consists of a CBL interface, a temperature probe, a light probe, a voltage probe, an experiment workbook, a user's guidebook, batteries, and a carrying case. Other probes—such as an ultrasonic motion detector, force sensor, pH system, colorimeter, and barometer—can be connected to the CBL interface, which is a graphing calculator rather than a computer as in MBL. Since the CBL is battery operated, experiments can take place anywhere. For example, accelerations can be measured in amusement rides. The temperature and pH of a stream of water can be monitored. Data can be collected as quickly as 10,000 points per second or as slowly as one sample every 4 hours. The calculator collects and graphs the data during the experiment. Students may analyze the data later. The calculator can then be connected to a computer to print the graph or to download or upload data and programs. Since the CBL has its own microprocessor and memory, it can be disconnected from the calculator, allowing it to act as a stand-alone data logger. It is also possible to simultaneously collect data from five channels. You can collect data in real time and plot the data on the calculator as they are collected. The CBL provides a low-cost alternative to computers. Teachers and students are now able to collect and analyze real-life data with much ease.

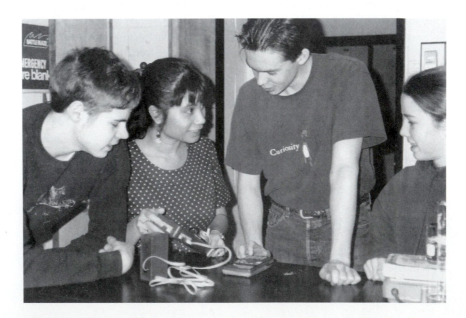

MBL, PSL, and CBL provide students with an easy, meaningful way to learn certain scientific concepts and principles. These electronic learning tools can be effectively used to mediate science concepts and principles.

TEACHER PRACTICE

Electronic Laboratories for Problem Solving

Learn how to conduct laboratories using probes such as light, sound, temperature, and pH sensors.

☒ COMPUTER-BASED SEMANTIC NETWORKS

In Chapter 8, we learned to create concept maps on paper. We alluded to the fact that computer programs are available to construct concept maps. SemNet (Fisher et al., 1990; Fisher, 1992), Learning Tool (Kozma, 1987, 1992), TextVision (Kommers, 1989), CMap, and Inspiration are powerful computer programs that "provide visual and verbal screen tools for developing concept maps" (Jonassen, 1996, p. 93). Jonassen argues that concept maps or "semantic nets are spatial representations of ideas and their interrelationships. They enable learners to interrelate the ideas they are studying in multidimensional networks of concepts, to label the relationships between those concepts, and to describe the nature of the relationships among all of the ideas in the network" (p. 93).

Concept maps that represent semantic networks in memory are composed of nodes (concepts of ideas) connected by links (statements of relationships). In computer-based semantic networks, nodes are represented as information blocks or cards (that is, "structural knowledge"—articulation of declarative and procedural knowledge) and the links are labeled lines. Semantic network programs provide the capabilities of adding text and pictures to each node. The purpose of semantic networks is to represent the organization of someone's ideas or the underlying organization of ideas in a content domain. The process of creating semantic networks engages learners in an analysis of their own knowledge structures, which helps them to integrate new knowledge with what they already know. Learners with better structural knowledge are better problem solvers. Since semantic networks describe what a learner knows, they can be used as evaluation tools for assessing learners' changes in thinking. The semantic networks that learners generate before and after instruction should reflect growth in their knowledge structures.

Features and availability of semantic network programs are described in Figure 10-8.

FIGURE 10-8
Features and availability of
semantic programs (*NOTE:*
From *Computers in the
Classroom: Mindtools for
Critical Thinking* (pp.
102–106), by D. H.
Jonassen, 1996, Englewood
Cliffs, NJ: Prentice-Hall.
Copyright 1996 by Prentice
Hall. Adapted with
permission.)

SemNet

FEATURES
Pull-down menus
Creates nodes for text and pictures
Creates links using a clockwise direction
A central node/screen surrounded by related concepts
A full web of interrelated concepts located in a special menu

AVAILABILITY
SemNet Research Group, 1060 Johnson Avenue, San Diego, CA 92103

Learning Tool

FEATURES
Creates and labels nodes in the form of folders
Connects nodes with labeled links
Displays a large number of interlinked concepts on the same screen
Nodes have intervening links on the same screen
Creates detailed submaps and text
Creates the net in a graphic mode or in an outlining mode
Easy to learn, use, and revise
Much text can be included

AVAILABILITY
Intellimation software company

CMap

FEATURES
Creates concept nodes and links
Copies, moves, and traces links
Links are elastic and follow the concepts
Easy to use; an excellent mapping tool for beginners

AVAILABILITY
ThinkTechnologies, Ithaca, NY
Distributed as "freeware."
CMap was developed by Hunter and Stahl to provide a tool for creating
concept maps as described by Novak and Gowin (1984).

Inspiration

FEATURES
Develops ideas and plans
Integrates diagrams (graphic) and outlines (text)
Creates mind maps, cluster diagrams, and idea maps

AVAILABILITY
Inspiration Software, Inc.
7412 SW Beaverton Hillsdale Hwy.
Suite 102
Portland, OR 97225

SemNet Semantic Networking Tool (Kathleen Fisher, a science educator at San Diego State University)

The SemNet software is a tool designed to promote and support personal knowledge construction. It has a number of qualitative and quantitative features that are useful to learners and researchers alike. Students in my biology course for prospective elementary school teachers use it regularly. They work in groups to construct their networks of biology knowledge. In a general education course about human heredity, I use SemNet as a presentation tool. I also make nets that I have constructed available to students as study tools. Last semester about a third of the students in this course chose to construct a semantic network rather than write a paper.

The SemNet software runs on any Macintosh computer with System 6.0 or higher and is available free to any interested individual. It can be downloaded from http://www.biologylessons.sdsu.edu/about/semnetdown. html. The SemNet User Guide is also available from those sites at no charge, in Microsoft Word 5.1 format.

Here is the reaction of one prospective schoolteacher to working with SemNet:

> My experiences in working with SemNet have been nothing but rewarding. I have found this program quite useful as a learning tool and as a mode of connecting ideas and concepts together. Because connections are a key to understanding what is being learned, this type of concept mapping can help students visually perceive the way things work.
>
> Organizing the information and choosing the appropriate relations in SemNet allowed me to recognize and build a network of my ideas, as I considered hierarchies, cohesiveness, and how each concept ties into the bigger ideas.
>
> One of the things I liked most about SemNet is that it is very easy to use and read. The processes for creating nets are straightforward and user-friendly. SemNet offers several versatile functions and features, such as the merging of nets, the masking of concepts in order to study from, and some previously programmed inverse relations to save time with the input of data.
>
> This program has helped me organize my ideas and establish connections to further understand how things come together. As a future educator, I would certainly consider using SemNet with my students because it would give them the opportunity to do hands-on knowledge mapping and it is a fun way to visualize and learn. (Student X)

Student X is a good student—one who spontaneously puts ideas together in her mind and who routinely builds meaning. Working with SemNet comes easily to such students because the computer simply makes external and explicit those cognitive processes that had previously been internal and implicit. For students who do not automatically engage in meaning-making as they study academic subjects, but who instead rely heavily on rote learning, SemNet can be a bit of a challenge at first. It can be difficult for concrete-oriented memorizers to conceive of and envision a network of interconnected ideas. Yet these are the students who, in the end, probably gain the most. They acquire a new way of thinking and in the course of a semester are able to master many of the cognitive and metacognitive skills associated with personal knowledge construction.

What is sad is that such students have to wait until their senior year in college to discover such skills. I believe that SemNet would be most powerful if employed with young people who are beginning to master abstract thought—say fifth to ninth grades. It is an excellent tool with which to construct hierarchies of ideas, organize ideas into categories, and lay out temporal flows. Further, it is easy to do all these things within one interconnected network of ideas.

With SemNet, it is possible for a teacher to see what each student is thinking and to give feedback at a level of detail heretofore impossible. Students likewise enjoy reviewing one another's nets, largely because of the insights they gain regarding different ways to represent the same ideas. They usually discover both more and less powerful ways of organizing knowledge than they themselves used. This is because there is no one right way to organize a given set of knowledge, but there are definitely more effective and less effective ways.

My students' nets usually contain one to several hundred concepts. SemNet displays each concept graphically with all its links to other concepts (see Figure 10-9). A concept in SemNet terms is any idea that is featured in a bubble—and is usually represented by a noun or noun phrase. A relation is shown by a line connecting two or more concepts and is usually designated by a verb or verb phrase. An instance is a simple proposition—two concepts connected by a relation. The graphic display in Figure 10-9 comes from a population net created by Student X and her Group X. It contains 281 concepts, 41 relations, and 644 instances.

Dormancy is linked to six related concepts by named relation rays. Since the net shown in Figure 10-9 contains 281 concepts, it can generate 281 graphic displays like this one—one for each concept. Students construct nets simply by entering simple propositions or instances in the Create an

FIGURE 10-9

Graphic display of the concept *dormancy* from a population net constructed by Student X and her Group X.

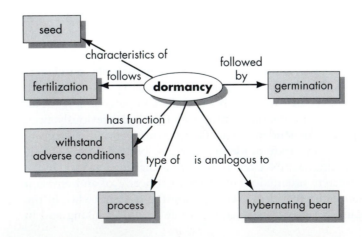

Instance dialog on the Instance menu. For example, we may want to add the following instance to the frame in Figure 10-9:

CENTRAL CONCEPT: DORMANCY
Relation: characteristic of
Related Concept: *deciduous trees in winter*

SemNet automatically does all the drawing, allowing the user to focus entirely on the content. SemNet would place *deciduous trees in winter* at the end of the "characteristic of" relation pointing to 10:00, under the concept *seed*. Each relation can be and usually is used many times in constructing a network.

SemNet keeps continuous count of elements in a net and offers many different ways to view the data. There are sixteen different static views on the Display menu and two dynamic views on the Move menu. The first view I routinely check when reviewing a student net is About Net (Figure 10-10).

In the top section, I can review the number of each type of element in a net. This net not only has a large number of concepts, relations, and instances, but it also has a good number of synonyms, texts, and pictures attached to concepts. I am especially interested in the ratio of instances to concepts, which provides an indication of the degree of interconnectivity in a net. This net has an unusually high ratio of 2.29 times as many instances as concepts. I am usually satisfied if there are at least a third more instances.

The middle section displays the concepts according to the number of instances in which they participate. Thirty-nine-and-a-half percent of the

About Net:	5 H40 population				
Net Elements	# Elements	# Synonyms	# Texts	# Pictures	# Names
Concepts	281	43	2	38	324
Relations	41	—	0	0	78
Instances	644				

Counts of Concepts Having Various Numbers of Instances

# Instances	# Concepts	% of Total Concepts
0	0	0.0
1–2	170	60.5
3 or more	111	39.5
6 or more	66	23.5
10 or more	41	14.6
20 or more	12	4.3

Maximums
  Most developed concept(s) with 42 instances: *insect*
  Most embedded concept(s) with embeddedness of 617: *insect*
  Most used relation(s) used in 233 instances: *eats/eaten by*

FIGURE 10-10
About Net view from the population net by Group X.

concepts in this net have three or more connections—the minimum necessary for an adequate description. I am usually satisfied if I see at least 25 percent. I can also see that this net has no loose ends—every concept is connected to the network.

In the third section I can see the main ideas in the net. The population net contains a forest food web with an unusually high degree of interconnectivity. It shows up here with the concept *insects* being the most embedded and the relation "eats/eaten by" being used most frequently. *Embeddedness* is the number of unique paths from a concept to two nodes away and it is calculated automatically by SemNet. Its practical value is in revealing the most highly developed ideas in a network. You can check the list of concepts by embeddedness to see the main ideas in the network.

It is possible to extract a hierarchy or temporal flow from a net. For example, Figure 10-11 shows the flow of meiosis from the population net by Group X. This says that *interphase* is followed by *meiosis,* specifically *prophase I,* and that each subsequent phase of meiosis follows in succession after *prophase I.* Flows and hierarchies are extracted by identifying a beginning concept and selecting one or more relations to follow. In this case we used one relation, "follows/followed by." You will notice that in SemNet every relation is bidirectional (that is, they point from concept A to concept B and vice versa) and most are asymmetric (that is, they are described by different words in each direction). This adds a richness to the nets but, at the same time, adds to the challenge of net construction.

In summary, SemNet is a useful tool for encouraging meaningful, mindful learning through systematic knowledge construction. It also provides many insights to teachers about how students think, and can be a powerful research tool for cognitive analysis. Further, it is easy to learn and fun to use.

FIGURE 10-11

A temporal flow composed of the stages of meiosis and cell division (extracted from the population net by Group X)

Hierarchy following relation "followed by/follows"
interphase
   followed by meiosis
   followed by prophase I
      followed by metaphase I
         followed by anaphase I
            followed by telophase I
               followed by cytokinesis I
                  followed by prophase II
                     followed by metaphase II
                        followed by anaphase II
                           followed by telophase II
                              followed by cytokinesis II

TEACHER PRACTICE

Drawing a Concept Map

Draw a concept map of a science topic using one of the computer software programs previously mentioned, or one with which you are familiar.

⚙ OTHER COMPUTER-BASED ELECTRONIC MEDIA

CDs

There are many types of CDs that can be used in the science classroom, ranging from simulations to creation to databases. The database CDs are an important resource for the students because, in most cases, they incorporate many different ways of viewing information. For example, the Microsoft Encarta 97 Encyclopedia includes video clips, sound clips, animations, and hyperlinks along with standard text and graphics. These features are important reasons for integrating CD database resources into research projects and presentations.

Videodiscs

Videodiscs are another source of a variety of information. Videodiscs hold still frames, video, and sound, and in some cases can be controlled by a computer. The advantage videodiscs have over videotapes is that each frame is indexed and can be accessed simply by entering its frame number into a remote control.

Videodiscs are meant to supplement and enhance instruction, not replace it. Most of the videodiscs are databases of charts, images, and video clips. There are some amazing discs that interact with the student through the computer interface. Our textbook shows many experiments that are simply not possible to do in the schools. By showing short clips, you can expose your students to the reactions without the costs and safety precautions. Examples are "Liquid Nitrogen" (boiling point), "Hindenberg Explosion," "Plastic Recycling," and "Magnesium Burning" (on dry CO_2).

Spreadsheets

Spreadsheets are particularly useful in science classes because of the high level of student-computer interactivity that can be built into each document.

The purpose of using a spreadsheet to compute and provide meaningful output for a given set of data is to eliminate the amount of attentional resources required by the student when doing mathematical computations.

Shelby Primmet, a secondary science preservice teacher, walked her peers through the following electronic means for science teaching and learning as part of her seminar at the 1998 P-STAR Conference.

By freeing these resources, students will be able to increase their understanding of the concept, instead of concerning themselves with the difficulties of "doing powers" or other mathematical skills. In this way, the student has the opportunity to develop his or her science skills without viewing the activity as an arduous mathematical task. The beauty of this instructional tool is found when the student who normally has difficulties performing multiplication or solving equations with variables suddenly is given the opportunity to understand how and why the concept (equation, proportionality) is utilized in science.

Personal Web Pages

Teachers can create their very own Web pages using HTML editors (like any word processing program) and use them in their classroom in the same fashion as they might use externally created pages or as mini-lesson environments. These hypermedia documents are important instructional tools because they allow the author the flexibility of including original text, imported and original graphics, video clips, simulations, animations, and sound clips that are specific to their classroom content. Graphics can be copied from the World Wide Web or imported from clip art, individual frames can be captured from video or digital cameras, photos and textbooks can be scanned, and, of course, images can be created using the various paint programs available. These elements help the author add the necessary instructional and personal touches to the content. For example, as an introduction to a frog dissection lab, the teacher may author a site that includes step-by-step graphics of specimens taken from past years. In order to maximize the capability of the page, the document may also include sound clips of the instructions, animations, labels, and links to external sites that simulate the dissection. The teacher would also have the option of posting the page to the World Wide Web or accessing it on a local server.

Hypertext, also known as links, creates a networklike structure among Web pages in hypermedia documents that is similar to the networklike structure of the student's mind (schemata). Documents that offer bite-sized chunks of information that are interconnected by hypertext in a networklike fashion allow students to intuitively explore the content and build their own natural knowledge schema. The connections between concepts are naturally understood because the student navigates his or her own ship in the sea of knowledge. In the preceding frog dissection document, the teacher may choose to incorporate content into the instruction; when introducing the heart, the author may give the students the opportunity to explore how the heart works, where it is, and what its evolutionary history is. The students can then follow the links that intuitively engage their interest. Offering hypertext links to all sets of information is critical to give students the opportunity to be independent learners, escaping the linear routine of a textbook, and allowing them to make choices about their learning and actively engage in the connection of the new material to their prior knowledge.

An important issue to consider when authoring Web pages for instruction is document design. The document should not detain the student's attention with flashy backgrounds or fonts. Layout, colors, images, backgrounds, and fonts should be purposefully chosen so that the student's attention can be devoted to the content rather than the interface. Another important feature an author should build into a document is navigational cues. A student should never feel lost in a maze of links, but rather comforted by a consistent link back to the first page, which is usually found in one of the corners of the page or at the bottom. Background colors can also be effectively used to categorize pages. Lastly, Web pages should adhere to the same standards of "chunking" of information as any other presentation tool. "Miller's magic number" of seven plus or minus two suggests that the mind can consider only between five and nine pieces of information at any given time. When authoring a Web page, the teacher must adhere to this standard and chunk content, graphics, sound and video clips, animations, and simulations appropriately to maximize students' learning.

TEACHER PRACTICE

Create Your Own Science Web Page
Try creating a Web page for science activities.

CHAPTER REVIEW

Secondary preservice teachers are increasingly using computers to teach science in their practicum classrooms. This attitude may result from two reasons. Current teacher education programs offer mandatory or optional courses in computer applications. In these courses, preservice teachers are introduced to multimedia programs such as PowerPoint, HyperStudio, and HyperCard. Also, preservice teachers are encouraged by their cooperating teachers to use computers in science. During practicum, computer-literate preservice teachers attempt to use computers in a variety of ways, particularly when they are encouraged by cooperating teachers who use computers to facilitate scientific inquiry.

This chapter has taken you through various forms of electronic-based interactive learning: surfing the Internet, searching through SemNet for representing knowledge structures in science, and creating your own Web pages. Conceptual-change teaching is possible with teacher- and/or student-constructed computer simulations, animations, and concept maps.

Increasing number of science teachers are learning to augment their teaching with computer tools.

PROBES

1. Search the Internet for science-related projects. List the appropriate URL for each source cited.
2. Search the Internet to write a two-page report on one of the following topics. Cite all locations used for evidence of research.
   - Thalidomide was a drug given to pregnant women in the early 1960s to reduce morning sickness. Unfortunately, the drug caused irreparable damage to the developing fetus. Explain how the Ames test could have prevented this tragedy.
   - How did the lowly lichen play a part in the 1986 accident at Chernobyl?
   - Is Fluosol the blood replacement of the future? Explain.
   - Investigate the Human Genome Project, which represents seventeen nations and has a budget of over $1 billion. Why do you think this project has been compared to the Manhattan Project?
   - Recombinant DNA has produced human insulin in bacteria. Because millions of people suffer from diabetes, the market for human insulin is enormous and so are the profits. Because of economic pressures, the nature of scientific research has changed from one of sharing information through publishing to one of patents and secretiveness. Companies are unwilling to release any breakthroughs for fear that their ideas might stolen. Scientific research, at least in some fields, is no longer controlled by researchers, but by investors who seek the advice of accountants and lawyers. Should government remove biotechnology from private enterprise? (Barker, 1997)
3. Examine a hypermedia program to illustrate Howard Gardner's theory of multiple intelligences such as text (linguistic), statistical charts (logical-mathematical), illustrations (spatial), sound (musical), video presentation (bodily-kinesthetic), discussing a hypertext (interpersonal), and personal reflections in the electronic journal (intrapersonal).
4. In your practicum, help students do a hypermedia project that will illustrate some of White's memory elements.
5. What are some of the computer microworlds available to the secondary teachers? (Find out!)

CHAPTER 11

The Science-Technology-Society-Environment Connection

STUDY QUESTIONS

1. What is meant by the term "designed world?"

2. What are the differences between science and technology?

3. What arguments would you advance for integrating science-technology-society-environment (STSE) in the existing science curriculum?

4. What is meant by the term "sustainable development?"

5. What are some principles and guidelines for sustainable development?

6. What are some appropriate teaching strategies for STSE teaching?

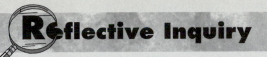

Reflective Inquiry

PAWEL'S VOICE

The Science-Technology-Society-Environment (STSE) model sets the basis for an in-depth exploration of chemistry curriculum sections that in most cases are labeled as "optional extensions." To my knowledge not too many science teachers are currently considering such extensions. And that is a sad reality. As a student teacher I have witnessed that most valuable learning takes place through the process of inquiry. Consider for example the section on chemical equilibrium. It is ultimately the study of chemical industries that provides students with a clear understanding of equilibrium laws and principles. The optional environment-technology project of the Haber process allowed my grade 12 students to fully comprehend the concepts of Le Chatelier's principle. Through the translation of their knowledge about equilibrium from their textbook to a real-life setting, students not only mastered the theory but also discovered meaningful and fascinating conjunctions leading to that "otherwise tedious information."

JOURNAL ACTIVITY

Different Ways of Teaching Science Content

In high school, science is usually taught as facts from the textbook and notes from the teacher. How else might a teacher teach science content? Write about your experiences or observations of another teacher or speculate on other approaches to teaching science.

In Chapter 1, we stated that science can be legitimately taught from a science-technology-society-environment (STSE) perspective. Besides teaching theoretical science we also attached technological, social, and environmental characteristics to science. In the last eight chapters we focused on a variety of ways of learning *about* science. In this chapter we would like to pay closer attention to technology education (the *use* of science) and also to explore the social character of science in more detail.

K–12 education reforms underscore the importance of technology education and the social aspects of science for all young people. Influential documents such as *A Nation at Risk* (National Commission on Excellence in Education, 1983), *Educating Americans for the 21st Century* (National Science Board, 1983), *Science for All Americans* (AAAS, 1989), and *Benchmarks for Science Literacy* (AAAS, 1993) have promoted including technology and issue-based science in the context of science education. Two of the content standards in the National Science Education Standards (NRC, 1996) are concerned with *science and technology* and the *personal and social character of science*.

⊠ THE DESIGNED WORLD

Understanding the designed world through the eyes of science is important if we are to understand the relevance of science in our lives. We can use technology to do science. We also discuss applications of science in designing technological products. Scientific knowledge and understanding are applied to design an artifact. Design technology "involves practical reasoning and relevance in authentic contexts and provides for dynamic and reflective practice among both students and teachers" (Raizen, Sellwood, Todd & Vickers, 1995, p. 18). When students contextualize the learned concepts in real-world problems, they are engaged in creative and complex thinking. Figure 11-1 illustrates the relationship between science and technology.

Students should have an experiential basis from which to understand the role science plays in the development and application of technology, as well as the role technology plays in the practice of science. A problem-solving approach, with a combination of knowledge and skills from different fields such as mathematics, social sciences, and art, is used in the design process. Figure 11-2 illustrates a dynamic design process model in which the learner may enter and exit at any point.

The nine elements of the design process model and descriptions of each element are:

Analysis and investigation. Identify a problem in the real-world setting for authentic analysis and investigation.

Framing of a design brief. Generate a statement of what the solution to the problem will do. List the constraints in reaching the solution. Refer to this brief throughout the design process so that your task remains on track.

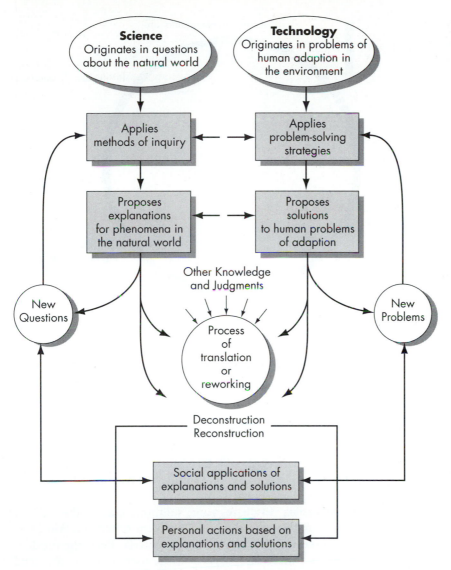

FIGURE 11-1
The relationship between science and technology (*NOTE: From Technology Education in the Classroom* (p. 12), by S. A. Raizen, P. Sellwood, R. D. Todd, and M. Vickers, 1995, San Francisco: Jossey-Bass. Copyright 1995 by Jossey-Bass. Reprinted with permission.)

Information gathering. Before attempting to develop solutions, research what others have done to solve this problem. Find out what factors influence the problem.

Generation of alternative solutions. Look at many possible alternative solutions to the problem. Defer criticism until you have proposed a range of solutions. This stage calls for originality, flexibility, and self-confidence. Initiate thoughts in your own mind and then share your ideas with others so that you can clarify and refine your ideas. This process is called *cognitive modeling.*

FIGURE 11-2
The design process model
(*NOTE:* From *Report of the
Commission on Technology
Education for the State of
New Jersey,* 1987. © 1986
P. Hutchinson, *TIES*
magazine.)

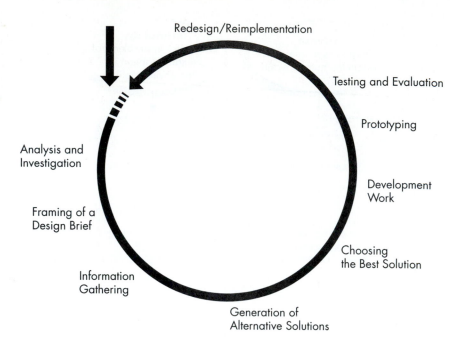

Choosing the best solution. Choose the best solution and be able to
defend your position based on your own situation and your design
brief.

Development work. Make various models. Use sketches and color
drawings, evolutionary models in flexible materials, mathematical
simulations, and technical drawings. Refer to your design brief and
initial statement of criteria for the final outcome of this step.

Prototyping. Develop a full-size model after you have decided on the
size and materials. Appearance is important.

Testing and evaluation. Evaluate your solution against the criteria
developed in your brief and the initial problem statement. Also, test
the solution in terms of the overall design criteria. Does the product
work properly and meet the purpose of the user? Is there any need
for improvements? What is required to enhance future design work?

Redesign and reimplementation. Fine-tune the solution if the product is
produced in any quantity. How does this solution change the
condition? School design work often does not reach the real-world
application.

Dick Hopkins teaches manufacturing and industrial physics in a secondary school in Ontario. He involves his students in project-based learning that teaches them how to solve open-ended "real-world" problems.
Students learn how to work together with peers and the community. They
take on community projects from conception to completion. The teacher
is a fellow learner with his students. Projects have included the following

(Hopkins, 1993, p.3): solar cars entered in the secondary school race for the Solar Energy Society (grade 10); a collapsible sheep shelter for the Ministry of Natural Resources (grade 10); an automatic sheep watering station for remote applications for the Ministry of Natural Resources (grade 10); and a mobilization bed for patients needing physiotherapy treatments, which is microprocessor controlled and pneumatically operated (grade 12).

 PEER TALK

Conceptual Analysis of the Design Process Model

Identify several real-world problems based on major ideas in your science curriculum. Choose one of the problems and carry out a conceptual analysis based on the components of the design process model in Figure 11-2. Examples might be designing a robot using your knowledge of electricity or a toy glider using the principles of flight.

An Experiential Learning Model for Science and Technology

The design process engages students in hands-on learning such as investigating, designing, building, and testing a product. As mentioned earlier, experiential learning in the design process model also involves students in critical thinking—questioning, rethinking, and reconstructing their understanding. Figure 11-3 is an example of an experiential teaching model for both science and technology education developed by the National Center for Improving Science Education.

FIGURE 11-3

A teaching model for science and technology (*NOTE:* From *Technology Education in the Classroom* (p. 55), by S. A. Raizen, P. Sellwood, R. D. Todd, and M. Vickers, 1995, San Francisco: Jossey-Bass. Copyright 1995 by Jossey-Bass. Reprinted with permission.)

Stages	Examples for Science	Examples for Technology
Invitation	Observe the natural world. Ask questions about the natural world. State possible hypothesis.	Observe the world made by humans. Recognize a human problem. Identify possible solutions.
Exploration, Discovery, Creativity	Engage in focused play. Look for information. Observe specific phenomena. Collect and organize data. Select appropriate resources. Design and conduct experiments. Engage in debate. Define parameters of an investigation.	Brainstorm possible alternatives. Experiment with materials. Design a model. Employ problem-solving strategies. Discuss solutions with others. Evaluate choices. Identify risks and consequences. Analyze data.
Proposing Explanations and Solutions	Communicate information and ideas. Construct a new explanation. Undergo evaluation by peers. Determine appropriate closure.	Construct and explain a model. Constructively review a solution. Express multiple answers/ solutions. Integrate a solution with existing knowledge and experiences.
Taking Action	Apply knowledge and skills. Share information and ideas. Ask new questions.	Make decisions. Transfer knowledge and skills. Develop products and promote ideas.

Technology education ought to co-exist with the science program. It is important to give more prominence to design and problem solving in science, thereby integrating the theoretical and practical strands of science and technology. Since science teachers are normally specialists in teaching science, it is often helpful to collaborate with technology teachers to develop lesson sequences that combine science and technology. Sharing of equipment, tools, and facilities is also a possibility. All secondary students should be given at least a few opportunities to translate their theoretical and practical knowledge learned in science to designing and building a technological artifact or device.

Implementing a Design Approach

Raizen et al. (1995) suggest the following ideas (pp. 128–129):

- Provide students opportunities to work collaboratively on design projects so that social discourse is carried on—to communicate their ideas, to suggest approaches and solutions, and to use data and persuasive argument about some aspect of learning.
- Build in opportunities for student groups to present their work to their classmates.
- See that the groups work successfully—students assign responsibility, ensure equal access by all participants, listen and consider all students' input, and use direct and honest talk.
- Allow students to group with friends, as this may enhance the work.
- Take affirmative steps to encourage girls' access and full participation. Same-sex groups may eliminate the gender problem associated with boys dominating the construction of activities.
- Establish clear expectations for group work and communication; use of cooperative working groups provides a foundation for effective teamwork.

Assessment

A design process naturally involves hands-on and minds-on learning. Traditional paper-and-pencil tests will not suffice. It is necessary to "[r]ethink how to assess and measure changes in student knowledge and development" (Raizen et al., 1995, p. 140). Teachers should gather data about student learning at several key points: discussions between teacher and students; students' views on open-ended questions; peer discourse; observations of students' work; and a review of final products. A range of assessment activities must be consciously ongoing and systematic. Engaging students in active inquiry, observing and questioning students, and regularly reflecting upon and documenting the results of students' work all help the teacher become proficient.

It is important to ensure that recording assessment data does not interfere with teaching and learning. You can record assessment information while you facilitate activities and monitor students' performance. Inform your students and their parents about your practices, criteria, standards, and language you will use to assess the quality of students' work so that a shared view is established.

Assessment criteria may be developed based on the components of the design process model described earlier. Performance indicators can reflect a Likert-type scale: *poor, fair, satisfactory, good,* and *excellent.* Some items for the assessment scale could be as follows:

1. Identifies real-world problems using human or nonhuman factors.
2. Frames the statement of the problem.

3. Applies scientific knowledge.
4. Applies knowledge of materials and use of tools.
5. Develops a range of solutions.
6. Selects the best solution based on defensible criteria.
7. Constructs the model using predetermined criteria.
8. Communicates the design process through words, graphs, and models.
9. Takes responsibility.

We have attempted to indicate the interdisciplinary character of science and technology. Teachers must deliberately make this connection for students. The world's economic progress depends on future citizens. The vision and mission of uniting science and technology in our schools may continue to make our world prosperous.

TEACHER PRACTICE

Implementation of the Design Process Model

Design a product based on your conceptual analysis of a real-world problem in the preceding "Peer Talk" box. This can be a term project carried out by small groups. Maintain a portfolio of your work: making the product, meeting the requirements of the design brief, using appropriate and cost-effective materials, developing mechanical graphics or computer-aided design (CAD), understanding of the subject knowledge, displaying knowledge of marketing skills, and relating to the needs of the user.

THE SCIENCE-TECHNOLOGY-SOCIETY (STS) INCLUSIVE SCIENCE CURRICULUM

STS science education is a movement with multiple strands, each having its own origins, history, and tensions. Unfortunately, it lacks a coherent and well-articulated message; nevertheless, STS educators have developed conceptual frameworks, curriculum, and implementation strategies. There are many possibilities for infusing STS education into the school curriculum (Solomon & Aikenhead, 1994): S-STS (Science through Science, Technology, and Society) was developed in the USA in 1985, and Science in Society, developed in Canada in 1988, and SISCON (Science in Social Context), initiated in Britain in 1983, are examples of separate, free-standing STS courses.

Until recently, science educators and teachers typically were prepared and interested in teaching only "valid" science (Ziman, 1994). Currently, STS advocates have made science education "relevant"; the fruits of their labor during the last three decades are clearly evident in research reports, policy documents, textbooks, and curriculum materials, as well as both secondary and postsecondary education. STS education is one of the seven science content standards identified for K–12 students in the 1996 National Research Council report. The council has spelled out the relationship between science and technology and detailed the relevance of science to students' personal and social lives. Social events of today's world have indeed played a timely role in making STS goals and ideas more relevant in school science curricula. But the extent to which the school science curriculum should include STS ideas has been always a contentious issue.

McConnell (1982) argues that STS education requires developing particular skills for evaluating and using appropriate knowledge, a commitment to particular beliefs and values, and converting attitudes, skills, and values into action. Earlier STS programs were targeted toward high school students only. Currently the National Science Teachers Association (NSTA) acknowledges that STS represents an authentic context for learning science for all students (NSTA, 1990). STS is relevant for the future scientist as well as the rest of the population.

> Project Synthesis, funded by the National Science Foundation in 1978, was an endeavor by an STS group to arrive at recommendations for an integrated STS approach to science education.

Significance of STS Education

Learning to lead a healthy life is important for adolescents. This is the age when students experiment with tobacco, alcohol, drugs, and sex. Consuming unnecessary foods is part of most adolescents' lifestyles. The consequences of unhealthy habits are costly and risky. Guiding adolescents in the understanding of science to make informed decisions about health-related issues is a worthwhile goal in science education.

At a more societal level, students are aware of ecological problems such as acid rain, waste management, and ozone depletion. The study of natural hazards such as floods, earthquakes, wildfires, and volcanic eruptions should not be ignored. STS education encourages adolescents to become socially and morally responsible—to think, decide, and act on issues.

The Character of STS Science

With the advent of STS curricula in the 20th century, science truly reveals its human, social, and technological character. STS education addresses what "valid" science "leaves unsaid" (Ziman, 1994, p. 22). "The movement for STS education springs from so many different sources, and flows in so many different channels, that it does not have a shape that can be grasped mentally and described as a whole" (p. 21). Although the "sources and channels" metaphor portrays a multidisciplinary character, in this book we are mainly concerned about the science education orientation. Even from a science education perspective, STS education is a complex web.

Curricular Frameworks of STS Teaching

Aikenhead (1994) identifies four aspects to be considered when planning for STS teaching:

1. *Function*—what are the goals for teaching science through STS?
2. *Content*—what should be taught?

3. *Structure*—how should the science and STS content be integrated?
4. *Sequence*—how can we design STS instruction (p. 47)?

The goals of teaching science through STS are the following:

- To reverse the existing negative trends in enrollments, achievement, and science career choice.
- To increase general interest in and public understanding of science, particularly for the bright creative students who are discouraged by a boring and irrelevant curriculum.
- To fill a critical void in the traditional curriculum—the social responsibility in collective decision making on issues related to science and technology (Aikenhead, 1994, p. 49).

The priorities among these and other similar goals might be different, but they have guided curriculum development in STS science. An intended outcome of these goals is scientific literacy for all students: future scientists and engineers and future "attentive" citizens who would make well-informed intellectual decisions. In this process science content is not neglected.

STS science includes both traditional and STS content. Aikenhead (1994, p. 52) offers the following examples of STS content:

- A technological artifact, process, or expertise
- The interactions between technology and society
- A societal issue related to science or technology
- Social science content that sheds light on a societal issue related to science and technology
- A philosophical, historical, or social issue within the scientific or technological community

There are many ways of integrating science with STS content, ranging from traditional science with a mere mention of STS to STS content with a mere mention of science. We will focus on the following three "categories of STS science" (Aikenhead, 1994, pp. 55–56).

Purposeful Infusion of STS Content

This category consists of traditional school science plus a series of short studies (about one-half to two hours in length) of STS content integrated into science topics. Students are partially assessed on their understanding of the STS content (for instance, 10 percent STS and 90 percent science). North American STS programs in this category include the following: *Harvard Project Physics* (U. S.: Holt, Rinehart, & Winston); *Science and Social Issues* (U. S.: Walch), *Science and Societal Issues* (U. S.: Iowa State University), *Nelson Chemistry* (Canada: Nelson); and *Science, Technology and Society,* Block J (U. S.: New York State Education).

Singular Discipline through STS Content

STS content serves as the organizer for the science content, which is selected from one discipline. Students are partially assessed on their understanding of the STS content (for instance, 20 percent STS and 80 percent science). North American STS programs in this category include the following: *ChemCon* (U. S.: American Chemical Society); *Science and Society Teaching Units* (Toronto, Canada: Ontario Institute for Studies in Education); *Chemical Education for Public Understanding* (U. S.: Addison-Wesley); and *Science Education for Public Understanding Program* (Berkeley, CA: University of California at Berkeley).

Science through STS Content

STS content serves as the organizer for the science content, which is multidisciplinary, as dictated by the STS content. The science topics represent important science topics from a variety of traditional school science courses. Students are assessed on their understanding of the STS content, but still not as extensively as they are on the pure science content (for example, 30 percent STS and 70 percent science). North American STS programs in this category include: *Logical Reasoning in Science and Technology* (Toronto, Canada: Wiley of Canada); *Modular STS* (U. S.: Wausau, Wisconsin); and *Global Science* (U. S.: Kendall/Hunt).

In each of these categories, STS content dictates the organization and sequence of science content (Aikenhead, 1994, p. 54). Students draw upon science content to address STS issues.

According to Aikenhead, the instructional sequence of a lesson or a unit is cyclical. The teaching sequence begins with a societal problem (a real-life situation). To understand and to respond to this societal problem, technology is used. To fully understand the technological and societal issues, students must study the science content (on a need-to-know basis). With the learning and understanding of science, technology can be focused and redeveloped. Finally, students address the original social problem and arrive at a decision. "Students make thoughtful decisions informed by (1) an in-depth understanding of the underlying science, (2) a grasp of the relevant technology, and (3) an awareness of the guiding values" (Aikenhead, 1994, p. 58). Alternatively, students may begin with technology or science and then move to society. The teacher plans the time allotted to each component of the STS sequence.

In STS science, science is studied in a social-technological context. Students constantly link science with their everyday world. A good STS education is relevant, realistic, and rigorous.

The Science Education for Public Understanding Program (SEPUP) is an issue-oriented program that develops an "understanding of the science and the problem-solving processes related to social issues, without taking an advocacy position" (Thier & Nagle, 1994, p. 76). Teaching and learning strategies include "activities and investigations, discussions and debates, themes, and questions" (p. 76). Students "learn to understand scientific evidence and its limitations, assess risks and benefits, ask questions, and make decisions based on evidence rather than on pure emotion.

Teachers in issue-oriented classrooms create situations where understanding can grow, where issues can be explored, and where students can interact. The teacher models tentativeness, objectivity, and nonadvocacy, and is willing to say, 'I don't know, let's find out.' . . . The SEPUP approach facilitates understanding of the available evidence so that students can come to their own conclusions about the issues. . . . This kind of science education helps students develop the knowledge and judgment necessary to make effective, evidence-based decisions regarding both their own health and welfare and the variety of science-based public issues they will encounter as participating members of a democratic society" (pp. 76–77). In SEPUP, the science content is not "viewed as enriching the science content, but as providing absolutely essential evidence, necessary for an understanding of the issue and possible decisions. The central role of evidence-based decision-making results in a program in which key science concepts and processes are studied in depth" (p. 77).

STS science is student oriented rather than scientist oriented, as in the case of traditional science. In Figure 11-4, the student occupies the central position. Students attempt to make sense of their everyday experiences, which involves the integration of their social environment (social), their constructed environment (technology), and their natural environment (science) (see the solid arrows in Figure 11-4). The broken arrows in Figure 11-4 represent the teaching of science (natural phenomena) through students' technological and social environments. Managing these environments contributes to sustainable living.

Five Domains for STS Assessment

The five domains for STS teaching and assessment are the following (Yager, 1994, p. 35):

- Concept domain (mastering basic content constructs)
- Process domain (learning the skills scientists use)
- Application and connection domain (using concepts and processes in new situations)

FIGURE 11-4
The essence of STS education (*NOTE:* Excerpted by permission of the publisher from Solomon, J., & Aikenhead, G. (Eds.), *STS Education: International Perspectives on Reform* (New York: Teachers College Press, © by Teachers College, Columbia University. All rights reserved, p. 48.)

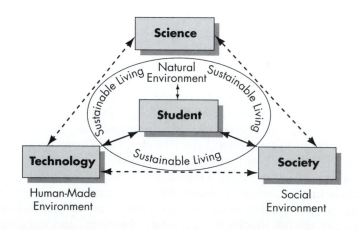

- Creativity domain (improving quantity and quality of questions, explanations, and tests for the validity of personally generated explanations)
- Attitudinal domain (developing more positive feelings concerning the usefulness of science, science study, science teachers, and science careers)

 TEACHER PRACTICE

Role Playing an STS Problem

Select an STS problem—for example, forgery. Role play this problem. Incorporate the learning of science principles as part of this play.

✵ ENVIRONMENTAL ETHICS AND SUSTAINABLE LIVING

What Do We Mean by Environmental Ethics?

There is a story that in 1855, President Franklin Pierce offered to buy a large area of Native American land (now occupied by the city of Seattle), and ordered Chief Seathl's people to move to a reservation. This is a brief excerpt from his reply to the President:

> If I decide to accept your offer, I will make one condition. The white man must treat the beasts of this land as his brothers. I am a savage and do not understand any other way. I have seen a thousand rotting buffaloes on the prairies left by the white man who shot them from a passing train. I am a savage and I do not understand how the smoking iron horse can be more important than the buffalo that we kill only to stay alive. What is man without beasts? If all the beasts were gone, men would die from great loneliness of spirit, for whatever happens to the beasts also happens to man. All things are connected. (Miller, 1990, p. 35)

Environmental ethics is concerned with the paradox of decentering humans and at the same time placing humanity at the center of things (Torgerson, 1985). It explores the fundamental question of the place of human beings in the natural order, and the respect and protection we owe to other forms of life. When students study sustainable development issues, they automatically participate in environmental problems (for example, locating a new landfill), in ethics and value-based conflict resolutions, and in making moral choices. For example, an ethical question about preservation of wildlife might be, "Do we exploit or sustain wildlife?" How do students "manage and enhance their own environment and economy for the benefit of the present and the future" (Soprovich,

When students discuss the issues raised in Chief Seathl's letter, they become aware of the cultural differences in the way humans relate to their environment.

1990; The World Commission and Environment and Development, 1987)? High school students at Vincent Massey Collegiate in Winnipeg, working as electronic multimedia ethnographers, are learning about the Seine River ecosystem in order to make a difference in their future urban lives. Learning science in this manner involves personal responsibility, collective agreement, decision making, and action taking in preserving wildlife and protecting the river ecosystem. When students attempt to deal with scientific problems from an ethical point of view, they become an integral part of nature.

Challenge to Teachers

Amid classroom realities, how do teachers bring their students to meaningful conceptual understandings that include genuine experiences with ethical issues? The classroom and its resources are a fixed locale, both physical and temporal. It is easy to outline sustainable development principles and guidelines such as **stewardship, shared responsibility, prevention, conservation,** and **recycling,** but it is a challenge to put these into practice in the classroom.

Yet for students to be successful in tackling ethical issues, it may be necessary to break the boundaries of the closed educational system. How does one get students involved in attempting to resolve environmental and economic issues? How do teachers enhance "relational learning" (Ebenezer & Gaskell, 1995) and examine scientific knowledge claims based on "contextual values" (Bingle & Gaskell, 1994)? What might be some of the more ecologically sound approaches to making ethical decisions? How might students make and defend appropriate value judgments based on personal values and belief system (Zoller, 1987)?

Eijkelhof (1985) outlines three main aims of ethics in science education: (1) learning to recognize ethical issues; (2) developing analytical skills; and (3) tolerating and reducing disagreement. Students must learn to recognize that often several alternative solutions are possible and that the choice among these depends not only on facts, but also the opinions, beliefs, and ethical considerations of those concerned. It is reasonable to expect students to be able to discuss value issues rationally, to justify their moral judgments, and to describe the process of their ethical thinking. Since ethical issues give rise to emotional reactions, students need to experience and learn how to express their feelings and ideas on an issue without fear of reproach, and to learn how and on what basis to accept, seek, and reconcile other points of view.

Adolescents are intellectually capable of learning how to reflect on the nature and role of ethics in science-related issues. They are also capable of making responsible decisions and taking appropriate actions when dealing with controversial issues. They can learn to cope with a democratic and pluralistic society that gives rise to complex ethical dilemmas, and can be taught how to make moral choices based on trade-offs, benefits, and costs. Science education, therefore, should make use of controversial issues in

Stewardship requires us to manage the environment and economy for the benefit of present and future generations.

Shared responsibility requires each of us to be responsible for decisions and actions for sustaining the environment and economy.

Prevention requires taking care of adverse environmental and economic impacts of policies, programs, and decisions.

Conservation requires that we maintain ecological and biological balance by making wise and efficient use of our renewable and nonrenewable resources.

Recycling requires that we endeavor to reduce, reuse, and recover the products of our society.

which scientific knowledge and skills can be used in the context of ethics and moral values.

 TEACHER PRACTICE

Searching the Internet for Environment-Related Ethical Issues
Search the Internet for environment-related ethical issues. List the appropriate URL for each source cited.

Toward More Socially and Personally Relevant Science

Education about *sustainable development* (the interdependence and balancing of the opposite poles of environmental preservation and economic growth) inherently addresses ethical objectives in science education. For instance, science concepts belong to highly developed and systematically structured disciplines, whereas the vocabulary required for examining ethical issues in sustainable development is more disparate; it is drawn from a variety of disciplinary and nondisciplinary language domains. Based on the idea that sustainable development is an educative process, the K–12 science curriculum emphasizes the integration of science with societal issues, economic decisions, ethics, and values. This integration characterizes the "multi-disciplinary nature of environmental studies encouraging students to think critically about problems, to form opinions, to shape beliefs, and to make choices that contribute to quality of life" (Derkach, 1990, p. 161). Thus, inherent in *any* discussion of sustainable development in science education are ethical issues as well as the discipline content knowledge. Any classroom discussion of ethical problems warns against adopting an authoritarian stance of "right" or "wrong." Instead, it emphasizes the need to place the learners in decision-making situations involving value judgments and, through this process, to guide them in developing ethical ways of thinking. Science education should help today's adolescents to consider ethical issues, think about systems, view the world, and work with others, ultimately resulting in students being able to understand and apply scientific evidence, weigh and take responsibility for trade-offs, and live in greater harmony with their environment.

Chisman and Holbrook (1990) have established three important criteria for developing citizens who are literate in sustainable development: relevance, practicality, and value orientation. "Relevance implies the use of community resources and the incorporation of local issues and practices into the curriculum; practicality means activity-based learning (doing and acting), with the inclusion of gaining balanced points of view and training in the recognition of bias; and values involve cultural issues, personal interdependence and informed judgments, both from a holistic view for the world and from a local society perspective" (Chisman & Holbrook, p. 235). To adopt these criteria for teaching and learning science, science teachers must choose to move from a *positivist* paradigm to a *personal-social constructivist* paradigm. The latter involves exploring students' views of socio-scientific issues and, through a negotiating process, helping them make decisions and take actions based on moral values and ethical principles. To practice ethics in science education from a constructivist paradigm, teachers must be able to break out of traditional teaching models and willing to take professional risks (Agne, 1986).

For alternative directions in science education to take place, science teachers must respond to the global challenge of the 1990s. There is a need for students to understand the concept of sustainable development that falls within the framework of the Native American notion of stewardship—communion with nature and the planet as well as managing and enhancing environment and economy for the benefit of present and future generations (Soprovich, 1990). Similarly, the United Nations Commission on Environment and Development describes sustainable development as a "path of environmental, economic, social, and political progress that meets the needs of the present without compromising the ability of future generations to meet their own needs" (World Commission on Environment and Development, 1987, p. 18). Francisco Madrid, a biology teacher educator, teaches his students the concept of sustainable development through the following experimental activity.

ACTIVITY 11-1

THE EFFECT OF ACID RAIN ON THE SOIL FAUNA

Purpose:

To create increased awareness and understanding of the concept of sustainable development and living
To recognize the importance of maintaining biological diversity
To better understand ecosystems
To develop scientific inquiry skills

Foci:

Students will:

- extract organisms from the soil samples
- tabulate and analyze the data obtained from the extraction of organisms from the soil samples

- simulate the effect of acid rain on several soil samples
- explain the concept of pH and its influence on diversity of organisms in a soil sample
- research the issue of acid rain and its diverse societal consequences
- assess the impact of pollutants on the population level of organisms and species diversity

I. Determination of Animal Diversity

Materials for One Sample:
2-L soda pop bottle
60-watt desk lamp
¼-inch mesh screen (diameter of the bottle)

20 ml alcohol (70%, as a preser-
vative)
soil collected from the schoolyard
15 ml vinegar or acetic acid to
treat the soil
stereoscopic microscope

The experimental procedure for soil
fauna sampling involves the following
steps:

a. collecting soil samples

b. mounting the extraction apparatus

c. treating soil samples

d. counting and identifying specimens

Collecting Soil Samples

Collect soil samples in an undisturbed
area at the back of the school, close
to trees or a park near the school,

preferably from soil littered with
leaves from previous years.

1. Place the inverted section of the
funnel collector bottle to determine
the area of soil to be sampled.

2. Scoop the soil with the small
shovel to a depth of 3–5 cm.

3. Place the sample in a plastic bag
for further analysis in the laboratory.

4. Repeat this procedure to collect
several soil samples.

Mounting the Soda Bottle Funnel Collector Apparatus

Design the funnel collector apparatus
from a soda bottle as shown in Figure
11-5. Take this opportunity to discuss
the technological problems.

FIGURE 11-5
Soda bottle funnel collector
system

30 cm

① cut here

② 2-liter soda bottle

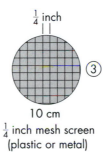

$\frac{1}{4}$ inch

③

10 cm

$\frac{1}{4}$ inch mesh screen
(plastic or metal)

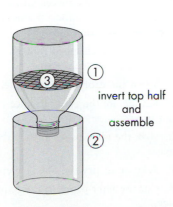

③ ①

invert top half
and
assemble

②

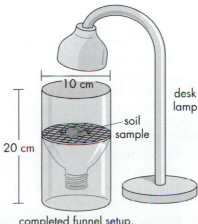

10 cm

desk lamp

soil sample

20 cm

completed funnel setup,
ready for operation

Treating Soil Samples

1. Place the soil samples in several funnel collectors.

2. Treat half the soil samples by adding approximately 15 ml vinegar or acetic acid *(treated soil sample)*.

3. Add 15 ml tap water to the other half of the soil samples *(untreated soil sample)*.

4. Allow all soil samples to rest for about 5 minutes.

5. Install a 60-watt lamp directly above each soil sample.

Note: Predict and explain the results of the contaminated and the noncontaminated samples, and what will happen to the soil sample when it is placed under the lamp.

6. Add 20 ml 70% alcohol to the bottom of the funnel collector apparatus. (*Note:* Add a drop of liquid detergent to break the surface tension of the solution so that the organisms will sink.)

7. Leave the system to work overnight.

Counting and Identifying Specimens

1. Transfer the contents (mixture of 20 ml alcohol with organisms) of the lower section of the funnel collector system to a 10-by-10-by-4-cm plastic or glass tray.

2. Observe the contents of the mixture under a stereoscopic microscope or a powerful magnifying glass.

3. Count the number of organisms in the sample of mixture.

Note: Why does the contaminated soil sample present so few and the uncontaminated soil present so many?

4. Sort and tabulate the organisms according to their shape.

5. Identify the specimens using a pictorial book of soil fauna.

6. Tabulate the results in a chart.

Note: Are students' predictions and assumptions validated? Grade 11 or 12 students may conduct statistical analysis and calculate the index of diversity.

Discussion Questions

1. What are the effects of polluted or contaminated soil?

2. What is meant by species diversity? How does it affect environmental health?

3. What are the social and economic implications of acid rain–contaminated soils?

4. How does acid rain affect the sustainability of the soil?

II. Determination of Soil Acidity

Materials

treated and untreated soil samples prepared as in Part I
funnel collector system
70% alcohol
one red cabbage
water
hot plate
beaker
filter paper or bleached coffee filters

Red Cabbage Water: Indicator for pH

1. Chop cabbage into small pieces.

2. Put the cabbage pieces into a beaker and add a sufficient amount of water to cover the cabbage.

3. Simmer the chopped cabbage until the water turns deep purple.

4. Strain the cabbage juice and cool.

5. Refrigerate the cabbage juice when not in use.

6. Soak the filter paper in the cabbage juice.

7. Bake or air-dry the filter paper.

8. Cut the filter paper to the required size.

Testing the Acidity of Soil

1. Wash and dry the bottom section of the funnel collector system.

2. Place a piece of filter paper treated with red cabbage solution in the bottom of all containers before resetting the funnel collector system.

3. Re-install the funnel collector system with the soil samples (treated and untreated).

4. Add water carefully so it slowly percolates through the soil samples.

5. Observe the change in color of the filter paper.

6. Document the results.

Discussion Questions

1. Where does acid rain come from?

2. What are the effects of acid rain on aquatic systems (for example, lakes, rivers), plants and animals, buildings, and statues (for example, concrete, marble)?

3. What can we do to control acid rain?

4. Suggest solutions to improve living conditions for the numerous and diverse species of microorganisms living in the soil.

5. How would solutions to the problem of acid rain affect the workers in fossil-fuel-run industries (for example, thermoelectric plants)?

Summary

This activity guides students in laboratory techniques such as extracting soil, comparing soil samples of different pH values, measuring the number of organisms and species diversity, and simulating the impact of acid rain on soil fauna. The experimental results are used as the basis for discussion of the issues of acid rain pollution and need for economic development and job production (thermoelectric plants). Additional research via the Internet and implications on sustainable living may be discussed.

Pink indicates an acid; green or blue indicates a base.

P-STAR CONFERENCE PAPER (11-1)

Debate and Argumentation

Karen Knight

Karen conducted the following lesson plan in her junior secondary science class. Karen taught her students how to debate by having them take part in a real debate. Her work with students also appeared in the local newspaper.

Unit: Human Impacts on the Environment

Strategy: Debate and Argumentation
Topic: Environmental Ethics: Shallow vs. Deep Ecology, The Gaia Theory

Resolution: "Be it resolved that a central goal of human activity is the preservation of ecosystems, where human beings work with and not against nature."

What Is a Debate? A debate contains a resolution on an issue and is an argument between two teams that follows a set of rules and time limits. One team is in favor of the resolution and wants change (the government), and one team is opposed to the resolution (the opposition). Each team tries to convince the *audience* of their position—not each other.

Two Types of Debates:

1. Policy: "We should do something about . . ."
2. Value: "This is better than . . ."

Strategy:

1. Define and discuss the resolution with the class so that all students understand the issue being debated. Essentially this discussion is a brief review of the unit just studied on human impacts on the environment.
2. Divide the class into groups of five or six students. Each group needs one large sheet of paper and a marker. They must come up with five arguments or ideas that support the resolution and five ideas or arguments against the resolution (students may use ideas from the sample activity chart to activate prior knowledge).
3. Each group elects one speaker to present their ten points to the class (some points will be presented by more than one group). Groups post their sheets at the front of the class.
4. *Flow chart on students' conceptions:* An exercise to keep the class engaged in the issue. After all groups have presented their ten arguments, the class develops a flow chart that combines ideas from all groups into one large sheet.

   Write down reasons why humans need to work in cooperation with nature. Continue with four to six different examples so that the entire class has an understanding of the resolution at hand, and an understanding of some of the issues on both sides of the argument.
5. *In-class debate:* Two teams are formed with two or four students on each side. Allow the students to pick their own partners. The debate may be set up so that each team must debate both sides of the resolution, or each team may choose to debate one side of the resolution. Using the in-class flow

TABLE 11-1

Humans need to work in cooperation with nature

For	Against	For	Against
President (government) Example: Chemical fertilizers used by farmers work against nature	→ Leader of the opposition Farmers need weed control to grow crops	2nd government speaker Chemical fertilizers increase the greenhouse effect	→ 2nd opposition speaker Fertilization increases the crop yields

chart and ideas from all the group work, the students on the debate teams write point-form speeches to be presented at a later date. The format of the speeches may be as follows:

a. *Introduction:* grabs the attention of the audience (the President defines the resolution)

b. *Argument #1:*
   • example/reason
   • example/reason
   • example/reason

   Argument #2
   • example/reason
   • example/reason
   • example/reason

   Argument #3
   • example/reason
   • example/reason
   • example/reason

c. *Conclusion:* briefly reiterates the two or three arguments presented, and ends on one solid concluding point. The rest of the class will vote for the debaters who have convinced them of their stand on the issue.

6. *Speeches from the floor:* These involve the entire class; students who have not prepared formal "speeches" on teams will have an opportunity to make impromptu comments on either side of the resolution. This may be done after the President and the leader of the opposition have spoken (half-time), or before the rebuttals.

The teacher calls on any student to give a 30- or 60-second opinion on the issue and keeps an ongoing list of student names to check off participants that have been called on.

Switching speakers in floor speeches: The first student starts speaking; then the teacher calls on the second student to jump in, or the second student is told to take the opposing view.

Personal Reflection

Debating in any subject area gives the teacher a fabulous opportunity to develop the following skills in the students:

- speaking and presentation
- research skills
- listening skills
- logic and listening
- understanding of different viewpoints

Since most of our personal interactions are oral rather than written, debating and public speaking are vital skills that are incredibly useful in real life. I can see a connection between subjects across the curriculum (Language Arts and Science, Language Arts and Social Studies, and so on).

Debating in the classroom is a very exciting and motivating strategy in any subject area. Students get caught up in the "argumentation" of issues, and they love to give their opinions and try to prove their points! The one drawback that I noticed in my grade 8 class was that it was the same students volunteering over and over again. Teachers have successfully used debating with the understanding that eventually everyone will have an opportunity to be involved in debate teams, in speeches from the floor, and as voting members of the audience. The teacher must keep an ongoing record of students' involvement to ensure inclusivity in the debate procedure. Introducing debating by allowing the students to choose their own topic in science class is a great way to get students motivated initially.

 TEACHER PRACTICE

Debating an STS Issue

Two groups of students will debate the issue of whether suntan lotions can prevent skin cancer caused by exposure to UV rays. One group of students will defend the notion that these lotions (for example, Coppertone SPF 45) have a high-performance sunblock formula that bonds to human skin and prevents UV absorption, ultimately preventing skin cancer caused by UV rays. The second group will argue the issue that the sunblock lotions are not as effective as they claim to be, and that prolonged usage of these lotions will have some negative side effects such as skin irritation and disorder.

⊗ CHAPTER REVIEW

In this chapter we have emphasized the importance of the designed world and issue-based teaching within science curricula. Through considering well-documented work of international experts, we have offered a few models to think about the STSE connection. Our preservice teachers' practice in a curriculum-and-instruction class and field setting suggests that issue-based teaching can easily be integrated into the science curricula.

The incorporation of environmental ethics in science curricula offers much promise for the improvement and maintenance of the earth's vital resources. Our students need to become aware of what it means to become "stewards" of the earth and to realize the need to embrace this role as responsible, caring citizens. Thus active participation in projects in which students learn about the environment, the economy, and social well-being must become a natural part of our science curricula.

PROBES

1. Develop a unit plan that reflects science through STSE teaching.
2. Teach your S-STSE unit and write a reflective report.
3. Identify a science-related societal problem. Have students research and write a simple play illustrating the societal problem chosen. Have students act out the play. What attitudes and dispositions do students display when they are engaged in a science activity of this type?
4. Identify STSE projects on the Internet. Give examples of projects in which students are engaged. Select one or two projects and write a report about the value of these projects.
5. Choose an STSE project from question 4 and design a scoring scheme using Yager's domains of assessment.

Suggestions for STSE projects include endangered species, waterfowl habitat, fisheries management, agroforestry, water resource management, biotechnology, and hazardous wastes.

CHAPTER 12

Science for All Students

STUDY QUESTIONS

1. What is meant by "science for all students"?

2. What considerations are essential to reach multicultural students?

3. What are the characteristics of special-needs students? How would you accommodate their needs?

4. How would you prepare students for further studies and scientific careers?

MICHELLE'S VOICE

I believe that science teachers need to take into account the needs of all of the students in their classes. Every student has his or her own individual needs, whether they are multicultural students, girls or boys, or special-needs students. I think it is difficult for teachers to adapt their styles and do research on what these students need because our time is limited. However, as teachers we should reach all our students. We have to continually be trying out different methods and strategies if we hope to reach all our students. Scientific literacy for all means a better nation.

JOURNAL ACTIVITY

Experience with Diverse Learners

What have your experiences been with diverse groups of students: those from minority groups, those who have special needs, and so on? Write about your experiences in your journal and share them with one of your peers.

At the end of her methods course in science, Michelle pointed out in her special-project paper that teachers must consider the needs of all their students. Michelle's goal is to develop a better nation by educating adolescents in science. We address her concerns about equity in this chapter by looking at additional curricular areas.

Thus far we have been considering several curricular areas that would contribute to the development of a scientifically literate person, and we have focused on the subject matter. This chapter will discuss some often-neglected areas that directly involve the learner:

- recognizing all cultures in the science class
- paying attention to girls in science
- meeting the needs of special students
- preparing for further studies in science
- developing career awareness in science

We often assume that science is for all. Science is objective and unbiased. Anyone can become interested in science. If a person is not interested in scientific matters, that is his or her own decision. Such was the accepted view for many years: science was what it was and it was up to the individual to determine whether he or she was interested in pursuing science.

It may be of interest to briefly consider the origins of modern science to explore how science came to be seen as objective and unbiased. Evelyn Fox Keller has noted that the modern view of science dates back to the seventeenth century. When the British Royal Society was founded, its stated purpose was to establish a "Masculine Philosophy . . . whereby the mind of Man may be ennobled with the knowledge of Solid Truths" (Keller, 1985, p. 52), in contrast to the traditional Greek science, which was considered weak and effeminate. Keller (1983) quotes Francis Bacon as describing the then new science as a "Chaste and lawful marriage between Mind and Nature, the purpose of which was to lead Nature to you with all her children and bind her to your service and make her your slave" (pp. 24–25). This was a view of science that reflected power and control. It also represented a change in the way of doing science, a change that has dominated scientific endeavor ever since. Science no longer involved merely learning to understand nature—its purpose was to control nature. Such a view is closely tied to the modern Judeo-Christian ethic prescribed in the Hebrew Bible or Old Testament:

> [B]e fruitful and multiply; fill the earth and subdue it; have dominion over the fish of the sea, over the birds of the air; and over every living thing that moves on the earth. (Genesis 1:28, New King James version)

When middle school and high school students are asked what they think about studying science in school, we find that the older they are, the less positive their views are about school science. More and more of our young people are being "turned off" by science. As science teachers, we can no longer ignore this. We are very concerned that so many young

---

The curricular areas that we have examined are science, content, scientific world views, inquiry, enterprise, and science for personal and social relevance.

Special students include those who are underachievers because of various disabilities, as well as those who have particularly high aspirations and intellectual capabilities to learn science.

people reject science, as we believe it is important for everyone to be familiar with some of the fundamental concepts of science—to be scientifically literate.

In this chapter we will look at some of the research that has addressed this aim of "inclusive science." Three broad groups will be considered: minority students, including those from non-Western cultures; females; and students with special needs. We will present some of the current findings about these groups of people and their views of science, and in particular we will discuss how science might be taught so as to be more inclusive and respectful of those who in the past have rejected (and often been rejected by) Western science.

⊗ CULTURAL WAYS OF KNOWING SCIENCE

Ursula's Voice

As a school board we have anti-racist and other policies that we're trying to put into place and policies to try to help the kids assimilate into our society, and I think it helps. It's really supportive of the elementary schools where the kids are, I think, young enough to be molded. But by the time they come into secondary schools, particularly if they're adults and they've never been to school at all, it's very difficult to change attitudes.

Not long ago one of the present authors attended a session about Native American science at a science teachers' conference. The speaker, who was Native American himself, told of his experiences as a graduate student in a large, prestigious university. He enrolled in a doctoral program in biology and told his advisor he wanted to do his thesis on aboriginal science. The advisor responded that there was no such thing! Fortunately few people would make such a statement today. We now know that prior to the "white man's discovery" of the Americas, Australia, or Africa, many indigenous peoples practiced very effective land management and had developed a broad knowledge of the medicinal use of the plants of their region. Unfortunately, the European view that all such "primitive" cultures were inferior and ought to be replaced by Western culture has resulted in the loss of much of this valuable knowledge (Selin, 1993).

In recent years, schools have become more aware that students from minority cultures often have different needs than middle-class students. Today there is an emphasis on allowing members of all cultural groups to have an equal opportunity to achieve, and this has been coming about through a restructuring of the educational system.

Science education is not excluded from this movement, and has been undergoing several structural changes in the past few years. These changes include the following:

- The inclusion of lessons that address the scientific achievements of many cultural groups
- Ensuring that students have a personal connection with science
- Identifying students' prior knowledge and beliefs about a subject area and building upon them in curriculum planning
- Relating science to everyday life, society, and technology
- Creating a positive self-image in order to raise students' confidence levels in their abilities to do science (Hodson, 1993)

All of these changes are strongly linked to the needs of multicultural learners.

Who Are Multicultural Learners?

Look at a present-day high school classroom in America. It represents adolescents from different races and ethnic backgrounds. Often recent immigrants and visible minority groups such as Hispanics, Asians, and Africans are referred to as *multicultural*. This is a narrow perspective, and to isolate these groups as multicultural is a mistake. Even those who have been living here for many centuries represent many different races and cultures.

The prosperous and the intellectuals who wish to make North America their home are encouraged to invest their assets, energy, and time in this great continent. Others may be given refuge in North America so that they may find comfort, peace, and rest. North America is home to recent immigrants and refugees as well as to individuals who have longtime roots in America. All adolescents, regardless of culture, must be treated with dignity and respect and granted equal opportunities to achieve in school.

Multicultural Education

Multicultural education is in the forefront in our society. Teachers are expected to become more culturally aware to meet the needs of an ethnically and culturally diverse student population. Science educators are faced with the challenge of designing curricula that are "not only content-sensitive to cultural differences (e.g., exposing students to the beliefs, background, and foundations of individual cultures), but also process-sensitive (e.g., helping students understand the many 'ways of knowing' that different cultures process" (Armstrong, 1994, p. 161). Multiple intelligences theory provides a model that is culturally sensitive to such differences. As such, it provides educators with a valuable tool to help celebrate the ways in which different cultures think (Armstrong, 1994). Multicultural education focuses on the following:

- The use of language in the classroom that promotes learning by all cultural groups
- An awareness by the teacher of his or her students' cultural beliefs and customs

- Student understanding and tolerance of others' cultural commitments, beliefs, interests, strengths, and contributions
- The inclusion of lessons that address the scientific achievements of many cultural groups

The science education community has been continually striving to meet the needs of all cultures through research and classroom practice. Science educators are reaching out to students in at least three important ways:

- Identifying students' prior ideas and beliefs of science concepts and systematically incorporating these into science units of study
- Becoming increasingly aware of customs and influences of different cultures
- Including lessons that focus on a variety of cultural achievements and contributions in science

Ideas and Beliefs

Existing ideas, knowledge, and experiences that multicultural students bring to the classroom cannot be ignored. Some religious and cultural beliefs may not mesh with the scientific concepts that are being taught. It is important for teachers to find the source of their students' beliefs; when there is a conflict of beliefs, we must acknowledge it and allow students time to research their views. Teachers should present scientific views and evidence for students to consider as an alternative viewpoint to their existing beliefs.

Cultural Customs and Influences

Adolescents from east and west, north and south may have difficulty adjusting to science teaching that explores students' ideas and encourages students to question the ideas of their peers and teachers. Why is this so? Adolescents have grown up to view learning science as learning "facts" presented by their teachers and/or their textbooks. Science is seen to be culturally transmitted from one generation to the next as "truths". You may have noticed that students in science classes typically spend much of their time copying teacher-prepared notes, answering questions at the end of textbook chapters, and completing worksheets. Students rarely speak *real* science in class.

In North American schools it may be noted that adolescents belonging to African, Indian, and Islamic cultures are less likely to speak up in class because they value and respect the knowledge of their elders and teachers. Islamic girls may find it particularly difficult to address and question a male teacher. Islamic boys may be uncomfortable recognizing a female teacher as an authority. Polynesian adolescents may find it difficult to compete with others, because they are raised in a cooperative cultural environment. A teacher must be aware of such cultural beliefs in their students, and respect and build on them, just as we build on their scientific beliefs.

Scientific "truths" are culturally negotiated and established ideas.

Cultural Achievements and Contributions

When students feel a connection to what they are learning, they are more likely to be motivated and interested. It is important for students from other cultural groups to see themselves and their groups represented in school. One way to achieve this is through lessons and activities that include and explore advances made by members of their cultural group. Just as we focus on the accomplishments of Western European and American scientists, we should also consider the historic pre-Renaissance advances of many other cultures. The theories of Kepler, Copernicus, and Einstein and the deeper origins upon which these advances were based must be probed. If we are to reach students of all cultures, a study of these historical components, as well as the scientific and technological inventions and contributions made by different cultures and communities, must be given consideration.

Studies show that students learn best and are more highly motivated when the subject matter they are studying reflects their own culture, perspectives, and experiences. If we ignore the scientific advances of other cultures, we are not providing all cultural groups an equal opportunity to succeed. Students are strongly influenced by their cultures, and if they are exposed to the major achievements of people from the same culture, it may result in a more positive self-image and a higher level of confidence.

It is equally important to expose students of the majority culture to the achievements of other cultures to avoid a Eurocentric view of science and technology. Exploring the advances made by other cultures informs all students that Western science is not the only science that has made such advances. Similarly, minority groups must respect the advancements made by Western science. Following are three lesson plans that give examples of various ways of incorporating scientific methods and achievements of different cultures into science classrooms.

Lesson 1: Homemade Batteries

Cultural Connection: Ancient Persia, modern Turkey and Iraq
Theme: Changes in Matter and Energy
Topic: Electric charges

Objectives

- To demonstrate that a culture discovered how to create low-voltage batteries over 2,000 years ago
- To demonstrate how an electrical current can be produced by chemical means
- To observe that two different metals can produce an electrical current when they are placed in an acid solution or a salt solution

Materials Required

map of the world
plastic cups or a clay jar
tin strips
copper strips
strong solutions of lemon juice, orange juice, salt water, and/or vinegar
miniature light bulbs
insulated copper wires
drawing/replica of ancient battery

You should have enough of these materials for the number of groups or students in your class.

Teaching Strategies

1. Explain to students that over 2,000 years ago, in about 250 B.P., the Persians created and used small batteries, or electrochemical storage batteries. They were made of clay pots filled with vinegar. A copper tube was placed in them, along with an iron or bronze rod. These batteries were able to emit 0.5–2.0 volts of electricity. The Persians apparently had a thorough understanding of currents and conductors, and were therefore able to create the first batteries. An example, replica, or drawing can be made ahead of time to show to students. The teacher may want to use a map to show students where ancient Persia was located.

2. Tell the students that they will be creating their own homemade batteries in class today.

3. Split the class into small groups of two to four students. Supply each group with a cup, a tin strip, a copper strip, insulated copper wire, and a miniature light bulb. Demonstrate in front of the class the steps that they should follow to produce their batteries.

4. Fill each cup three-quarters full of the solution. Attach one insulated copper wire to the tin strip at one end, and another to the copper strip. Attach the light bulb to the other ends of the insulated wires. Place both metal strips into the solution. The bulb should light.

5. This process can be repeated using a variety of solutions as well as other metals, such as aluminum or iron. Discuss with students how they think the Persians discovered how to make batteries. Encourage them to be imaginative and creative. A follow-up activity could involve creative writing of stories on how the battery was invented.

Lesson 2: Model Solar System

Cultural Connection: Islamic heliocentric theories
Theme: Earth, Space, and Time
Topic: Earth and the solar system

Objectives

- To learn the names and order of the planets in the solar system
- To discuss ancient beliefs about the solar system, and the discovery of its actual organization by the Islamic people centuries before Western scientists did so
- To construct a model of the solar system that accurately depicts the distances between the planets, and to gain an understanding of the relative distances involved

Materials Required

paper plate
9 round balloons or Styrofoam balls
string, yarn, or fishing line
hole puncher
meterstick or measuring tape
chalkboard
markers

Teaching Strategies

1. Describe ancient beliefs about the solar system and the relations of the planets. This should include the geocentric theory of Ptolemy that was widely accepted in Western Europe until the time of Copernicus 2,000 years later. It should be stressed here that astronomers from the Islamic culture created, and followed, a heliocentric view of the solar system centuries before Copernicus. Remind the students that we now follow the heliocentric theory: that the Sun is the center of our system and the planets revolve around it.

2. List the names of the planets, in order, on the chalkboard. Beside each planet, write its distance from the sun in kilometers. Group each student with a partner. Give a balloon to each of nine students and have them blow it up. Then assign a planet to each group, and have the partners write the name of their planet on each balloon with the markers.

3. Involve the remaining students in the activity by having them measure the lengths of string. Using a scale of 1 cm = 1 million Km should result in the following lengths of string:
   - Mercury: 49 cm
   - Venus: 99 cm
   - Earth: 1 m 48 cm
   - Mars: 2 m 23 cm
   - Jupiter: 7 m 44 cm
   - Saturn: 14 m 48 cm
   - Uranus: 29 m 76 cm
   - Neptune: 47 m 52 cm
   - Pluto: 59 m 52 cm

4. Punch nine holes in the paper plate and have each group attach their string to their balloon.
5. Go out to the schoolyard and attach the free ends of each string to the paper plate in the proper order. As each string is attached, have that group walk out until the string is completely extended.
6. Observe the resulting model of the solar system and allow the students time to grasp the concept of the vast distances between the planets. Explore ideas about how Islamic astronomers could have recognized the movement of the planets by observing the sky.

Lesson 3: Constellations

Cultural Connection: Native Americans
Theme: Earth, Space, and Time
Topic: The observable universe

Objectives

- To listen to an Anishinabe legend of how the Big Dipper constellation was formed and gain an understanding of how legends were used in the past to account for why things were the way they were
- To become familiar with five major constellations and where they are located in the night sky using a star chart
- To determine the position of true north
- To differentiate between apparent motion and real motion, thus explaining why some constellations are visible only at certain times of the year

Materials Required

star chart
chalkboard
Keepers of the Earth legends
meterstick

Teaching Strategies

1. The teacher will read the students the Anishinabe legend "How Fisher Went to the Skyland: The Origin of the Big Dipper." This is a Native American legend from a tribe of the Great Lakes region. It is available in the book *Keepers of the Earth: Native Stories and Environmental Activities for Children* by Michael J. Caduto and Joseph Bruchac (1991, Saskatoon, Canada: Fifth House Publishers). The legend describes the traditional view of how the animals brought warm weather to the Earth for six months of the year. It also includes a legend explaining how The Big Dipper was formed and why its orientation changes throughout the year.

2. Discuss with students what a constellation is, and the names of any that they are familiar with. List the five major constellations that are visible throughout the year in much of North America (those from the southern United States will not be able to view all of these at all times): the Big Dipper, the Little Dipper, Cassiopeia, Cepheus, and Draco. Find the locations of these constellations on a star chart and stress their positions in reference to the North Star, or Polaris.

3. Take the students outside. Remind students that the Earth travels in an elliptical orbit around the Sun. Set one student in the center as the Sun. Create an elliptical orbit around this student, with the smallest distance being 3 m from the Sun. Designate another student as the Earth, and have him or her follow the path in a counterclockwise direction. Set twelve other students around the orbit, 3 m away. They are the stars and constellations. Have the "earth" walk around the oval, while looking over his or her right shoulder at the "constellations" and "stars." Certain constellations will only be visible at certain times. This should allow students to understand why the objects appear to move, when in actuality, it is the earth moving. The students can take turns being the "Earth."

The issue of multicultural science education has been developing for several decades. The needs of minority students are finally being acknowledged, as are the benefits of having these students in our classes. As teachers we will be required to find methods to teach these students to the best of our abilities, and hopefully to make science an enjoyable experience for them. Familiarity with students' cultural beliefs and how they relate to science concepts will allow you to adapt your approach and avoid confrontations or confusion. Being aware of how young people are expected to act in a certain culture will also help you deal with your students and any differences that may arise. Understanding and acceptance are the keys to multicultural education. Incorporating that understanding into your teaching methods will allow you to unlock the door to their understanding.

 TEACHER PRACTICE

Activities for Multicultural Science
Research or develop several activities that have a multicultural flavor.

⚛ PARTICIPATION OF GIRLS IN SCIENCE

HANNA'S VOICE

Female students don't think that they're good at science. . . . I know I'm a role model, being a female, but that's not good enough. Just me up there in front of the class as a woman is not enough. Make sure you include and have answers equally from the girls and the boys. Boys tend to shout out answers and say things to disrupt the class and they will get your attention a lot more than the girls will; you'll pay a lot more attention to them.

Gender and science is a hot topic in education today. Few educators are neutral about gender. Some would say it is crucial that we make science more appealing to girls and women; others would argue that there is already far too much attention being paid to girls, and boys have become disadvantaged as a result (*Ottawa Citizen*, 1997). Some probably just wish it would go away.

In this section we will review some of the recent findings about gender and science and see what some preservice teachers have to say about the matter. Once again, you will be asked to reflect on your own past experiences as we explore some of the gender and science issues.

What is it like to be a girl or woman in science today? Many of you will have direct experience, being women who have studied science at a university. Those of you who are male will have female friends and relatives who have studied science. Some of you may be sympathetic with the view expressed by one female student teacher, who said she was sick of hearing about the plight of poor women in science.

Kahle (1988) reported that nearly 50 percent of the workforce in the United States consisted of females, but that only 9 percent of scientists and engineers were women. These numbers are typical throughout North America. Why is this happening? Why is there still such a significant difference between the numbers of men and women who have careers in science?

There have been many studies done and suggestions made that have attempted to solve these questions. Some feel that biological differences between men and women predispose men to the sciences and women to the arts and humanities. Other theories suggest that the dichotomy is due to years of society's influence on women. Regardless of the reasons why this occurs, we as teachers must do our best to accommodate the needs of both genders in our classes.

Adolescent males tend to have a higher level of interest in the sciences than do females. They are in the majority in many science classes, especially in secondary physics. Males tend to answer more questions, offer more theories, attempt more difficult problems, and suggest higher-level solutions. They are also usually the ones who do the hands-on part of the experiments: measuring, manipulating, and exploring. This seems to make a major difference in their understanding of concepts. Boys appear more confident of their abilities and may apply themselves more to science and math than to other subject areas. As a result, they are the ones who continue their studies in the area of science, and therefore make up the majority of the scientific workforce. Science has traditionally been a male-dominated area. Why is this so? What is it in the science classroom that appeals to males so strongly?

In many schools, most secondary science teachers are men. If males and females learn differently, then perhaps the male teachers have been teaching science in the manner in which they learned it—a male-oriented style of teaching. Girls in science courses may not excel because the teaching style is not geared toward their style of learning. This theory makes some sense, but does not account for girls who lose interest when taught by women science teachers.

Girls' interests in science seem to wane as they reach adolescence and enter high school. Here girls tend to opt for fewer science and more humanities courses. They may have a feeling that "girls can't do science." Where does this come from? Studies by Baker (1988), Kahle and Rennie (1993), and Scantlebury and Kahle (1993) suggest that these negative feelings often develop as a result of the attitudes and behaviors, whether conscious or subconscious, of their science teachers. The kinds of behaviors that perpetuate male domination in science include the following common practices in science classrooms:

- Calling on boys more often than girls
- Allowing boys to interrupt more often, and scolding girls when they do
- Asking boys higher-order questions and girls lower-order questions
- Giving more feedback and more encouragement, both verbal and nonverbal, to boys
- Using a longer wait time with boys than with girls
- Choosing boys to help with experiments and demonstrations more often than girls
- Using gender-biased language, such as always using male names and pronouns
- Using textbooks that do not represent or depict women as scientists, or that do not mention the achievements of women in science (other than Marie Curie)
- Assigning group roles according to gender, or allowing girls to always be observers and recorders (Baker, 1988; Canadian Teachers' Federation, 1988).

All of these attitudes and behaviors affect the self-confidence and enjoyment that girls develop about science. By asking boys more and harder questions, we imply that girls are not at the same level. By scolding girls more often than boys for interrupting, we imply that girls should be passive observers. This is further reinforced by the allocation of roles in group activities to specific genders. By giving boys more feedback and encouragement, we are again suggesting that females do not need to worry about learning or achieving in sciences. The lack of textbook photographs depicting women as scientists reinforces the opinion that women are not scientists (Bazler & Simonis, 1990, 1991).

How can we as teachers become aware of our own behaviors and attitudes that may be perpetuating the situation? Baker (1988) suggests the following:

1. Have an observer watch your behavior during several science lessons and make notes on the following:
   - List the names and number of times you call upon certain students
   - List the names of students who were not called upon and their gender
   - Note biased language use
   - Note the level of difficulty of the questions posed to members of each gender
   - Note the amount of positive and negative feedback given to males and females
   - Note disciplinary and social interactions with genders
   - Note wait time given to members of each gender
2. After you have noted the areas in which you need to improve, Baker suggests that you attempt some of the following:
   - Use a class list and check off each name as you ask that student a question
   - Ensure that you vary your questions from girl to boy to girl
   - Make a list of higher-and lower-level questions before class and make sure that you address them equally
   - Assign each group specific roles, and rotate the roles each class
   - Teach a class using all female names and pronouns, and later discuss the students' feelings and opinions about it
   - Bring women who work in scientific careers to class as role models and have them discuss their occupations and their academic training
   - If the textbook has a notable absence of females depicted in it, infuse lessons with notes on the achievements of females in that area
   - Set up a peer tutoring situation, where older girls can tutor younger ones

Kahle (1988) supports several of the preceding ideas and also makes several other useful suggestions on how to make your classroom more "female friendly." She says that the following elements encourage girls to succeed in the sciences:

   - An organized, well-equipped classroom that is perceptually stimulating

- The use of labs, discussions, and quizzes as the main method of teaching
- Stressing creativity and basic skills
- Providing information on career opportunities

How you choose to implement these ideas will depend on your own beliefs and flexibility. The options are innumerable.

It has been suggested that girls and women are more in tune with cooperative rather than competitive education. Classes can be organized to highlight the collaborative approach and hopefully be more appealing to girls (Peltz, 1990). Their lack of interest in science may be related to taking a passive role when doing science experiments and activities. Girls often opt to be the recorder or observer and leave the actual working of the experiment to the boys. Doing an experiment leads to a greater understanding of the concept, as well as a greater level of interest (Peltz, 1990). By relegating themselves to background roles, girls create a negative learning environment for themselves without realizing it. It is important for teachers to ensure that both girls and boys take an active role in the science classroom.

Pollina (1995) suggests that teachers must be aware of how girls learn science. For example, a physics teacher was willing to learn from his students rather than imposing his own pedagogy. He used collaborative processes, hands-on experimentation, and connected abstract concepts with practical applications. To build their self-image, the teacher acknowledged to the girls that these are valid and important methods of scientific inquiry.

Female scientists' approaches to scientific inquiry shed light on how we may want to teach science. Pollina (1995) states:

> Jane Goodall and Dian Fossey, who revolutionized the understanding of primate behavior, did not hypothesize and then corroborate by observing a group of apes. Instead they took a relational approach and focused on a single ape, tracing that primate's interactions. (p. 30)

Pollina (1995) offers ten tips to reaching girls:

- Connect mathematics, science, and technology to the real world. For example, what effect did Newton's law of motion have on the thinking of the Enlightenment?
- Choose metaphors carefully, and have students develop their own.
- Foster an atmosphere of true collaboration. All members of a group should be taught to listen and are responsible for one another's learning. Both teacher and students should feel free to ask questions, admit mistakes, take risks, and express confusion. This creates a powerful sense of one's own learning and that of others. Students become a teacher's intellectual friends.
- Encourage girls to act as experts. Have the groups be responsible for verifying their own logic and critique their own work and that of their peers like scientists.

- Give girls the opportunity to be in control of technology.
- Portray technology as a way to solve problems as well as a plaything.
- Capitalize on girls' verbal strengths. Encourage students to express the logic behind their solutions in essay or picture form.
- Experiment with testing and evaluation. Give topics related to real-world experiments so that girls can show their ability to synthesize, make connections, and use their practical intelligence. Alternate strategies that work well for girls include **embedded** and **circus** assessments.
- Give frequent feedback and keep expectations high. Girls may need more encouragement than boys. Continual praise and verbalization of expectations are critical. Reinforce students' control of their materials through homework checks, quizzes, and comments. Help students develop the self-reliance that all students need to survive in an inquiry-based classroom.
- Experiment with note-taking techniques. Girls become so absorbed in taking every note and copying every diagram that they are too pre-occupied to take part in discussions. Give students copies of lecture notes or make them available on the computer (Pollina, 1995, pp. 30–32).

Embedded assessments are activities in which students, usually working in groups, perform experiments, identify patterns, and arrive at hypotheses. A teacher circulates and observes student performance for evaluation.

Circus assessments consist of stations with reflection questions or experiments set up around a room. Students go from station to station and are evaluated on the quality of their investigation at each.

What we learn from Pollina's work is that we must stop trying to change girls. Rather, we must include a feminist approach to science in our pedagogy. Pollina (1995) asserts that we "will see some exciting results for boys and girls and for science and technology" (p. 33).

Consideration of gender issues in science is very important, but is often ignored by teachers. Some teachers believe it takes too much time and effort to change their way of teaching. Others feel that it is not an issue at all, that they already treat their students equally. Still others believe that any differences are due to heredity and are therefore irreversible. These teachers fail to take into consideration the ways in which experiences shape a learner's understanding and outlook, and how vastly different the experiences of boys and girls are in the science classroom. As a pre-service teacher you need to reflect on your own views and willingness to implement change in your classroom based on the needs and potential of your female students.

The following lesson plans take into account gender issues in science. The first lesson incorporates the suggestions of Kahle (1988), Baker (1988), and the Canadian Teachers' Federation (1988) in a normal science lesson. The second lesson recognizes women's achievements in science.

Lesson 1: Altering Freezing and Boiling Points

Theme: Changes in Matter and Energy
Topic: Physical properties and physical changes of matter

Objectives

- To observe the effects of adding substances (salt, sugar) on the boiling and freezing points of water
- To understand that addition of substances to water will affect the boiling and freezing points
- To recognize ways in which we use and apply this knowledge in everyday life

Materials Required

3 beakers
water
hot plate
3 thermometers
salt
ice cubes
graph paper

Teaching Strategies

1. *Eliciting Phase:* Ask students why city work crews spread salt and sand on icy streets in the winter. Record their responses on the chalkboard and ask students to explain why they feel their theory or idea is relevant. Use the class list to ensure that you address your questions equally among boys and girls. Check off student names as they are asked a question or offer an idea. Then ask if anyone can think of an example of how one might change the boiling point of water.
2. Ask students to suggest how they might design an experiment to alter the freezing and boiling points of water. Develop a procedure for the experiment. Ask several girls in the class to perform the experiment. Ask several boys to act as the recorders.
3. Develop a procedure such as the following: Pour 1 L of water into each of two beakers. Add 75 mL salt to one of the beakers. Place a thermometer in each beaker, and put the beakers on the hot plate. Begin heating. Have the recorders record the results of how long the water takes to boil and at what temperature it boils.
4. Discuss the results with the class. Does the salt appear to affect the boiling point? How? You can repeat the experiment using another substance, such as sugar, and compare the results.
5. Move on to the next part of the lesson. Now you are dealing with the freezing point of water. Ask the boys to be the experimenters for this section, and the girls to be the recorders. Place half of the ice cubes and a thermometer into the third beaker. Have the recorders make a graph showing the temperature changes in 10-minute intervals. Note when the temperature begins to rise steadily, and when it levels off. Repeat the experiment, adding salt to the ice. Record the results on the graph.
6. Discuss the effects of salt on the freezing point of water.

7. Discuss both experiments with the class and ask for their suggestions on other ways we apply this knowledge to our daily lives. Look for answers that include the use of antifreeze in car radiators, how to make ice cream, and so on.

A follow-up lesson could involve actually making ice cream in class using only salt, ice, flavoring, and milk.

This lesson incorporates several of the ideas mentioned earlier on how to make your science class more "female friendly." The use of the class list ensures that both genders are called upon equally, and that everyone gets a chance to speak. It also ensures that the higher- and lower-level questions are equally dispersed. Asking girls to perform the hands-on part of the experiment ensures their participation and helps their level of understanding. Switching roles for the second half of the lesson ensures that there is no gender bias in the classroom.

It is important to create an environment that will make science more appealing for our female students, but we must be cautious that we do not end up alienating the boys in our classes. We are not suggesting that you use only female names and pronouns, nor that you involve only girls in the activities, ask girls all of the higher-level questions, or give only girls a longer wait time. We want to support and give our female students positive science experiences, but we do not want to coddle and patronize them. Keeping this in mind can ensure a positive experience for both genders in your classroom.

Lesson 2: Roberta Bondar

Theme: Earth, Space, and Time
Topic: Can vary according to grade level

Objectives
- To show the accomplishments of Canada's first female astronaut
- To expose the students to how the life of an average girl can change as she becomes a famous scientist through continued education in science
- To discuss Canada's contributions to space exploration and the space program

Materials Required
book: *Roberta Bondar: Leading Science into Space* by Michael Webb (1993)
photographs of the CANADARM

Instructional Strategies

1. Introduce the lesson by asking the students to name some famous astronauts. Make a list of these on the board. Note whether the astronauts are American, Russian, or Canadian. If someone mentions Roberta Bondar, great! Otherwise, ask them specifically for female astronauts.

2. Show the students the book about Roberta Bondar. Ask them if they have ever heard of her, and where she is from. You can read the book to the class, or pick out the parts that you wish to focus on, such as her education and how she became an astronaut. Discuss the book or portions of it with your students. Note their feelings and whether they think such an opportunity might be available to them. Stress that Roberta was an average Canadian girl who aspired to achieve in the sciences.

3. Elicit ideas from the class on what science careers they feel are possible for them. Make a list. In the future, you may want to contact a university in your area and have a speaker come in to discuss these careers.

4. Have a list of books about other women in science posted in your classroom, or have the books on display. Include science-related careers that are at a technical or technological level as well as professional careers. You can obtain ideas from your school librarian. If resources are not available in your school, make a note of this to your principal and librarian.

The issue of science education for females is important and needs to be addressed. The lack of girls' participation in school science courses reveals that something is missing from how science is being taught. We are, in effect, not reaching half of our students. This cannot be allowed to continue. We do not suggest that girls deserve special treatment in the classroom, but rather that they require different approaches. In this section we have outlined several ideas that are easily implemented in any classroom. As science educators, our primary concern must be that all of our students are encouraged to learn; this cannot be achieved by treating everyone the same. The need for flexibility in teaching styles is readily apparent for special-needs and multicultural students. We must do no less for our female students.

 PEER TALK

Feminizing Scientific Inquiry

Should we focus on "remedial masculinity" for girls in a science class? That is, should we strive to make girls more aggressive, more analytical, more competitive, rougher so that they will survive in science and technology? Why or why not?

How *do* many girls and women learn science and conduct scientific inquiry? Can they help us learn better ways to teach them science?

An article in the *Ottawa Citizen* (1997) stated: "[A]s long as schools expect boys to be like girls, boys will increasingly fall behind." Comment on this statement, considering the following statement from the same article: "Boys need discipline. Boys need competition. Boys, in short, need to be taught differently."

⊗ SCIENCE FOR SPECIAL-NEEDS STUDENTS

BILL'S VOICE

You're trying to teach the average student. Personally, I've never found an average student in any one of my classes. And I find it very difficult to say that you're going to have a generic set of tools that you're going to use. In terms of things like classroom management and dealing with the students, there are some very generic rules, like the one about mutual respect and projecting a comfortable classroom. But in terms of communicating information for promoting discussion, if you go to some other areas of typology, you can't expect one set of rules to work from person to person, when you're trying to have a discussion. And when you're working with one student's answers, for all effective purposes, that's a one-on-one discussion. The fact that there are 28 other students in the room affects how you respond to it in the sense that you're making it heard for everybody, but it doesn't change the basic tenet that you were having a communication with one other person.

A brief section in one book cannot possibly provide a comprehensive guide to working with students who have special needs. Hopefully you will have the opportunity to study those needs in more detail in a special-education course. This section will consider ways of accommodating special students when they are placed in a regular classroom, either because the school has a policy of mainstreaming or because the student has not been identified as having special needs.

This may be an appropriate time to remind ourselves of a few things. First, all students have particular talents and particular weaknesses. Naturally, all parents want the best for their children, and in the case of special-needs students, that may not easily be achieved, especially given the constraints of a typical classroom of 25 to 35 students. Some parents believe that their special child is best served in a classroom with "normal" children of the same age, rather than in an isolated setting.

Remember, in Chapter 4 we discussed Howard Gardner's theory of multiple intelligences. One argument in support of MI theory was the special way that disabled people use their intelligence.

Sometimes school district policies are contrary to parent wishes, and this can be very difficult for the parents to accept. We must remember that parents know their child better than anyone. They know what the child is like when he or she is away from the influence of his or her peers. And this may be very different from how the child behaves in a classroom in the presence of those peers.

In this section we will consider two broad categories of special needs: gifted and talented students and physically and mentally challenged students. In many cases, students have multiple handicaps, and so will be in both of the latter two categories. Moreover, some gifted students also have disabilities.

Gifted and Talented Students

What is it like to be a gifted student in our schools today? Perhaps you or someone you know is gifted. What special accommodation do schools provide for such students? What should they provide? Some schools and educators believe that in times of budgetary restrictions, providing special programs for gifted students is a misuse of valuable resources. Statements such as "Gifted children can get along very well on their own," and "Disadvantaged students are much more in need of our scarce resources," are not uncommon. But do gifted students really get along well on their own? We frequently hear stories of people such as Albert Einstein or Winston Churchill, who did poorly in school, yet were very successful as adults. But what if they had experienced a school program that was challenging and stimulating for them? Would their lives have been any different? What about the numbers of gifted students languishing in our classrooms today? Is it good enough to say that they will do well enough on their own, that they do not need extra resources?

Some gifted children are very unhappy. They may not have the same interests as other children their own age. They may become rebellious or, alternatively, they may withdraw from participating in class activities. Sharon Haggerty clearly remembers several students from her years of teaching high school science who remained quiet and passive, working only enough to receive average grades in her classes—not standing out in any way. It was only through personal conversations or by seeing IQ scores in their files that she became aware that these were bright people. Many went on to do outstanding work in college and/or have successful careers, but their high school work was not in any way outstanding. What has happened to such students in their years of schooling? And, more important for our purposes here, what can we, their teachers, do to encourage these students to realize their full potential?

Some students become very successful in school science by focusing on learning what is taught, without subjecting that learning to any critical analysis. Some of these students may be very able, but others are not. How can we recognize which of our students are truly gifted, and which are merely successful at reproducing what they have been "taught"? How can we convince students who are very successful at this sort of "learning" that it is in their best interests to strive for understanding, rather than merely reproducing factual knowledge?

These are some of the issues facing teachers of gifted children. How can we deal with these issues, rather than leaving our gifted students to get by on their own? How are we to know which of our students are truly gifted? And, once we have identified a gifted student, what can (and should) we do with him or her in a typical mixed-ability class? These questions will be considered in this section, but first we will clarify what we mean by *gifted* and *talented*.

Sometimes the terms *gifted* and *talented* are used interchangeably. Gagné (1991) distinguishes them as follows: giftedness refers to natural abilities or aptitudes, whereas a talent is a developed ability or skill (p. 66). Here we are considering only students who are gifted.

As we have already noted, it is now generally accepted that there is no single category of intelligence, but rather multiple forms of intelligences. Different experts recognize different types of intelligences. We have previously considered Gardner's multiple intelligences: linguistic, logical-mathematical, spatial, bodily-kinesthetic, musical, interpersonal, and intrapersonal (Ramos-Ford & Gardner, 1991). In the same volume, Gagné (1991) names four categories of aptitudes or gifts: intellectual, creative, socioaffective, and sensorimotor. The first of these, along with Gardner's linguistic and logical-mathematical intelligences, corresponds with what is measured in the classical IQ score. It is these abilities that are typically drawn upon and valued in most traditional academic work, including science. In this book, however, we have been asking you to draw on the other intelligences as well, in order to make science more accessible and relevant to all of the students you teach.

Gifted students can be an invaluable source of information during discussions and introductory lessons. These students are often able to explain concepts at an appropriate level for other students and take ideas beyond where they would normally go. Other students in the class can then be challenged in their own way, and they will often benefit from further discussions. In your teaching, be sure to incorporate the ideas and opinions of other students in your class so that the gifted student is not always targeted to give the answers.

Gifted students can also be encouraged to do enrichment work. They tend to complete their work more quickly than other children and it is when they have nothing to occupy themselves that inappropriate behavior may occur. Supplementary projects may provide enough work to occupy them after their regular assignments are finished. Having them present their finished projects at the end of the unit will be beneficial to the other students in the class as well.

The following lesson plan is an example of how to encourage and challenge the gifted students in your class.

Lesson 3: Challenges for Gifted Students

Theme: Changes in Matter and Energy
Topic: Light

Objectives

- To challenge the gifted students in the class to strive for further knowledge in the area of light
- To have the gifted students share their finished products with the class and enable the others to also learn more about the topic

Materials Required

up-to-date resources that deal with holograms, holographs, lasers, fiber optics, and optical illusions, *or*
access to a school library that is equipped with such resources.

Teaching Strategies

1. Arrange time for a conversation with your gifted students at the beginning of the unit. Tell them that you have noticed that they tend to finish their assigned work well ahead of the others, and that you want to challenge them during this unit. Tell students the topic of the new unit, and ask for opinions on what they think it might involve.
2. Tell students that when they finish their work ahead of the others, you want them to work on a small research report on a topic of their choice. Give them a choice of holograms, holographs, lasers, fiber optics, or optical illusions. Encourage them to research not only how we use these phenomena in society, but also how they work, and who invented them. It is important to suggest topics that students will find interesting. Some students will want to identify their own topics; this should be encouraged.
3. Allow students to go to the library for their research, and to keep their resources in the classroom so they are available when needed.
4. Allow students extra time to finish their projects if needed.
5. At the end of the unit, have the students present their projects to the rest of the class so that the other students may learn about these areas.

Such projects should not be restricted only to gifted learners. Other students who have a strong interest in science can also be allowed to do projects on their own time.

Physically and Mentally Challenged Students

The term *physically challenged* covers a broad range of students with many different needs. More and more such children are being integrated into regular classrooms. Few would now deny that wherever possible, most intellectually able students belong in regular classrooms, regardless of physical disability. Children who are visually impaired and hearing impaired, as well as those with mobility impairment, are now in fully integrated classes. What are the implications of this integration for teachers? What about the other students in the class? How do disabled students affect the other students? To what extent should a teacher be asked to modify his or her science program to accommodate such students?

Both physically and mentally challenged (PMC) students are becoming a part of every classroom. These children should not be prevented from experiencing science. In the past, PMC students have often missed out on the experiences of a regular science program for various reasons. Many PMC children are being denied a complete science education program because they are isolated in separate learning environments, and being taught different curricula (Idol, 1994). Studies have shown that these students can reap several benefits from participating in a mainstreamed science class (Mastropieri and Scruggs, 1992):

- Expansion of experiential knowledge for those whose experiences have been limited
- Acquisition of skills that will be needed in adult life
- Use of concrete, hands-on learning activities
- Development of problem-solving and reasoning skills

This study also found that able children are also given an opportunity to learn and grow through interaction with the mentally challenged students in their classes. Many PMC children have one of the following disabilities: language/literacy, cognitive/conceptual, psychological, or physical-sensory.

PMC students have as much right to an education as any other student. They have the right to study with children their own age and to receive required support services (Idol, 1994); as a result, PMC students are being mainstreamed into classrooms across the country. The needs of these students must be met; however, many science teachers have little or no training in the area of special education, and those with training in special education have little or no science training (Cawley, 1994). The resulting dilemma is only now beginning to be a subject of educational research.

Current research has identified several factors that influence the success of the learning environment. For example, textbook-based teaching has been found to be inhibiting for challenged students, whereas activity-based learning has been found to be more in tune with the needs of these students. Textbook teaching is problematic for a number of reasons: it is typically dominated by lectures and teacher demonstrations, with the students as passive learners who are expected to absorb and memorize a series of seemingly unrelated facts. In such classrooms, students are often assigned independent reading, which often requires understanding new, undefined vocabulary. Assessment is based on paper-and-pencil tests. Studies have noted that under such conditions, an extensive amount of content may be covered, but little understanding develops.

This form of teaching is especially inappropriate for students with language/literacy problems. Cawley, Miller, and Carr (1989) found that reading comprehension scores for students with mild disabilities on science texts were, on average, only 33 percent correct. That is, a PMC child in a textbook-based science class will miss much of the information. The same holds true for students with comprehension/conceptual challenges. Children with psychological disorders may find this format too restrictive and act out in class. Students with learning disabilities will require added support and training in the areas of reading and comprehension, writing, and study skills, memory strategies, and test-taking skills (Mastropieri & Scruggs, 1994). All in all, this approach to teaching is largely ineffective for many learners.

An alternative approach is an activities-oriented science program. An activities-oriented program involves the use of hands-on experiences, performed by the students themselves, as the main method of teaching. Vocabulary and the acquisition of facts are deemphasized, and the main focus is on understanding broad concepts. Science is seen as an ongoing process of discovery and exploration. Assessment is generally performance based.

This approach to teaching is beneficial to special-needs students in a number of ways. Students with language/literacy disabilities benefit because little emphasis is placed on reading and writing. Those with cognitive/conceptual disabilities may require extra attention to ensure that they have understood the topic, but seeing a concept in concrete form is usually a better learning tool for them than trying to visualize it mentally. Children with social/behavioral problems will have to be closely monitored during hands-on activities, and cooperative behavior management programs may need to be put in place. Students with physical/sensory challenges may have difficulties manipulating the equipment. Peers can help each other in this area, and group work would be a good solution.

When a student with mild mental retardation is placed in a classroom, there are several more areas to be taken into consideration. Mastropieri and Scruggs (1995) outlined four areas in which these learners often have difficulties: memory, attention span, logical reasoning, and outer-directedness.

How does this affect their learning abilities? In the area of memory, it often involves retrieval difficulties that can impede the communication process and interrupt the flow of the lesson. This can be lessened through the use of vocabulary cards, charts, and written outlines that list the main vocabulary words. When planning group discussions, allow yourself extra class time in anticipation of this. Attention spans can also be short, requiring the teacher to monitor to make sure that the students are on task. This area may improve through praising students for attending to their work, giving verbal reminders to refocus, and staying in close proximity as a physical reminder. Logical-reasoning disabilities can be difficult to recognize in some students because the disability is often affected by the student's attention span. As teachers, we need to focus the learner on his or her work, and be explicit in what we are trying to teach. Avoid broad terms and vague examples. Ideas must be thoroughly explained. Outer-directedness is a condition in which children rely on others for clues on how to act and respond, resulting in copied answers and a reluctance to pursue their own ideas. These behaviors can be resolved only through repeated practice and acceptance of the learner's ideas by the teacher and peers.

Mastropieri and Scruggs (1995) make several other suggestions on how to meet the needs of children with mild mental retardation, including the following:

- Limiting the amount of reading to be done
- Emphasizing vocabulary
- Asking clear questions and presenting ideas clearly
- Being well-organized
- Monitoring and reinforcing attention to work
- Encouraging responses and accepting all answers
- Monitoring for understanding
- Using peers in the classroom as support for yourself and PMC students

When a child with mild mental retardation is placed in your class, there are many methods you can use to ensure that the child learns to the best of his or her capabilities, and that learning is not negatively affected for other students in the class.

Theme work has been seen to have a positive effect on special-needs students; it allows them to see the concepts as "sets of relationships and meanings that are process related rather than as sets of isolated" concepts (Cawley, 1994). Themes can be incorporated across the curriculum, or they can focus on science, relating topics from the physical, life and earth sciences under one main idea. Cawley (1994) suggests combining topics under such themes as motion, stability, or energy. For example, energy can be used in reference to physical forces, energy exerted by living things, and the energy forces of the earth.

The following lesson plan will give you an idea of how to modify a lesson to meet the individual requirements of special-needs students in a class.

Lesson 4: Introduction to Energy

Theme: Changes in Matter and Energy
Topic: Alternative forms of energy

Objectives

- To introduce students to the topic of energy
- To suggest various forms of energy and how we use those forms
- To identify the source from which the energy is generated.

Materials Required

pictures of windmills, oil rigs, hydroelectric dams, solar panels, and so on
chalkboard or overhead projector

Instructional Strategies

1. Tell the students that you will be discussing a new theme today. Remind them of the class rules for discussions to ensure that those with social/behavioral problems are aware of what is expected of them. Write the word ENERGY on the chalkboard in large letters. Ask the students what that word means to them. Record their answers on the board.

2. Ask the students to describe the ways in which we use energy in our homes, schools, offices, and so on. Make a web or concept map of these ideas, stemming from the heading USES OF ENERGY. Get as many ideas as you can from the students. Elicit the ideas of the gifted students to see if they can lead you into another area that the others may not have considered, such as windsurfers, sailboats, and bicycles. Be sure to repeat all answers for the visually and hearing-impaired children in the room. Writing the answers on the board will aid those who are mainly visual learners. Also, tell the visually impaired students that you are writing the responses on the board, so that they are aware of why pauses are occurring in the discussion.

3. Next, ask the students where we get these forms of energy. Identify sources such as fossil fuels, sun, wind, water, and so on. Make another web on the board, stemming from the heading SOURCES.

4. Ask the students to give examples of how we transform these sources into usable energy. Record these on the previous web, connecting "sun" to "solar panels," "wind" to "windmill," and so on. Show the pictures of hydroelectric dams, windmills, and so on, and describe each in as much detail as possible.

5. End the class by having pairs of students work on lists of the different energy sources that they used the previous day. Pair the gifted students with those who are conceptually or language impaired.

PMC students have a wide range of abilities and disabilities. Each classroom situation will be different, and each child will respond differently to your teaching. As a science teacher, you must be able to judge what you feel will work for you in your classroom, as well as what will work for your students. It is only through trial and error with each student that you will be able to find the technique most effective in teaching and reaching them.

PEER TALK

Special-Needs Students

Identify the characteristics of special-needs students.

How would you address the needs of at least one group of special-needs students in your classroom?

⚛ PREPARING FOR FURTHER STUDIES

Once students have completed the required science courses in the middle school and junior high school years, they must choose which science courses, if any, they wish to pursue. This is often a difficult decision for many students. We noted earlier that this is the point where most girls opt out of science courses. Some simply do not continue in science because they believe that science is useful only for those who intend to continue to study science at college. We need to ensure that our students are aware of the consequences of such a decision, and that they are aware of the many positive aspects and benefits of science education. We want them to recognize how science affects their lives, and how it will continue to do so. How can science teachers help students make well-informed decisions as to further science studies?

To begin, we need to help our students recognize the many uses of science in our daily lives. One means of addressing this is through a science-technology-society approach to science. Young people should be aware of the role that science and technology play in their lives. Students need to understand how technology can alter the environment if it is misused or misunderstood (for example, pollution and its negative effects on our environment). Encourage your students to continue their studies in the sciences so that they can learn to understand the links between science, technology, and society. Let them realize that through understanding these links, they are empowering themselves for the future.

Developing an attitude of lifelong learning is also important. Students should be encouraged to look at their secondary school days as but a small part of a lifelong process of learning. All of our students should see science as an integral part of everyone's future, not just those in scientific careers. We need to teach students about processes that are relevant to their lives, not concepts that are beyond their capabilities. The National Research Council (1996) and the Science Council of Canada (1984) suggest that excellence in the basic training of future scientists does not mean that students should be subjected only to abstractions, but they should also be able to relate science to their personal lives. If we hope to have our students continue to study the sciences, we need to make science relevant to them and their lives.

Students can often be heard exclaiming, "When am I ever going to use this in my life?" This is often a cry of desperation over a concept that has no meaning to students and is beyond their grasp. As science teachers we need to help our students to see how that concept is applied in their lives, especially when its presence is hidden from the untrained eye. Making science relevant and enjoyable for our students is an important way of ensuring that they will want to continue their studies of science through high school and beyond.

Another aspect to this topic is to ensure that science is enjoyable and understood by all of our students. This includes multicultural, female, and special-needs students. We need to help these students in every way possible to ensure that their career options are not limited—that we have not lost another Roberta Bondar or Stephen Hawking.

⊠ AWARENESS OF SCIENTIFIC CAREERS

Students who leave high school having completed only the required science courses are often unaware of science and technology career options available to them. Those who have a genuine interest in the sciences are often unwilling to continue their studies at the university level because the only science career they recognize is doing lab work. Students need to be informed of the vast array of careers that is available to them if they continue their science studies.

How do we as teachers help prepare our students for future career choices? One way is to integrate discussion of employment opportunities with each topic throughout the year. For example, when studying earth science, jobs that are involved in the study of the earth, such as geologist, surveyor, seismographer, biologist, zoologist, climatographer, and so on, can be identified. When you continually expose your students to the choices that exist, they will realize that there are many more options than testing chemicals in a lab every day.

Another way that you can encourage your students to consider a science or technology career path is to ask them what careers they are interested in or would like to learn more about. Invite a speaker from a local college or university to come in and speak about the options and what high school preparation is required. The students can ask specific questions and get specific answers.

A third option is to have someone who works in a science or technology career speak to the class. This speaker can be an invaluable source to respond to questions regarding the level of difficulty of certain programs, why he or she chose that path, what education was required, what the speaker enjoys about his or her chosen field, and so on. It is also important to have speakers who are willing to talk about their personal lives and how they are able to balance their career and family life. Guest speakers should include women and young people as much as possible to show the students that not all scientists are eccentric old men. The students will learn what the speaker particularly enjoys about his or her career, as well as learning about some of the recent advances in that area.

A fourth option would be to take students to a local business in which science is a major aspect of the business. This could include research and other labs in a university or hospital, an airplane or automobile plant, a weather station, a chemical or pharmaceutical company, a garden nursery, the local pharmacy, and so on. Arrange a tour that describes how science and technology are involved. Try to arrange to see staff at work and, if possible, to speak to them about their work to give the students an even better idea of what their futures may hold.

Yet another option would be to have the students choose a career that interests them and prepare a short report on it. The reports could include educational requirements, what kind of work the job entails, expected salary, need for that particular career, and so forth. Students should be encouraged to get information from a variety of sources, including interviews with people from a college or university, those presently employed in that career, career counselors, and so on. Try to make this an interesting assignment for the students. If they enjoy learning about a career, they may choose to work toward that career.

Careers in general are becoming more demanding as more unskilled workers are being replaced by technology, resulting in a shift to a technologically based workplace. To be assured of a place in a technological society, our current students will need to have a basic understanding of just how technology functions and how to work with it. Continuing studies in science and technology can give today's students the tools necessary to understand these concepts, and possibly to apply them to create further technological advances. As teachers we must help our students see the benefits of further studies in science and technology.

 PEER TALK

Advanced Studies in Science and Career Planning

How would you encourage students to continue to advanced studies in science? Elaborate on at least one way of helping students plan for a scientific or technological career.

⚙ CHAPTER REVIEW

This chapter has examined several different and very important areas in science education. Multicultural students have specific needs and ideas that the science teacher must consider. Both girls and boys need to be encouraged to continue in the sciences, and teaching methods may need to be altered to address this need. Special-needs students, including gifted students, require special consideration.

Students' future studies, as well as an awareness of the scientific careers that are available to all of them, cannot be neglected in the science classroom. As science teachers, we have much to attend to as we organize and plan our teaching. Developing scientific understanding is our major focus, but in order to achieve that we must focus on the needs of all of our adolescent learners.

PROBES

1. Prepare lesson plans in several science areas, taking into account the key principles of diversity and inclusivity with respect to gender, global education, multiculturalism, and special-needs students.

2. Write a research report on a scientist or inventor and his or her contributions. What research characteristics does the scientist/inventor display? What pedagogical principles can you abstract from his or her scientific inquiry?
   - female scientists/inventors
   - American scientists/inventors
   - Third World scientists/inventors

CHAPTER 13

Authentic Assessment Practices in Science

STUDY QUESTIONS

1. What are the characteristics of standardized tests?

2. What is an alternative way of constructing multiple-choice questions?

3. Discuss continuous- and culminating-assessment strategies. What are the differences between these two types of assessment?

4. Why are rubrics important?

5. Why is it necessary for teachers to experience conceptual change about the nature of science in order to practice authentic assessment?

Reflective Inquiry

GEOFF'S VOICE

I like the idea of using several different methods for culminating assessment. This is important because in our schools we will be dealing with a wide variety of students with a variety of abilities and learning styles. Having a range of assessment strategies will cover those kids who learn and explain best by manipulating objects as well as those who can write down what they know. I really like the strategy of using students' ideas to create multiple-choice tests. I think this will give a clear indication of whether or not students have progressed past their initial beliefs about a phenomenon. Additionally, I would rely on the students' journals as a source for continuous assessment.

JOURNAL ACTIVITY

Tests and Examinations

In your journal, write down your personal experiences and views about your science tests and exams. What sorts of questions did the teacher ask? What are your present feelings with regard to school tests?

⌘ ASSESSMENT IN THE CONVENTIONAL CLASSROOM

Assessment is an integral part of teaching. Too often, we use paper-and-pencil tests that consist of fill-in-the-blanks; multiple choice; true or false; and questions that elicit one word, a sentence, or short answers. Most questions require only recall answers that satisfy the first level of Bloom's taxonomy of educational objectives, which tests for knowledge. However, there might be one or two questions that reflect Bloom's higher-order thinking skills. Some teachers consciously construct questions based on several levels of Bloom's taxonomy, which indicates six levels of cognitive complexity (Bloom, 1956):

> *Knowledge:* Rote memory skills (knowing facts, terms, procedures, classification systems)
> *Comprehension:* The ability to translate, paraphrase, interpret, or extrapolate material
> *Application:* The capacity to transfer knowledge from one setting to another
> *Analysis:* Discovering and differentiating the component parts of a larger whole
> *Synthesis:* Weaving together component parts into a coherent whole
> *Evaluation:* Judging the value or utility of information using a set of standards (Armstrong, 1994, p. 154)

Many teachers also depend upon and use ready-made tests that accompany commercially developed science programs. Standardized tests are also administered to students by teachers and by the state.

Appendix 13-1 provides a chart that illustrates multiple intelligences theory and Bloom's taxonomy in a unit on ecology.

⌘ STANDARDIZED TESTS

What are the features of standardized tests? Standardized tests are *reliable* because subject performance is consistent, and *valid* because they measure the expected knowledge and skills outcomes. The standardized tests are reliable and valid when used for the purposes for which they are designed. They are objective and scientific, and we can analyze, sort, categorize, compare, and rank the results through computer-based statistical packages. When reviewed, the advantages of this form of assessment seem to be beneficial only to teachers and administrators. But how do they affect the students?

Standardized tests do not assess students' creativity or their ability to communicate scientifically. They also do not look at the students' ability to find new solutions to problems, or the level of skills that they possess. Standardized tests only assess the breadth of low-level cognitive information that a student possesses. Through standardized tests, we tend to ignore higher-level thinking skills such as analysis, synthesis, application, and prediction. However, Linn, Baker and Dunbar (1991) have expanded the validity framework of standardized tests to include new aspects such as consequence, fairness, transfer and generalizability, cognitive complexity, content quality and coverage, meaningfulness, and cost/efficiency. Those involved with school science are seeking authentic ways of assessing students' cognitive and problem-solving abilities.

☒ AUTHENTIC ASSESSMENT

Authentic assessment involves both continuous assessment as well as culminating assessment. *Continuous* or *formative assessment* allows a teacher to monitor and assess students' progress in "multiple dimensions of reasoning" (Gardner, 1991) for the purpose of making curriculum and pedagogical decisions. *Culminating* or *summative assessment* takes place at the end of a unit of study and assesses students' ideas about the topic of study. At the end of the school term, **evaluation** of students' work also becomes necessary to give a final report to parents and principals. At parent-teacher meetings, teachers are encouraged to show parents samples of students' work as evidence of their intellectual growth and to seek ways of improving students' learning.

Assessment must be carried out as students engage in scientific reasoning and discourse within the contexts of multiple representations of knowledge: strings, propositions, images, episodes, intellectual skills, motor skills, and cognitive strategies (White, 1988). These knowledge types are the bases for language development in science, scientific discourse practices, communication, and reasoning (Gitomer & Duschl, in press; Lemke, 1990). Since scientific reasoning or inquiry is determined by a knowledge domain and shaped by the context in which the cognitive process occurs, assessment must arise from particular knowledge domains.

Authentic assessments provide a vehicle to explore students' thinking and the conceptual changes they make. Authentic-assessment practices are developmental and thus characterize the complementary nature of learning and assessment. Further, evaluation of assessment methods as they portray student understanding involves assessing students' employing the processes of science for data gathering, their ability to use reasoning skills that are necessary for "scientific argumentation"—making meaning in data analysis and drawing scientific conclusions (Gitomer & Duschl, 1995).

Authentic assessment involves *imagery stimuli* such as metaphors and analogies (Treagust, 1993, 1995); concept mapping (Novak & Gowin, 1984); chemical systems (Ebenezer & Erickson, 1996); discrepant events (Nussbaum & Novick, 1981); the prediction, observation, and explanation (POE) strategy (White & Gunstone, 1992); textual reading (Roth, 1991); hypermedia (Duffy & Jonassen, 1992; Gabel, 1994); and projects, performance-based assessment, and portfolios (Collins, 1992; Lorsbach, Tobin, Briscoe, & LaMaster, 1992; Lundberg, 1997; Wiggins, 1992). Hence, criteria for evaluating students' conceptions through these assessment methods must be guided by the following questions: Do students'

Evaluation is a process of using assessment data to judge the value of an instructional procedure or program. Evaluation has predetermined criteria by which the success of the program is judged, whereas continuous and culminating assessment are the systematic gathering of information about student competencies and achievements. Both assessment and evaluation are vital components of science education.

reasoning and argumentation reflect the association of different types of knowledge? Is there a sufficient intersection and overlapping between what students know and what teachers aim to teach? For example, Gitomer and Duschl (1995) incorporate the philosophy of science and the principles of assessment to amass evidence from classroom-based portfolios and to validate inferences about the kinds of social values and subject-matter domain assumptions that exist in and across classrooms, schools, and districts.

Valid inferences lead a teacher to promote teaching and learning that "maintains the triadic relationship between theories, aims and methods" in science (Gitomer & Duschl, 1995). Theoretical adequacy is a necessary driving force for scientific thinking (Gitomer & Duschl, 1995). Thus, a learning environment should focus on scientific thinking—knowing the theoretical ideas and practical skills within the scientific domain that are needed to examine a real problem, using evidence to support an argument or a knowledge claim and consider alternative explanations. Students' habits of mind such as curiosity, openness, flexibility, tolerance, and honesty may be assessed in problem-oriented contexts. Scientific attitudes and dispositions such as identifying and framing a problem, collecting and sifting through pertinent data, proposing multiple means of analyzing the problem, weighing possible solutions, looking at trade-offs, making decisions, and taking actions may be assessed in problem-solving activities. We must also aim to assess intra- and interpersonal understandings of scientific knowledge and social interactions that occur within scientific inquiry. In this sense we are continually monitoring and assessing students' progress not only through paper-and-pencil tests but by different means, as is appropriate or related to the objectives of the assessment. Hence, assessment may be described as tracing students' understandings, points of view, scientific attitudes, and habits of mind through multiple ways in multiple contexts based upon defensible criteria.

To carry out authentic assessments in class, a teacher must believe in learning as conceptual change, and his or her practice must involve formative assessments of students' conceptions. Teachers must experience changes in conceptions of the nature of science, of the learner and the different ways in which learning occurs, and in the practices and functions of assessment. Teachers should understand that inferences obtained from formative or continuous assessments must be valid not only for reporting students' learning progress to parents and the educational community at large, but also for shaping "decisions concerning the curriculum and the instructional practices used" (Gitomer & Duschl, in press).

Authentic assessment serves multiple purposes: evaluation of student progress, student achievement, or the success of a type of teaching method. It also provides teachers with better teaching tools, with an emphasis on teaching relevant skills. Authentic assessment can also promote instruction at deeper levels of thinking and understanding that incorporate alternative solutions and cooperation among students.

The drawbacks to authentic-assessment methods are that reliability is difficult to obtain and grading is subjective. These two doubts can be erased through the introduction of *rubrics* into the grading process. Rubrics will be discussed in greater detail later in the chapter. Another concern is that authentic assessment is more time-consuming to create, administer, and evaluate than standardized tests. This may be true, but the benefits far outweigh the inconvenience that more preparation time may cause. As one becomes more experienced with authentic assessment, the time required to create, administer, and evaluate will decrease.

Whatever information is gathered during authentic assessment should be shared with the student, with a focus on what has been achieved. Students should always be given the opportunity to comment on the findings and the progress that they have made in science. The most effective part of authentic assessment is the involvement of students in the assessment phase of learning. Students need to know that their opinions are valued throughout the learning process. This allows students to become personally involved in and responsible for their learning. This is the first step toward scientific literacy and lifelong learning.

Continuous-Assessment Strategies

There are many different forms of continuous assessment for science teachers to choose from to meet the assessment needs of both teacher and students. Assessment methods should be chosen based on the type of activity to be assessed, the goal of the assessment, the teacher's instructional style, the students' learning styles, and how these elements fit into the unit of study. Not all assessment strategies are suited to all assessment situations; you must take care to choose the most appropriate strategy for your class. The following assessment strategies are useful when carrying out continuous forms of assessment in the classroom.

Science Journals and Notebooks

Using a personal journal and notebook in the science classroom allows the teacher valuable insight into the students' thoughts, feelings, attitudes, and understanding of science skills. Students should be encouraged to make daily entries in their journals and notebooks so that reflection becomes an integral part of their science experience.

Science notebooks can be used daily by students as a form of a log in which they record and describe experiment procedures, observations, and conclusions. They are used to reflect on work that is accomplished and attempted. Journals, in comparison, can be used as a tool to enhance and encourage students' higher-level thinking. Shepardson and Britsch (1997) suggest the use of a four-phase journal: pre-investigation, investigation, post-investigation, and communication. During the *pre-investigation phase,* students describe the purpose of the day's experiment, write their predictions, and then plan their approach. This allows students to become focused on the lesson. In the *investigation phase,* students organize their data, reflect on their prior knowledge, and record new ideas as they occur. The *post-investigation phase* involves interpretation of, explanation of, and reflection on their findings, and the use of a *KWL strategy,* in which they record what they knew, what they wanted to learn, and what they learned. Students can also create concept maps and charts during this phase. The final phase is the *communication phase,* in which students are required to create a product from the investigation (or at least describe one) that could be used to help them communicate their understandings to someone else. The product can be in the form of a presentation, article, poster, poem, song, and so on.

The use of journals and notebooks in the science classroom allows teachers, and students, to assess student understandings of facts and concepts over a period of time. It also enables teachers to assess students' familiarity with science procedures and processes, as well as their attitudes toward science. Progress and evolution of thought can be more easily noted if one is familiar with students' original realms of knowledge. Journals also enable students to become more familiar with their own ideas and concepts, and how they change over a period of time. Figure 13-1 is an example of a student's journal entry.

Berenson and Carter (1995) makes several suggestions about the use of science journals in the classroom. When introducing the use of journals, encourage students to write about their feelings toward science and the lesson. Students are more willing to write about themselves, and hopefully this will develop into more in-depth reflections about the concepts of the lesson. Berenson and Carter suggest the use of a model to ensure that students are aware of what is expected of them in their writings. Teachers should try to respond to entries on a regular basis. This does not have to be every day, but frequently enough to let students know that their work is important and that it is being read.

FIGURE 13-1

A seventh-grade student's journal entry

Some big concerns for society with lightening are the potential of danger it presents. For example, if the lightening hit your house it could require a lightening rod. If perhaps a bolt of lightening hits a tree in a forest things could get messy. There are many deaths caused by this massive amount of electricity. If, as society says, you're stuck in a storm with lightening, never hide under a tree for lightening hits high points. It is better to lay flat on the ground.

I, as well as almost everyone else, use electricity every day. We use current electricity to cook, watch television, listen to music, create light, to keep our food cool, etc. Life would be more laid back, the crime rates would probably go down, however, there would be way less jobs available. I can't really say how I miss it. However, if I had know it existed but then disappeared, I would be depressed. Electricity is fabricated in plants, that is power plants, and through cities, town, almost everywhere aided by power lines.

Interviews

An interview is a conversation with one student or a group of students to get a better understanding of what students are thinking before, during, and after teaching. It also allows the student and teacher to engage in discussions about the student's thought process and ability to reason. In a teacher-student(s) conversational interview, students talk while the teacher listens with keen interest.

Bell (1995) suggests several points to keep in mind with regard to pre- and post-instruction interviews:

- the purpose of the interview
- the wording of the interview questions
- putting the students at ease
- recording the interview
- keeping the conversation going (p. 353)

The purpose of the interview is to find out what students are thinking. It is not meant for eliciting factual answers or leading them to right answers by a process of questioning.

The wording of the interview questions must be phrased so that it is open-ended and encourages students to talk about their personal ideas. For example: Show a picture of the moon. Ask questions such as, "I am interested in your meaning of the word *gravity*. Can you tell me about gravity on the moon?" (Bell, 1995, p. 353). Bell suggests *avoiding* questions that lead to right answers: "Do you know if (think) there is

gravity on the moon?" (p. 354). "Have you seen the film of the men walking on the moon? Did they float around or could they stand upright?" These elicit yes or no answers. The answers are either right or wrong!

Putting the students at ease is important because students are not used to interview assessment. They might wonder if this is a remedial session. Students also expect teachers to affirm their right answers; they want to please the teacher with the right answer. Hence, you must explain the purpose of the interview. Mention that you will speak to them individually to find out about their ideas, for example, of how sound travels, so that appropriate activities may be planned for a unit on sound. Some students appreciate the fact that the teacher is genuinely interested in using their ideas in teaching. Others need time to get used to this type of assessment activity. A preservice teacher, Mohammed Razai, states the following about teacher-student interviews:

MOHAMMED'S VOICE

According to my own experience, the process of interviewing is not as simple as I thought it would be. It is a very delicate process that needs to be handled with care and expertise. It is a task that requires a great amount of preparation. It also requires a better understanding of the students and the way they think.

Recording the interview may be done with an audiotape or video recorder for subsequent listening and transcribing and for better analysis and interpretation of students' ideas. Since students own the data, they must be given control over them. For ethical implications and considerations, Bell (1995) offers the following suggestions: Ask permission from the student before recording the interview by electronic means; play a portion of the recording before the student leaves; and give the student a copy of the transcribed data so that the student can validate your analysis and interpretation.

Keeping the conversation going during an interview is important. Taking the focus away from the interviewer is the key here. This can be accomplished easily when the activity is the center of focus. For example, the *interview-about-instances technique* (Osborne & Gilbert, 1980) consists of giving students a set of cards with line drawings or pictures to illustrate instances and non-instances of a single concept such as burning, energy, force and motion, and animals. For example, consider Figure 13-2, which consists of a set of cards for the instances and non-instances of burning.

Bell (1995) suggests the following questions:

I am interested in your meaning of burning. In your meaning of the word, would you say burning is taking place? What tells you that? (p. 355)

For a detailed discussion about the interview-about-instances technique, read Osborne, R., & Freyberg, P. (1985). *Learning in science.* London: Heinemann.

1 — A lighted candle	2 — Glowing light bulb	3 — Toast getting blackened
4 — Smouldering paper	5 — Gas cooker flame	6 — Fireworks skyrocket exploding
7 — Accidentally touching hot pot	8 — Strong acid spilling on cloth	9 — Sun shining
10 — Lightning striking on tree	11 — Rockets firing on space shuttle in space	12 — Camera flash

FIGURE 13-2

Interview-about-instances on burning (*NOTE:* From "Interviewing: A Technique for Assessing Science Knowledge" (p. 356), by B. Bell, 1995, in S. M. Glynn & R. Duit (Eds.), *Learning science in the schools: Research reforming practice*, Mahwah, NJ: Erlbaum. Copyright 1995 by Lawrence Erlbaum Associates. Reprinted with permission.)

To keep the conversation going, teachers can ask questions with phrases termed *view finders* (Bell, 1995):

- That's an interesting idea. I wonder if other people think like that?
- What would happen if . . .
- Can you tell me more about that?
- What tells you that?
- Can you think of other examples when that might happen too?
- I don't quite understand. Could you explain that to me again? (p. 355)

Considerations for interview assessment are as follows (Bell, 1995; Berenson, & Carter 1995):

- Give adequate time for students to think and respond to questions.
- Impress that their ideas are valuable.

Interviews may also be conducted with small groups of students. Students may feel more comfortable in a group situation and they may also provide insights based on their peers' ideas.

For a detailed discussion on interview techniques read White and Gunstone (1992, pp. 65–97).

Conducting interviews is time-consuming. But if time permits and opportunities are there, the techniques given in this section should be helpful.

- Speak with a kind and caring tone.
- Create a relaxed atmosphere.
- Keep the interview format consistent so that students know what to expect.
- Do not turn the interview into an instructional session.
- Encourage students through positive body language, but do not lead their answers.
- Plan questions ahead of time and use probes to draw out more information.

Questions on management: Do you need help to calibrate the pH probe? Did you all take accurate readings of the thermometer? Have you put the beakers away?

Questions to explore understanding: That's interesting. Tell me more about what you just said. Why do you think the color of the liquid in the conical flask changes to pink at a certain point? How would you interpret this graph?

Conversational interviews can be conducted *during* a unit of study or a lesson to elicit students' current understandings. For example, informal talk may be carried out with students to elicit their understandings when they perform laboratory or field investigations. Besides asking questions that pertain to lesson management, ask questions that would explore and probe students' understanding about what they are thinking and doing. In doing so, you are "helping the students clarify and reflect on their ideas, challenging the students' ideas, giving the students further information to consider, helping the students to change their ideas, helping the students find answers for their questions, getting the students thinking for themselves, helping the students test out their own ideas, or helping the students to reflect on their own ideas about learning" (Bell, 1995, p. 359). Students' new understandings and their questions can contribute to future lessons, activities, and investigations.

Bell (1995) sees much value and benefit in letting students talk during science lessons while teachers listen. The values and benefits include:

- Students will realize that the teacher is not the only legitimate member of the class who can contribute to the lesson. Students will readily see that they are also contributing members of the class.
- Students will recognize that their contributions are worthwhile to the lesson.
- Students will come to value their own ideas, to consider the views of others, to reflect personal ideas, to construct and test out personal and collective ideas, to accept new ideas, and to use their ideas with confidence.
- Students will get the impression that their ideas, regardless of scientific merit, are worthy of the teacher's and their peers' consideration.
- Students will have the opportunity to assess, develop, and change their ideas.
- Students will develop their thinking skills.
- Students will enjoy themselves, get involved, build confidence, and develop skills of cooperation (pp. 359–360).

Data obtained from interviews before, during, and after instruction can be used for planning teaching activities. Students can also trace their conceptual development and conceptual changes. They can compare their ideas with scientific ideas in their journal writing and in self-assessment activities. Records of student interviews can be part of their science portfolio.

Teacher-Made Observations

Teachers can observe students throughout the science lesson: in individual and group work situations, during interviews, and during group discussions. These observations can be recorded in a number of ways. Checklists can be created and used to monitor student achievement and to note when certain skills and techniques have been exhibited. The checklist can include such areas as curricular goals, attitudes, and processes used by the student. When the teacher notices these skills, he or she can merely check them off on the list. This gives the teacher an idea of where additional work and instruction may be necessary. Students can also use checklists to monitor their own achievements and to become aware of what is expected and required of them for the unit. Again, this makes students more responsible for their own learning.

Anecdotal records are another quick method of recording student observations. These are short notes that are jotted down about certain teacher-made observations, which can include student behavior, comments, questions, and ideas. The notes can be made on Post-it notes and then transferred to students' portfolios. The student's name and the date of the observation must be recorded for quick reference in the future.

Self-Assessment

Self-assessment is an effective method of making students aware of and responsible for their own learning and productivity. Self-assessment guides students in the learning process and gives them the opportunity to reflect on what they have learned and where they may require additional practice and/or instruction. Self-assessments can take many forms. As mentioned earlier, students can use checklists to monitor their progress. Journals are another valuable form of reflection. Questionnaires can also be used to guide and focus students' thinking (see Figure 13-3).

Name: _____   Date: _____

1. What was the most important thing that I learned from today's activity?
2. What was my favorite part of the activity? My least favorite part?
3. What was the most difficult part?
4. What did I not understand? Did I ask the teacher about it?
5. Did anything surprise me about the activity?
6. How did I feel about the activity?
7. How does this activity explain an everyday occurrence to me?

FIGURE 13-3
Student self-assessment questionnaire

FIGURE 13-4

Peer assessment questionnaire (*NOTE:* From *Science Assessment Program, Grade 8 Performance Component,* by Manitoba Education and Training, 1994, Winnipeg, Canada: Author. Copyright 1994 by Manitoba Education and Training. Adapted with permission.)

Name: _____   Date: _____

Partner's/Group Members' Name(s): _____

Please rate the questions using the following rating scale:
1. Always   2. Often   3. Sometimes   4. Never

1. I enjoyed working in groups.   _____
2. I shared my ideas.   _____
3. I helped my partner/group.   _____
4. We cooperated in group activity.   _____
5. I did more work than the others.   _____
6. I did less work than the others.   _____
7. I finished my work on time.   _____
8. My partner helped me.   _____
9. My partner suggested ideas.   _____
10. My partner was reliable.   _____

Comments:

Peer Assessment

Peer assessment can be used to assess students' abilities to work together in groups, but it can also be used to enable students to reflect on each other's accomplishments. Group-work assessment usually takes the form of a questionnaire that asks students to reflect on how they and their partners worked together. When assessing each other's accomplishments, the class should set procedures and criteria to be followed. Students should be encouraged to assess each other without bias, and to leave personal feelings out of the classroom. This form of assessment allows students to see different thought patterns and different manners of approaching and solving problems (see Figure 13-4). Students then respond jointly to the statements shown in Figure 13-5:

The group assessment sheet in Figure 13-5 enables students to reflect on their performance as a group and helps students think about improvements that they can make on future tasks. Teachers also have a way of examining group skills.

Graphic Organizers

Graphic organizers are an effective method for both teacher and students to assess students' understanding of a particular concept or fact. Students can organize the information as they understand it into several different forms of graphic organizers, including concept maps, diagrams, word webs, or idea balloons. Students should be encouraged to use whatever method of organization they are most comfortable with. The use of

Statements

1. Write the names of your group members.
2. Discuss how you worked together.
3. Briefly state the nature of your discussion before you started the problem.
4. Describe each member's responsibility and workload.
5. State how you designed your solution.
6. Discuss how you feel about what you have achieved.
7. Describe what you did as you carried out your research.
8. State what you learned from the research.

FIGURE 13-5

A group assessment (*NOTE: Reproduced from The Science of Problem-Solving: A Practical Guide for Science Teachers* (p. 123), by M. Watts, 1991, Portsmouth, NH: Heinemann. Used by permission of Cassel Plc, Wellington House, 125 Strand, London, England.)

graphic organizers helps students to organize all of the information that they have learned into an easily referenced graphic form. It enables them to focus on and review the information that they have learned. Graphic organizers also allow teachers to review student understandings in a relatively quick manner. The use of concept maps will enable teachers to note exactly where the student's conceptions may originate. For example, based on a series of concept maps constructed by the same group of students with Inspiration (see Figures 13-6a, 13-6b, and 13-6c), Greg Lupal, a high school teacher, states the following:

> In addition, seeing a series of maps produced as a topic is developed gives students and myself inner views into students' schemata. This is useful pedagogically. Further, I can see if a certain portion of a topic needs to be reviewed (say too many students are not making the connections I intended). I can also see connections that I didn't think of. This helps me in my own thinking and teaching. I have also noticed that the maps of students who have difficulty with calculations lack specific reference to actual examples, whereas students who have a greater facility include more detailed solutions to actual problems. Also, when students work in pairs to create these maps there is a dynamic interplay of their ideas as they construct these maps.

Products

Products can be used in the science classroom as an extension of the communication phase in journal entries, or as part of a project for summative assessment. Products are various creations that students use to express their understanding of a science concept. They can be in the form of models, drawings, stories, videos, and any other method that students feel help to demonstrate their knowledge. Products enable students to express their knowledge in a form that they feel is most suited to them.

Portfolios

Portfolios are becoming a popular means of assessment in science (Gitomer & Duschl, 1995); they are gaining so much attention because of their versatility, involvement of students, and ability to show evidence of growth

FIGURE 13-6a
Student concept map of
acids and bases—concept
map 1

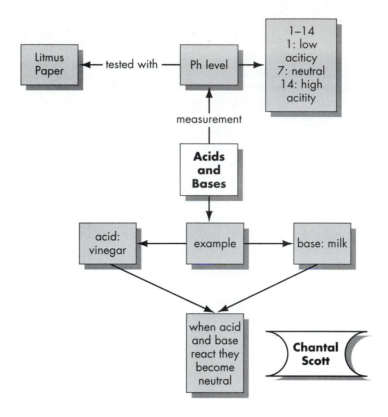

over time. A portfolio is a collection of a student's work over an extended period of time. The portfolio can be used to mark progress made during a unit of study, throughout the school year, or throughout the student's career at the school. The information gathered in the portfolio can be used to measure students' progress and growth in their understandings, skills, and attitudes. It can be used to show evidence of the student development to students, their parents, and school administrators.

Portfolios are a container of evidence collected to meet a purpose (Collins, 1992). This evidence can be in the form of artifacts (documents of students' work), reproductions (charts, photographs), attestations (letters from people other than the student about the student's work), and productions (reflections, goal statements, and captions developed especially for the portfolio). All of these forms of evidence are to be used to exhibit the student's skill, knowledge, and/or attitude in science. In most situations, the teacher designs the portfolio, clearly stating the purpose and goal of the collection to students. Teachers should be aware of limitations in time, cost, ability, and opportunity when having students create portfolios. Possible portfolios can include evidence of skills in the follow-

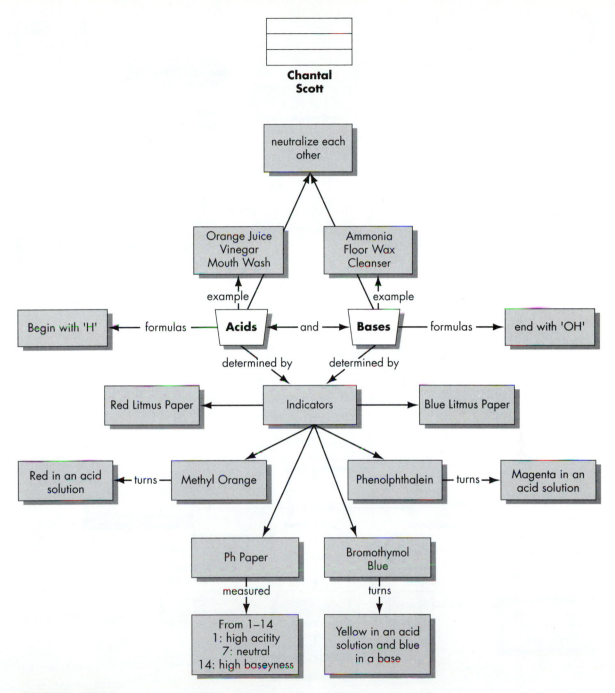

FIGURE 13-6b
Student concept map of acids and bases—concept map 2

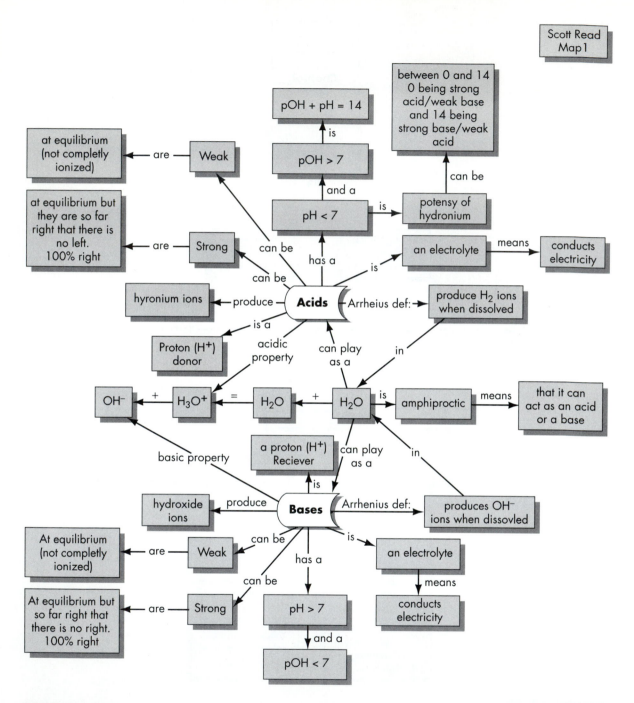

FIGURE 13-6c
Student concept map of acids and bases—concept map 3

ing areas: (1) a body of content that ranges from definitions to "conceptual structures that explain and predict" (Collins, 1992); (2) evidence of level-of-thinking skills ranging from precise, in-depth descriptions to the creation of scientifically based questions; and (3) expressions of an understanding of the social implications of science in our everyday lives (Collins, 1992).

When using portfolios in the classroom, teachers should strive to involve the students in decisions about what pieces to include and how to arrange the work. Portfolios can contain only the student's best examples of work, their best and their worst, or pieces that show a gradual improvement in their understanding. The teacher and student should decide what they want the portfolio to represent, and then choose the pieces to be included. Meeting on a regular basis with students, or giving them time each week to work on their portfolios, allows for continuous, unintrusive assessment to occur. In Appendices 13-2, 13-3, and 13-4, we have included "The Five C's of Portfolio Development," "What to Put in an MI Portfolio," and "An MI Portfolio Checklist," respectively.

 TEACHER PRACTICE

Construction of Continuous-Assessment Items

Examine several science topics. Develop items that reflect some of the continuous-assessment strategies.

Connect with a student and help that student develop a science portfolio. Share this student's portfolio with his or her peers in class, emphasizing the criteria used for assessing the portfolio.

Culminating-Assessment Strategies

Culminating assessment usually occurs in three different forms: written tests, performance-based tasks, and projects.

Written Tests

Students are required to give written responses to questions regarding their understanding of science concepts. Many students, however, find this form of assessment very difficult, especially those with reading and writing difficulties. If this form of assessment is to be used, alternative approaches should be created to meet the needs of these students. The questions used in this approach can take several forms: one-word answers, multiple-choice questions, a sentence, a paragraph, a diagram, or an illustration. Written answers can be done individually or in a group, and can be recorded in many fashions, such as on a worksheet, computer, or chalkboard.

Classroom assessment: Principles and practice for effective instruction by J. H. McMillan (1997), Boston: Allyn & Bacon is a useful reference for preparing assessment and test questions.

However, there are certain forms of written assessment that should be avoided because they rely on rote learning and memorization, and do not allow for creativity. They also give little indication of students' understandings and abilities, which is the main focus of assessment. Such questions include true-or-false, matching, and fill-in-the-blank questions. Even multiple-choice questions are not ideal, but if they are a must, try to create questions that require higher-level thinking on the part of the student. The following forms of written assessment allow for creativity and can show evidence of understanding.

Science Concept Stories. This form of assessment asks students to explain a concept in a scientific context. Students are given the choice of deciding what ideas and concepts they wish to include in their stories. Students may be also given a list of concepts:

Pretend that you are the egg that was used in today's experiment. Describe how you felt, as well as what caused you to be go through the small neck of the bottle.

You are a beam of light that is passing through a piece of red glass. Explain what happens and why it happens.

You are a seed and you have just been planted. Explain your life as you grow into a mature plant. Use as many of the following words as you can: germination, energy, primary leaves, cotyledons, radicle (embryonic root), stem, soil, elongated, roots, nutrients, seed coat, foliage leaves, sunlight, plumule (embryonic shoot), hook, photosynthesis, seedling.

Pretend that you are a marshmallow that is put under a vacuum pump. Describe what will you go through once the pump is turned on. (Boyle's law)

If you and your classmates are air molecules inside an air-filled balloon, what happens when the balloon is placed in liquid nitrogen? (Charles's law)

Concept Maps. As mentioned in continuous assessment, graphic organizers such as concept maps allow teachers to assess students' understanding of the unit of study by analyzing the way that the concepts are integrated into the students' concept maps. The maps can be used to form further questions, and to decide what areas need to be reviewed or retaught. In this form of assessment, students are given a list of words and are required to show the relationships between the words through the use of arrows and connecting words.

Draw a concept map using the following concept labels: solvent, solute, dissolving, solution, water, crystals, soluble, insoluble, solid, liquid, mixture.

See Figure 13-7 for an example of a concept map. From the concept map, the following questions can be formed:

- Explain how a mixture can be soluble or insoluble.
- Explain the relationship between a solute, solvent and solution, giving an example of each.

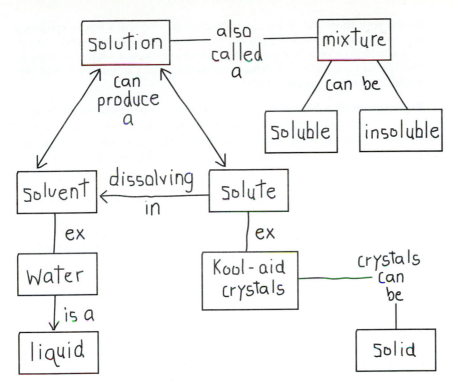

FIGURE 13-7
An eighth-grade student's concept map

Representations. This form of assessment asks students to draw or label a diagram. Teachers can gain a deeper insight into their students' understandings of science concepts. This also gives students who have difficulty expressing themselves in written form an alternative form of expression.

Draw a picture showing how lightning reaches the earth. Use labels (+, −) to show charges. Briefly describe what happens to cause lightning.

Draw a rough sketch of the human heart showing different concentrations of oxygen in the blood in the chambers of the heart. Describe the blood flow in the heart.

Problem-Solving Questions. Students are asked to solve a particular problem that has many possible solutions. This will allow the teacher to assess students' abilities to apply new meaning to science concepts, and how they are able to manipulate and apply their knowledge in different situations.

You have learned about circuits in science today. You want to show off to your little brother what you have learned. So you decide to demonstrate for him how a circuit works. You get the necessary supplies—wire, light bulb, and a battery—and you begin to put the circuit together. However, as you are putting it together you notice that there is a gap in your circuit. You quickly glance around your room and notice these objects: a jar of coins, a box of crayons, a cup with a metal spoon in it, and a glass with a straw in it. You don't want to look silly in front of your brother, so which objects do you ask him to bring so that you can conclude your demonstration for him? Explain briefly why you would ask for those specific objects.

Explanation of a Situation. This form of assessment allows the teacher to observe and assess students' abilities to recognize concepts in a new situation, as well as their understandings of the concepts. Students are asked to explain a specific event based on their understanding of a scientific concept.

> Many students use a magnifying glass to set paper on fire. How does this work?
>
> There is a large cruise ship leaving the harbor for the open seas. If this ship weighs thousands of pounds, how is it able to float on water?
>
> How can the mushroom live in the dark in the soil in the cave? Could roses or grass grow in this cave? Explain.

Explanation of a Diagram. The test items consist of an illustration, diagram or series of diagram, or graph. Students are asked to answer questions, solve a problem, or explain a situation based upon them (see Figures 13-8a and 13-8b).

Closed-Ended Questions. Students are asked to describe or explain scientific concepts in their own words, which makes this a useful method of assessment for all students.

> Your mom receives a crystal ornament for a birthday present. She sets it on the windowsill. Later that day, when the sun is shining through the window, dozens of tiny rainbows appear on your walls. Why does this happen?
>
> You and your classmates are involved in a game of tug-of-war; meanwhile a tenth-grade student passes by and tries to make fun of you. You try to explain to him that you are trying to understand the concept of balanced and unbalanced force. How could you use this demonstration to explain these phenomena to the tenth-grade student?

Traditional multiple-choice answers test only whether your students know a concept, not how much they know or how they learned it. There is only one right answer, which usually relies on rote memorization.

To construct alternative multiple-choice items, teachers must have information on students' conceptions on a particular topic because the distractors are based on students' conceptions.

Alternative Multiple-Choice Assessment. Treagust (1995) uses alternative multiple-choice items to diagnose students' conceptions before a unit of study begins or after the teaching of the topic. This different type of multiple-choice instrument uses propositional knowledge as well as students' conceptions.

DEVELOPMENT OF THE MULTIPLE-CHOICE QUESTIONNAIRE

Step 1:   List each of the propositional statements of a specific unit of study.

Step 2:   Make a concept map.

Step 3:   Relate propositional statements to the concept map to ensure internal consistency.

Step 4:   Examine the literature to identify students' conceptions. List these.

Step 5:   Develop multiple-choice items with free response. Each item contains a limited number of propositional statements. Each multiple-choice item is followed by a space for the student to complete the reason why the particular propositional statement was chosen.

Step 6:   Develop the two-tier diagnostic test. The first part of each item in the questionnaire is a multiple-choice question consisting of two or three choices. The second part of each item consists of a set of four possible

To earn points for a multiple-choice item, the student must make the correct choice and give the correct reason.

Please refer to the diagram below to answer questions 63, 64 and 65.

The following diagram illustrates the circulatory system of the human body.

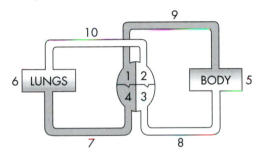

63. Which chamber receives oxygenated blood?

  A)   1
  B)   2
  C)   3
  D)   4

64. When blood is pumped from chamber 4, where does it travel to then?

  A)   7
  B)   8
  C)   9
  D)   10

64. Which sequence describes the pathway of the blood when it **returns** to the heart from the lungs?

  A)   1 to 4 to 7 to 6
  B)   2 to 3 to 8 to 5
  C)   9 to 1 to 4 to 7
  D)   10 to 2 to 3 to 8

FIGURE 13-8a
Explanation of a diagram (*NOTE:* From *Grade 8 Science Assessment Test Booklet* (p. 41), by Manitoba Education and Training, 1994, Winnipeg, Canada: Author. Copyright 1994 by Manitoba Education and Training. Reprinted with permission.)

reasons for the answer given to the first part. One of the reasons must be the correct reason. The other three reasons must be students' conceptions, obtained from steps 4 and 5.

AN EXAMPLE IN CHEMISTRY

The commercially available substance Vaseline has a smooth, thick, creamlike structure. Based on this, Vaseline would be classified as being

(1) a covalent molecular substance

FIGURE 13-8b

Questions on a graph (*NOTE:* From *Grade 8 Science Assessment Test Booklet* (p. 25), by Manitoba Education and Training, 1994, Winnipeg, Canada: Author. Copyright 1994 by Manitoba Education and Training. Reprinted with permission.)

Flight

A team of grade 8 students tried to control the height of a helium balloon by adding paper clips to a string attached to the balloon. They made the following graph.

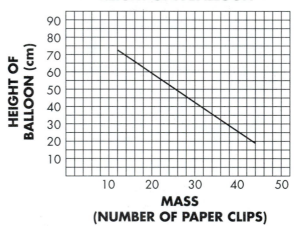

THE EFFECT OF MASS ON THE HEIGHT OF A BALLOON

a) How high would the helium balloon rise if 20 paper clips were attached to the string? _____

b) If the helium balloon is 50 cm above the floor, how many paper clips were attached to the string? _____

c) How many paper clips are needed to keep the balloon 80 cm above the floor? _____

d) The balloon rises from 20 cm, to 30 cm, to 70 cm, and, finally, to 100 cm. What happens to the number of paper clips required to hold the balloon as it rises to this height? _____

e) Explain why. _____
    _____
    _____
    _____

   (2) a covalent network (continuous covalent) substance
       Because
       (a) the substance has a continuous linear lattice structure.
       (b) the high viscosity of the substance results from the continuous covalent network.
       (c) the molecules in the substance experience weak intermolecular forces and easily move to accommodate changes in the shape of the solid.
       (d) the bonds within the molecules of the substance break easily to accommodate the changes in the shape of the solid (Peterson, Treagust, & Garnett, 1989, p. 305).

BLOOM'S TAXONOMY/MULTIPLE INTELLIGENCES TESTING

This test on acids and bases was presented by Mike Kattenfeld and Angela Poetteker at the 1998 P-STAR Conference Seminar. Identify which levels of Bloom's Taxonomy and which of the multiple intelligences (described by Gardner, 1993) are represented by each of the following test questions:

1. In Denver, Colorado, in April of 1983, nitric acid poured from a train car in a major acid spill. The acid attacked metals and emitted a yellowish-brown gas. How would you have combated the spill? Why? Show an equation.
   (4 points)
2. Mr. Kattenfeld had indigestion. He knew that the 150 mL of his stomach acid had a concentration of 0.050 M. How many grams of baking soda ($NaHCO_3$) did Mr. Kattenfeld need to ingest to get a good night's sleep? Explain how you solved the problem.
   (5 points)
3. (See Appendix 13-5 for the word cycle that would be presented to students.)
   (3 points)
4. Use a diagram (e.g., Venn, Double Bubble Map) to compare and contrast acids and bases. Include at least three characteristics unique to acids, three characteristics unique to bases, and three characteristics common to both acids and bases.
   (3 points)
5. Evaluate the following statement: "Acid rain is a global issue." Consider one side of the issue, providing three points to support your perspective. Make sure to include an introduction and a conclusion, while paying close attention to your grammar and spelling.
   (3 points)

                                              TOTAL: 18 points

Performance Tasks

Performance-based assessment involves completing a task or constructing a response that demonstrates a student's knowledge of a skill, process, or concept. These tasks are usually hands-on activities, but can also take the

form of open-ended questions, exhibits, group projects, interviews, oral presentations, demonstrations, computer simulations, or portfolio presentations. There are many different methods of assessing students through performance tasks, the most popular being hands-on activities.

Through the use of hands-on experiments, students can give evidence of their abilities to hypothesize, observe, record data, summarize, describe, and so on. Students are not required to memorize abstract formulas and definitions, but instead are given various materials and real-life objectives, and asked to perform certain hands-on activities. These activities must be practical and authentic, meaning that students can see the application of such activities in their daily lives. This allows students to demonstrate their understanding of a concept in a manner that is both familiar and important to them.

Hands-on performance activities can be designed in several ways. They can be set up as a series of centers where students move from task to task, or they can be in set places where students design and carry out their investigations. These tasks can involve finding a solution to a problem, or developing and carrying out the process of an investigation. The problems can have one or many solutions, and assess the creativity of the students.

Again, Berenson and Carter (1995) give several useful suggestions on how to run a successful performance assessment in your classroom. They suggest that four stations be set up in each corner of the room. Half of the class works at the stations, while the other half works on a written test. Students are to be told that there is no one right answer, but several. Give the students points for creative answers and approaches. The following are different forms that performance-based assessment can take.

Science Investigations. Investigations can allow the teacher to assess students' understanding of and ability to apply concepts, design experiments, and solve problems. They also allow observations of students' performance abilities in the areas of predicting, inferring, hypothesizing, controlling variables, observing, classifying, measuring, recording and interpreting data, and handling equipment. All of these skills are important and necessary for success in science, and by observing students performing these skills, teachers can discover where further instruction and practice may be required. Examples of science investigations are:

determining the rate of reaction
investigating magnetic field–current interactions
investigating the effects of temperature in enzyme activity
classifying and identifying unlabeled mineral samples using appropriate
    tests
investigating the effect of sound on the human body.
analyzing local water samples

The following performance-based assessment was constructed and presented at the 1998 P-STAR Conference by two chemistry preservice teachers.

P-STAR CONFERENCE PAPER (13-1)

Performance-Based Assessment: An "Alternate" Vee Diagram Activity

Mike Kattenfeld and Angela Poetteker

Students are placed at stations in pairs and are instructed to perform the task as outlined below. All required materials are provided to students, including four "unknown" antacids labeled A, B, C, and D. Student performance is observed by a tester as students perform the investigations.

1. You are a chemical analyst. Your employer has asked you to determine the most effective antacid.

    The equipment provided in front of you will help you to solve this problem. The four antacids are labeled. Study the four samples of antacids and predict which antacid would most effectively neutralize stomach acid.

    – Our prediction: Antacid name _____

– Why do you think so?

_____

_____

2. Develop and set up an investigation to find the answer to your problem and record your data in chart form.

ANTACID	*RESULT*
A	
B	
C	
D	

3. Which sample was the most effective antacid? _____
   – Why was this so?

_____

_____

Antacid Tests Observation and Comment Sheet

Category	Points	Comments:
Worked cooperatively to design and perform the investigation	/2	
Predicted	/1	
Controlled variables	/1	
Observed	/1	
Measured (pH, drops to neutralize)	/3	
Recorded data	/3	
Interpreted data	/1	
Handled equipment	/1	
Understood the problem	/1	
Solved the problem	/2	
Understood the concept of neutralization	/1	
Other comments:		

Science Activity Stations. Stations are appropriate for assessing students' understandings of certain concepts, as well as their abilities in certain areas. At each station, students will find a question or situation, as well as the equipment that they are to use to solve the problem. Students are required to complete the tasks in a certain period of time, and then continue on to the next station. There should be one station for each student in the class. Following are some examples:

Set out three different types of seeds. Have students observe and identify the three types. Have students cut each seed in half and locate the following structures: the seed coat, cotyledons, endosperm, radicle, and plumule. Students are required to draw the three seeds and label the structures listed.

Place seeds, a glass container, a plastic container (with four holes in the bottom), rocks, soil, and a few other materials (styrofoam, foil, plastic wrap) on the table. Instruct students to create an environment that would best promote the germination of a seed. Have the students list the materials that they chose, and why they chose them. Also have them list all other factors that are necessary.

Place half of an Alka-Seltzer tablet in a glass half-filled with water. Describe what is happening. Is this a physical or chemical change? Give a reason for your answer.

Explain what happens when two open containers (for example, watch glasses), one containing 2 mL of concentrated HCl acid and the other containing 3 mL of concentrated NH_3, are put side by side (no distance between them). What do you think is the white vapor that is produced as a result?

Teacher Demonstration. This alternative to stations and investigations can be used when there is a lack of equipment or when the task is potentially dangerous. This is especially useful in classes that contain students with behavioral problems, to ensure the safety of all students. Guidelines for teacher demonstrations include the following:

- Ensure that everyone can view the event.
- Speak in a loud, clear voice so that everyone can hear.
- Allow students to move to the front or change positions if the activity is difficult to see from a distance.
- Always try an activity before it is attempted in the classroom to ensure that you can obtain the expected results.

The following procedure is an example of a teacher demonstration:

3 g powdered iron is placed in a test tube; then 5 mL concentrated hydrochloric acid is added to the test tube. Immediately after adding the acid, place an empty test tube over the top of the test tube containing the iron and the acid. Make sure the test tubes are the same size. Collect the hydrogen gas that is produced as a result. Make sure you wait long enough to collect the gas—usually two or three minutes. While collecting the gas, invite students to touch the test tube in which the reaction is occurring; it should be very warm. They should also notice occasional color change. All of these characteristics—gas production, change in temperature, possible color change—are signs of chemical change. After the gas is collected, seal the test tube containing the hydrogen gas with your thumb. To confirm that the collected gas is hydrogen, do a pop flame test.

Creative Drama. Creative drama is a good assessment technique for students who have difficulty expressing their thoughts orally or in written form to give evidence of their understandings of science concepts. This can be in the form of mime or dramatic discourse, individually or in a group.

Have students choose a topic from a list given by the teacher. Have them create and act out a situation that involves the topic. Possible topics are:

- How does light affect our daily lives?
- What would happen if the sun did not rise?
- The invention of the electric light bulb
- Space travel; Apollo 13
- Act out the rotation and revolution of the Earth around the Sun, depicting day, night, and the seasons.

Following is an example of how to show the concept of equilibrium through creative drama:

Select eight students, and place four on each side of the room. Place 20 inflated balloons on the floor on each side. Ask students on each side to carry one balloon at a time and walk with it at a steady pace and place it on the other side. Carry out this "to and fro" process for five minutes. Count the number of balloons on each side. The number of balloons on each side should be more or less the same as when they started out, thus demonstrating the concept of equilibrium.

 TEACHER PRACTICE

Performance-Based Assessment Items
Examine several science topics. Develop performance-based items for investigations and stations.

Projects

Assessment also includes problem solving in open-ended projects. While science is a way of knowing, specially focused in a science class, it can also be translated to everyday life. Science-related problems are everywhere, needing multiple solutions. Open-ended projects require problem-solving standards and methodologies. Something becomes a problem when the learner cannot reach his or her goals or objectives without obstacles. Watts (1991) distinguishes three types of problems: "Given problems, where the solver is given both the goal and strategies; Goal problems, where the solver is given the goal and nothing else—the solvers have to decide and develop their own strategies; and Own problems, where solvers decide both the goal and the strategies" (p. 8). Examples of "given" problems in science are: "Given $f = ma$, where a is $4m\,s^{-2}$ and m is 3 kg, find f. What are the benefits, effects and disadvantages of color and flavor additives in food" (Watts, 1991, p. 12). Here the goals are specified. The problem statement may not be explicit (particularly in the second example), but solving it requires no more than looking at a textbook or teacher-given notes. For "goal" and "own" problems, students "choose the best strategies from a wide range of possibilities to achieve their goal" (Watts, 1991, p. 8). The design process and the scientific process constitute the "goal" and "own" problem-solving strategies. Examples of problems of the "goal" type for open-ended projects are as follows (Watts, 1991, pp. 9, 142–143):

- Monitor and adjust soil conditions to maximize vegetable growth.
- Explore dampness control in a house.
- Design and construct a light meter.
- Design and make a water salinity tester.
- Investigate the polyunsaturated, mono-unsaturated and/or saturated fatty acid content of some common foods, such as 2 percent milk and margarine.

These problems are not the type you find in ordinary textbooks, although the "goal" is set by a teacher. They are real-life problems that may be given as open-ended projects or as the starting point of "owning a problem." In these problem-solving tasks, not only the solutions or the products but also the processes or means are important. Best solutions can be identified based on scientific principles and relevant information.

Problem solving in open-ended, everyday-life contexts is useful for learners in the following ways:

- To take responsibility and ownership for learning
- To engage in decision making and many social skills
- To take part in active learning
- To learn many scientific skills
- To learn science content as needed
- To link cross-curricular content and methodologies
- To engage in the highest and most complex forms of human activity: problem solving and creative thinking
- To communicate effectively (Watts, 1991)

The focus is on the student as described in Chapter 12, which describes the science-technology-society-environment connection. "The adoption of problem-solving activities in school science . . . is a useful attempt to simulate and explore the roles of scientists 'doing' science" (Watts, 1991, p. 16).

How do we manage problem solving in the classroom? Watts (1991, p. 16) offers the following suggestions:

- Set the same problem for a whole class group so that different students generate different solutions.
- Set one large problem for all and ask different groups to tackle different aspects so that you build a composite picture at the end.
- Set different problems for different groups, or even a different problem for each individual, and allow them to work separately.

- Before beginning problem solving, deliberately teach all the facts, concepts, and skills so that the students will have all the relevant information at their fingertips.
- Use the motivating power of problem solving as a means of allowing the students to decide and satisfy their own knowledge needs.

Project-based learning and the assessment of such learning is complex. A set of skills or processes as well as the science concepts involved in a problem-solving approach may serve as criteria for assessment. The knowledge and skills involved in problem solving depend on the problem, the context in which the problem is embedded, and the possible means to a solution. Assessing the project depends on the application of science content knowledge and problem-solving skills used. A broad group of skills includes the following:

- *Problem-solving and creative skills:* the ability to diagnose the features of a problem, frame hypotheses, and design experiments to test those hypotheses and evaluate the results; the ability to draw on relevant ideas and use materials inventively
- *Observation and visual skills:* the ability to observe accurately; the ability to record distributions, patterns, and relationships, using scale, perspective, shape, and color; the ability to interpret observations
- *Numerical skills:* the ability to estimate and measure, and to understand the use of numerical relationships, shapes, and patterns
- *Imaginative skills:* the ability to put oneself into other situations, whether of time, place, or person, to visualize other experiences; the ability to discipline the imagination by evidence and experience, to reorder and reshape experiences and images
- *Organizational and study skills:* the ability to extract information, to arrange in sequence, to classify, to weigh and interpret evidence and to draw conclusions, to see relationships; the ability to make the best use of time
- *Physical and practical skills:* the ability to develop manual dexterity and a variety of coordinated body movements, to select appropriate tools and pieces of equipment and to use them effectively
- *Social skills:* the ability to cooperate, to negotiate, to express ideas in a variety of contexts, to consider other points of view, to recognize nonverbal communication
- *Communication skills:* the ability to use reading and writing, oral, aural, nonverbal, and graphical skills to receive and convey communication without the risk of misunderstanding (Watts, 1991, p. 41)

More specific skills include the following:

PROCESSES:

- communicating and discussing—which include questioning, thinking, seeking help, negotiating, listening

- processing information—which includes selecting, using relationships, designing, drawing conclusions, controlling interacting variables
- problem solving, experimentation, and decision making—which include predicting, inferring, interpreting, formulating hypotheses, modeling, evaluating, assessing, classifying, managing time, costing

SKILLS

- listening, talking, reasoning, drawing, numeracy, small-group skills, observing, nonverbal communication, searching, measuring, manipulation, graphically recording

ATTITUDES

- open-mindedness, self-criticism, responsibility, independence of thought, perseverance, cooperation, skepticism, desire to be well informed, confidence, respect, sensitivity, willingness to be involved, tolerance, persuasiveness, questioning, trust (Watts, 1991, p. 42)

You and your students can develop a Likert-style assessment scale (excellent, good, satisfactory, fair, and poor, ranging from a positive of 5 to a negative of 1 from left to right) for either a "goal" or "own" project.

TEACHER PRACTICE

Construction of Culminating-Assessment Items
Examine several science topics. Construct a written test that reflects a variety of the culminating-assessment strategies.

SCORING KEYS AND GUIDES

Authentic-assessment strategies have been criticized because they are difficult to grade and the grading is very subjective. This is true only if a teacher does not create a set of mastery criteria for the unit of study. Through the use of such scoring guides as rubrics, authentic assessment can easily be given a fair grade, and can stand as evidence to show why that grade was assigned. A *rubric* is a set of guidelines that are prepared in advance and designed for evaluating students' work, progress, and achievements.

   Lundberg (1997) strongly suggests the use of student-generated rubrics, especially at the senior level. To create a student-generated rubric, Lundberg suggests presenting students with a science problem and asking them to solve it. Students then work in pairs and review each other's work and grade it, giving reasons for the grades. Students' names can be replaced by numbers to ensure anonymity. The class as a whole lists the reasons for high and low grades. Students are then asked to work in threes to categorize the list; then they join into groups of six and compare categories. The class as a whole then reaches a consensus on what would constitute a high score and a low score for their rubrics. Such rubrics can be designed for lab procedures and write-ups, presentations, and research projects. Through the use of student-generated rubrics, students are well aware of what is expected of them, and rubrics allow for consistent grading for authentic assessments. There are presently four different forms of rubrics available for creating and arranging criteria to be used to judge students' progress. The rubrics will be illustrated based on the following test question:

> Observe and identify the three types of seeds that are displayed. Cut each seed in half and locate the following structures: seed coat, cotyledons, endosperm, radicle, and plumule. Draw a diagram of each and label the structures listed.

The Point System

The point system is probably one of the most popular forms of rubrics used in today's classrooms. A certain number of points is assigned for specific features that are deemed important or necessary parts of the response or process. Mastery criteria for each part of the solution are designed, with each feature being listed. As points decrease, the criteria for each subsequent level are lowered slightly. This system is suited to open-ended questions because it gives partial credit for incomplete responses. For the sample activity, a possible rubric based on a point scale may look like the following:

6 points: Correctly identifies, draws, and labels all parts of each seed.
4 points: Correctly identifies and draws each seed, but mislabels one or two structures.
2 points: Correctly identifies each seed, but drawing and labeling are incomplete.
0 points: Makes no attempt to draw or label seeds, or answers are incorrect.

Analytic Rating Scale

This form of scoring is very similar to the point scale, except that it assigns a descriptive phrase to the rating instead of a number. Students would receive a rating of excellent, very good, good, satisfactory, or unsatisfactory to express the level and quality of their work. The descriptive words and phrases used do not have to be restricted to the preceding list. There are many others that may be more meaningful to your students, and their input should be elicited when creating and using this type of rubric.

Focused Holistic Rating Scales

This is also one of the most popular scoring methods used for rubrics in the classroom. Focused holistic rating scales differ from the point scales in that the entire response is graded as a whole, whereas with point scales each section of the response is graded based on the criteria. This form of scoring is suited to grading students on their overall performance on tasks and products. The following is an example of a focused holistic rating scale based again on the sample activity:

4 points: Performs entire activity; identifies and draws each seed completely and accurately; labels each structure correctly; shows competence and understanding of the structures of a seed.

3 points: Performs activity; identifies and draws each seed fairly accurately; labels most of the structures correctly; exhibits a fairly good understanding of the structures.

2 points: Performs some of the activity; omits one of the seeds; omits some of the structures, or incorrectly labels them; shows a vague understanding of the structures.

1 point: Very little response; diagrams are incomplete; does not perform entire task; has at least one correct answer.

Checklists

As mentioned earlier under formative assessment strategies, checklists are also a useful method of scoring with a rubric. Checklists again allow students to see what was required of them, what they achieved, and where they lost points. Checklists can be used for both written and performance tasks. As with all forms of scoring, checklists should be created before the assessment occurs, to allow the teacher to address all of his or her attention to the students and their tasks. As each criterion on the list is noted, the teacher can check off the student's name. Individual checklists can be created for each student, and each skill is checked off as evidence of that skill is shown.

_____ 1. Correctly identifies each seed.
_____ 2. Cuts each seed in half and observes structures.
_____ 3. Draws each seed.
_____ 4. Labels the structures of each seed (McColskey and O'Sullivan, 1993, pp.41–44).

 TEACHER PRACTICE

Rubrics

Construct assessment items for various assessment strategies such as individual written tests, group problem-solving projects, performance-based tests, and STSE project-based tests. Develop rubrics for your assessment strategies.

⚛ CHAPTER REVIEW

In the past few years, there has been a shift toward authentic-assessment practices in the classroom. Authentic assessment includes interviews, journal writing, graphic organizers, performance-based assessment, and portfolios. Authentic assessment implies that the learning and assessment are complementary, and that assessment tasks are used to measure students' abilities to translate their knowledge in a real-world setting. Students are no longer confined to mere pencil-and-paper tests, because this way of assessment does not relate to the manner in which they learned the concepts. Authentic assessment allows students to be tested in situations that are similar to the manner in which the information was learned, and to assess their abilities to apply that knowledge in a situation that they may encounter in everyday life.

The assessment criteria and procedures provide teachers with a means to effectively judge students' progress for determining instructional goals, planning curricula, redesigning teaching and learning strategies, and rethinking ways of assessment. Assessment provides feedback to students about their work and progress, to teachers about the success of their teaching methods, to parents about their children's progress, and to districts and policymakers about the effectiveness of the curricula and programs. This feedback will enable those involved to make the changes needed to help students become scientifically literate. Teachers should develop assessment criteria, procedures, and tasks by learning to identify essential components of exemplary assessment practices.

PROBES

1. Using Gardner's multiple intelligences and Bloom's levels of cognitive complexity as your guides, examine a unit test that has been developed by a teacher. Write additional assessment items that will reflect Gardner's and Bloom's work.
2. Construct continuous-assessment items for a particular unit. Complete them with rubrics and scoring keys.
3. Develop a culminating test for a particular unit. Complete it with rubrics and scoring keys.

APPENDIX 13-1

Multiple Intelligences Theory and Bloom's Taxonomy
Ecology Unit: Local Environment—Trees in Your Neighborhood

	Bloom's Six Levels of Educational Objectives					
	Knowledge	**Comprehension**	**Application**	**Analysis**	**Synthesis**	**Evaluation**
Linguistic Intelligence	memorize names of trees	explain how trees receive nutrients	given description of tree diseases, suggest cause of each disease	list parts of tree	explain how a tree functions in relation to the ecosystem	rate different methods of controlling tree growth
Logical-Mathematical Intelligence	remember number of points on specific trees' leaves	convert English to metric in calculating height of tree	given height of smaller tree, estimate height of larger tree	analyze materials found in sap residue	given weather, soil, and other information, chart projected growth of a tree	rate different kinds of tree nutrients based on data
Spatial Intelligence	remember basic configurations of specific trees	look at diagrams of trees and tell what stage of growth they are in	use geometric principles to determine height of tree	draw cellular structure of tree root	create a landscaping plan using trees as central feature	evaluate practicality of different landscaping plans
Bodily-Kinesthetic Intelligence	identify tree by the feel of the bark	given array of tree fruits, identify seeds	given type of local tree, find an ideal location for planting it	create different parts of tree from clay	gather all materials needed for planting a tree	evaluate the quality of different kinds of fruit
Musical Intelligence	remember songs that deal with trees	explain how old tree songs came into being	change the lyrics of an old tree song to reflect current issues	classify songs by issue and historical period	create your own tree song based on information in this unit	rate the songs from best to worst and give reasons for your choices
Interpersonal Intelligence	record responses to the question "What is your favorite tree?"	determine the most popular tree in class by interviewing others	use survey results to pick location for field trip to orchard	classify kids into groups according to favorite tree	arrange field trip to orchard by contacting necessary people	rank three methods to ask others about tree preference
Intrapersonal Intelligence	remember a time you climbed a tree	share the primary feeling you had while up in the tree	develop "tree-climbing rules" based upon your experience	divide up your experience into "beginning," "middle," and "end"	plan a tree-climbing expedition based on your past experience	explain what you liked "best" and "least" about your experience

APPENDIX 13-2

The Five C's of Portfolio Development

The kinds of materials placed in an MI portfolio depend upon the educational purposes and goals of each portfolio. There are at least five fundamental uses of portfolios:

1. *Celebration:* To acknowledge and validate students' products and accomplishments during the year
2. *Cognition:* To help students reflect upon their own work
3. *Communication:* To let parents, administrators, and other teachers know about students' learning progress
4. *Cooperation:* To provide a means for groups of students to collectively produce and evaluate their own work
5. *Competency:* To establish criteria by which a student's work can be compared to that of other students or to a standard or benchmark

NOTE: From *Multiple Intelligences in the Classroom* (pp. 128, 129), by T. Armstrong, 1994. Alexandria, VA: Association for Supervision and Curriculum Development. Copyright © 1994 ASCD. Reprinted by permission. All rights reserved.

APPENDIX 13-3

What to Put in an MI Portfolio

To document linguistic intelligence:

- Research reports (journal jottings, preliminary drafts, and final report)
- Written description of investigations, POE
- Audiotapes of debates, discussions, problem-solving processes

To document logical-mathematical intelligence:

- Science skills checklists
- Samples of graphs
- Rough notes of mathematical problem solving in science, such as $f = m/a$
- Final write-ups of science lab experiments
- Photos of science fair projects
- Graphic organizers: hierarchical maps

To document spatial intelligence:

- Three-dimensional structures; for example, molecular models, complex structures—carbohydrates, proteins, fats, polymers

- Diagrams, flow charts, sketches, and/or mind maps of thinking
- Photos and videos of projects
- Multimedia computer simulations

To document bodily-kinesthetic intelligence:

- Videotapes of projects and demonstrations
- Samples of design projects
- Photos of hands-on projects
- Videotapes of creative drama, such as movement of molecules or atoms

To document musical intelligence:

- Samples of science principles in musical format

To document interpersonal intelligence

- Letters to and from others (STS and SDE issues)
- Traditional and electronic dialogue journals
- Written feedback from peers, teachers, and experts
- Teacher-student conference reports (summarized/transcribed)
- Peer-group research reports
- Photos, videos, or write-ups of cooperative learning projects
- Documentation of field studies in science

To document intrapersonal intelligence:

- Personal journal entries
- Self-assessment essays, checklists, drawings, activities
- Samples of self-reflection exercises
- Questionnaires
- Student-kept progress charts
- Notes of self-reflection on own work

NOTE: From *Multiple Intelligences in the Classroom* (Figure 10.5, pp. 128, 129), by T. Armstrong, 1994. Alexandria, VA: Association for Supervision and Curriculum Development. Copyright © 1994 ASCD. Adapted by permission. All rights reserved.

APPENDIX 13-4

An MI Portfolio Checklist

The process of assessing portfolios is very complex. Current reforms in assessment include development of benchmarks and holistic scoring. Armstrong (1994) argues that these tools are best suited for the competency dimension of portfolio development and to judge students against predetermined criteria and standards that promote competition and not cooperation. More empathetic assessment compares a student to his or her own past performance, thus measuring self-development and growth. Armstrong (1994) aptly states that: "MI theory provides an assessment framework within which students can have their rich and complex lives acknowledged, celebrated, and nurtured" (p. 132).

HOW WILL YOU USE THE PORTFOLIO?

_____ For student self-reflection (Cognition)
_____ As part of regular school evaluation/report card (Competency)
_____ At parent conferences (Communication, Competency)
_____ In IEP/SST meetings (Communication, Competency)
_____ In communicating to next year's teacher(s) (Communication, Competency)
_____ In curricular planning (Competency)
_____ In acknowledging students' accomplishments (Celebration)
_____ In creating cooperative learning activities (Cooperation)
_____ Other:

HOW WILL IT BE ORGANIZED?

_____ Only finished pieces from a variety of subjects
_____ Different expressions of a specific objective
_____ Charting of progress from first idea to final realization
_____ Representative samples of a week/month/year's work
_____ Only "best" work
_____ Include "group" work
_____ Other:

WHAT PROCEDURES WILL YOU USE IN PLACING ITEMS IN THE PORTFOLIO?

_____ Select regular times for pulling student work
_____ Train students to select (e.g., flagging with stickers)

_____ Pull items that meet preset criteria
_____ Random approach
_____ Other:

WHAT WILL THE PORTFOLIO LOOK LIKE?

_____ Two pieces of posterboard stapled or taped together
_____ Box or other container
_____ Scrapbook
_____ Diary or journal
_____ Manila folder
_____ Bound volume
_____ CD-ROM
_____ Other:

WHO WILL EVALUATE THE PORTFOLIO?

_____ Teacher alone
_____ Teacher working in collaboration with other teachers
_____ Student self-evaluation
_____ Peer evaluation
_____ Other:

HOW WILL THE WORKS IN THE PORTFOLIO BE ARRANGED?

_____ Chronologically
_____ By student: from "crummy" to "great" (with reasons given)
_____ By teacher: from poor to superior (with reasons given)
_____ From birth of an idea to its fruition
_____ By subject area
_____ Other:

WHAT FACTORS WILL GO INTO EVALUATING THE PORTFOLIO?

_____ Number of entries
_____ Range of entries
_____ Degree of self-reflection demonstrated
_____ Improvement from past performances
_____ Achievement of preset goals (student's, teacher's, school's)
_____ Interplay of production, perception, and reflection
_____ Responsiveness to feedback/mediation
_____ Depth of revision
_____ Group consensus (among teachers)
_____ Willingness to take a risk
_____ Development of themes
_____ Use of benchmarks or standards for comparison
_____ Other:

PART FOUR

PLANNING FOR TEACHING SCIENCE

One of the most frequent laments of preservice teachers comes from a perception that teacher education programs fail to address the real world of teaching and schools. There is a common view that teacher education courses are too theoretical, that they fail to effectively address teaching practice, and that the *real* learning goes on in the schools during practice teaching, not in the college or university classroom. We do not discount the critical role that practice teaching plays in any preservice program. But, at the same time, we do not discount the critical role that your education courses play in allowing you to make meaning from those practical experiences in the schools. We have kept these concerns in mind as we wrote this textbook and we conclude with two chapters that tie together the various aspects of science learning and teaching that have already been examined, providing concrete examples to illustrate how other preservice teachers have put this *theory* into *practice* and how you might do so.

Chapter 14 begins with some theoretical views on learning and then considers some ways of implementing those views in planning for teaching and assessing learning. The common knowledge construction model for unit planning is presented and illustrated in a chemistry unit prepared by two preservice students. The book concludes with a chapter that presents a biology unit plan on photosynthesis, drawing on various frameworks that are examined in earlier chapters of the text. These models provide you with concrete examples of how you can link the theory from this course with your teaching practice.

CHAPTER 14

Interactive Phases of Teaching and Learning

STUDY QUESTIONS

1. What are the interactive phases of a teaching and learning model?

2. Discuss how Marton and Booth's experiential learning underpins exploring students' conceptions for teaching science.

3. What are the implications of Bruner's culture's symbolic system for high school science?

4. Discuss Pedretti and her action research group's science-technology-society-environment teaching model from its base to the pinnacle.

5. What are the National Research Council's assessment standards? And what are their uses?

Reflective Inquiry

BOB AND SOFIA'S VOICE

The exploration objectives will be achieved through the critical examination of students' conceptions of corrosion. Students' conceptions provided by Andersson (1986) will serve as examples. We think students would find this exploration activity enjoyable because it starts off with a real-world application of chemistry. In other words, by relating the topic to their personal conceptions and their everyday experiences, students may be motivated to learn about corrosion in the subsequent lessons.

JOURNAL ACTIVITY

Experiential Learning

Write what you mean by experiential learning in science. Share your ideas with the class.

Teaching must promote experiential or conscious learning. We want students to be aware of their own personal ideas about physical phenomena. We also want them to learn the "science way"of knowing. In other words, we expect students to come to know of scientific ideas from a *science-cultural* point of view. Science becomes meaningful when students attach personal and social relevance to what they are learning. Finally, we want students to reflectively assess their learning. We will consider the following frameworks as we further explore how students learn science:

- relational learning
- language: cultures symbolic system
- science-technology-society-environment (STSE) model
- assessment standards
- common knowledge construction model

⚛ RELATIONAL LEARNING

Learning may be described as "coming to experience the world, or aspects of the world, in particular ways" (Marton & Booth, 1997, p. vii). As teachers, it is important that we understand our students' relations to the way they experience the world. We must become familiar with the variety of ways our students experience phenomena. We should be able to understand the way our students see physical or social phenomena. In science classes, we should develop students' capabilities for experiencing particular phenomena in the world in *particular* ways.

Individuals conceptualize in a limited number of qualitatively different ways when they read a text, listen to a presentation, try to solve a problem, or reflect upon a phenomenon. The different ways in which they experience these are logically related to each other and form a complex whole. Marton refers to this as the "outcome space." For example, an object in motion implies a range of variation within two possible states: rest and motion. Some ways of experiencing phenomenon are more complex than others.

The way one experiences something can be thought of as a relationship between the individual and the experienced. Marton and Booth (1997) state: "We cannot describe a world that is independent of our descriptions or of us as describers. We cannot separate out the describer from descriptions. Our world is a real world, but it is a described world, a world experienced by humans" (p. 113). Learning, according to Marton and Booth (1997), is "a change in internal relationship between person and world, . . . it concerns experience. . ." (p. 115). "A specific way of experiencing something may thus refer to the structural and referential aspects [that is, how a person structures the phenomenon, as well as how he or she relates it to other phenomena or referents] of a person's way of making sense of the phenomenon at a specific point in space and time" (p. 116). Hence, a teacher should ask, "How did you arrive at that answer? How did you think about the problem? What does the problem mean for you?" (p. 118). A teacher may compare a student's response to a problem with the theoretical structures in science; the response can be the starting point for the teacher to explore in depth the student's understanding of the problem. As teachers we should be able to "find out the extent to which learners have progressed toward the competence that the teaching aims to develop. On the other hand, to be better able to develop that competence through teaching, we have to find out why some learners have been more successful than others in making such progress" (p. 119).

As we learned earlier while studying the nature of scientific inquiry, we cannot dissociate the person's experience of the world from the world he or she is investigating. Students can tell us how they are experiencing the world, and as teachers we must be concerned with the various ways our students are doing so. Students' experiences are reflected in the statements they make, in the actions they take, and in the artifacts they produce. We should look at how these reflect students' ways of experiencing without subjecting them to tests of validity (how close is a student's statement to the established conceptual structure), skill (how skillful a person is), and functionality (how functional is the element).

How is Marton and Booth's relational learning played out in science classes? Once you have explored students' conceptions about a physical phenomenon, focus not on the learners but on the variations among their collective responses. Conceptions you have explored may reflect individual differences or differences within the same individual. Determining the qualitatively distinct ways in which all of your students experience the given phenomenon is the emphasis.

PEER TALK

Implications of Marton and Booth's Relational Learning

In small groups, discuss the main ideas of Marton and Booth's notions of relational learning. How do these ideas depart from Piaget's developmental principles of learning, which you learned in Chapter 3?

LANGUAGE: CULTURE'S SYMBOLIC SYSTEM

Students' experiences are subject to interpretation using *science-cultural* ideas. In other words, students' personal constructions and puzzlement about the physical world are assigned for interpretation to scientific ideas and canons. It is the fusion between students' personal ideas and the scientific ideas, through a process of discourse and negotiation in the medium of scientific language, that eventually forms their conceptual worlds. What they believe and what they think is true is *negotiated* and renegotiated with those around them. In the science class, student's ideas are influenced by the teacher and the textbook authors (who indirectly speak to students through their textbooks) as well as their peers. Thus students' personal constructions are never formed in isolation; they always conform to some set of ideals established by the culture.

Bruner (1986) suggests that culture comprises ambiguous text that is constantly in need of interpretation by those who participate in it; therefore, the role of language in creating social reality becomes important. The question is, What is the origin of a science "concept"? Is it out there in the world? In the perceiver's head? A result of interpersonal negotiation? Where is it formed?

We believe the meaning of science concepts comes as a result of reaching agreement through a process of creating, re-creating, interpreting, arguing, negotiating, and sharing. Science concepts are formed in the science-cultural forum, which is bounded by certain rules within that culture. Hence the student in the science classroom does not occupy the central position, as in Piaget's child-centered tradition; rather, the student becomes a part of the negotiation process through which his or her personal creations of the science world are re-created. The student does not become a knowledge inventor on his or her own (discovery learning); rather, knowledge is constructed through a process of personal-cultural negotiations. Science learning is therefore, a *communal activity,* a sharing of the science culture. In this view, science teaching should characterize the spirit of a forum, in which the members (students and teacher) nego-

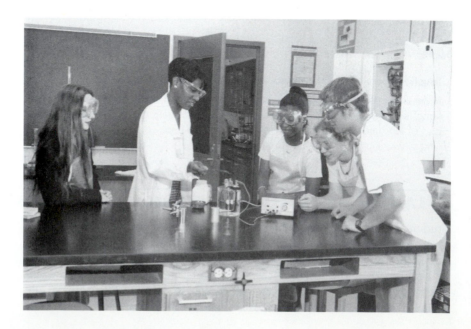

tiate and re-create meaning through a process of reflection. This indeed will produce a joint culture, or shared meaning within the science class. When the student learns to reflect, then he or she controls, selects, and guides the knowledge from within, rather than having the knowledge guide the student from the outside.

"Language imposes a perspective in which things are viewed" (Bruner, 1986, p. 121). For Bruner, language is a tool, and the standards of its use perfect the mind and the hand. Without language, the mind and the hand alone cannot construct knowledge about the world. Language is symbolic of our culture. Words are symbols for concepts.

 PEER TALK

Implications of Bruner's Framework for Science Teaching

In small groups, discuss the implications of Bruner's view of language as culture's symbolic system for science teaching. What might be the characteristics of your lessons? How would you organize your class to make sense of Bruner's notions of learning science? Make note in your journal of the important ideas that arise in your group. Contribute your groups' thoughts in a large group interpretive discussion with your science teacher educator.

SCIENCE-TECHNOLOGY-SOCIETY-ENVIRONMENT (STSE) MODEL

In her action research study, Pedretti (1996) and her teacher research group, after much discussion, reflection, reading, and debating, identified crucial elements of an STS education. These elements—critical social reconstruction, decision making, action, and sustainability—became the building blocks for this action research group's STSE model for curriculum development (Pedretti, 1996, p. 435, see Figure 14-1).

Critical Social Analysis

A primary goal of STSE education is to develop informed and responsible citizens. For students to take part in society, first of all students need to understand that science and technology are interdependent human enterprises that have an impact on their lives. They must recognize that underlying political, social, and cultural forces drive the development and distribution of scientific and technological knowledge and artifacts. A "critical thinking disposition" (Aikenhead, 1990) allows students to exercise both intellectual and ethical skills in investigating the pros and cons of any scientific and technological development, examining potential benefits and costs, and detecting underlying political and social forces driving the

FIGURE 14-1

An STSE model (*NOTE:* From "Learning about Science, Technology, and Society (STS) through an Action Research Project: Co-Constructing an Issue-Based Model for STS Education," by E. Pedretti, 1996, *School Science and Mathematics, 96*(8), p. 435. Copyright 1996 by the School Science and Mathematics Association. Reprinted with permission.)

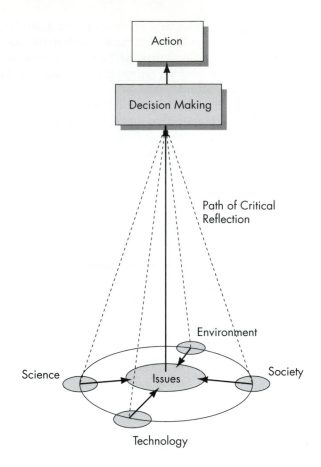

development. Social practices and decisions are underpinned by particular value positions, motivations, and vested interests.

Decision Making

STSE education is rooted in understanding and participating in the decision-making process (Aikenhead, 1987; Ebenezer & Zoller, 1993; and Fleming, 1989). Students may need assistance to gain a clear understanding of how decisions are made at every level. How can students effectively participate in decision-making processes?

Action

Preaching without practicing is futile. Pedretti's group came to the understanding that action is "critical"; it is the pinnacle of STSE education. This group of teachers believed that action empowers people, leads to personal and social change, and prepares individuals to function responsibly and effectively. Julie, a teacher in the action research group, noted the idea that learning to think critically alone is not sufficient; action must be included. However, she believed that action can be politically unpopular and difficult for teachers to implement. Malcolm, another teacher, stated that it is not necessarily the task of science teachers to engage their students in action—whether it be political or environmental.

In this action research group, the members felt constraints of time, content-process tensions, and problems in executing appropriate action. The teachers thought that fostering awareness, critical dispositions, and intellectual independence in their students is sufficient. Pedretti (1996) notes that action and social critique became inextricably linked. Thus the group questioned the very purpose of science education. What are the responsibilities of a science teacher? To what extent do science educators encourage action?

Sustainability

Sustainability (intrinsic worth of all life on earth) is grounded in the context of ethical, individual and collective responsibility (De Vore, 1987). For Pedretti's action research group (1996), the environment became one of the corner stones of their STSE model. Literacy, the group believed, involves systematic study and use of resources and the consideration of human needs in an effort to maintain a life-giving and life-sustaining environment. Concern for environmental improvement should be articulated and demonstrated through society and technology education (Zoller, 1987). Pedretti's action research group developed and approved of issue-based teaching to translate their STSE model.

Issue-Based Teaching

To this research group, issue-based teaching (waste management, genetic engineering, and nuclear power) was the central focus for developing STSE curricula. They believed that science conceptual structures (learning science) can be embedded in a social context (learning about science). The science content can be learned through social issues, problems, or contextual settings, leading ultimately to action. Thus for this group, STSE education was rooted in the critical analysis of social responsibility and issues: where they come from, how they develop, how they are controlled, and how they might be resolved.

The action research group suggests that the STSE model can be used in conjunction with existing science curricula to explore issues that are socially relevant and personally compelling. Rather than reconstructing the entire science curriculum around social issues, STSE can be integrated into appropriate units in the curriculum from an issue perspective. For example, Pedretti reports that two teachers in the research group decided to explore the codfish debate in Newfoundland as part of a tenth-grade ecology unit. Students examined many facets of the problem, including the scientific principles of food chains and webs, the concepts of food pyramids, biomass and carrying capacity; they also explored the sociological implications and human costs of closing fish processing plants and the political dimensions of offshore sovereignty.

Another teacher, rather than simply teaching students how to balance nuclear equations, embarked on a broader study of nuclear chemistry by exploring issues with an STSE perspective. The class examined some of the historical background of the discovery of radioactivity and the development of the atomic bomb. Students debated several controversial issues around the themes of nuclear power, nuclear disarmament, peace, and justice.

> "I have to admit I was one of those 'here's how a car battery works,' just the direct application, extension of what you learn in the classroom . . . And I didn't really give it too much thought about the much broader societal, political, emotional issues. There's a lot more to science than just a direct cause and effect relationship . . . I had wanted to do a controversial issue but really did not know how to go about it." (Pedretti, 1996, p. 438)

Challenges of STSE Education: A Model to Overcome

The group did not dismiss the challenges of STSE education; its inherent complexities are many. For example, one has to consider the nature and extent of action and politicization, the role of moral and ethical thinking, values, and the role of the teacher. Another set of constraints is that teachers work amid limited time and resources, curriculum demands, an excessive tide of content-oriented objectives, and school contexts. One possibility for addressing these challenges is to create an action research environment that supports and encourages groups of teachers to critically analyze, develop, implement, and evaluate curriculum by offering the following:

- the recognition that other teachers share many of the same sorts of problems
- a chance to look at things critically from a variety of perspectives
- an opportunity to listen to alternative arguments and rationales
- a chance to learn about someone else's solution to a common problem
- an opportunity to take part in brainstorming activities
- an occasion to engage in mutual support and criticism in a trusting and open environment (Pedretti, 1996, p. 438)

 PEER TALK

Implications of Pedretti's Action Research

In small groups discuss the implications of the approach Pedretti's action research group for STSE science teaching. What might be the characteristics of your lessons? How would you organize your class to carry out Pedretti's STSE- or issue-based science lessons? How might an action research group in your school overcome some of the challenges of STSE teaching? Make note in your journal of the important ideas that arose in your group. Contribute your group's thoughts in a large-group interpretive discussion with your science teacher educator.

✵ ASSESSMENT STANDARDS

Learning and assessment must be complementary. Assessment must be fair to meet all students' needs, and should focus on the most important content to be learned by students: the ability to inquire; knowledge and understanding of facts, concepts, principles, laws, and theories; the ability to reason scientifically; the ability to use science to make decisions and take positions on societal issues; and the ability to communicate knowledge effectively. Tests should rely on students' "active" knowledge (reasoning and understanding) rather than their "inert" knowledge (memorization) (National Research Council, 1996, p. 82).

A test should measure what it claims to measure. When triangulated, the test results must be congruent and valid. This means that an individual student's performance must be similar on more than two tasks that measure the same aspect of student achievement—indicating that the tasks are reliable. Students should also be given adequate opportunities to demonstrate their achievement based on understanding and ability. The tasks should also be developmentally appropriate, be set in contexts that the students are familiar with, be bias-free, and not require skills (such as reading and writing) that are beyond the grade level.

The National Science Education Standards suggest several ways in which the data can be used, which will be discussed in the following sections (National Research Council, 1996).

Improving Classroom Practice

Teachers use assessment continually in the classroom to measure student progress and achievement, and also to make adjustments to their teaching styles and methods. Assessment in the classroom should not only be used to assess students, but it should also be used by the teacher to assess the appropriateness of his or her own teaching, and to make changes when students are not grasping the intended information. Teachers should constantly observe students, then formulate a hypothesis about why a certain method may not be working, interview students to test the accuracy of the hypothesis, and interpret the information and adjust the lessons accordingly.

Planning Curricula

Assessment results can be used to select content, activities, and examples to be used in courses, modules, units, and lessons. Findings can also be used to judge whether the content is developmentally appropriate, whether students will have an interest in the content, the effectiveness of activities and examples, and the skills that students would require to benefit from the selections made for the course. There are three basic purposes for assessment data use in planning the curricula: to determine students' prior knowledge of the topic, to monitor progress made by students during the course, and to collect information about student achievement.

Developing Self-Directed Learners

Students need to know what their learning goals are in order to be able to self-assess. Students should be made aware of the mastery criteria for scientific literacy to allow them the opportunity to self-assess and reflect on their own learning. By making students aware that they can learn science, and what they need to learn to be successful, students can take responsibility for their own learning. The criteria developed in the science standards state that to show mastery in this area, students should be able to pick out a piece of their own work that shows evidence of their understanding, explain that piece orally or through writing, and constructively critique their own and others' work. Again, it is important for students to be made aware of these expectations in order to allow them the opportunity to self-monitor their progress toward mastery.

Reporting Student Progress

The traditional and most prevalent use of assessment in schools is to report on student achievement and progress in learning science. This reporting is based on the teacher's own standards and criteria, the student's progress during the past year, student mastery of the science curriculum, and student achievement. Each of these forms of assessment requires different information and different modes of assessment. It is necessary to realize that not all areas of assessment can be measured using the same method of data collection.

Researching Teaching Practices

Many forms of assessment can be used by teachers to assess the effectiveness of their own teaching. For a teacher to continually research and assess his or her own methods is a sign of a master teacher who places students' success as a top priority. Teachers need to constantly grow, learn, and adapt to the needs of their students in order to build success for themselves and their students. Remember this as you enter the classroom; do not blame the failure of a unit on your students, but rather realize that perhaps you were not successful in the methods you chose to teach the unit. Consistent reflection and research are necessary for every teacher.

PEER TALK

Implications of Alternative Assessment
In small groups, discuss the implications of the National Research Council's standards on assessment.

THE COMMON KNOWLEDGE CONSTRUCTION (CKC) MODEL

There are four interactive phases to the common knowledge construction model, developed by Ebenezer and Connor (1998). Figure 14-2 is an illustration of this model. In terms of science, students think about their own personal conceptions and subject these to science-cultural ways of

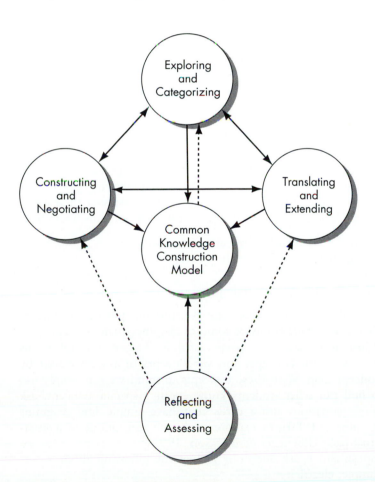

FIGURE 14-2
The common knowledge construction model (*NOTE: From Learning to Teach Science: A Model for the 21st Century* (p. 97), by J. V. Ebenezer and S. Connor, ©1998. Adapted by permission of Prentice-Hall, Inc., Upper Saddle River, NJ.)

knowing. With respect to STSE science education, students come to consensus in solving a problem or finding the best solution based on criteria, evidence, theoretical understanding, and the problem context.

The common knowledge construction model characterizes the principles of Marton's relational learning, Bruner's view of language as culture's symbolic system, Vygotsky's zone of proximal development, science-technology-society-environment connections, and alternative assessment. It also reflects postmodern thinking with respect to the history of scientific discourse and adopts personal-social constructivist views (Driver et al., 1994; Ebenezer & Erickson, 1996). The model uses a variety of teaching, learning, and assessment strategies (see Chapters 4–13). This chapter combines some of the important aspects discussed in earlier chapters.

The common knowledge construction model consists of four interactive phases:

- exploring and categorizing
- constructing and negotiating
- translating and extending
- reflecting and assessing

Phase 1: Exploring and Categorizing

Marton's relational learning leads us to explore students' conceptions throughout an entire science lesson sequence. We explore students' conceptions before we begin a unit of science study so that we and our students become consciously aware of their ideas. This is the beginning of conceptual-change teaching. We carry out ongoing explorations of students' conceptions throughout the unit so that students can trace their conceptual changes. At the end of the unit, we again take the opportunity to help students see the outcome of their learning by assessing their ideas.

Exploring students' conceptions can have a number of aims, including:

1. to brainstorm for what they know about a concept
2. to elicit terms that are related to the concept
3. to find out about a situation
4. to probe understanding of a single proposition

What we would like to know at this point are students' prior ideas, understandings, views, or mini-theories of some of the important concepts, situations, and instances related to a particular unit. We can accomplish this by identifying the major concepts and subconcepts of a science unit by drawing a concept map. With these concepts in mind we can simply use questions to find out what students know about a specific concept, ask questions about situations using cards that have simple line diagrams (Osborne & Gilbert, 1980), or explore students' conceptions of a situation with actual tasks (Ebenezer & Erickson, 1996).

To accomplish aim 1, ask questions such as the following about a *concept*—for example, electricity:

"Tell me what you know about electric current."

"Can you think of anything else?"

"Do you have any personal experiences relating to electric current?"

"Do you have any mental pictures relating to electric current?" (White, 1988, p. 69).

Such questions will reveal propositions, images, and episodes. Simply asking individuals what they know about a concept is not sufficiently focused and can lead to omission of significant knowledge.

In Chapter 8 we studied the construction and uses of concept maps. Concept maps are considered reflectors of understanding. To achieve aim 2, ask students to list concepts that are related to a major concept. Then, with the list of concepts, students can construct a concept map. An examination of a concept map can reveal students' understanding. If you are in doubt about certain connections in the concept map, ask students to explain them individually or collectively, depending on how the map was constructed.

To achieve aim 3, ask students to propose their theories *as* they observe a situation using a task that would depict a natural phenomenon. Similarly, for aim 4, ask students to propose theories to account for a particular proposition. The situation will stimulate a dialogue that will reveal students' views, beliefs, or theories (see Chapter 5 for PEOE strategy). Situation-based exploration tasks (using actual materials and equipment) stem from Piaget's work, although the previous focus was to support his theory of developmental stages and to find out students' conservation skills and logical relations. In current practice, situation-based exploration strategy is a form of assessment of a single concept. Students' theories may not always reflect their mental representations or schema, as cognitive theorists believe. The ideas might be on-site reflections.

Once students' ideas are gathered—for example, through the PEOE strategy and interpretive discussion (see Chapter 5)—it is important to look for common understandings. These commonalties are then grouped under teacher-made categories of descriptions that reflect students' reasoning. Figure 14-3 shows steps to categorize students' ideas. Categories

1. Color-code similar ideas.
2. Count out the ideas that have the same color.
3. Put all of the ideas that have the same color into a pile.
4. Decide on a label that reflects the concept in each pile. This label is referred to as a "teacher-made category."
5. Write the teacher-made category labels on your page, leaving room for the examples that best indicate the label.
6. Write one or two of the best examples under each teacher-made category label.

The labels must reflect students' ideas, not curricular words.

FIGURE 14-3
Steps to categorize students' ideas (NOTE: From *Learning to Teach Science: A Model for the 21st Century* (pp. 76–77), by J. V. Ebenezer & S. Connor, ©1998. Adapted by permission of Prentice-Hall, Inc., Upper Saddle River, NJ.)

of description help us develop teaching objectives. Teaching and learning become purposeful when students' ideas are used for constructing and negotiating meaning.

Since the 1970s, many studies have explored students' conceptions on various scientific concepts, propositions, and phenomena. You will be able to locate these articles in your university library. Our preservice teachers have found these articles very interesting and revealing; they contain categories of specific conceptions pertaining to concepts. More general knowledge claims that researchers have made and that teachers should understand from these studies are as follows: (a) Students' conceptions are found to be different from those of scientists; and (b) despite teaching, some deeply held alternative conceptions persist.

In Chapter 13 we taught you how to conduct interviews. We do not expect you to carry out personal interviews in class for determining students' conceptions, but we encourage you to use appropriate tasks to explore and incorporate students' ideas (see the next section).

Researchers have explored students' ideas of physical phenomena using different activities but mainly through interviews. Linder and Erickson (1989) found that physics preservice teachers had many conceptualizations about the concept of sound; some were alternative to those held by physicists. It is, therefore, important that as science teachers we strive for higher levels of competence and deeper levels of understanding science concepts through the use of "Christopherian encounters" (Gardner, 1991). Armstrong (1994) follows Gardner's example: "[J]ust as Christopher Columbus challenged the notion that the earth is flat by sailing 'beyond the edge' and thereby showing its curved shape, so, too, Gardner suggests that educators challenge students' limited beliefs by taking them 'over the edge' into areas where they must confront the contradictions and disjunctions in their own thinking" (p. 152).

 TEACHER PRACTICE

Exploring and Categorizing Students' Conceptions

Choose a science topic for your unit. Review at least one major article on exploring students' ideas about your topic. Develop an activity to explore students' ideas. State questions that you will ask. Describe the methodology you will use. Share these with your peers in class as well as your science teacher educator to refine your ideas about the exploration activity.

Explore a group of students' ideas on your topic. Categorize these ideas. Compare your findings with those in the article you reviewed. Share your findings and examples of students' work and diagrams with your peers.

See Chapter 1 for the format of this part of a unit plan.

Phase 2: Constructing and Negotiating Meaning

In the second phase, students' conceptions are explored and categorized. These categories of students' conceptions are used to develop a series of lessons to construct and negotiate meaning. The culture's symbolic system is negotiated with students through various activities and experiences. Students, the novice learners, traverse through the zone of proximal development with the help of expert teachers (see Chapter 3).

The lessons you prepare to construct and negotiate meaning should match students' conceptions. These lessons must move from macroscopic observations to mathematical reasoning, as illustrated in Chapter 4 with White's memory elements. The teaching and learning approaches should match the content taught, the objectives of the lesson, and students' learning preferences (see Chapters 5–12). Students' common knowledge and their understandings must be subject to continuous assessment (see Chapter 13).

 TEACHER PRACTICE

Developing Activities Based on a Conception

Select one of the students' conceptions from the previous "Teacher Practice" box. Prepare activities or lessons that will address this conception. Lessons should reflect macroscopic, microscopic, and symbolic ideas. See Chapter 1 for a lesson plan that incorporates students' conceptions.

Phase 3: Translating and Extending

As Pedretti (1996) and her action research group pointed out, the STSE model can be effectively infused into the existing curriculum. In every science unit there are opportunities to develop the elements of the STSE model. The study of science is undertaken within an STSE context.

After students' ideas are clarified and extended from science and history as well as from nature-of-science perspectives, students are ready to translate their understandings in everyday situations. Until students are comfortable developing their "own" problem-solving projects, teachers can initiate students into "goal-based" projects (see Chapter 12). Based on our present school system, a few well designed "goal" problem-solving projects are doable and manageable. The key pedagogical elements involved in STSE or design technology projects are students' views and understandings of a given problem; informed decision-making based on research, evidence, and so on; and taking actions in appropriate ways.

 TEACHER PRACTICE

Developing Issue-Based Activities

Identify STSE-based themes or everyday problems based on your science topic.

> Choose one STSE topic and prepare issue-based activities or lessons using Pedretti's STSE model.
>
> Include some of the elements of sustainable-development education listed in Chapter 12.

Phase 4: Reflecting and Assessing

This phase of the common knowledge construction model begins during the first phase. When we make sense of students' conceptions, we are reflectively assessing their understandings. Based on this assessment, we prepare a learner-appropriate sequence of lessons. During the "constructing and negotiating" and "translating and extending" phases we continue to assess our students using many different strategies to check their understandings of the subject matter, attitudes, and abilities. This includes lab work, portfolios, and projects. At the end of the unit it is appropriate to administer a congruent and valid written and performance-based test.

    TEACHER PRACTICE

Constructing Alternative-Assessment Items
Construct several written items for continuous and culminating assessment.
  Write out one detailed performance-based activity based on your theme.
  Write a "goal-based" problem-solving project. You may want to have students write a scientific research paper on the history of science or an STSE issue. The project can also involve a hands-on/minds-on design process activity or STSE activity.
  Include scoring criteria and a key for each of these authentic-assessment ideas. See Chapter 13.

P-STAR CONFERENCE PAPER 14-1

Phenomenographic Categories of Oxidation and Reduction: Curriculum Development and Implementation

Robert Lewin and Sofia Lukuszuk

This paper was presented by Robert and Sofia in their chemistry curriculum and instruction course at the University of Manitoba. Preservice teachers were required to choose a particular unit in chemistry and present a four-hour seminar in two consecutive periods. The content of the P-STAR seminar depicted preservice teachers' content knowledge and the four phases of the common knowledge construction model. They developed "phenomenographic categories" of oxidation and reduction for curriculum development and implementation.

Robert and Sofia examined their chemistry program materials to identify the concepts that need to be taught in a unit on oxidation and reduction. They then surveyed the literature to determine students' ideas. In particular, they found an article by Andersson (1986) very useful. These preservice teachers examined Andersson's tasks and questions for exploration. In turn, they prepared their own activities to explore students' ideas. They tested their exploratory activities on their peers. Robert and Sofia also presented their peers with students' ideas that they had found in the literature. Based on students' ideas, the two preservice teachers developed lessons. Their peers went through the lessons themselves as learners, then reversed their role to teachers and evaluated these lessons. Similarly, Robert and Sofia took their peers and their chemistry teacher educator through the remaining phases of the common knowledge construction model. Robert and Sofia's depiction of the common knowledge construction model follows.

Robert and Sofia were assisted by their chemistry teacher educator in preparing this unit. These preservice teachers' work has undergone revision before being included in this book. Due to lack of space, we have eliminated the introductory part of the multivoice unit plan presented in Chapter 1 and illustrated the teacher content knowledge as well as the phases of the common knowledge construction model.

Students' Conceptions of Corrosion

Scenario I

When a house was newly built, both the hot- and cold-water pipes in the kitchen were shiny. Before long, the outside of these pipes had become dull and tarnished (covered with a thin, dark coating). The outside of the hot-water pipe was more tarnished than the outside of the cold-water pipe. Explain how this coating is formed.

STUDENTS' CONCEPTIONS WITH RESPECT TO SCENARIO I
- Copper has become coated with verdigris.
- This is the way all copper pipes change.
- Rust is formed.

STUDENTS' CONCEPTIONS OF THE MACROSCOPIC WORLD
A. Displacement of a substance from the outside of the pipe
   - Hot water makes steam, which forms a coating on the pipe.
   - Some substance has penetrated the hot pipe.
   - There's so much lime in the water that it must be noticeable on the pipes.
B. Displacement of a substance from the air to the outside of the pipe
   - Although the house was newly built, there might have been some dust and dirt on the pipe. But you could not see it until the pipe was hot, because then it was stickier.
   - Heat attracts dirt.
   - There's air on the pipes, I think.

STUDENTS' CONCEPTIONS OF THE MICROSCOPIC WORLD
- Metal molecules in the air have stuck on the pipes and formed a coating.

Scenario II

Students are shown a shiny nail and a rusty nail. The students are informed that the rusty nail, which was shiny to start with, had stood half-immersed in water for about a week. What happened to the nail?

The majority of students respond that the nail is rusted.

STUDENTS' CONCEPTIONS OF THE MACROSCOPIC WORLD
A. Displacement of rust from the air to the outside of the nail
- Rust is sort of a chemical.
- It breeds in dampness.
- It's in the air all the time, and when any steel is damp or anything, it spreads all over and breaks it down . . . it's a sort of fungus.
B. Displacement of rust from the inside to the outside of the nail
- Water got into the steel and it has taken some stuff out of it and made the steel go like that and it weakens steel.
- The water got into the paint and the ingredients of the steel.

Discussion

It is not uncommon for secondary chemistry students to have some of the same conceptions. The goal of this lesson is to explore students' conceptions of corrosion, using the preceding examples of students' conceptions as guidelines for probing students' explanations. This exploration activity engages students to explore their conceptions of corrosion on cars, a real-world phenomenon.

ACTIVITY

STUDENT INVESTIGATION OF CORROSION

Distribute a Prediction-Observation-Explanation strategy sheet to students. Tell them that they will be predicting, observing, and explaining a natural phenomenon. In this exploration activity, students will explore their conceptions of corrosion by observing rust spots on cars.

This activity serves as an exploration activity to the oxidation-reduction unit in a chemistry curriculum. Also, this activity leads to other related activities to clarify and modify students' ideas. Moreover, this activity

provides students with an opportunity to raise important questions they may have about the process of rusting (oxidation-reduction reactions).

Exploration Questions

1. What is this spot?

2. What is the spot made of?

3. What do you think caused this spot?

4. If you were to observe the spot with an imaginary microscope, what

would you see? Explain how this spot came to be. Draw a picture to show your way of thinking.

Rusting as a Chemical Process

Students' Conceptions

Conceptualization 1: Displacement of rust from the air (airborne particles)
Conceptualization 2: Displacement of rust from the steel (an active ingredient)

Discussion

Students tend not to focus on chemical systems that include nonvisible, often gaseous reactants and products, such as oxygen in the case of rusting. The objective of the lesson is to clarify students' conceptions and help students form chemical conceptions by making microscopic and macroscopic connections. This lesson will help students understand the basics of redox reactions.

Objectives

1. Students will state what rust is in terms of a chemical compound.

2. Students will state the half reactions involved and write the complete reaction.

3. Students will draw a diagram explaining rusting from a microscopic perspective.

Teaching and Learning Approaches

1. Drawing diagrams
2. Journal writing

Materials and Resources

list of questions
notes on rusting and redox reactions
chalk
chalkboard
journal

Activities and Procedures

1. To help students become consciously aware of their ideas from the exploration activity, display concept maps consisting of their own conceptions (see Appendix 14-1).

2. Develop the macroscopic ideas about the makeup of the car—the chemical components and properties in detail.

3. Then attach the symbolic knowledge. Introduce students to the idea that rust is hydrated iron(III) oxide. Write the chemical formula on the chalkboard:

– $Fe_2O_3 \bullet xH_2O$

4. Write the half-reactions on the chalkboard and have students suggest which half-reaction is oxidation and which is reduction. Make sure students provide justification for their responses.

– $Fe(s) \rightarrow Fe^{2+} + 2e^-$ (oxidation)
– $O_2(g) + 4H^+ + 4e^- \rightarrow 2H_2O$ (reduction)   H$^+$ is supplied by carbonic acid.

5. Explain to students that oxygen is reduced in the presence of hydrogen carbonate, which is formed from dissolved carbon dioxide.

– $H_2O + CO_2 \rightarrow H_2CO_3$
– $H_2CO_3 + H_2O \rightarrow H_3O^+ + HCO_3$
– $CO_2 + HCO_3^-$ (net equation)

6. Based on the half-reactions in step 4, have students write the complete reaction.

7. Explain that the Fe^{2+} ions are further oxidized to rust by atmospheric oxygen, and write the reaction on the chalkboard.

– $4Fe^{2+} + O_2(g) + 4H_2O \rightarrow 4Fe_2O_3(s)$ (rust) $+ 8H^+$

8. Help students draw a diagram showing the chemical process of rusting (see Appendix 14-2).

9. Students brainstorm to write all the concepts that they have learned so far—create a web first.

10. In small groups, students put the concepts in a hierarchical or chain concept map with the help of the textbook (conceptual change through the textbook) or the teacher-given notes.

11. Share the concept maps with other groups.

12. Compare these concept maps to the web that you created with students' conceptions from step 1.

Revisiting original conceptions

13. Have students do a journal entry about their conceptual growth.

14. Have students include their concept maps and journal entries in their portfolios.

Assessment

A directed journal entry is used to assess students' understanding of the material taught in the lesson. Students are required to describe the chemical process involved in rusting using chemical reactions and diagrams. In the journal, students also state any difficulties they have or concepts that need clarifying. Furthermore, students are required to identify with another type of corrosion (for example, tarnishing of silver) to generate ideas for an independent investigation of chemistry.

Reflection

The goal of this lesson is for students to clarify their conceptions on the chemical theory of rusting. This instructional objective is achieved through the critical examination of the specific reaction involved in rusting. Specifically, students will break down rusting into half-reactions. The teacher leads explanations in terms of the composite reactions of rusting, aimed at clarifying the conceptions of students. In order to further clarify their conceptions, students will draw diagrams

to support their explanation of rusting. By making connections between microscopic and macroscopic explanations, students will truly understand rusting as a redox reaction.

A Physical Model of Redox Reactions

Students' Conceptions

ASSIGNING OXIDATION STATES

The oxidation state of an element is the same as the charge of the monatomic ion of that element.

Oxidation numbers or states can be assigned to a polyatomic molecule and/or polyatomic ions.

The charge of a polyatomic species indicates the oxidation state of the molecule or ion.

Discussion

In order to elaborate on the preceding conceptions of the assigning of oxidation states, students will work in groups of three or four and try to explain why these conceptions are scientifically incorrect. In addition, students will restate the conceptions in a scientifically correct manner. In working with the conceptions, students will use the text and other resource materials as references. A large-group discussion will follow, and each group will present its "scientifically correct" versions of the initial conceptions. Once students are clear on the true science conceptions, they can progress to the physical model of redox reactions. In this activity students will elaborate and apply their conceptions in demonstrating various redox reactions, using balloons to signify the transfer of electrons.

Objectives

1. Students will restate the initial conceptions in a scientifically correct manner.

2. Students will explain the transfer of electrons in redox reactions using balloons.

Teaching and Learning Approaches

1. Group sharing and discussion

2. Student-led demonstrations

3. Journal writing

Materials and Resources

list of rules for assigning oxidation states

list of students' conceptions of assigning oxidation states

balloons

double-sided tape

anode and cathode labels

list of redox reactions to be demonstrated

textbook and other resource materials

Activities and Procedures

1. Introduce the lesson with a review of the rules for assigning oxidation states (see a chemistry textbook). Have students generate the rules by asking questions—for example, "What is the sum of the oxidation numbers in a neutral molecule?"

2. Present students with the list of students' conceptions of assigning oxidation states. Students will work in groups of three or four to come up with the correct science conceptions. Students may refer to the text and other available resource materials.

3. In a large-group discussion, each group will present its "scientifically correct" versions of the initial conceptions. Discussion will take place to ensure that the new versions are in fact correct. This may be accomplished through questioning—for example, "Explain why you think that oxidation states cannot be assigned to polyatomic molecules or ions."

4. A physical demonstration of redox reactions follows. Students will physi-cally demonstrate redox reactions (see the examples in Appendix 14-3), using balloons to signify electron transfer. The activity initiates with students acting out simple half-reactions, and progresses to more complex redox reactions. Students will determine the oxidation states of monatomic species and state which species is being oxidized, which species is being reduced, the oxidizing agent, and the reducing agent. Students will then determine the process of electron transfer that the ion/element undergoes, as well as at which electrode this process takes place.

Assessment

Student understanding will be assessed during the large-group sharing/discussion of students' redesigned versions of the initial conceptions. Further assessment may occur by observing the student-led demonstrations of some redox reactions. During the demonstrations, students should be able to answer a number of questions: Which chemical species is being oxidized? At which chemical cell does reduction occur? Which chemical species is the oxidizing agent? How many electrons are being transferred? and so on. A final assessment will be the journal entry, which will require students to give a detailed explanation of a redox reaction, showing the half-reactions, the transfer of electrons, and the complete balanced reaction.

Reflection

The initial activity of working with conceptions allows students to elaborate on their conceptions. By researching the true science conceptions, students are actively engaging in a critical cognitive process of coming to understand. This activity reinforces the rules for assigning oxidation states, which may be extended to develop a sound understanding of redox reactions. This physical demonstration of redox reactions provides students with an opportunity to demonstrate the transfer of electrons. Students gain a better understanding of redox reactions as they are able to act out the atomic level within given reactions. By actively engaging students in such an activity, the teacher will make connections between microscopic and macroscopic levels. This particular activity may also be enjoyable for students, and serve as a motivating factor for learning and understanding redox reactions. This activity may be challenging to most students.

Electron Transfer Reactions

Students' Conceptions

Students have a very difficult time understanding that science is a time-consuming process and that the facts that the students presently have at their fingertips took years of inquiry, research, and experimentation. Explain these ideas to students and give them a timeline of some major scientific discoveries.

Discussion

Students need to be exposed to the history of science. Lessons in the history of oxidation-reduction are an important portion of the unit. The concepts that students are exploring took years to discover. It is important to give credit to the individuals who worked so hard to make these discoveries. Students might also be able to see some connections between themselves and these scientists; many of the preconceptions that students have today were the same as the ones these scientists had many years ago. The question for this activity is, "Why are electron transfer reactions called *oxidation* and *reduction*?"

Objectives

1. Students will identify from a list of scientists those scientists who made significant contributions to our knowledge of oxidation-reduction and electric currents (see Appendix 14-4).

2. Students will identify the contributions of at least three scientists to the topics of oxidation-reduction and electric currents.

Teaching and Learning Approaches

1. Group work and peer sharing

2. Research

3. Small-group and large-group discussion

4. Journal writing

Materials and Resources

research materials (a library setting should do)
list of historical figures
journal
notebook

Activities and Procedures

1. Students will be placed into groups of two and will receive a teacher-created list of historical figures in the area of chemistry. (The teacher may choose to limit the number of scientists.)

2. Students will be required to look at what each scientist has contributed and decide which of these scientists have made contributions to the area of oxidation-reduction. They should then separate the scientists involved in oxidation-reduction from the rest.

3. Students will then search to find the specific contributions of these scientists and write this information down.

4. Once all groups have gathered this information, the class will be split into two groups, with one member of each pair going into each group. In these

large groups, they will discuss why they have chosen these scientists and why they feel their contributions are so important.

It is important to have a facilitator in each group to guide the discussion. The teacher should move from group to group to verify that the discussions are working well.

5. After some discussion, students will return to their partners and share with each other what happened in the large-group session. They will then be expected to produce write-ups on the scientists that they feel contributed to oxidation-reduction. They will be expected to specify the scientist, give a short life history (for example, place of birth, schooling, important influences), explain the person's contribution to science, and explain why they feel this scientist's discoveries are a contribution to oxidation-reduction reactions.

Journal

Each student chooses one specific scientist that he or she has an appreciation for and explains how he or she would interact with that person now. Does the student have any questions, ideas, or suggestions for this scientist? Why does the student admire him or her?

Assessment

Students will be assessed on their write-ups as well as their contributions during group work. Hopefully, they will have gained an appreciation for the work that scientists have done in the past and are doing today. Each student will have a write-up of a scientist who has contributed to various areas of oxidation-reduction, as well as an overview of the work of scientists in other areas of chemistry. The journal write-ups will give the teacher an idea of how in-depth the stu-

dents went with their research on specific scientists.

Reflection

Most people like learning about others, especially when the people they are learning about have encountered great obstacles. Unfortunately, the majority of scientists encounter great obstacles, but this makes the exploration of their discoveries all the more exciting. Through discussions and research papers, the students will not only be able to identify the scientists who have contributed to oxidation-reduction chemistry, but will be able to explain those contributions. Through looking at the whole list of scientists, the students will also be able to look at where these scientists fit in the overall picture. Through their journal writing, they will also form a connection with the scientist of their choice, which will place their learning experience on a personal level. Ideally, students will now want to inquire about the lives of all the scientists on the list, not only those involved in redox.

Dealing with an Everyday Redox Reaction

Students' Conceptions

"Molecules in the air stick on the metal and form a coating."

"Rust is sort of a chemical. It breeds in dampness. Its in the air all the time, and when any steel is damp or anything, it spreads all over and breaks it down . . . its a sort of fungus."

"Water go into the steel and it has taken some stuff out of it and it made the steel go like that and it weakened steel. the water got into the paint and ingredients of the steel."

Have students look at these conceptions and identify by themselves where the problems are. (If they have trouble, do the activity and revisit at the end.)

Discussion

Students need to be able to use their chemical knowledge and apply it to the world they live in. They are expected to make decisions about the world around them. By having a good knowledge background in chemistry, they will be able to make informed decisions about issues that are of a chemical nature. One of the most publicized issues within oxidation-reduction chemistry surrounds corrosion. The economy could greatly benefit if less metal needed to be produced to replace metal that is corroding. Students will look at this issue and see whether they can discover some way to prevent this process. They should already have extensive knowledge about corrosion from previous lessons; this will be an extension of those lessons. They will learn how to analyze a situation and make decisions about how to resolve it.

Objectives

1. Students will look at multiple variables and alternative solutions when making a decision.

2. Students will predict, look at, and evaluate the results of corrosion in various cities.

3. Students will use their knowledge of the process of corrosion to come up with the best possible solution.

Teaching and Learning Approaches

1. Interviews
2. Small-group work
3. Library research
4. STSE connections
5. Small-group reports
6. Internet research

Materials and Resources

human resources
library resources
computer/Internet resources

Activities and Procedures

1. Students will be paired and given the assignment.

2. The assignment is as follows:

   – You are forced to move to another city. Since you just spent $45,000 on a new sports car, a major factor in your decision on which city to move to will be the tendency of your car to form rust in that city. Using your chemistry knowledge, the Internet, and research materials, explain how you would go about gathering the information necessary. To what city would you relocate? Why would this be the best place for your car? Write your answer in the form of a report.

   – Using your knowledge of corrosion, think of some way that it could be prevented.

3. Students will then need to formulate a plan to approach these problems.

4. Once the students have decided how to proceed, they will be required to check their plan with the teacher. The teacher and student will discuss and negotiate the plan. What their plan says decides what their future steps will be.

Assessment

The students will be assessed on their written reports as well as their plans of action. It is just as important to properly think out how one will go about resolving a decision as it is to make the actual decision. The students will need to go back to their information on corrosion to see which variables in each city need to be studied. They will need to look at the actual effects of corrosion on cars in various cities and the factors that promote rust formation. They will also need to examine the various chemical changes that occur in order to prevent rust formation. By taking these steps, students will have achieved the goals stated within the objectives.

Reflection

It is very important that students be able to effectively apply their chemistry knowledge. The students will be motivated by the fact that if they own a nice sports car (that idea alone is exciting to many), they would want to take on the responsibility of caring for it. By taking an issue that is so com-

mon to many of the students, they will be able to focus on the chemistry behind it. They will be required to look at corrosion from a personal/social perspective as well as a scientific perspective. The process that they go through to get information will make them informed decision makers. They will look at how to plan the information-gathering process as well as how to make decisions based on that information. Those skills could be transferred to many other areas, both chemistry and non-chemistry related. Students should know how to apply their chemistry knowledge to benefit them in the decisions they need to make.

Continuous-Assessment Items

Constructing and Negotiating Lessons

Allot each student 10 points for the three "constructing and negotiating" lesson journal entries. The following assessment techniques may be used.

A. Group assessment

In groups of four, you will assess each other's work. After you finish, we will discuss the answers as a class.

B. Self-assessment (journal writing)

Do journal writing after examining your own work again in the light of class discussion. In your journal, answer the following questions:

– What did you think of these activities?

– Were you able to translate chemistry concepts in understanding these everyday applications?

– Discuss your personal struggle to understand what was happening.

The teacher should facilitate the discussion.

After the discussion, students compare their answers to the actual process. This post-assessment will be easier for them for they will now have an idea of where they went wrong and will be able to see where they had difficulties.

Research Paper

Write a research paper on the history of oxidation and reduction in groups of two or three. Follow some of the principles of research paper writing (given in Chapter 6). Use a multimedia program to organize your report and present it to the class. (Assign 30 points for students' research reports and multimedia presentations.)

Design Technology Project

Identify a problem such as tarnishing of silver spoons. Follow the design model discussed in Chapter 11 to produce the silvery shine. Include a description of the chemical understanding and equations you will use in this design technology. (Assign 25 points for this project.)

Portfolio

(Assign 20 points for student portfolios on oxidation and reduction. Scientific arguments must be presented for including each piece of work in the oxidation-reduction portfolio.)

Culminating-Assessment Items

Discussion

The culminating-assessment items will consist of a written component and a performance-based item.

Objectives

1. Students will demonstrate their construction and mastery of the chemical concepts.
2. Students will use the chemical ideas that they have constructed within the unit to explain how some common applications of oxidation and reduction reactions work.

Assessment Approaches

1. POE
2. Research
3. Critical self-evaluation
4. Peer evaluations
5. Experimental observation
6. Journal writing

Materials and Resources

  resource materials
  journal
  chart paper

Written Test

1. Using computer software, construct a concept map with the following concepts:

    oxidation, reduction, electric current, ion, atom, mass, charge, electron, proton, oxidation number, charge, electrochemical, electrolytic, electrolyte, battery, conduction, salt bridge, anode, cathode, electroplating, electrode. (20 points: 1 point for each concept correctly used)

2. Observe what happens to a strip of zinc when added to a copper(II) sulfate solution. Explain what happened to the zinc strip and the copper sulfate solution. Draw a diagram that illustrates the microsopic process. Write equations. (10 points: 4 points for the paragraph if chemically correct, 2 points for the correctly labeled diagram illustrat-

ing the microscopic process, 1 point for the chemical equation, 1 point for the oxidation equation, 1 point for the reduction equation, and 1 point for the net ionic equation.)

3. Why is the corrosion of iron undesirable? Include a chemical equation to illustrate rust formation. What are some solutions to the problem of corrosion? (10 points: 5 points for valid arguments from the sustainable development perspective, 2 points for the correct chemcial equation for rust formation, and 3 points for listing ways of preventing corrosion.)

Performance-Based Items

A. You are supplied with a well reaction plate; dilute hydrochloric acid; pieces of magnesium, zinc, and copper; and a chart listing "Activity Series of Metal."

– Observe each metal's reaction with dilute hydrochloric acid. Prepare a data table and record your observations. (8 points: 2 points for making each observation and recording the observation in the data table, and 2 points for the data table.)

– Which metal did not react with dilute hydrochloric acid? (1 point for correct observation.)

– What is the name of the gas produced by the reactions? (1 point for naming the gas.)

– How can you tell? Perform a test. (3 points for testing.)

– Write a half-reaction for one of the reactions. (2 points for the correct half-reaction.)

(15 points total for Part A)

B. Use the same well reaction plate. You are given (1) copper(II) nitrate solution and zinc, and (2) zinc nitrate solution and copper.

– Observe what happens in each reaction. Record your observations in the data table. (3 points for making observations.)

– Based on the reactions, which is more easily reduced: Cu or Zn? (1 point for making the correct observation.)

– Write a chemical equation and a corresponding net ionic equation for each of the reactions. (6 points: 1 point for the chemical equation and 2 points for the net ionic equation for each of the reactions.)

(10 points total for Part B)

The total possible score for both continuous and culminating assessment is 150 points.

Reflection

Students will have looked at their knowledge in the area of chemistry by applying the concepts they have explored throughout the unit to actual examples and practical applications. A teacher can assess the students' conceptions based on their responses to the experimental activity as well as to the applications that they were asked to explore. The teacher can also use the students' self-evaluations and peer evaluations. By being expected to explain the chemical processes behind these examples, students demonstrate whether they have mastered the concepts within the unit. By comparing their answers to the actual processes they are looking at their own progress through the unit; this is a very important step in giving students the ability to assess their own preconceptions.

The lesson looks at students' conceptions from the students' as well as the teacher's perspective. It is important for the teacher to have the students' input on evaluation, because only the students know where they began and how far they've come. Therefore, to assess students' conceptions means that not only will the teacher assess the students, but also the students will assess themselves and each other as well. Students are given the opportunity to explore what they know by explaining common everyday things. The fact that they are familiar with these applications puts the emphasis not on the application but on the process behind the application. Through these activities, both students and the teacher will be able to assess how well each student has progressed through the unit and identify any alternative conceptions that each student still holds.

☒ CHAPTER REVIEW

This chapter has brought together the frameworks of Marton and Booth (relational learning), Bruner (culture's symbolic system), Pedretti (STSE), and the National Research Council (alternative assessment) to illustrate the common knowledge construction model (Ebenezer & Connor, 1998). This teaching model consists of four interactive phases depicting the voices of science education researchers and practitioners. Subsequently, we have depicted these multiple voices through a unit written by two preservice teachers on the chemical concepts of oxidation and reduction.

PROBES

1. Choose a unit from any of the science domains and prepare activities following the common knowledge construction model and the unit on oxidation and reduction presented in this chapter.
2. Organize a Pre-Service Teacher As Researcher (P-STAR) conference. In a seminar format, present and critically evaluate your activities. Your reflections may be based on the notions presented in this chapter as well as your personal science education (high school and/or university) experiences.
3. Based on the experience you have had in your science teacher education program, whose voices do you hear in Robert and Sofia's work? In groups of three or four, prepare a chart indicating names of researchers and their corresponding work. Indicate the curriculum contexts, teaching methodologies, and science outcomes that would contribute to developing scientific literacy.

APPENDIX 14-1

Students' theories

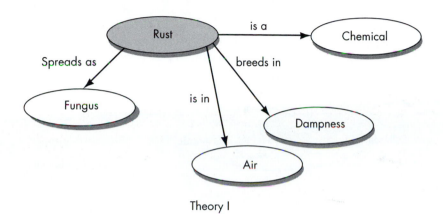

Theory I

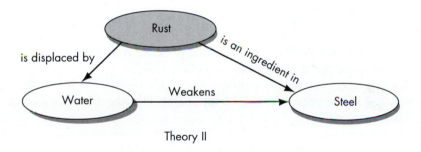

Theory II

APPENDIX 14-2

Sample Diagram of the Process of Rusting

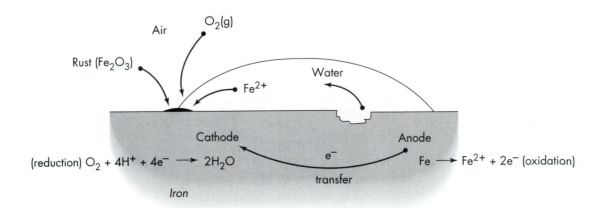

Explanation

1. Rust is hydrated Fe_2O_3; it forms in the presence of O_2 and H_2O
2. Oxidation occurs at the anode; $Fe \rightarrow Fe^{2+} + 2e^-$
3. Reduction occurs at the cathode; $O_2 + 4H^+ + 4e^- \rightarrow 2H_2O$; O_2 is reduced in the presence of H^+ supplied by H_2CO_3, which is formed from dissolved CO_2
4. Overall reaction:
$$2Fe(s) + 4H^+ + O_2 \rightarrow Fe^{2+} + 2H_2O$$
5. Fe^{2+} is further oxidized to rust by atmospheric oxygen:
$$4Fe^{2+} + O_2\ (g) + 4H_2O \rightarrow 4Fe_2O_3\ (s) + 8H^+$$

Example of Redox Reactions for Physical Demonstrations

(1) $Na^+ + e^- \rightarrow Na$

(2) $Zn(s) + Cu^{2+} (aq) \rightarrow Zn^{2+} (aq) + Cu(s)$

(3) $Cu + 2H_2SO_4 \rightarrow CuSO_4 + SO_2 + 2H_2O$

(4) $2Fe(s) + 4H^+ + O_2(g) \rightarrow Fe^{2+} + 2H_2O$

(5) $Ni^{2+} (aq) + Cd(s) \rightarrow Ni(s) + Cd^{2+} (aq)$

Consider example 5: $Cd(s) \rightarrow Cd^{2+} + 2e^-$ (oxidation)

$Ni^{2+} (aq) + 2e^- \rightarrow Ni(s)$ (reduction)

oxidizing agent: Ni^{2+} (aq)

reducing agent: $Cd(s)$

Analytical Description: Electrochemical Cell

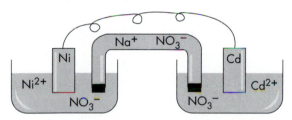

*Physical Description:

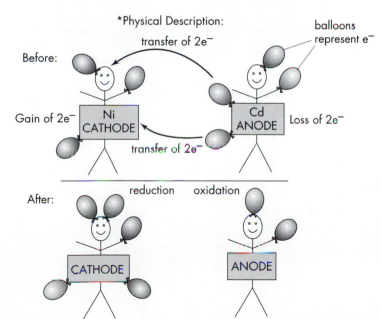

APPENDIX 14-4

Prominent Figures in the History of Chemistry

1. John Dalton
2. Marie Curie
3. Michael Faraday
4. St. Elmo Brady
5. Joseph Louis Proust
6. John Humphrey Davy
7. Dmitri Ivanovich Mendeleev
8. Jons Jakob Berzelius
9. Norbert Rillieux
10. Jane Haldimond Marcet
11. Charles Hall
12. Amadeo Avogadro

CHAPTER 15

Multiple Voices in Unit Planning

STUDY QUESTIONS

1. What are the many voices and visions that have influenced the progression of science education?

2. How are these voices and visions translated into considerations for planning?

3. From how many perspectives can science teaching be approached?

4. How can a sequence of lessons integrate the four phases of the common knowledge construction model?

Reflective Inquiry

RICHARD'S VOICE

Understanding the conceptual basis of the common knowledge construction model has provided me with a different way of planning units and lessons. Progressing from the exploration phase, each lesson is designed to provide students with positive experiences and an opportunity to better focus their own theories about the topic. This model, perhaps most importantly, ensures that I consider the multidisciplinary nature of science, thus meeting the needs of all my students.

JOURNAL ACTIVITY

Unit and Lesson Planning

Describe your personal ideas of unit and lesson planning. What are the special features of your unit plan?

✿ MULTIPLE VOICES INFLUENCING SCIENCE EDUCATION

During the last three decades, science educators have been calling for the renewal of science education—for school sciences that would characterize the social nature of the scientific enterprise (AAAS, 1989; Orpwood, 1984). The voices represent the following research communities: history and philosophy of science (HPS); sociology of science; language in science; relationship between science and technology; connections of science, technology, science, and environment (STSE); psychology; multicultural-ism in science education; feminist science; and personal-social construc-tivist science. The new multi-models of science education originate from the study of science from the following perspectives:

Historical and philosophical—falsification of ideas in science (Popper, 1979), evolutionary changes (Toulmin, 1972), normal science and evolutionary paradigm shifts (Kuhn, 1970)

Sociological—internal convictions and persuasions: scientists' discourse (Latour & Woolgar, 1986); external convictions and persuasions: the sociological study of the cultural milieu in which scientific ideas arise (Cobern, 1991), political economic analysis (Hodson, 1993)

Language—using the specialized language of science to make sense of the world, and to make sense of and to one another; doing science and the scientific process through the medium of language (Lemke, 1990; Sutton, 1992)

Science and technology—understanding the designed world (Raizen, Sellwood, Todd, & Vickers, 1995)

Science-technology-society-environment—teaching the connections among science, technology, society, and environment is considered relevant and is accessible to all students. Decision making and action taking are fundamental to issue-based teaching (Bybee, 1986, 1993; Solomon & Aikenhead, 1994)

Psychological—cognitive structural wholes: person-world dichotomy (Ausubel, 1968; Piaget, 1973), person-world dialectical relationships (Marton, 1981, 1984; Marton & Booth, 1997)

Multicultural—interpersonal relationship and learning styles as cultural factors, multi-sciences where *multi-science* refers to science in various cultural contexts (Atwater & Riley, 1993; Hodson, 1993; Keller, 1985)

Feminism—sociologically motivated (Tuana, 1989); feminist-philosophy oriented but includes social context as a critical feature of scientific work (Longino, 1990)

Constructivism—Children's science (Osborne & Freyberg, 1985); radical constructivism (Glasersfeld, 1989); common knowledge (Edwards & Mercer, 1987); students' ideas (Driver, Asoko, Leach, Mortimer, & Scott, 1994); relational conceptions (Ebenezer & Erickson, 1996)

 PEER TALK

Voices and Visions
Based on the foregoing voices and visions in science education, what elements of teaching and learning would you include in a unit of science?

A Unit on Photosynthesis

Richard Hechter,
diagrams adapted from drawings by Francisco Madrid

This unit may be used at the more senior level in biology.

During the 1997–1998 academic year, Richard Hechter took the chemistry curriculum and instruction course with Jazlin Ebenezer, the first author of this book, at the University of Manitoba. Richard was invited to write a unit on photosynthesis at the tenth-grade level with the help of Jazlin Ebenezer and biology educator Francisco Madrid. Currently, Richard teaches biology, chemistry, and physics in Winnipeg, Manitoba, Canada. In this unit, the Group 1 activity in Lesson 1 was contributed by Wendy Chase, previously a student of Jazlin Ebenezer and currently a teacher in Winnipeg.

In Chapter 1 we outlined a general unit plan based on post-modern voices in science. Subsequent chapters developed the content for this unit. In this final chapter, we bring some of the already discussed pedagogical elements into the development of a unit in science.

Curriculum

Manitoba Education and Training Curriculum Guide

Grade Level

Grade 10

Nature of Students

In my Grade 10 practicum classroom, there are 24 students—15 females and 9 males. There are no special-needs students. There is a broad spectrum of ethnicities and races among these individuals. Most students are self-motivated and very keen on participating in classroom discussions and activities.

Purpose of Unit

The purpose of the unit is to explore students' conceptions about the role photosynthesis plays in the biosphere. Students will participate in numerous hands-on activities in both group and individual settings to explore and validate their ideas. This unit will provide contexts that will encourage students to ask questions and explore additional ideas.

Overview

Photosynthesis occurs within the organelles of the cells called chloroplasts. It is described as the conversion of carbon dioxide into glucose, which is rich in chemical energy. This process, in its intricacies, has transformed the earth into a hospitable environment. How so? Photosynthesis, perhaps the most important biological process we know of, liberates oxygen while consuming carbon dioxide in the presence of light, chlorophyll, and water. In the "big picture" or as a large context problem, photosynthesis is responsible directly or indirectly for our nourishment and sustenance. Not only is it part of our food, but it provides building materials and energy storage in petroleum, coal, natural gas, and firewood as well. It is clear that the study of photosynthesis has science-technology-society-environment connections and implications.

Curricular Content Development

Photosynthesis is a process by which plants manufacture food in the presence of sunlight. During photosynthesis, the light energy is captured by chlorophyll pigment molecules located in the thylakoid membrane in the chloroplasts and is converted into chemical energy. Oxygen is released as a by-product. The chemical energy produced in this manner is used in carbon fixation, which involves a series of reactions in the stroma in the chloroplast to assemble sugar molecules. More specifically, photosynthesis proceeds in the thylakoid membranes and stroma, where the light reaction and carbon fixation occur, respectively (see Figure 15-1). Photosynthesis is a redox process in which carbon dioxide is reduced and water is oxidized (low energy) to produce glucose and oxygen (high energy).

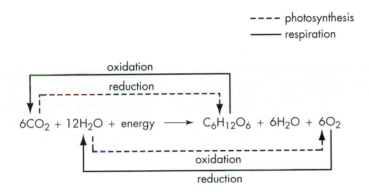

Suzuki (1991) states: "Eventually life learned to eat sunlight through photosynthesis to stay alive" (p. 116). At the same time, life learned to reverse this photosynthesis process through cellular respiration, a meta-

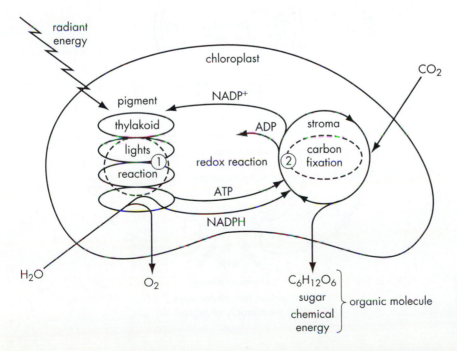

FIGURE 15-1

Photosynthetic process (diagram by Francisco Madrid)

bolic mechanism, to release energy that will allow the plant to grow (see Figure 15-2).

Figure 15-3 is a concept map representing the concept of photosynthesis and related concepts. Figure 15-4 is a Vee diagram that structures the separation of pigments in leaves. Figure 15-5 is a Vee diagram that structures how plants produce oxygen. (Appendix 15-1 indicates how to determine the number of carbon dioxide molecules and water molecules that are necessary to produce one molecule of glucose.)

Historical Context

Much of what we know today about photosynthesis comes from many experiments that have been performed throughout history. The first individual to comment on plant growth was Jean-Baptiste van Helmont, a seventeenth-century Belgian physician and scientist. He did experiments that determined that the addition of mass, or growth, was from the plant or the earth it grew in. From his experiment, which was carried out over five years, he concluded that the earth had no change in

FIGURE 15-2

Energy flow from radiant energy (sun) to chemical energy (organic molecule)

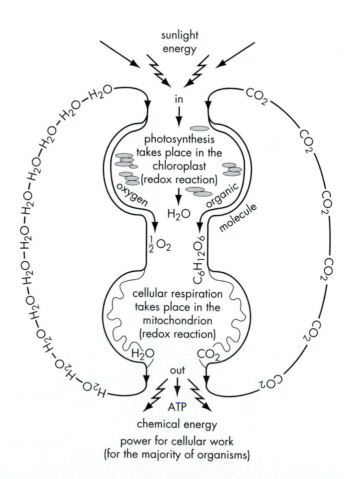

sunlight energy

in

CO_2

photosynthesis takes place in the chloroplast (redox reaction)

H_2O

oxygen

organic molecule

$\frac{1}{2} O_2$

$C_6H_{12}O_6$

cellular respiration takes place in the mitochondrion (redox reaction)

H_2O CO_2

out

ATP

chemical energy

power for cellular work
(for the majority of organisms)

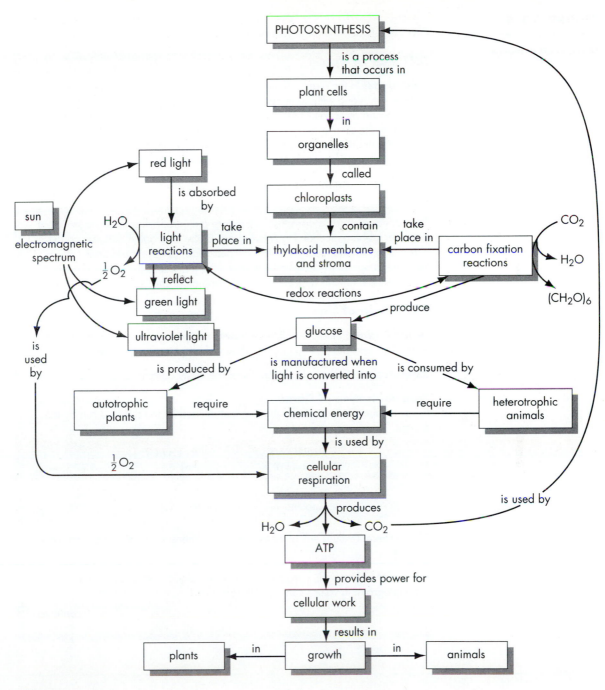

FIGURE 15-3
A concept map of photosynthesis

FIGURE 15-4
Vee diagram of separation
of pigments in leaves

Focus question: What pigments are present in plants?

Left Side of Vee

Key Ideas: In the plant cell there are many pigments. Chlorophyll *a* and *b* are present, along with xanthophylls, carotenes, and phycobilins. These pigments can be separated by paper chromatography. The pigments are carried up the chromatogram by capillary action. The solvent (petroleum ether) carries the lightest, most easily dissolvable pigments up the chromatogram more rapidly and less easily dissolvable pigments more slowly.

Concepts: photosynthesis, pigments, solubility, absorption, chromatography, capillarity

Event: Paper chromatography. To prepare a chlorophyll solution, crush plant leaves in rubbing alcohol. Place two drops of the chlorophyll solution on the chromatogram and let dry. Put 1–2 mL petroleum ether in the cylinder. Place the chromatogram in the cylinder with a drop just above the petroleum ether. Observe the pigments migrating up the chromatogram.

Right Side of Vee

Value Claims: Students will learn how to use paper chromatography as a method to separate plant pigments. They will also learn to interpret results.

Knowledge Claims: In a plant there are many different pigments.

Transformation of Data:
R_f value = the distance run by the pigment divided by the distance run by the solvent.

PIGMENT	R_f *VALUE*
Chlorophyll *b*	0.61
Chlorophyll *a*	0.57
Xanthophyll	0.35
Carotenoids	0.95

Note: Different values will be obtained using different solvents, pigments, and techniques

Records: Chlorophyll, carotenes, and xanthophylls were seen on the chromatogram. R_f values can now be calculated.

continued

My Understanding

Focus Question

What pigments are present in plants?

My Doing

Key Ideas

In the plant cell there are many pigments. Chlorophyll *a* and *b* are present, along with xanthophylls, carotenes, and phycobilins. These pigments can be separated by paper chromatography. The pigments are carried up the chromatogram by capillary action. The solvent (petroleum ether) carries the lightest, most easily dissolvable pigments up the chromatogram more rapidly, and less easily dissolvable pigments more slowly.

Concepts

photosynthesis, pigments, solubility, absorption, chromatography, capillarity

Value Claims

Students will learn how to use paper chromatography as a method to separate plant pigments. They will also learn to interpret results.

Knowledge Claims

In a plant there are many different pigments.

Transformation of Data

R_f value = the distance run by pigment ÷ the distance run by solvent

Pigment	R_f value
Chlorophyll *b*	0.61
Chlorophyll *a*	0.57
Xanthophyll	0.35
Carotenoids	0.95

Records

Chlorophyll, carotenes, and xanthophylls were seen on the chromatogram. R_f values can now be calculated.

Event

Paper chromatography. To prepare a chlorophyll solution, crush plant leaves in rubbing alcohol. Place two drops of the chlorophyll solution on the chromatogram and let dry. Put 1–2 mL petroleum ether in the cylinder. Place the chromatogram in the cylinder with a drop just above the petroleum ether. Observe the pigments migrating up the chromatogram.

FIGURE 15-5
Vee diagram of how plants produce oxygen

Focus question: How do plants produce oxygen during photosynthesis?

Left Side of Vee

Key Ideas:
Photosynthesis takes place in the presence of light.
Photosynthesis occurs in plant cells in the presence of chlorophyll pigments.
Photosynthesis is a redox reaction where carbon dioxide, water, and light energy produce glucose, water, and oxygen.
Light triggers a redox reaction in the presence of chlorophyll, carbon dioxide, and water. As a result of this redox reaction, the molecules of water split into oxygen and hydrogen. Carbon dioxide combines with hydrogen from the molecules of water, forming organic molecular glucose. Simultaneously, water is also formed:

$$6CO_2 + 12H_2O \rightarrow C_6H_{12}O_6 + 6H_2O + 6O_2$$

The O_2 associated with H_2O is represented by the O^{18} isotope.

Concepts: redox reaction, compound, chlorophyll, photosynthesis, glucose, isotope

Event: Count various atoms in the glucose molecule to determine the number of carbon dioxide molecules and water molecules that combine to produce one glucose molecule (for details of this activity, see Appendix 15-1).

Right Side of Vee

Value Claims: Building the structural models of glucose, carbon dioxide, and water, students should be able to state how many molecules of water and carbon dioxide are needed to produce glucose, water, and oxygen in the process of photosynthesis.

Knowledge Claims: There is a precise proportion of atoms of various elements (C, H, O), in the ratio of 1:2:1, in a molecule of glucose. Water splits into oxygen and hydrogen.

Transformation of Data: none

Records: There are six carbon atoms, six oxygen atoms, and twelve hydrogen atoms in glucose. Therefore, six molecules of carbon dioxide and twelve molecules of water are needed to produce one molecule of glucose, six molecules of water, and six molecules of oxygen.

continued

My Understanding	Focus Question	My Doing

Focus Question: How do plants produce oxygen during photosynthesis?

My Understanding

Key Ideas

Photosynthesis takes place in the presence of light. Photosynthesis occurs in plant cells in the presence of chlorophyll pigments.

Photosynthesis is a redox reaction where carbon dioxide, water, and light energy produce glucose, water, and oxygen.

Light triggers a redox reaction in the presence of chlorophyll, carbon dioxide, and water. As a result of this redox reaction, the molecules of water split into oxygen and hydrogen. Carbon dioxide combines with hydrogen from the molecules of water, forming organic molecular glucose. Simultaneously, water is also formed:

$6CO_2 + 12H_2O \rightarrow C_6H_{12}O_6 + 6H_2O + 6O_2$

The O_2 associated with H_2O is represented by the O^{18} isotope.

Concepts

Redox reaction, compound, glucose, chlorophyll, isotope

My Doing

Value Claims

Building the structural models of glucose, carbon dioxide, and water, students should be able to state how many molecules of water and carbon dioxide are needed to produce glucose, water, and oxygen in the process of photosynthesis.

Knowledge Claims

There is a precise proportion of atoms of various elements (C, H, O), in the ratio of 1:2:1, in a molecule of glucose. Water splits into oxygen and hydrogen.

Transformation of data: NA

Records

There are six carbon atoms, six oxygen atoms, and twelve hydrogen atoms in glucose. Therefore, six molecules of carbon dioxide, and twelve molecules of water are needed to produce one molecule of glucose, six molecules of water, and six molecules of oxygen.

Event

Count various atoms in the glucose molecule to determine the number of carbon dioxide molecules and water molecules that combine to produce one glucose molecule.

---

mass, while the plant itself had an enormous increase in mass. Subsequent to Helmont's work, many scientists performed complementary experiments (see Table 15-1).

TABLE 15-1

The Historical Account of Photosynthesis

Scientist	Year	Study
Joseph Priestley	1772	Plants exchange air by giving off oxygen
Jan Ingenhousz	1779	The green plants give off oxygen only in the presence of light
Nicholas de Saussure	1804	Plants take in CO_2 as well as produce oxygen during photosynthesis
Julius Robert von Mayer	1845	Sunlight contributes energy to make food from CO_2 and water
C. B. van Niel	1930	Plants split water as a source of hydrogen, releasing oxygen as a by-product
Melvin Calvin	1960	There are many chemical steps in the forming of glucose

Technological and Societal Context of Inquiry

From food to fibers, energy production, agriculture, environment control and regulation, and medicine, photosynthesis has an enormous impact on and part in our society and culture.

Teaching and Learning Approaches

For this unit, I will be using many different types of teaching and learning approaches. I believe that a variety of approaches is useful and essential, as there is more than one type of learning style in the classroom. Moreover, I must remember that science is for all students. I should also take the opportunity to match teaching methodologies with different knowledge types in science. Developing students' intelligences also fosters various approaches to teaching and learning.

Small-Group Work

Students will work together as a community of inquirers—experimenting, sharing, debating, negotiating, clarifying, and reaching agreement or coming to consensus based on evidence and justification. This will emulate the multidisciplinary nature of scientific work and how scientific knowledge is generated and validated. The group work helps students develop interpersonal intelligence.

Teacher-Students Negotiation

Negotiation will take place between the teacher and students in large-group interpretive discussion so that common knowledge and meanings may be achieved.

Personal Journals

Students will record "insider" accounts of photosynthesis in their journals. In other words, the students will record their personal understandings, draw their diagrams and images, and raise questions that might puzzle them. Journal entries will enable students to trace their conceptual growth. Students' personal accounts will help the teacher see how students are thinking and what sorts of meaning students are attaching to the teacher-students-negotiated biology concepts. In addition, the teacher is better able to gear lessons to students' personal ideas and understandings of specific concepts.

Concept Mapping

Students will identify the concepts related to photosynthesis (see Figure 15-3) as they progress through the unit. Through concept mapping, individually or in small groups, students will relate concepts of photosynthesis at the end of each lesson. This will enable students to trace their conceptual growth as well as to see the interrelationships of concepts.

Vee Diagramming

Students will record their investigations in the form of a Vee diagram. This knowledge-generating tool will help students visualize the relationships between the biologists' conceptual meanings and their laboratory investigation in answering the teacher-students-developed focus question based on a biological event (see Figure 15-4).

Research

Students will research the personal histories and the works of biologists who studied plants (see the section on history). Through traditional research or multimedia ethnographies, students will discuss STSE issues related to photosynthesis, such as global warming, acid rain, and oxygen depletion. The Internet will be an excellent resource for identifying activities, conducting scientific inquiries, and communicating with remote mentors and students.

Common Knowledge Construction Model

Phase I: Exploring and Categorizing

A. Exploring Students' Conceptions of Photosynthesis. I carried out the following exploration activity in class.

EXPLORATION ACTIVITIES
- I asked students to look out the window at plants in the school yard.
- I had students individually explain in writing, "How do plants grow?"
- I told students to answer the following question: "If you had special glasses that would allow you to see how plants grow, what would you see happening?"

An alternative idea is to bring a plant to class and focus students' attention on this plant.

While students recorded their explanations and drew diagrams, I walked around and asked pertinent questions based on what the students had written and drawn. Each student submitted his or her idea sheet to me.

B. Categorizing Students' Conceptions. Based on the two-part question, I allowed students to separate each idea sheet into two parts. I spread out the separated anonymous responses over the main desk. Initially, acting as a facilitator, I asked students to group their ideas, justifying each one. Then, together with students, I refined their initial categories. The phenomenographic categories of plant growth are as follows:

Along with some students' diagrams, we have included the expert diagrams contributed by Dr. Francisco Madrid.

1. Plants get their energy from the sunlight.
   - "The stem of the plant will grow toward the light."
   - "They get their energy from the sunlight."
   - "Plants have leaves, which collect sunlight for energy. . . ."

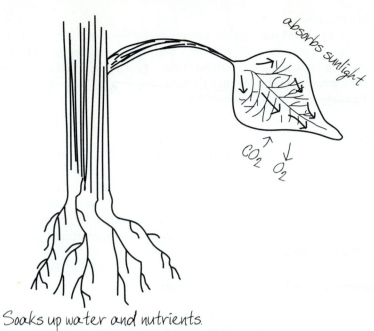

Soaks up water and nutrients.

Student Diagram 1

2. Plants take their nutrients and water from the soil.
   – "A seed starts to germinate to form a tiny root. After this, the root
     will grow downward into the soil taking nutrients and water from the
     soil. The stem of the plant will grow toward the light."

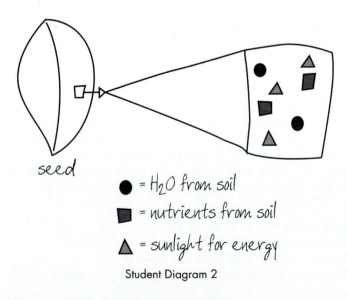

seed

- = H_2O from soil
- = nutrients from soil
- = sunlight for energy

Student Diagram 2

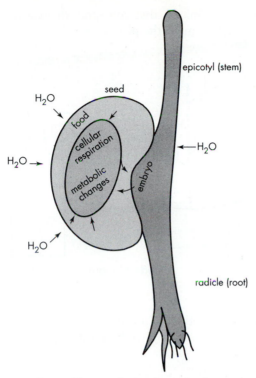

Expert Diagram 1: Seed germination, stage 1

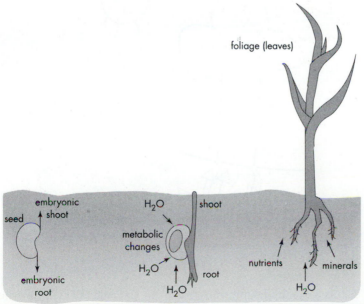

Expert Diagram 2: Seed germination, stage 2

– "Fertilizers, or chemicals, that you spray them with will have nutrients and water that make the plants grow."

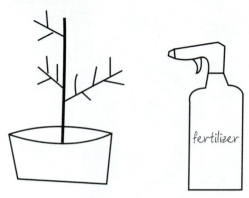

Student Diagram 3

– "Plants get their food from nutrients in the soil like water and food. The nutrients are sucked up to the plant using roots."

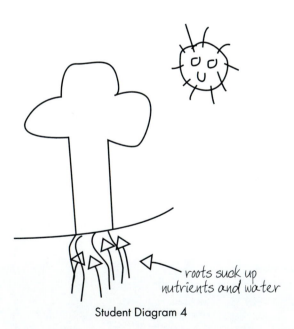

Student Diagram 4

– "Plants grow by taking nutrients from the soil. All nutrients needed for growth can be found there. The plant gets energy from the sun."

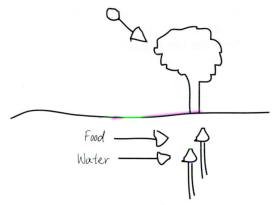

Student Diagram 5

3. Plants grow through a chemical reaction, referred to as photosynthesis.
   – "Plants grow from the use of photosynthesis, which contains sunlight, glucose, carbon dioxide, oxygen and water."

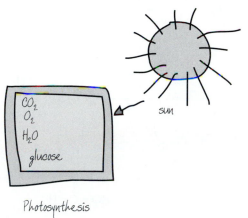

Photosynthesis

Student Diagram 6

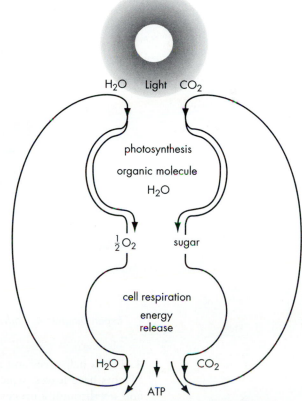

Expert Diagram 3: Energy flow in photosynthesis

– "Plants grow through a chemical reaction involving CO_2, H_2O (from rain or soil), and chlorophyll, which react with the energy from the sun to produce glucose, which is their food. This is called photosynthesis."

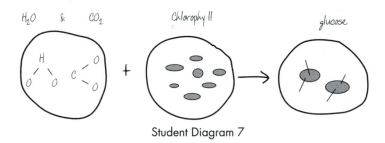

Student Diagram 7

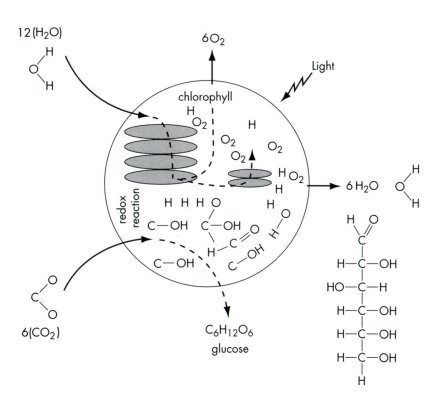

Expert Diagram 4: Conversion of carbon dioxide and water into glucose

4. Plants help trees and animals.
"Plants have leaves, which collect sunlight for energy and carbon dioxide and go through a process called photosynthesis, which helps the tree and oxygen-breathing mammals grow and live."

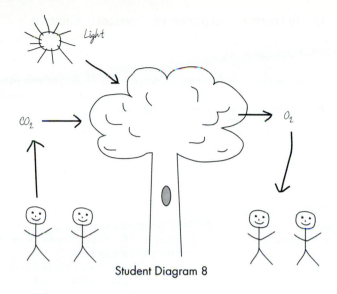

Student Diagram 8

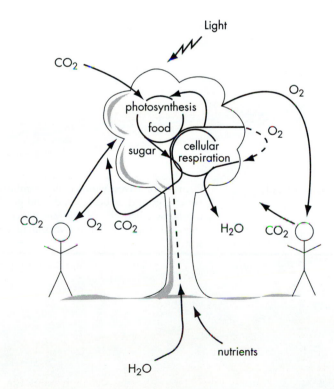

Expert Diagram 5: Recycling of carbon dioxide, water, and oxygen

C. Relating Students' Conceptions to Curricular Content

TABLE 15-2

The Relationships between Curricular Content and Tenth-Grade Students' Conceptions of Photosynthesis ($n = 24$)

Curricular Content	Teacher-Made Categories	Students' Conceptions
Plants get their energy from the sunlight and cellular respiration.	Plants get their energy from the sunlight.	"They get their energy from the sunlight."
Plants grow by capturing energy from sunlight and storing it in the organic molecules in their bonds.		"The stem of the plant will grow toward the light." "The plant gets energy from the sun."
Water and nutrients are absorbed from the soil by the roots.	Plants take nutrients and water from the soil.	*"Plants get their food from nutrients in the soil like water and food. The nutrients are sucked up to the plant using roots."
Plants grow as a result of a chemical redox reaction, referred to as photosynthesis and cellular respiration.	Plants grow through a chemical reaction, referred to as photosynthesis.	"Plants grow through a chemical reaction involving CO_2, H_2O (from rain or soil), and chlorophyll, which react with the energy from the sun to produce glucose, which is their food. This is called photosynthesis."
Photosynthesis is a process of consuming carbon dioxide and water and producing oxygen and sugar. Light energy is converted into chemical energy that is stored in sugar molecules.		
In cellular respiration, sugar is oxidized into carbon dioxide and oxygen is reduced to water.		
Photosynthesis converts light energy to chemical energy and stores it in sugar molecules.		
Plants produce oxygen, which is used by animals. Animals breathe out carbon dioxide, which is used by plants.	Plants help trees and animals.	"Plants have leaves, which collect sunlight for energy and carbon dioxide and go through a process called photosynthesis, which helps the tree and oxygen-breathing mammals grow and live."

*Alternative conception

D. Teacher Reflections. The nine individuals represented in teacher-made category 1 identified the energy requirement as the dominant variable in plant growth. This is likely indicative of prior knowledge these students may have had about placing plants in the windows of their home to maximize light availability.

Seven students detailed nutrient absorption from the soil as the primary factor in plant growth (see category 2). This response suggests substrate as a determining step. Two students in category 2 also suggested that plants require applied fertilizers to grow successfully. I believe that these students may have had a mental picture of a houseplant that requires special chemical fertilizers to help the plant grow.

Seven other students were very specific in suggesting that plant growth is due to a chemical/biological process termed photosynthesis. These students remembered what was taught in their previous grades and used the term *photosynthesis* to explain how plants grow. One student brought a previously unmentioned "extension" to the table. This student focused on the benefits of photosynthesis for trees and animals. The ideas that plants help animals by providing fresh, clean oxygen, and that they are *autotrophic* because they make their own food energy, are wonderful extensions to this unit.

E. Relating Students' Ideas to Previous Studies. Anderson, Sheldon and Dubay (1990) studied the concepts of respiration and photosynthesis of mostly elementary preservice teachers. These researchers found that many elementary preservice teachers used the words *respiration* and *breathing* synonymously. The preservice teachers in this study also did not give sufficient explanation of how photosynthesis works. These authors' work illustrates the conceptions individuals have about plant respiration. But, more important, the study indicates that students do not know how photosynthesis works. For example, one preservice teacher in this study said, "Green plants turn sun and CO_2 into chlorophyll".

Roth and Anderson's findings (1985) denote that plants produce oxygen via photosynthesis not for their own benefit, but rather the benefit of other animals (especially people). The authors cite the exchange of gases as the most important link. This finding correlates with a conception in my study: "Plants help trees and animals."

Bell and Brook (1984) report in their study, "Aspects of Secondary Students' Understanding of Plant Nutrition," that most students appear to understand that plants need energy to grow and that plants get the energy from their food. However, many students also said that plants get their food from the soil via the roots. Students need to learn that light energy is required and chlorophyll is a green pigment that absorbs light energy in the presence of carbon dioxide and water to prepare food. Students also need to be aware that plants growth depends not only on the process of photosynthesis, but also on cellular respiration.

Simpson (1984), Simpson and Arnold (1982), and Bell and Brook (1984) all suggest that some students do not understand the role of chlorophyll. Some students reported that chlorophyll made the plants green so to look pretty and attractive. Others suggested that chlorophyll in plants is analogous to blood in animals. Hence, the photosynthetic process deserves careful and detailed attention in a biology curriculum.

F. Direction for Subsequent Work. Using students' conceptions as a foundation for conceptual development, I decided on the following lesson sequence:

> *Lesson 1:* Courtroom drama on photosynthesis (constructing and negotiating)
> *Lesson 2:* History of photosynthesis (constructing and negotiating)
> *Lesson 3:* Design technology (solarium) (translating and extending)
> *Lesson 4:* Why study photosynthesis? (translating and extending)
> *Lesson 5:* Global warming (STSE) (translating and extending)
> *Culminating Assessment:* Written test and performance-based test

Phase II: Constructing and Negotiating

Lesson 1: The Courtroom Drama

Students' conceptions

"Plants get their energy from the sunlight."
"Plants take their nutrients and water from the soil."
"Plants grow through a chemical reaction referred to as photosynthesis."
"Plants help trees and animals."

Discussion

This activity-based lesson facilitates many aspects of learning. In terms of photosynthesis, this lesson provides students the opportunity to debate the various conceptions developed during the exploration activity. From a pedagogical view, this lesson utilizes role playing, group sharing, group cohesiveness, and allocation of responsibility.

Objectives

Students will:

- demonstrate the ability to work successfully in groups.
- determine the most plausible conception about plant growth by analyzing and observing the proceedings.

Teaching and Learning Approaches

- Students will use a variety of processes, including experimenting, analyzing, and sharing, to determine the most plausible conception.

- Students will also work in small groups, but will effectively assign a division of labor of tasks.
- Students will record observations and notes and answer questions in their journals.

Materials and Resources

paper
scissors
stations
list of student conceptions
list of available times the lab can be used for the "new" activity.

Activities and Procedures

1. Have students arrive and sit in preselected groups corresponding to one of the six stations.
2. Explain the activity as follows:
   a. The groups are to defend their conceptions in court.
   b. Each group will need an opening statement.
   c. The judge will allow time for each opening statement.
   d. The judge will start the proceedings.
   e. The groups may present their evidence.
   f. Groups may also call witnesses for defense of their conception.
   g. Each group is to make up name tags, stations, cases, evidence sheets, and desired questions. (*Note:* Be aggressive when defending your case.)

While the procedure is the skeleton of the lesson I planned, the following is essentially a play-by-play recourse of how the lesson proceeded.

Entering the class on the first day of the unit, the students looked out the window and answered the exploration question, "How does a plant grow?" Based on students' conceptions, the students and I developed four categories. The examples of students' conceptions representing the four categories are as follows (important concepts are italicized):

1. "They (plants) get their energy from the *sunlight.*"
2. "Plants get their food from nutrients in the soil like water and food. The *nutrients* are sucked up to the plant using roots."
3. "Plants go through a chemical reaction involving CO_2 . . . and *chlorophyll,* which react with the energy from the sun to produce *glucose.*"
4. "Plants help the tree and *oxygen*-breathing mammals grow and live."

From these categories of conceptions, I developed six activities that would help students clarify and elaborate on their personal ideas. The activities are as follows:

1. Plants and sunlight
2. Absorption of nutrients from the soil
3. Carbon dioxide intake
4. Presence of chlorophyll

These activities will give students sufficient experience in the fundamentals of photosynthesis before they encounter the enormously complex biological, biochemical process and more sophisticated models at the senior secondary level.

We wish to remind you that students require extensive learning experiences through activities designed to allow them to construct and negotiate meaning regarding the concept of photosynthesis. Just as students have a network of ideas, scientific ideas are interrelated. Hence, we cannot conduct only one corresponding lesson, thinking that scientific ideas will be made more intelligible. A series of lessons will provide both awareness and understanding of interrelationships among scientific concepts.

5. Presence of glucose
6. Oxygen production

Each group of four students (making six groups) was then provided with one of the conceptions and a supporting activity. Each group was given separate class time to conduct the activity I had selected for them. At a specified time, there was only one group working with me in the laboratory. No other group knew the experimental procedure or experimental results.

During the laboratory activity with one group, the other groups searched the Internet to find resources that supported their conception. This procedure helped each group to hold their conception private until "the day in court," when they were expected to present their findings and ideas to the other groups. The different groups spent the next few classes in the library, using the computer and resources there, except for one group that met with me in the laboratory. Finding adequate resources and conducting laboratory activities were vital to make scientific arguments in the court. The purpose of this lesson is for students to contribute their knowledge claims about the photosynthetic process.

Experimental Activities.

GROUP 1 ACTIVITY
PLANTS AND SUNLIGHT

This activity was presented by Wendy Chase, a preservice teacher, at our annual P-STAR Conference at the University of Manitoba.

This activity is one in a series of activities on photosynthesis so that students will come to believe that without light energy, photosynthesis cannot occur, and that chlorophyll is the green pigment in plants that absorbs light energy for use in photosynthesis.

In this activity, students will be able to:

- *demonstrate* that when parts of a leaf are covered, the leaf becomes paler because the leaf is not receiving light energy.
- *observe* that if a leaf does not receive light energy, then chlorophyll, the green pigment in leaves, cannot act to combine water and carbon dioxide from the air to form sugar.

Materials and Resources

a plant with large wide leaves
black construction paper
scissors, paper clips, and masking tape
student journal

Procedure

1. Have students cut out several patterns (circle, square, triangle) from the same piece of black construction paper (see diagram).

2. Have students draw a diagram of three different leaves in their personal journals.

3. Have students cover the leaves as much as possible with the cut-out

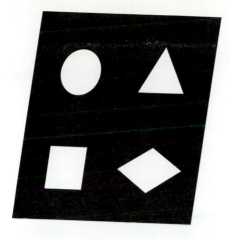

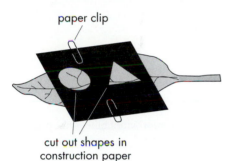

paper clip

cut out shapes in
construction paper

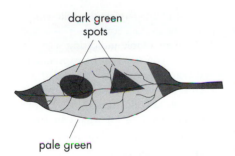

dark green
spots

pale green

construction paper by attaching it with a paper clip or masking tape (see diagram).

4. Leave the paper attached for 2–3 days, exposed to intense light.

5. After several days, have students remove the attached paper and observe the leaves. (*Note:* Save these leaves for the Group 5 activity, step 6.)

6. Have students draw a diagram of each of the leaves in their journals.

7. Have students record their observations and explanations in their journals.

8. Have a group discussion revolving around students' questions, such as the following: How did the covered portions of the leaves compare to the uncovered portions of the leaves? What does this tell about the role of light energy? What is the role of chlorophyll in the leaves of green plants?

Assessment

Observe students' participation in the activity. Collect students' journals to examine their diagrams and personal notes.

Reflection

Through this activity students will come to understand that plants require light energy to manufacture their own food through a process called photosynthesis.

GROUP 2 ACTIVITY

ABSORPTION OF NUTRIENTS FROM THE SOIL

Focus on the microscopic ideas of the xylem and the phloem.

Materials

> 3 carnations
> water
> food coloring (red, blue, and
>   green)
> 3 beakers
> light source

Procedure

1. Fill each beaker with warm water.
2. Place a few drops of food coloring in the water (a different color in each beaker).
3. Place one carnation in each beaker.
4. Allow to rest for 24 hours.

Assessment

Have students answer the following questions in their journals:
1. What happened to the petals?
2. How did the color get from the beaker to the petals?
3. Draw a picture of how this was done.

GROUP 3 ACTIVITY

CARBON DIOXIDE INTAKE

Materials

> bromothymol blue
> *Elodea*
> test tubes
> drinking straws
> carbonated water

Procedure

1. Place a straw in the test tube filled with bromothymol blue. Breathe into the straw to create bubbles, and watch the color change.

2. To separate test tube filled with bromothymol blue, add a few drops of carbonated water. Is there any color change? Describe the change. What similarities can you draw between your breath and the carbonated water?

3. Design an experiment, using the findings from steps 1 and 2 and the *Elodea*.

Note: Bromothymol blue is not poisonous to *Elodea*.

Assessment

Have students answer the following questions in their journal:
1. Prepare a table indicating what materials you used in the experiment. For example, list what you added to each tube, what you expected, and what you saw. Be sure to provide possible explanations for what you saw.

2. Do you have any reason to believe that light alone does not change the color of the indicator?

3. Which combination of materials indicates the necessity of light for photosynthesis?

4. Which tube demonstrates the role of CO_2 in photosynthesis? How?

5. What, if any, are the differences in what you predicted and what you actually saw?

GROUP 4 ACTIVITY

PRESENCE OF CHLOROPHYLL

Materials

lab equipment
leaves
bottle
prism
projector
colored slides or plates
student journal

Procedure

1. Pour chlorophyll solution into a flat-sided bottle until it is almost full.

2. Shine a bright light on one side of the bottle (use a slide projector). View the solution from directly above. Record your observation.

3. Place a prism in front of the light beam coming from the projector. Position the prism so that the best possible spectrum can be seen on the wall screen. Record these colors from red to violet.

4. Place the bottle of chlorophyll solution behind the prism. Observe again the spectral rays that fall on the wall. Record these.

5. Hold a red glass plate in the light beam coming from the projector. Record what light is transmitted.

6. Hold a green leaf behind the red glass plate. What color does the leaf appear to be? Record.

Assessment

Have students answer the following questions in their journals:

1. The chlorophyll extract that you obtained was green. The presence of a green pigment created this color. Is it possible that pigments with colors other than green were present? Why do they not show up?

2. What did you observe when you looked down on the chlorophyll solution that was being illuminated from the side?

3. What color wavelengths of light were able to pass through the chlorophyll solution?

4. What colors were absorbed?

5. Which of these wavelengths—the transmitted ones or the absorbed ones—do you think would be used in the photosynthetic process?

6. Why does a geranium leaf appear green in the daylight?

7. What colors did the geranium leaf that was illuminated with red light appear to be? How do you account for this appearance?

The event in the Vee diagram indicated in Figure 15-4 describes how to prepare chlorophyll solution.

GROUP 5 ACTIVITY

PRESENCE OF GLUCOSE

Materials

2 *Coleus* plants (one that has been in the dark for 48 hours)
ethyl alcohol (50–70%)
forceps
two 250-mL beakers

iodine solution
hot plate

Procedure

1. Take one leaf from the healthy plant that has been exposed to light

and draw it in your journal, indicating the distribution of chlorophyll.

2. Place the leaf in a beaker of boiling water and let it cook for two to three minutes.

3. Remove the leaf from the boiling water (using forceps) and submerge it in boiling alcohol for about three minutes. **Caution: do not heat alcohol over an open flame.**

4. Remove the leaf from the alcohol and let it dry. After drying, submerge the leaf in a beaker of iodine solution for a minute or two. Sketch this in your journal.

5. Repeat steps 2–4 with a leaf from the plant that has spent the last 48 hours in the dark.

6. You may also repeat steps 2–4 with the leaves obtained from the Group 1 activity to observe the pattern between the exposed part and the unexposed part of the leaf.

Assessment

Have students answer the following questions in their journal:

1. What effect does the alcohol have on the leaves?

2. Did you notice a conversion from sugar into starch in any leaf cells? Discuss. (The iodine test for starch will show chemically that light is essential for glucose formation.)

3. Do all green parts of a leaf necessarily have starch? Explain.

4. The conversion of sugar to starch is a complex procedure involving the unification of many small molecules into fewer larger molecules. What must be present in the cell for this chemical reaction to occur?

5. This activity identifies two things that a plant must have in order to produce food. Name them.

GROUP 6 ACTIVITY

OXYGEN PRODUCTION

Materials

6 sprigs *Elodea*
water
large beaker
a large clear glass funnel that fits
   the beaker
small test tube
wooden splint

Procedure

1. Invert the funnel inside the beaker.

2. Put as much *Elodea* under the funnel as can fit.

3. Boil the water and then let it cool to room temperature

4. Pour the water into the beaker until the neck of the funnel is totally submerged; however, do not let any water into the funnel—cover it with your thumb.

5. Place the test tube over the neck of the funnel.

6. Water will fill part of the test tube, but it will be displaced as oxygen is produced.

7. Place the beaker in sunlight and wait until the level of the water in the test tube is halfway between the top and the bottom. At this point there is enough gas to test for oxygen.

8. Remove the tube, covering it immediately.

9. Light a wooden splint and let it
burn. When it is burning well, blow it
out and quickly place the glowing
splint in the tube.

Assessment

Did the splint burst into flame?
Why did this happen?

For each of the activities, students were expected to construct a Vee dia-
gram-concept map combination.

The Trial

After four or five days of research, the students are to appear, with their
team, in "court." The room is set up like a courtroom—a table for the
judge and six more tables, one for each group. Each group has now
researched their conception through experimental activities that have provided them with scientific evidence. I, playing the judge but acting merely
as a facilitator, began the hearings:

> "I call your attention to order. Docket number 01201998 now comes to order.
> Welcome to the court case of the century—aside from O.J., of course. Today
> we are gathered here to find out exactly how plants grow. We begin the pro-
> ceedings with an opening statement from each group."

Each group then proceeded to make an opening statement. For example,
Group 1's statement was as follows:

> "Good afternoon, Judge Hechter and fellow scientists. Today, it is our inten-
> tion to demonstrate that the sun provides the energy a plant needs to grow. We
> will call experts to the stand to confirm our findings. Thank you."

As another example, this was Group 4's statement:

> "Ah yes. You have heard some of the other contestants now, but now it's time
> to hear the real deal. We stand here today to confirm that without our pres-
> ence—that is, the presence of chlorophyll—the plant would not survive, never
> mind grow. Today we will show, beyond doubt, that chlorophyll is the answer
> to this growth question. Thank you."

Each group made a statement of intention, and, more important, gave
the rest of the class their position (in our terms, their conception). From
here we went right to the heart of the matter—the sharing of scientific
ideas, arguments, and evidence.

Each group, in randomly drawn order, presented their case to me and
to the class. The presentation consisted of various components, as in the
following example from Group 6:

> "Good afternoon. First we are going to share our conception with you again.
> We are here to say that plants produce oxygen and take in carbon dioxide and
> water (oxygen comes from water), which in turn helps oxygen-breathing ani-
> mals on the earth. While this is true, how do we really know that it is oxygen
> that the plants are producing? To answer this question, we call our expert to the

stand." (Here, another group member wearing a lab coat; big, black, taped glasses; hair fashioned Kramer-style (from *Seinfeld*); a plaid shirt; and a pocket protector filled with pens and a calculator approached the judge's table and sat down in the witness stand. The "courtroom" filled with laughter.)

GROUP MEMBER:	"Dr. Knowitall, tell us about your research."
DR. KNOWITALL:	"Sure. I have developed a way to test for oxygen in the gas produced by plants."
GM:	"Please explain."
DR. K:	"I captured the gas as it was produced in an inverted test tube." (She demonstrates the experiment with the apparatus in hands.)
GM:	"First, how did you know a gas was produced?"
DR. K:	"Well, the water displaces inside the apparatus when a gas lighter than water is produced."
GM:	"Okay, so now what?"
DR. K:	"Well, I thought of what would be a definitive test for oxygen. I mean, how could I show by doing something, that it had to be oxygen in the test tube?"
GM:	"So how did you do it?"
DR. K:	"Easy. Oxygen will ignite a glowing splint, as oxygen is combustible."
GM:	"I see."
DR. K:	"And if I placed a glowing splint into the test tube, the splint would ignite and create a flame only if oxygen is the gas present."
GM:	"Did it work?"
DR. K:	"It sure did. Not only that, it let off this eerie sound that scared half my research team." (A laugh from the gallery)
GM:	"Thank you, Dr. Knowitall."
DR. K:	"Anytime, anytime . . . now back to the lab."

The "doctor" then got up and returned to the group's table. The other students applauded her performance. The "lawyer" (the group member who questioned Dr. Knowitall) continued:

"So, as you can see, Your Honor, plants grow by a process called photosynthesis, but more important, they provide clean, fresh oxygen to the world. This should not be overlooked. Thank you."

And he sat down, to the roaring applause of his classmates.

After each presentation, the other groups were provided an opportunity to ask questions. After all the presentations were done, the groups were asked for their closing remarks. Group 2 concluded by saying this:

"Friends, biologists, teacher . . . lend me your ears. I come to praise photo-synthesis, not bury it. While it is important to consider the many facets of pho-tosynthesis, there is little doubt as to the vital importance of having the roots absorb the nutrients and water from the soil, or substrate, that they live in. We have demonstrated the transport system of the plants by using food coloring in carnations. Here, we are introduced to the xylem and phloem, the main com-ponents of the plant transport system. From this simple, yet very informative activity, we can see that the most important aspect of plant growth is plant health and nutrient availability. Without the roots doing this work, plants would simply perish, and certainly no growth would occur. Thank you."

Ah, yes, a fine, fine ending. Each group tried to convince me and their classmates that their conception was the only plausible one. By the time this lesson had come to an end, most of the students had already figured out the intentions of this week-long activity. Each one focused on a dif-ferent conception that contributed to the big picture of photosynthesis and plant growth. It was the students teaching the students. It is true that I "set them up," as they exclaimed when they realized how this lesson would end. But I did so in a way that was fun, interesting, and creative, yet still covered the major ideas of the topic. Even after reading this over several times, I continue to develop this lesson in hopes that it will be improved by next year.

Assessment. In the "post-trial" the students filled in a form that indicated whether or not the court proceedings had changed what they perceive happens—for example, "Has your conception about plant growth changed from what has happened here today?"

Lesson 2: History of Photosynthesis

Students' Conceptions

"How did the idea of photosynthesis come about?"

Discussion

Through this lesson, students will trace the historical events that have led to the construction and development of the photosynthetic process. This lesson, filled with historic role playing, will provide students an opportunity to move through time on a historic journey. This unconventional lesson may help students see the great value of integrating scientific history into everyday lessons.

Objectives

Students will:

- trace the historical pathway in which the photosynthetic process has come to be understood.

- identify and describe the major experiments performed during each stage of this discovery process.

Teaching and Learning Approaches

- Students will use role playing, predicting, observing, explaining and interpreting during this lesson,
- Students will use organizing skills (chart making) and journal writing to record their observations
- Students will participate in large group activities and research using role play to help facilitate learning

Materials and Resources

research materials
lab equipment (for demonstration)
props for role-playing activity
student journal
book: BSCS. (1968). *Biological science*. Boston: Houghton Mifflin.
Internet: "Why Study Photosynthesis?"
            http://www.photoscience.la.asc.edu/photosyn/study.html
journals: *Nature* archives: http://www.nature.com/
            Science archives: http://www.sciencemag.org/
CD-ROM (for example, Bio-Sci II)

Activities and Procedures

1. Place students into six groups for research activity (prior to the lesson).
2. Assign each group a scientist and the corresponding key historical finding about photosynthesis (prior to the lesson). Choose from the following list:
   a. Jean-Baptiste von Helmont
   b. Joseph Priestley
   c. Jan Ingenhousz
   d. Nicholas de Saussure
   e. Julius Robert von Mayer
   f. C. B. van Niel
   g. Melvin Calvin
3. Each group will present a 15- to 20-minute presentation about their respective scientist and the major contribution he made to the idea of photosynthesis.
4. The presentation itself is to be creative, informative, and clear. Ideas for this presentation, similar to a short P-STAR conference, include a short skit detailing the scientist and his work, a re-enactment of the experiment, and a discussion about the implications of this scientist's findings. The following is an example of what students may present during this lesson about the work of Melvin Calvin:

A group of four students to represent the C^{14} molecule, the plant, Melvin Calvin, and the narrator.

NARRATOR:	"One day, in Melvin Calvin's lab, way back in 1961 . . ."
CALVIN:	"I am now putting a tag on you [C^{14} molecule] so I can trace you through the plant."
C^{14} MOLECULE:	"Sure, just make sure it's on tight. I don't want to lose it during chromatography."
CALVIN:	"I'm sure you won't!"
	The C^{14} isotopic tagged molecule then runs around the plant, weaving in and out of the arms of the plant until it stops and hides behind the plant.
CALVIN:	"Hmmm. The molecule is in the plant. Now, let me use chromatography to separate the pigments and find out where the carbon went."
C^{14} MOLECULE:	"I'm changing, I'm changing. . . ."

The molecule comes out of the plant in a new form (the finished products of assimilation) with the tag still on it.

| CALVIN: | "Eureka—oh no, that was Archimedes. I've got it!" |
| NARRATOR: | "And so it was that Calvin traced the path of the C^{14} molecule through the plant, and he was given a Nobel Prize!" |

In this short dramatization, the students will visually demonstrate the work Calvin did in relation to photosynthesis.

5. After each presentation, the other students will positively critique the presentation.

Assessment

The teacher will collect and analyze the comment sheets. Ask students to discuss questions they may have had during the presentation. Collect students' journals to examine personal notes.

Reflection

From this activity students will get a better understanding of the many historical events from which we now learn about photosynthesis.

Phase III: Translating and Extending

Lesson 3: Design Technology

Discussion

The students will follow the "Design Process" (as suggested in Chapter 11) to develop a product that uses one or more of the concepts learned in this unit. I have used this strategy to develop the example I used in class. This example is presented here.

Activities and Procedures

1. *Analysis and investigation:* The real-world problem I have chosen is, "Which plants should be put in solariums?"
2. *Framing of a design brief:* This problem will help solarium decorators select the best photosynthetic plants to put in these special rooms. The constraints of this study are that often, the best photosynthetic plants are not the most visually appealing. Thus, the room decorator would need to compromise when purchasing plants.
3. *Information Gathering:* I have used botany journals, textbooks, and other resources to gather information on the photosynthetic rates of various different house plants.
4. *Generating of alternative solutions:* I have generated the following ideas on how I can find the best photosynthetic plant to place in a solarium:
   A. Take the three "best" houseplants for gas exchange and place them in a solarium for several weeks. After this time I would collect data as to growth, color, and shape, all of which indicate photosynthetic abilities.
   B. Take samples of the leaves, stems, and roots of each plant and study them microscopically. Here I could determine cellular abilities of each plant.
   C. Place representatives in a small-scale solarium, which could be analyzed and observed easily. The small-scale environment could be an open fish tank.
5. *Choosing the best solution:* I chose idea C. Here, I can place the plants in the tank and manage them easily. Also, this method allows me to change variables such as carbon dioxide levels, light intensity, and water and food supplements. The small-scale solarium will be set up in an abandoned fish tank. This provides a solution to the problem of which plants to put in a solarium for maximum oxygen production.
6. *Developmental work:* After many attempts to find the best way to pursue this project, I determined that the one with hydroponics lights, a fish tank, plants, enriched soil, and a watering can provided the best chance of success.
7. *Testing and Evaluating:* The design of this small-scale solarium worked well for many reasons. First, the manageability of this setup was ideal, as it fit nicely in the lab. Second, the results I was pursuing came to fruition. One plant grew remarkably, while the others did not. This is relative to each plant's average size, as suggested in the research. Since each was in its own

pot, with equivalent soil and water levels, I was able to reduce the number of variables that would contaminate the validity of this project.

   In terms of universal applicability, this method is ideal. Different solariums have varying amounts of sunlight, as determined by room layout and window placement. Thus, each solarium has different qualities. With sunlight as a determining factor, this small-scale experiment could be repeated with different variables where specific light intensity, duration of sunlight, and window position are known.

8. *Redesign and Reimplementation:* The way I would redo this is by doing more than one trial. Due to lack of available resources and time, I could only experiment once. Furthermore, the materials and procedures I used were limited by what was available. Every science lab is different. Thus, this experiment might have taken a different shape if I had been in another lab with different resources.

Assessment

Assessment of the design technology is not based on the success or failure of the product. Rather, it is based on the process that went into developing it—specifically, the steps of the design process. Points are awarded on the basis of creativity, originality, and comprehensibility.

Reflection

This is a wonderful lesson, but very time-consuming. It requires a lot of extracurricular work and time. As a result, students must be self-motivated.

Lesson 4: Why Study Photosynthesis?

Students' Conceptions

"I don't know how plants grow, but what does it matter anyway?"

Discussion

Students have already learned the biological processes of photosynthesis. The students will now turn to the application and relationship of photosynthesis to the real world in which we live. What are the functions of photosynthesis?

Objectives

Students will:

- describe the importance of photosynthesis in terms of agriculture, food, energy production, environmental control, electronics, and medicine.

Teaching and Learning Approaches

- Students will participate in discussion, large-group sharing, teacher-student debate, and student negotiation in this lesson.

- Students will use journal writing to record their thoughts and new ideas.
- Students will work cooperatively in a large group to develop ideas about the importance of photosynthesis.

Materials and Resources

Search the Internet for up-to-date sites.

Activities and Procedures

1. Conduct an open forum on the importance of photosynthesis.
2. Have students record their ideas in their personal journals.
3. Incorporate ideas about agriculture, food, energy production, environmental control, electronics, and medicine in relation to the biological process of photosynthesis.

Assessment

The teacher should assess this lesson through observation of students' participation and insight during the discussion and journal writing. Students should identify at least five important reasons for studying photosynthesis and record these in their journals.

Reflection

Through this lesson students will learn the many important extensions and real-life connections of photosynthesis. It's not just about plant growth!

Lesson 5: Global Warming

Students' Conceptions

"Photosynthesis only affects plants."

Discussion

This lesson discusses photosynthesis in the real world. As the research and literature suggest, there is an unexpected increase in photosynthetic activity paralleled to the global warming trend in the Northern Hemisphere. This lesson focuses students' attention on the relationship between photosynthetic rates and global warming. More important, this discussion is a perfect example of an STSE issue–based lesson.

Objectives

Students will:

- suggest reasons for the increase in photosynthesis in the Northern Hemisphere.
- suggest plausible methods to control the rate of photosynthesis.
- participate actively in open forum discussions about global warming.

Teaching and Learning Approaches

- Students will participate in discussion forums in large and small groups.
- Students will use critical-thinking skills to suggest reasonable solutions to this trend.
- Students will record ideas and thoughts in reflective writing in their journals.

Materials and Resources

http://gene.com/ae/WN/SUA10/glowarm497.html
http://gene.com/ae/WN/SU/soil496.html

Activities and Procedures

1. Assign students to groups.
2. Have students do research about global warming and its relationship to photosynthesis.
3. Have students discuss their findings. They may ask the following questions:
   a. Why do you think global warming is happening?
   b. Should we prevent or control global warming? Why or why not?
   c. If we should prevent or control global warming, suggest a method for doing so.
4. Give the students adequate time to answer the preceding questions.
5. Ask a representative from each group to share the group's answers with the class.
6. Invite questions from each group and have the groups field the answers.
7. In the last five minutes of class, have students reflect on the discussion and write their views in their journal.

Decision making

Action taking

Assessment

Collect journals and read reflective statements. Also, note students' views, group participation, and interaction.

Reflection

This type of lesson allows students to use the ideas learned in the previous lessons to help facilitate discussion around the questions posed here.

Phase IV: Reflecting and Assessing

Written Test

Part A: Examples of Multiple-Choice Questions
(20 points)

1. Animals depend on plants for:
   A. carbon dioxide and water
   B. oxygen and food
      1. I chose A because plants produce carbon dioxide and food.

2. I chose A because plants use carbon dioxide and food.

3. I chose B because plants produce oxygen and food.

4. I chose B because plants use oxygen and food.

2. The four essential factors for photosynthesis in plant cells are carbon dioxide, water, light energy and:

   A. chlorophyll

   B. starch

      1. I chose A because it is the blood of the plant.

      2. I chose A because this is where photosynthesis takes place.

      3. I chose B because it is the blood of the plant.

      4. I chose B because it is where photosynthesis takes place.

3. Leaves appear green because they:

   A. absorb only green wavelengths of light.

   B. reflect green wavelengths while absorbing other wavelengths.

      1. chose A because the objects appear to be the color of the wavelengths that are absorbed.

      2. I chose A because the green light has the highest frequency.

      3. I chose B because the chlorophyll absorbs all wavelengths.

      4. I chose B because objects appear to be the color of light that is reflected.

Part B: Examples of Essay Questions

1.   Plants grown in the shade often have larger leaves than the same plants grown in direct sunlight. Of what advantage is this to the plant? (3 points)

2a. Distinguish between absorption, transmission, and reflection of light. (3 points)

2b. What is the visible spectrum? What physical characteristics distinguish the different portions of it? (2 points)

2c. How is chlorophyll affected by the visible spectrum? (2 points)

3.   Using as many of the concepts listed as possible, write a paragraph that indicates that you understand *one* of the following processes: (10 points)

   A. noncyclic photophosphorylation

   B. CO_2 fixation

   Underline the words from the list that you include in your paragraph.

List of concepts:

ADP	excited electrons	oxygen	reduced
ATP	G-3-P	PGA	ribulose
biphosphate	glucose	phosphorylated	starch
C_6 compound	ground state	photon	thylakoid membrane
chlorophyll	NADP	photosystem I	unstable
CO_2	NADPH	photosystem II	water
electron	oxidized	proton	Z-scheme

4. Design an experiment with a good control that will confirm the following hypothesis:
   – Light is necessary for photosynthesis.
   Be sure to explain what tests you would use to show that photosynthesis has or has not taken place. Give a conclusion. (10 points)

Performance-Based Test
Using the apparatus for chromatography activity, perform an experiment that separates plant pigments. (15 points)

Term Work (labs, homework): 20 points
Design Technology: 25 points
Portfolio/Student Journal: 15 points
Overall Score for This Unit: 125 points

⊠ CHAPTER REVIEW

In this chapter we have suggested a format for unit planning that incorporates multiple voices. We have also included a unit on photosynthesis that was prepared by a preservice teacher. This unit brings together some teaching ideas mentioned in the previous chapters. The lessons in the unit plan have been developed by analyzing students' conceptions and organizing them into categories. Each lesson provides suggestions on how you can put the ideas into practice in your classroom. As preservice teacher Richard Hechter said, "The more we seek to improve, the better we will become."

PROBES

1. Observe a science class in action. What voices in science education do you hear? Illustrate with examples.
2. Observe a science class in action. How does the teacher account for scientific objectivity in this class?
3. Prepare and teach a unit that reflects multiple voices in science. What are the students' attitudes and dispositions in your science classes? Support your claims with examples.

APPENDIX 15-1

Event for Vee Diagram Activity (see Figure 15-5)

1. Write a photosynthesis equation and balance it.
   $$6CO_2 + 12H_2O \rightarrow C_6H_{12}O_6 + 6H_2O + 6O_2$$
2. Draw molecular structures for carbon dioxide, water, and glucose.

carbon dioxide   water   glucose

3. Prepare a paper strip with the molecular structure of $CO_2[C<^O_O]$; number the carbons as C_1, C_2, C_3, and so on (cut on the perforated lines).

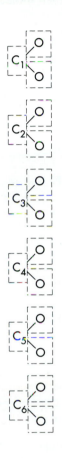

4. Prepare a paper strip showing the molecular structure of H_2O $[O^{18}{<}^H_H]$; mark oxygen associated with water as O^{18}. (Cut along the perforated lines; repeat for each molecule of water.)

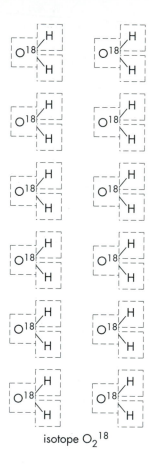

isotope $O_2{}^{18}$

5. From steps 3 and 4, assemble a glucose molecule by cutting CO_2 and H_2O molecules and rearranging them into the C, O, and H atoms of a glucose molecule.

    Count the oxygen (O) atoms that did not participate in the glucose molecule formation.

    Count the hydrogen (H) atoms that did not participate in the glucose molecule formation.

6. Assemble H_2O molecules using the extra O_2 from the CO_2 and the H to form new molecules. How many water molecules did you form?

    Count the free O^{18} ($6O_2 = 12O$).

    Count the H_2O ($6H_2O = 12H, 6O$).

    Count the glucose ($C_6H_{12}O_6 = 6C, 12H, 6O$).

What is the purpose of marking the O_2 as oxygen isotope O^{18}?

PARTING MESSAGE

TEACHER TRANSFORMATION

The perspectives and pedagogy of science teaching and learning presented in this book were in many cases somewhat different to the ones that you may have experienced in the past. You have indeed "lived in another province" of teaching and learning. However, the primary aim of this book was not to impose "foreign" ways of teaching science, but to give you opportunities to ponder your ways of teaching science and to introduce additional ideas for your consideration.

In learning to teach science, you worked through many mini–research studies and the practical experiences of previous preservice teachers. You also engaged in much reflective thinking, writing, and talking through pedagogical elements such as journal activities, peer talk, teacher practice, and probes. These ways of learning to teach were carried out in a very supportive, nonthreatening collaborative context from a constructivist perspective (examining your own beliefs and values) and through a type of reflective practice (framing and reframing problems in action) so that professional change would come from within, or from the self.

Constructivist reflective practices, as well as the collaborative relationships and inquiry that we encouraged you to develop, are two ways of developing shared vision and understanding in science education. Just as we "talked the talk" and "walked the walk" with you, we would like you to metaphorically join hands and walk with your students, fellow teachers, curriculum developers, administrators, and university researchers who participate in the inquiry of science education. Your professional knowing will then be continually nurtured and facilitated.

In her editorial comments in a special issue on teacher development in the *International Journal of Science Education,* Bell (1994) explains that teacher development may be viewed as professional, personal, and social. As our parting message, we would like you to focus on these aspects of teacher development. We will discuss Bell's notion of teacher development through inservice teachers' voices and experiences.

☒ TEACHER PROFESSIONAL DEVELOPMENT

MARY-ANN'S VOICE

Professional growth is a process a teacher continually goes through to learn new teaching techniques, update curriculum knowledge, and become aware of contemporary changes in science education and how to implement these changes in the classroom.

This book has indeed focused on the ideas expressed in Mary-Ann's voice by presenting many contemporary professional ideas for the practice of science teaching and learning. For example, we outlined two learning tools (concept mapping and Vee diagramming) to develop your knowledge in the science that you will be teaching; we provided you with alternative concepts of teaching and learning (sytematically assessing and incorporating students' conceptions of science concepts and scientific inquiry in your lessons); and we introduced to you the learning processes of teaching science (a constructivist reflective practice and collaborative inquiry). These important aspects of professional development require your attention. However, you can develop personally and socially as well.

✹ TEACHER PERSONAL DEVELOPMENT

DENISE'S VOICE

To me personally, it means learning more about myself so that I can be the best I can be.

Bell (1994) discusses teacher development as a "personal" experience that involves "feelings associated with becoming a different teacher" (p. 494). In reconsidering your conceptions, beliefs, and values of science teaching and learning, you may have experienced mental disequilibrium that was created intentionally. A feeling of insecurity may have occurred for a period of time. Or you may have fumbled through a negotiatory interpretive discourse with your students while developing a science concept (for example, magnetic effects) in practice teaching. You may have felt that you did not answer students' questions and left them hanging as they walked out of your classroom. But with a supportive collaborative environment, teachers find ways to "deal with the feelings associated with the change process" (p. 494). Bell suggests that managing uncomfortable feelings as you learn to teach science is "a part of personal development" (p. 494). When you try different ways of doing science with your students and when you learn to manage your feelings about teaching acts when they appear to be unsuccessful, you are empowered!

✹ TEACHER SOCIAL DEVELOPMENT

DENISE'S VOICE

It's always fun to work on any professional development committee. So many great ideas evolve from working with others. It has been a great pleasure to work with various science-related committees and inservices. These professionals have the knack of making people want to try new ideas and extend themselves. As a result of their support and encouragement I have been able to try additional science-related activities that are beneficial to our school, the university, and other school divisions.

Denise considers professional committees and inservices as opportunities and contexts for working with others for teacher development. Pay attention to Ken's voice; he has similar conceptions about working with others.

KEN'S VOICE

There were many stages of professional growth in my teaching career. When I began as a teacher my primary objective was to learn the curriculum and my focus was on my classroom performance. As I gained experience, I became more involved in committee work for a variety of reasons. Firstly, you had responsibility to improve the quality of your teaching. Secondly, it was important to develop contact with colleagues. As an experienced teacher, you wish to continue contributing and provide leadership when you feel confident that you have skills to offer.

Bell (1994) thinks of working with other teachers as social development. Involved with committee work and planning or participating in inservices are important avenues of working with others. However, teacher development is external to the teacher. What Denise and Ken refer to is "collaborative collegiality" (Hargreaves, 1994). Collaborative collegiality is imposing on other teachers in order to implement a new program, encourage team planning or peer coaching, and promote cooperative learning. "Collaborative culture," on the other hand, consists of collaborative working relationships between teachers and their colleagues that tend to be spontaneous, voluntary, development oriented, and pervasive across time and space; it is unpredictable (Hargreaves, 1994).

Bell (1994) accepts the notion of collaborative collegiality, the form of collaboration that Denise and Ken identified. However, she states that the latest debate on teacher development is leaning more toward collaborative culture, where the collaboration is not contrived. She points to developing new ways of working with other teachers. Joining a group of teachers in a long-term study of teaching will provide opportunities for new ideas, support, and feedback that will nurture and facilitate the change process. Bell does warn about the risks involved in becoming a group learner; however, she claims that the benefits are greater and learning is superior because collaborative teacher development is viewed as self-initiated (it comes from the teacher) rather than authority-imposed (arranged by the school district or university). For example, Rodelyn Stoeber, a science teacher, had her colleague, an English teacher, in her class as a "critical friend" when the former learned to work with micro-computer-based laboratories in her eighth-grade class. In her action research of teaching, Rodelyn recognized that she must focus on developing her eighth-grade students' ideas of chemical changes in relationship to the computer-produced graphs. That year she was recognized as the science teacher of the year, and two articles appeared in the local newspaper about her classroom success stories. Remember, not every teacher's effort is rewarded, but there is "knowledge and power," and both knowledge and power can result when teachers engage in self-initiated action research.

Some teachers collaboratively work with university-based teachers and researchers to enhance their social development. Usually, such work is initiated by science teacher educators with the view that collaborative work with teachers is the responsibility of the educational research community (Ebenezer & Erickson, 1996; Erickson, 1991). The idea here is that without outlining recommendations for teachers, it is better to work with them in the classroom in their own institutional setting, which is filled with complexities (facilities and constraints). Such classroom-based collaborative efforts between school classroom teachers and university teachers and researchers result in enriched practices for both because professional distinctions and boundaries become blurred. Now that you are a teacher leaving the university, you should seek opportunities to belong to similar, locally based groups of committed teachers who are working together toward mutually designed goals in science education. Throughout the world there are collaborative action research groups where practicing teachers, preservice teachers, and teacher educators research teaching and learning. Projects consist of personal reflection on teaching, narrative inquiry, and storying about personal practical knowledge. While some groups focus on personal practice, others are engaged in assessing students' conceptions of science concepts and reflecting about how best to incorporate them into science lessons using multiple strategies such as analogy mapping, classroom discourse, and hypermedia.

These are only a few examples of classroom-based collaborative projects. If your educational community has a classroom-based collaborative research group, we recommend that you join this group. A collaborative action research group will provide you with a forum for the exchange of ideas. If there is no such group, create one. The exchange of ideas will promote reflection and develop both a language of professional knowledge and classroom inquiry. It will encourage open communication and criticism among collaborators to achieve professional growth and improved practice.

⬚ SUMMARY

In the words of Leslie Wurtak, coordinator of the science program in her school division, "Teacher development is a reflective process. It is ongoing and continuous as one continues to learn new ideas of teaching."

Teacher development begins with preservice teaching, when preservice teachers learn to teach. It begins in a linear fashion with "self," "task," and "students" (Gunstone, Slattery, Baird, & Northfield, 1993); through reflection and collaboration, *self, task,* and *students* become integrated.

Teacher development is ongoing and is seen through many "lenses." Teacher development consists of many lenses in the sense that teacher development can take place while attending after-school, noon, and day-long inservices in knowledge areas such as studying the curriculum, training in new curriculum "thrusts," expanding knowledge in computers, learning about portfolio assessments, or studying cooperative learning. A teacher develops professionally when planning a project or inservice. Working on school committees such as science fairs or science Olympics and looking at possible ways of integrating subject areas involve teacher development. Pursuing personal-interest initiatives is another form of teacher development. Teacher development is multifaceted. One form is not superior to another. A teacher should seek opportunities for sustained dialogue in his or her professional development.

Appendix A

Some Ideas for Your Teaching Portfolio

This is a collection of ideas and suggested questions for you to ask yourself as you choose the items for your portfolio and as you write your justification for each artifact. The justifications are the most important part of your teaching portfolio—these will be the major aspect to be evaluated.

Developing Goal Statements

What do you hope to learn from this course? The following are some possible goals you may include in your portfolio:

- How to elicit students' conceptions, preconceptions, prior knowledge, and so on
- How to build on students' preconceptions to facilitate meaningful learning
- How to clarify your own ideas about your educational problems, questions, and concerns to facilitate problem solving
- How to develop an introductory knowledge and understanding of science content in an area in which you do not have a strong background (see the reminder at the end of this appendix)
- How to develop a more detailed understanding of the nature of science and why it is important to take the nature of science into consideration
- How to learn what factors have to be considered to become an effective teacher

Ask yourself the following questions:

What are some steps I can take to help me move toward achieving each of my goals?

What have I already done that has helped me make some progress toward achieving one of my goals?

What new ideas or understandings do I have now?

Why did I change my ideas?

How can I demonstrate my progress to someone reading my portfolio?

Choose one *artifact* (a reading, class discussion, or piece of information) that was significant for you and your knowledge and/or understanding about learning to be a great science teacher. *What is it about this artifact* that makes it significant?

Write a reflective piece about something that happened in class that was meaningful for you. It may have been a small-group discussion, information presented by your science teacher educator or another student, an activity you did in class, a conversation, or even a brief statement or comment by someone. Consider questions such as the preceding ones in your reflection.

Further writing can be based on these questions:

What still frustrates you about trying to understand how to become a better teacher, or about a particular approach to teaching?

What extra reading have you done? How did that help you?

Whom have you talked to? How did that help you?

What else can you do? How can you find more resources? Whom can you talk to to get more information?

Remember: There is far more to teaching than mastering the content. Accordingly, there is far more to *learning how to teach* than learning the content you have to teach. The key is *transforming* that content to make it readily accessible and meaningful to your students. This is the really big challenge in becoming a great teacher, and it is what your teaching portfolio should emphasize.

Appendix B

Your Professional Portfolio

A *professional portfolio* is a collection of work that may be used for a variety of purposes:

- It provides a professional person with a *structure* for documenting personal and professional growth over an extended period of time—during a practicum, an education course or program, or a career.
- It provides *evidence* of achievement.
- It serves as a guide for personal *goal setting* and *reflection* on growth and development.
- It provides a focus for *collaboration* with peers, associate teachers, professors, and others you will encounter during your professional career.

Key questions you should ask yourself throughout your professional education and career include the following:

What are my goals for this (practicum/course/other program)?
How can I most effectively demonstrate my progress?

Barton and Collins (1993) have identified seven characteristics of teaching portfolios (from their point of view):

1. The purposes or goals of the portfolio are made explicit.
2. The documents demonstrate the integration of theory and practice—that is, they link the content of education courses with teaching practice.
3. They are drawn from a variety of sources.
4. They are authentic—that is, they are based on actual experiences.
5. They demonstrate growth and development in the learner/teacher over a period of time.
6. They demonstrate that the student/teacher takes ownership, or responsibility, for his or her own professional development.
7. They are multipurposed. They may include assignments, evaluation documents, and so forth, and may be used for student evaluation, program evaluation, or a job search.

We have assigned portfolios for the following reasons:

1. The portfolio provides a focus for you, the student, to articulate personal purposes and/or goals for this course and for your practicum experiences, and to develop and collect evidence that you have met or have made progress toward meeting your purposes and goals.
2. The portfolio provides a focus for personal, individual reflection in and on practice (Schön, 1991).

3. The portfolio provides a focus for professional collaboration with peers, associate teachers, professors, faculty liaison representatives, and the like.

4. The portfolio provides a framework for you as a student teacher to link theory and practice.

5. The portfolio provides a focus for your teacher educator to evaluate your progress throughout the year.

Planning Your Professional Portfolio

1. *Identify explicit purposes and goals*. What do you really want and expect to learn about teaching and learning this year? How will you go about your learning to ensure that you make optimum use of your time and the resources available to you? How can you demonstrate your progress toward achieving your long-range goals?

2. *Gather evidence*. How can you collect and assemble evidence that will demonstrate your proficiency in or progress toward achieving your goals? Some examples of kinds of evidence include the following:

   a. *Artifacts,* which are items developed during the normal course of your university courses and practice teaching. Examples are assignments, lesson plans, notes made by those who observed you teaching, photos of you teaching or doing other activities with children, examples of work done by your students during student teaching, and so on.

   b. *Attestations,* or materials prepared by others about your work, such as student teaching reports or other kinds of evaluations or responses to your work, including assignments.

   c. *Items produced especially for your portfolio,* including a table of contents and goal statements, justifications for other items, and so on. These elements transform a collection of items into evidence of your growth and development. They should describe and analyze the item as a piece of evidence indicating the extent to which you have achieved your goals.

      You may wish to include items that provide evidence that you have understood and internalized the implications of students' preconceptions for teaching; related your class readings to your teaching practice; done additional reading about teaching science; developed skills and habits of reflection and self-evaluation; regularly and systematically reflected on your practice teaching experiences; regularly and systematically reflected on your learning experiences in your education courses; and so on.

Compiling Your Professional Portfolio

1. Select one item that provides the most compelling evidence of the purpose of your portfolio: to demonstrate your development toward achieving your goals.

2. Choose a second item and decide what will be added to the portfolio if you include this piece; then decide whether you should include it or not. Continue this process until you believe you have made a convincing case.
3. Decide how to best organize the items to ensure that the portfolio provides an adequate demonstration of your knowledge and skills.
4. Create a table of contents and write a justification for each item so that it makes a compelling argument about your abilities and achievements.

As a final check, answer the following questions:

1. Does your portfolio have a *goal statement* and a *rationale* for your goals?
2. Does each item have a *caption* that presents a *justification* and *reflective explanation*?
3. Is there *concrete evidence* of progress toward your stated goals?
4. What needs to be added to ensure that the first three items are achieved?

APPENDIX C

SUGGESTED PEOE ACTIVITIES

The first four junior-high-school-level PEOE activities in this appendix are taken from various issues of the $(SI)^2$ *Network Newsletter*. They were contributed by Tony Williams, a science teacher at Dr. Charles Best Jr. Secondary School in Coquitlam, British Columbia. The author of the fifth activity is unknown.

Phase Changes

You have seen that when water is heated to a high enough temperature it will go through a change of state; it evaporates to form water vapor, a gas. When it is cooled enough, it will go through a different change of state as it freezes to form ice, a solid.

Imagine that you had a microscope that was so powerful that you could see how water is made. What do you think it would look like? Draw your magnified view in the circle below the water drop.

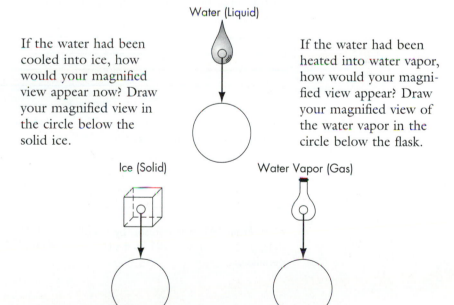

Water (Liquid)

If the water had been cooled into ice, how would your magnified view appear now? Draw your magnified view in the circle below the solid ice.

If the water had been heated into water vapor, how would your magnified view appear? Draw your magnified view of the water vapor in the circle below the flask.

Ice (Solid)

Water Vapor (Gas)

NOTE: From "Phase Changes," by T. Williams, 1991, $(SI)^2$ *Network Newsletter, 4*(2), p. 4. Copyright 1991 by the University of British Columbia. Reprinted with permission.

Water in a Rush

The apparatus on the right shows a test tube half full of water being heated as shown by a bunsen burner. When the surface of the water is boiling and steam is readily coming out of the test tube, the test tube is rapidly turned upside down into a beaker of cold water as shown.

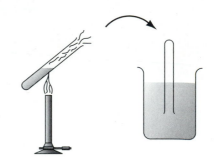

PREDICTION

In the space below, write down what you predict will happen in the test tube when it is turned upside down in the cold water. Also, mark your prediction on the diagram.

_____

_____

_____

_____

OBSERVATIONS

In the space below, and on the diagram, write down your observations.

_____

_____

_____

_____

EXPLANATION

In the space below, write down, in terms of the particle model, your explanation of what you saw.

_____

_____

_____

_____

NOTE: From "Water in a Rush," by T. Williams, 1991, (SI)² Network Newsletter, 4(1), p. 2. Copyright 1991 by the University of British Columbia. Reprinted with permission.

Flying Paper

The picture on the right shows a student holding a narrow strip of paper close to the mouth
so that the paper hangs freely. The student then
blows steadily across the top of the paper strip
as shown.

PREDICTION

In the space below, write down what you predict will happen to the paper strip. Also, mark
your prediction on the diagram.

20 cm

2 cm

_____
_____
_____
_____
_____

OBSERVATIONS

In the space below, and on the diagram, write
down your observations.

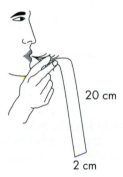

20 cm

2 cm

_____
_____
_____
_____
_____

EXPLANATION

In the space below, write down, in terms of the
particle model, your explanation of what you
saw.

_____
_____
_____
_____
_____
_____
_____
_____

NOTE: From "Flying Paper," by T. Williams, 1990, *(SI)*² *Network Newsletter, 2*(6), p.
2. Copyright 1990 by the University of British Columbia. Reprinted with permission.

Balloons

The picture on the right shows two sealed balloons, one filled with air, the other with hydrogen gas. The strings are tied to a stand and the balloons are left for two days.

PREDICTION

In the space below, write down what you predict will happen to each of the balloons. Also, mark your prediction on the diagram.

_____
_____
_____
_____
_____

OBSERVATIONS

In the space below, and on the diagram, write down your observations.

_____
_____
_____
_____
_____

EXPLANATION

In the space below, write down, in terms of the particle model, your explanation of what you saw.

_____
_____
_____
_____
_____
_____
_____

NOTE: From "Balloons," by T. Williams, 1991, *(SI)² Network Newsletter, 3*(4), p. 2. Copyright 1991 by the University of British Columbia. Reprinted with permission.

Gravity

A. 500 g mass hanging freely.

B. Glass dome with all the air removed
    – 500 g mass suspended in a
    vacuum.

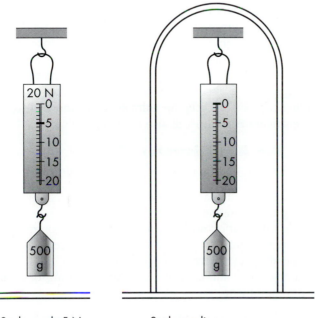

Scale reads 5 N   Scale reading = _____

Explain how you decided what the correct reading should be.

_____
_____
_____
_____

Form into a group of four to five students. *As a group,* decide what the
reading would be. Give the group reasons below.

_____
_____
_____

If the group answer or reason was different from your original answer or
reason, how do you feel about that? Are you comfortable with the decision? Why or why not?

_____
_____

APPENDIX D

PRACTICING SCIENCE SAFETY

Learning to practice safety in the science class is useful for personal and social well-being—an important aspect of scientific literacy. When students are doing science investigations, safety in the science class should not be taken lightly. The administrator, the teacher, and the student all have responsibility. In this section, we will examine each of these individuals' responsibilities and also offer suggestions for safety in the science class, including topics from keeping animals to storing and using equipment. Your curriculum guides will also list safety rules.

What Can the Administrators Do?

The administrators should be responsible for the following:

- Providing sufficient space for science
- Supplying safe equipment
- Supplying information and resources through an ongoing school science safety committee in the school and inservice education
- The general upkeep of the science facilities
- Conducting safety audits once a year and repairing or replacing substandard equipment

Although the administrator has indirect responsibility, you are directly responsible for students' safety when students do science activities. You should be knowledgeable about safety rules. You should be also able to apply safety rules in the storage, use, and care of the materials used by students.

What Can You Do about Safety?

1. Develop and enforce a set of safety rules.
2. Chart and post safety rules in class so that every student can see them. Students can take part in this activity; it will help them remember as well as obey the rules that they have developed.
3. Wear goggles if necessary.
4. Instruct everyone to keep long hair tied at the back and leave jewelry at home.

Some Specific Cautions

Animal Care

When keeping animals, you should think of the safety of students and the animals. The housing must be spacious and sanitary, and disposal of the animal must be humane. Incubation of eggs may be allowed only if a home can be found for the chicks; otherwise the gestation period must be ended after nineteen days. Venomous creatures should not be kept. If animals are brought to the classroom they should be checked by a veterinarian and given rabies shots. If an animal dies, the cage should be disinfected to prevent the spreading of any diseases. The students should wash their hands after handling an animal to prevent spreading disease. Animals should be handled properly to teach students to have a reverence for all animal life forms.

Place aquariums away from direct sunlight because the glass can crack. Empty the aquarium before moving it; a filled aquarium can be very heavy and it can break. To empty a tank, do not use the mouth suction method, as the water may be contaminated. Dying or dead fish should not be handled with bare hands—use gloves.

Plants and Seeds

Poisonous seeds should not be found in the science room. Plants grown with insecticides and pesticides may be harmful to students who are exposed to them in excessive amounts; the same is true for bread molds and spores. When handling plants, students should be reminded not to put anything in their mouths. They should also wash their hands after handling plants, as insecticides can be transferred from plant leaves to hand to mouth.

Heat

Open flames must be used cautiously. Have access to a fire extinguisher, a bucket of sand, a first aid kit, and a fire blanket.

Electricity

Students should be allowed to use only controlled voltages such as batteries and dry cells.

Chemicals

Keep all chemicals out of students' reach—store them in closed containers in a locked area. Know the risks and hazards involved as well as first aid measures. Common household chemicals such as aerosols and cleaners should be handled with care.

Glass

Check glass for splits and cracks. If glass breaks, the teacher should clean it up. Never pick up broken glass with bare fingers. The bigger pieces can be collected using tongs and the glass slivers can be gathered using a damp cloth.

REFERENCES

Introduction

Clarke, A. (1994). Student-teacher reflection: Developing and defining a practice that is uniquely one's own. *International Journal of Science Education, 16*(5), 497–509.

Connelly, F. M., & Clandinen, D. J. (1988). Teachers as curriculum planners. New York: Teachers College Press.

Ebenezer, J. V., & Hay, A. (1995). Preservice teachers' meaning-making in science instruction: A case study in Manitoba. *International Journal of Science Education, 17,* 93–105.

Erickson, F. (1986). Qualitative methods in research on teaching. In M. Wittrock (Ed.), *Handbook of research on teaching* (3rd ed., pp. 119–161). New York: Macmillan.

Erickson, G., Mayer-Smith, J., Rodriguez, A., Chin, P., & Mitchell, I. (1994). Perspectives on learning to teach science: Insights and dilemmas from a collaborative practicum project. *International Journal of Science Education, 16*(5), 585–597.

Feiman-Nemser, S., & Buchmann, M. (1986). The first year of teacher preparation: Transition to pedagogical thinking? *Journal of Curriculum Studies, 18,* 239–256.

Gunstone, R. F., Slattery, M., Baird, J. R., & Northfield, J. R. (1993). A case study exploration of development in preservice science teachers. *Science Education, 77*(1), 47–73.

Kagan, D. M. (1992). Professional growth among preservice teachers. *Review of Educational Research, 62*(2), 129–169.

Schön, D. A. (1983). *The reflective practitioner: How professionals think in action.* New York: Basic Books.

Schön, D. A. (1987). *Educating the reflective practitioner.* San Francisco: Jossey-Bass.

Stofflett, R. T. (1994). The accommodation of science pedagogical knowledge: The application of conceptual change constructs to teacher education. *Journal of Research in Science Teaching, 31*(8), 787–810.

Part One

White, R. T. (1988). *Learning science.* Oxford, England: Basil Blackwell.

Chapter 1

Aikenhead, G. (1980). *Science in social issues: Implications for teaching.* Ottawa, Canada: Science Council of Canada.

American Association for the Advancement of Science. (1989). *Project 2061: Science for all americans.* Washington, DC: American Association for the Advancement of Science.

American Association for the Advancement of Science. (1993). *Benchmarks for science literacy.* Washington, DC: American Association for the Advancement of Science.

Carnegie Forum on Education and the Economy. (1986). *A nation prepared: Teachers for the 21st century.* The report of the Task Force on Teaching as a Profession. New York: Carnegie Corporation of New York.

Driver, R., Squires, A., Rushworth, P., & Wood-Robinson, V. (1994). *Making sense of secondary science: Research into children's ideas.* London: Routledge.

Ebenezer, J. V., & Connor, S. (1998). *Learning to teach science: A model for the 21st century.* Upper Saddle River, NJ: Prentice-Hall.

Ebenezer, J. V., & Zoller, U. (1993). The no change in high school students' attitudes toward science in a period of change: A probe into the case of British Columbia. *School Science and Mathematics, 93*(2), 96–102.

Fleming, R. (1986). Adolescent reasoning in socio-scientific issues, Part I: Social cognition. *Journal of Research in Science Teaching, 23*(8), 677–687.

Hurd, P. D. (1987). A nation reflects: The modernization of science education. *Bulletin of Science Technology Society, 7*(1), 9–13.

Hurd, P. D. (1994). New minds for a new age: Prologue to modernizing the science curriculum. *Science Education, 78*(1), 103–116.

Marton, F. (1981). Phenomenography—describing conceptions of the world around us. *Instructional Science, 10,* 177–200.

National Commission on Excellence in Education. (1983). *A nation at risk: The imperative for educational reform.* Washington, DC: U.S. Department of Education.

National Research Council. (1996). *National Science Education Standards.* Washington, DC: National Academy Press.

Shulman, L.S. (1986). Knowledge and teaching: Foundations of the new reform. *Harvard Educational Review, 57*(1), 1–22.

Uzwyshyn, E. (1990). Foreword. Principles of sustainable development. In J. E. Penick & J. R. Stiles (Eds.), *Sustainable development for a new world agenda* (pp. v–viii). Proceedings of the World Environment Energy and Economic Conference, Oct. 1990. Winnipeg, Canada: STAM/ CASE/ICASE.

Chapter 2

Alexander, P., Schallert, D., & Hare, V. (1991). Coming to terms: How researchers in learning and literacy talk about knowledge. *Review of Educational Research, 61,* 315–343.

Avegelis, N. (1989). Lakatos on the evaluation of scientific theories. In K. Gauroglu, Y. Goudaroulis, & P. Nicolacopoulos, *Imre Lakatos and theories of scientific change* (pp. 157–167). Dordrecht, The Netherlands: Kluwer Academic Publishing.

Brickhouse, N. (1990). Teachers' beliefs about the nature of science and their relationship to classroom practice. *Journal of Teacher Education, 41,* 53–62.

Candido, J. L., James, E. S., Phillips, R. E., Kaufman, B. D., & Wiley, G. W. (1988). *Heath science connections 10.* Toronto: D. C. Heath Canada.

Charlesworth, M. (1982). *Science, non-science and pseudo-science.* Geelong, Australia: Deakin University Press.

Claxton, G. (1991). *Educating the inquiring mind: The challenge for school science.* London: Harvester Wheatsheaf.

Elgin, C. Z. (1996). *Considered judgment.* Princeton, NJ: Princeton University Press.

Fenstermacher, G. D. (1994). The knower and the known: The nature of knowledge in research on teaching. *Review of Research in Education, 20,* 3–56.

Gallagher, J. J. (1991). Prospective and practicing secondary school science teachers' knowledge and beliefs about the philosophy of science. *Science Education, 75,* 121–134.

Greene, M. (1994). Epistemology and educational research: The influence of recent approaches to knowledge. *Review of Research in Education, 20,* 423–464.

Haggerty, S. M. (1986). *Learning about heat and temperature: A case study of a grade nine science class.* Unpublished doctoral thesis, University of British Columbia.

Harding, S. (1991). *Whose science? Whose knowledge?* Ithaca, NY: Cornell University Press.

Hubbard, R. (1989). Science, facts and feminism. In N. Tuana (Ed.), *Feminism and science* (pp. 119–131). Bloomington, IN: Indiana University Press.

Koulaidis, V., & Ogborn, J. (1995). Science teachers' philosophical assumptions: How well do we understand them? *International Journal of Science Education, 17,* 273-283.

Kuhn, T. S. (1962). *The structure of scientific revolutions.* Chicago: University of Chicago Press.

Kuhn, T. S. (1977). Objectivity, value judgement, and theory choice. In T. S. Kuhn, *The essential tension: Selected studies in scientific tradition and change* (pp. 320–339). Chicago: University of Chicago Press.

Lederman, N. G. (1992). Students and teachers' conceptions of the nature of science: A review of the research. *Journal of Research in Science Teaching, 29,* 331–359.

MacIvor, M. (1995). Redefining science education for Aboriginal students. In M. Battiste & J. Barman (Eds.) *First Nations education in Canada: The circle unfolds* (pp. 73–98). Vancouver, Canada: University of British Columbia Press.

National Research Council (1996). *National Science Education Standards.* Washington, DC: National Academy Press.

Osborne, R., & Freyberg, P. (1985). *Learning in science: The implications of children's science.* London: Heinemann.

Roberts, D. A., Winter, M. K., Bullard, D., Hirsch, A. J., Gore, G. R., Grace, E. S., Emerson, B., & McClelland, L. W. (1991). *Science directions 9.* Toronto, New York: Wiley.

Schwab, J. J. (1962). *The teaching of science as inquiry.* The Inglis Lecture of 1961. Cambridge, MA.: Harvard University Press.

Selin, H. (1997). *Encyclopaedia of the history of science, technology, and medicine in non-western cultures.* Dordrecht, The Netherlands: Kluwer Academic Press.

Zeidler, D. L. & Lederman, N. G. (1989). The effects of teachers' language on students' conceptions of the nature of science. *Journal of Research in Science Teaching, 26,* 771–783.

Chapter 3

Barman, C. R. (1996). Bridging the gap between the old and the new: Helping teachers move towards a new vision of science education. In R. Rhoton & P. Bowers (Eds.), *Issues in science education* (p. 156). Arlington, VA: National Science Teachers Association.

Bell, B. F., & Brook, A. (1984). *Aspects of secondary students' understanding of plant nutrition.* Leeds, England: Children's Learning in Science Project, Centre for Studies in Science and Mathematics Education, University of Leeds.

Bruner, J. (1986). *Actual minds, possible worlds.* Cambridge, MA: Harvard University Press.

Bruner, J. (1990). *Acts of meaning.* Cambridge, MA: Harvard University Press.

Champagne, A. B., Klopfer, L. E., & Anderson, J. H. (1980). Factors influencing the learning of classical mechanics. *American Journal of Physics, 48,* 1074–1079.

Driver, R. (1983, June–July). An approach to documenting the understanding of fifteen-year-old British children about particulate theory of matter. In *Research on Physics Education,* proceedings of the First International Workshop, Éditions du Centre National de la Recherche Scientifique 1984, (pp. 339–346), La Londe-les-Maures, France.

Gunstone, R., White, R., & Fensham, P. (1988). Developments in style and purpose of research on the learning of science. *Journal of Research in Science Teaching, 25*(7), 513–530.

Gurney, B. F. (1995). Tugboats and tennis games: Preservice conceptions of teaching and learning revealed through metaphors. *Journal of Research in Science Teaching, 32*(6), 569–583.

Hand, B. M., & Treagust, D. F. (1988). Application of a conceptual conflict teaching strategy to enhance student learning of acids and bases. *Research in Science Education, 18,* 53–63.

Hewson, P. (1981). A conceptual change approach to learning science. *European Journal of Science Education, 3*(4), 383–396.

Karplus, R. (1977). *Science teaching and the development of reasoning.* Berkeley, CA: University of California.

Kuhn, T. (1970). *The structure of scientific revolutions* (2nd ed.). Chicago: University of Chicago Press.

Needham, R., & Hill, P. (1987). *Teaching strategies for developing understanding in science.* Leeds, England: Centre for Studies in Science and Mathematics Education, University of Leeds.

Nussbaum, J. (1976). Children's conceptions of the earth as a cosmic body: A cross-age study. *Science Education, 63*(1), 83–93.

Nussbaum, J. (1985). The particulate nature of matter in the gaseous phase. In R. Driver, E. Guesne, & A. Tiberghien (Eds.), *Children's ideas in science* (pp. 124–144). Philadelphia: Open University Press.

Nussbaum, J. (1989). Classroom conceptual change: Philosophical perspectives. *International Journal of Science Education, 11*(5), 530–540.

Nussbaum, J., & Novick, S. (1981). *Creating cognitive dissonance between students' preconceptions to encourage individual cognitive accommodation and a group cooperative construction of a scientific model.* Paper presented at the Annual Convention of the American Educational Research Association (AERA), Los Angeles, CA.

Osborne, R. J., & Cosgrove, M. M. (1983). Children's conceptions of the changes of state of matter. *Journal of Research in Science Teaching, 20*(9), 825–838.

Posner, G., Strike, K., Hewson, P., & Gertzog, W. (1982). Accommodation of a scientific conception: Toward a theory of conceptual change. *Science Education, 66,* 211–227.

Renner, J. (1982). The power of purpose. *Science Education, 66*(5), 709–716.

Scott, P., & Dyson, T. (1987). *A constructivist view of learning and teaching in science.* Leeds, England: Centre for Studies in Science and Mathematics Education, University of Leeds.

Shapere, D. (1974). Scientific theories and their domains. In F. Suppe (Ed.), *The structure of scientific theories* (pp. 518–600). Urbana, IL: The University of Illinois Press as cited in Loving, C. C. (1992). From constructive realism to deconstructive anti-realism: Helping science teachers find a balanced philosophy of science. In S. Hills (Ed.), *The history and philosophy of science in science education* (Vol. 2, pp. 45–70). Kingston, Canada: Queen's University Faculty of Education.

Skinner, B. F. (1953). *Science and human behavior.* New York: Macmillan.

Stinner, A. (1992). Science textbooks and science teaching: From logic to evidence. *Science Education, 76,* 1–16.

Stinner, A. (1995). Science textbooks: Their present role and future form. In S. M. Glynn & R. Duit (Eds.). (1995). *Learning science in the schools: Research reforming practice.* Mahwah, NJ: Erlbaum.

Strike, K., & Posner, G. (1992). A revisionist theory of conceptual change. In R. Duschl & R. Hamilton (Eds.), *Philosophy of science, cognitive psychology, and educational theory and practice* (pp. 147–176). New York: State University of New York Press.

Toulmin, S. (1972). *Human understanding: An inquiry into the aims of science.* Princeton, NJ: Princeton University Press.

Treagust, D. (1995). Enhancing students' understanding of science using analogies. In B. Hand & V. Prain, *Teaching and learning in science: The constructivist classroom.* Sydney, Fort Worth, & Toronto: Harcourt Brace.

White, R. (1993). *Insights on conceptional change derived from extensive attempts to promote metacognition.* Paper presented at the annual convention of the American Educational Research Association (AERA), Atlanta, GA.

Vygotsky, L. (1968). *Mind in society: The development of higher psychological processes.* Cambridge, MA: Harvard University Press.

Chapter 4

Armstrong, T. (1994). *Multiple intelligences in the classroom.* Alexandria, VA: Association for Supervision and Curriculum Development.

Gardner, H. (1983). *Frames of mind: The theory of multiple intelligences.* New York: Basic Books.

Gardner, H. (1985). *The mind's new science: A history of the cognitive revolution.* New York: Basic Books.

Gardner, H. (1993). *Multiple intelligences: The theory in practice.* New York: Basic Books.

Gardner, H. (1995). Reflections on multiple intelligences. *Phi Delta Kappa 77,* 203–209.

Johnson, D. W., & Johnson, R. T. (1989). *Cooperation and competition: Theory and research.* Edina, MN: Interaction Books.

Johnson, D. W., Johnson, R. T., & Holubec, E. J. (1993). *Circles of learning: Cooperation in the classroom* (4th ed.). Edina, MN: Interaction Books.

Longino, H. (1990). *Science as social knowledge: Values and objectivity in scientific inquiry.* Princeton, NJ: Princeton University Press.

Putnam, J. (1997). *Cooperative learning in diverse classrooms.* Columbus, OH: Prentice-Hall.

Schank, R. C. & Abelson, R. P. (1977). *Scripts, plans, goals, and understanding: An inquiry into human knowledge structures.* Hillsdale, NJ: Erlbaum.

Slavin, R. E. (1990). *Cooperative learning: Theory, research and practice.* Englewood Cliffs, NJ: Prentice-Hall.

Slavin, R. E. (1995). *Cooperative learning: Theory, research and practice* (2nd ed.). Boston: Allyn & Bacon.

White, R. T. (1988). *Learning science.* Oxford, England: Basil Blackwell.

Yager, R. E. (1995). Constructivism and the learning of science. In S. M. Glynn & R. Duit (1995), *Learning science in the schools: Research reforming practice.* Mahwah, NJ: Erlbaum.

Chapter 5

Barnes, D. (1988). Oral language and learning. In S. Hynds & D. Rubin (Eds.), *Perspectives on talk and learning.* Urbana, IL: NCTE.

Carson, B. (1992). *Think big: Unleashing your potential.* New York: HarperCollins.

Champagne, A. B., Klopfer, L. E., & Anderson, J. H. (1980). Factors influencing the learning of classical mechanics. *American Journal of Physics, 48,* 1074–1079.

Damon, W., & Phelps, E. (1989). Critical distinctions among three approaches to peer education. *International Journal of Educational Research, 13,* 9–19.

Giancoli, D. C. (1991). *Physics: Principles with applications* (3rd ed.). Englewood Cliffs, NJ: Prentice-Hall.

Driver, R. (1989). Students' conceptions and the learning of science. *International Journal of Science Education, 11*(5), 481–490.

Erickson, G. (1992). Some suggestions for running an interpretive discussion. In *(SI)² Newsletter, 5*(1). The University of British Columbia, Vancouver, Canada.

Gitomer, D. H., & Duschl, R. A. (1995). Moving toward a portfolio culture in science education. In S. M. Glynn & D. Reinders (Eds.), *Learning science in the schools: Research reforming practice* (pp. 299–326). Mahwah, NJ: Erlbaum.

Haury, D. L, & Rillero, P. (1994). Perspectives of hands-on science teaching [Online]. Introduction. Available: http://www.ncrel.org/sdrs/areas/issues/content/cntareas/science/eric/eric-toc.htm. Columbus, OH: The ERIC Clearinghouse for Science, Mathematics, and Environmental Education [Producer and Distributor].

Hofstein, A., & Lunetta, V. N. (1982). The tool of the laboratory in science teaching: Neglected aspects of research. *Review of Educational Research, 52*(2), 201–217.

Jones, B. F., Palinscar, A. S., Ogle, D. S., & Carr, E. G. (Eds.) (1987). *Strategic teaching and learning: Cognitive instruction in the content areas.* Alexandria, VA: Association for Supervision and Curriculum Development.

Lehman, J. R. (1990). Students' verbal interactions during chemistry laboratories. *School Science and Mathematics, 90*(2), 142–150.

Liem, T. L. (1991). *Invitations to science inquiry* (2nd ed.). Chino Hills, CA: Science Inquiry Enterprises.

Lunetta, V., & Tamir, P. (1979). Matching lab activities with teaching goals. *The Science Teacher, 46*(5), 22–24.

Novak, J. D. (1988). Learning science and the science of learning. *Studies in Science Education, 15,* 77–101.

Piaget, J. (1974). *The child and reality: Problems of genetic psychology.* London: Frederic Muller.

Putnam, J. (1997). *Cooperative learning in diverse classrooms.* Columbus, OH: Prentice-Hall.

Roth, K. J. (1991). Reading science texts for conceptual change. In C. M. Santa & D. E. Alvermann (Eds.), *Science learning: Processes and applications* (pp. 48–63). Newark, DE: International Reading Association. Copyright by the International Reading Association. All rights reserved.

Sharan, Y., & Sharan, S. (1992). *Expanding cooperative learning through group investigation.* New York: Teachers College Press.

Stinner, A. (1993). Contextual teaching in physics: From science stories to large-context problems. *Alberta Science Education Journal, 26*(1), 20–29.

Tobin, K. (1990). Research on science laboratory activities: In pursuit of better questions and answers to improve learning. *School Science and Mathematics, 90,* 403–418.

Tobin, K. G., & Gallagher, J. J. (1987). What happens in high school science classrooms? *Journal of Curriculum Studies, 19,* 549–560.

White, R. T. (1988). *Learning science.* Oxford, England: Basil Blackwell.

White, R., & Gunstone, R. (1992). *Probing understanding.* London, England: Falmer Press.

Chapter 6

Aldridge, J. (1995). Some topics for chemistry reports or projects [Online]. Available: http://rampages.onramp.net/~jaldr/topics.html.

Assiniboine South School Division (1998). Info Zone research skills area [Online]. Available: http://www.mbnet.mb.ca/~mstimson/. Winnipeg, Canada: Assiniboine South School Division.

Bloom, B. (1956). *Taxonomy of educational objectives.* New York: David McKay.

Driver, R., Guesne, E. & Tiberghien, A. (Eds.). (1985). *Children's ideas in science.* Milton Keynes, England: Open University Press.

Driver, R., Squires, R., Rushworth, P., & Wood-Robinson, V. (1994). Making sense of secondary science: Research into children's ideas. London: Routledge.

Edwards, P. R. (1991). Using dialectical journals to teach thinking skills. *Journal of Reading, 35*(4), 312–316.

Gardner, H. (1983). *Frames of mind: The theory of multiple intelligences.* New York: Basic Books.

Johnson, D. W., & Johnson, R. T. (1994). *Learning together and alone: Cooperative, competitive, and individualistic learning* (4th ed.). Needham Heights, MA: Allyn & Bacon.

Jonassen, D. H. (1996). Computers in the classroom: Mindtools for critical thinking. Englewood Cliffs, NJ: Prentice Hall.

Kuhn, K. (1989). The journal method. SI^2 *Network Newsletter, 1*(2), 2.

Kuhn, K., & Aguirre, J. (1987). A case study on the journal method: A method designed to enable the implementation of constructivist teaching in the classroom. In J. D. Novak (Ed.), *Proceedings of the Second International Seminar: Misconceptions and educational strategies in science and mathematics* (Vol. 2, pp. 262–274). Ithaca, NY: Cornell University.

McClintock Collective. (1989, August). Creative writing ideas. *Australian Science Teachers Journal, 35*(3), 72.

Nussbaum, J. (1985). The particulate nature of matter in the gaseous phase. In R. Driver, E. Guesne, & A. Tiberghien (Eds.), *Childrens ideas in science.* (pp. 124–144). Milton Keynes, England: Open University Press.

Pradl, G. M., & Mayher, J. S. (1985). Reinvigorating learning through writing. *Educational Leadership, 42*(5), 4–8.

Putnam, J. (1997). *Cooperative learning in diverse classrooms.* Columbus, OH: Prentice-Hall.

Sanders, A. (1985). Learning logs: A communication strategy for all subject areas. *Educational Leadership, 42*(5), 7.

Slavin, R. E. (1990). *Cooperative learning: Theory, research and practice.* Englewood Cliffs, NJ: Prentice-Hall.

Tompkins, G., & Hoskisson, K. (1991). *Language arts: Content and teaching strategies* (2nd ed.). New York: Merrill.

Chapter 7

Cosgrove, M. (1991). *Learning science: A place for learners' analogies.* Paper presented at the annual meeting of the Australasian Society for Educational Research, Brisbane, Australia.

Duit, R. (1991). On the role of analogies and metaphors in learning science. *Science Education, 75*(6), 649–672.

Harrison, A. G., & Treagust, D. F. (1993). Teaching with analogies: A case study in grade-10 optics.

Journal of Research in Science Teaching, 30, 1291–1307.

Hopkins, D., Legros, J. (Producers), & Mills, M. (Producer/Director). (1991). *S.P.L.A.S.H.* [Film]. Available from the National Film Board of Canada, Montreal, Canada.

Lenburg, J. (1991). *The encyclopedia of animated cartoons.* New York, Oxford: Facts on File.

Maxwell, R. (1996). *Writing across the curriculum in Middle and High Schools.* Boston, MA: Allyn & Bacon.

McClintock Collective. (1989, August). Creative writing ideas. *The Australian Science Teachers Journal, 35*(3), 72.

Tompkins, G., & Hoskisson, K. (1991). *Language arts: Content and teaching strategies* (2nd ed.). New York: Merrill.

Treagust, D. (1993). The evolution of an approach for using analogies in teaching and learning science. *Research in Science Education, 23,* 293–301.

Van Matre, S. (1990). *Sunship earth.* Warrenville, IL: I.E.E.

Wheatley, E., & Kuhn, K. (1989). Cartoon capers for science students. *(SI)^2 Network Newsletter, 1* (1), 2.

Williams, T. (1991, November/December). Creative writing in science. *(SI)^2 Network Newsletter, 4*(2), 1–4.

Chapter 8

Ausubel, D. P. (1968). *Educational psychology.* New York: Holt, Rinehart, & Winston.

Ausubel, D. P., Novak, J. D., & Hanesian, H. (1978). *Educational psychology: A cognitive view.* New York: Holt, Rinehart, & Winston.

Briscoe, C. (1993). *Building contexts for learning and generating knowledge: Students' use of language in a small group concept mapping activity.* Paper presented to the annual meeting of the American Educational Research Association, Atlanta GA.

Ebenezer, J. V. (1992). Making chemistry learning more meaningful. *Journal of Chemical Education, 69,* 464–467.

Jones, B. F., Palinscar, A. S., Ogle, D. S., & Carr, E. G. (Eds.). (1987). *Strategic teaching and learning: Cognitive instruction in the content areas.* Alexandria, VA: Association for Supervision and Curriculum Development.

Novak, J. (1995). *Concept mapping: A strategy for organizing knowledge*. Mahwah, NJ: Erlbaum.

Novak, J. D. (1991). Clarify with concept maps. *The Science Teacher, 58*(7), 45–49.

Novak, J. D. (1977). *A theory of education*. Ithaca, NY: Cornell University Press.

Novak, J. D. (1978). An alternative to Piagetian psychology for science and mathematics education. *Studies in Science Education, 5*, 1–30.

Novak, J. D. (1985). Metalearning and metaknowledge strategies to help students learn how to learn. In L. H. T. West & A. L. Pines (Eds.), *Cognitive structure and conceptual change* (pp. 189–209). Orlando, FL: Academic Press.

Novak, J. D. (1988). Learning science and the science of learning. *Studies in Science Education, 15*, 77–101.

Novak, J. D., & Gowin, D. B. (1984). *Learning how to learn*. Cambridge, England: Cambridge University Press.

Okebukola, P. (1990). Attaining meaningful learning of concepts in genetics and ecology: An examination of the potency of the concept mapping technique. *Journal of Research in Science Teaching, 27*(5), 493–504.

Roth, W.-M., & Verechaka, G. (1993, January) Plotting a course with Vee maps. *Science and Children, 30*, 24–27.

Roth, W.-M. (1990, April). Map your way to a better lab. *The Science Teacher, 57*(4), 30–34.

Ruiz-Primo, M. A., & Shavelson, R. J. (1996). Problems and issues in the use of concept maps in science assessment. *Journal of Research in Science Teaching, 33*, 569–600.

Ruiz-Primo, M. A., Shavelson, R. J., & Schultz, S. E. (1997). *On the validity of concept map–based assessment interpretations: An experiment testing the assumption of hierarchical concept maps in science*. Paper presented at the annual meeting of the American Educational Research Association, Chicago, IL.

Slavin, R. E. (1968). *Educational psychology: Theory into practice* (2nd ed). Englewood Cliffs, NJ: Prentice Hall.

West, C. K., Farmer, J. A., & Wolff, P. M. (1991). *Instructional design: Implications from cognitive science*. Boston: Allyn & Bacon.

White, R., & Gunstone, R. (1992). *Probing understanding*. London: Falmer Press.

Chapter 9

Kenealy, P. (1989). Telling a coherent "story": A role for the history and philosophy of science in a physical science course. In D. E. Herget (Ed.), *The history & philosophy of science in science teaching*. Proceedings of the First International Conference (pp. 209–220). Tallahassee, FL: Florida State University.

McMillan, B., & Walker, A. (1991). Large context problem: Newton's optical experiments. An assignment submitted for 81.203: Development of Science Education. Winnipeg, Canada: The Faculty of Education, The University of Manitoba.

Piaget, J. & Garcia, R. (1989). *Psychogenesis and the history of science*. (H. Feider, Trans.). New York: Columbia University.

Stinner, A. (1993). A brief history of force. *Physics in Canada, 49*, 135–144.

Stinner, A. (1993). Contextual teaching in physics: From science stories to large-context problems. *Alberta Science Education Journal, 26*(1), 20–29.

Stinner, A. (1994). The large context problem approach: Providing a contextual base and a theoretical structure to guide the teaching of high school physics. *Physics in Canada, 50*(1), 45–51.

Whitehead, A. N. (1967). *The aims of education*. New York: Free Press.

Chapter 10

Barker, G. (1997). Biotechnology and societal issues. In V. Timmons, X. Liu, R. Macmillan, L. MacDonald, & R. MacKinnon, *Integration of technology into the secondary curriculum: Appendixes*. Antigonish, Canada: Office of Learning Technologies, St. Francis Xavier University.

diSessa, A. (1987). The third revolution in computers and education. *Journal of Research in Science Teaching, 24*, 343–367.

Fisher, K. M. (1992). SemNet: A tool for personal knowledge construction. In P. A. M. Kommers, D. H. Jonassen, & J. T. Mayes (Eds.), *Cognitive tools for learning* (pp. 63–75). Berlin, Germany: Springer-Verlag.

Fisher, K. M., Faletti, J., Patterson, H., Thornton, R., Lipson, J., & Spring, C. (1990). Computer-assisted concept mapping. *Journal of College Science Teaching, 19*(6), 347–352.

Friedler, Y., Nachmias, R., & Linn, M. (1990). Learning scientific reasoning skills in microcomputer-based laboratories. *Journal of Research in Science Teaching, 27*(2), 173–191.

Friedman, E. A., Baron, J. D., & Addison, C. J. (1996). Universal access to science study via Internet. *THE Journal (Technological Horizons in Education), 23*(11), 83–86.

Gabel, D. L. (Ed.). (1994). *Handbook of research on science teaching and learning.* New York: Macmillan.

Gardner, H. (1991). *The unschooled mind.* New York: Basic Books.

Greenbowe, T. J. (1994). An interactive multimedia software program for exploring electrochemical cells. *Journal of Chemical Education, 71,* 555–557.

Hameed, H., Hackling, M. W., & Garnett, P. J. (1993). Facilitating conceptual change in chemical equilibrium using a CAI approach. *International Journal of Science Education, 15,* 221–230.

Hennessy, S., Twigger, D., Driver, R., O'Shea, T., O'Malley, C., Byard, M., Draper, S., Hartley, R., Mohamed, R., & Scanlon, E. (1995a). Design of a computer-augmented curriculum for mechanics. *International Journal of Science Education, 17*(1), 75–92.

Hennessy, S., Twigger, D., Driver, R., O'Shea, T., O'Malley, C., Byard, M., Draper, S., Hartley, R., Mohamed, R., & Scanlon, E. (1995b). A classroom intervention using a computer-augmented curriculum for mechanics. *International Journal of Science Education, 17*(1), 189–206.

Johnstone, A. H. (1991). Why is science difficult to learn? Things are seldom what they seem. *Journal of Computer Assisted Learning, 7,* 75–83.

Jonassen, D. H. (1996). *Computers in the classroom: Mindtools for critical thinking.* Englewood Cliffs, NJ: Prentice-Hall.

Kommers, P. A. M. (1989). *Text Vision.* Enschede, Netherlands: University of Twente, Faculty of Education.

Kozma, R. B. (1987). The implications of cognitive psychology for computer-based learning tools. *Educational Technology 24*(11), 20–24.

Kozma, R. B. (1992). Constructing knowledge with Learning Tool. In P. A. M. Kommers, D. H.

Jonassen, & J. T. Mayes (Eds.), *Cognitive tools for learning* (pp. 23–32). Berlin, Germany: Springer-Verlag.

Krajcik, J. S., & Layman, J. W. (1993). Microcomputer-based laboratories in the science classroom. In NARST News: Research matters—to the science teacher. *National Association for Research in Science Teaching, 35*(1), 3–6.

Kroeker, M. (1997). It's science fair time. *The Manitoba Science Teacher, 39*(2), 33–35.

Langley, D., Ronen, M., & Eylon, B. (1997). Light propagation and visual patterns: Preinstruction learners' conceptions. *Journal of Research in Science Teaching, 34*(4), 399–424.

Marsh, E. J., & Kumar, D. D. (1992). Hypermedia: A conceptual framework for science education and review of scientific findings. *Journal of Educational Media and Hypermedia, 1,* 25–37.

Nachmias, R., & Linn, M. (1987). Evaluations of science laboratory data: The role of computer-presented information. *Journal of Research in Science Teaching, 24*(5), 491–506.

Novak, J. D., & Gowin, D. B. (1984). *Learning how to learn.* Cambridge, England: Cambridge University Press.

O'Neil, J. (1995, October). On technology schools: A conversation with Chris Dede. *Educational Leadership,* 6–12.

Perkins, D. (1991). Technology meets constructivism: Do they make a marriage? *Educational Technology, 35*(5), 18–23.

Ronen, M., Eylon, B., Rivlin, O., & Ganiel, U. (1993). Designing and using an open interface for instruction in geometrical optics. *Computers & Education, 20,* 299–309.

Ronen, M., & Rivlin, O. (1995). *RAY: Users Guide* [Physics Academic Software], Raleigh, NC: North Carolina University.

Salomon, G., Perkins, D. N., & Globerson, T. (1991). Partners in cognition: Extending human intelligence with intelligent technologies. *Educational Researcher, 20*(3), 2–9.

Sanger, M. J., & Greenbowe, T. J. (1997a). Common student misconceptions in electrochemistry: Galvanic, electrolytic, and concentration cells. *Journal of Research in Science Teaching, 34,* 377–398.

Sanger, M. J., & Greenbowe, T. J. (1997b). Students' misconceptions in electrochemistry: Current flow in electrolyte solutions and the salt bridge. *Journal of Chemical Education, 74*, 819–823.

Steed, M. (1992). Stella, a simulation construction kit: Cognitive process and educational implications. *Journal of Computers in Science and Mathematics Teaching, 11*(1), 39–52.

Tek, G. (1994). Visual Physics Optics Simulation [Computer software]. Raanana, Israel: G. Tek Technologies.

Twigger, D., Byard, M., Draper, S., Driver, R., Hartley, R., Hennessy, S., Mallen, C., Mohamed, R., O'Malley, C. E., O'Shea, T., & Scanlon, E. (1991). The conceptual change in science project. *Journal of Computer Assisted Learning, 7*, 144–155.

Twigger, D., Byard, M., Driver, R., Draper, S., Hennessy, S., Mohamed, R., O'Malley, C. E., O'Shea, T., & Scanlon, E. (1994). The conception of force and motion of students aged between 10 and 15 years: An interview study designed to guide instruction. *International Journal of Science Education, 16*, 215–229.

Updegrove, K. H. (1995). Teaching on the Internet [Online]. Available: http://pobox.upenn.edu/~kimu/teaching.html.

White, R. (1993). *Insights on conceptional change derived from extensive attempts to promote metacognition.* Paper presented at the annual convention of the American Educational Research Association (AERA), Atlanta, GA.

White, R. T. (1988). *Learning science.* Oxford, England: Basil Blackwell.

White, B., & Horwitz, P. (1988). Computer microworlds and conceptual change: A new approach to science education. In P. Ramsden (Ed.), *Improving learning new perspectives* (pp. 69–80). New York, NY: Nichols Publishing Co.

Williamson, V. M., & Abraham, M. R. (1995). The effects of computer animation on the particulate mental models of college chemistry students. *Journal of Research in Science Teaching, 32*, 521–534.

Zietsman, A. I., & Hewson, P. W. (1986). Effects of instruction using microcomputer simulations and cognitive change strategies on science learning. *Journal of Research in Science Teaching, 23*, 27–39.

Chapter 11

Agne, R. M. (1986). Teaching strategies for presenting ethical dilemmas. In M. J. Frazer & A. Kornhauser (Eds.)., *Ethics and social responsibility in science education* (pp. 165–174). Ontario, Canada: Pergamon Press.

Aikenhead, G. (1994). What is STS science teaching? In J. Solomon & G. Aikenhead (Eds.). *STS education: International perspectives on reform* (pp. 47–59). New York: Teachers College Press.

American Association for the Advancement of Science. (1989). *Project 2061: Science for all Americans.* Washington, DC: American Association for the Advancement of Science.

American Association for the Advancement of Science. (1993). *Benchmarks for science literacy.* Washington, DC: American Association for the Advancement of Science.

Bingle, W. H., & Gaskell, J. P. (1994). Scientific literacy for decisionmaking and the social construction of scientific knowledge. *Science Education, 78*(2), 185–201.

Chisman, D., & Holbrook, J. (1990). The future direction of sustainable development in the curriculum. In J. E. Penick and J. R. Stiles (Eds.), *Sustainable development for a new world agenda* (pp. 233–240). Proceedings of the World Environment, Energy and Economic Conference, Winnipeg, Manitoba, Canada.

Derkach, L. (1990). The link between education and sustainable development. In J. E. Penick and J. R. Stiles (Eds.), *Sustainable development for a new world agenda* (pp. 161–163). Proceedings of the World Environment, Energy and Economic Conference, Winnipeg, Manitoba, Canada.

Ebenezer, J. V., & Gaskell, J. (1995). Relational conceptual change in solution chemistry. *Science Education, 79*(1), 1–19.

Eijkelhof, H. (1985). Ethics in the classroom: Goals and experiences. In D. Gosling and B. Musschenga (Eds.), *Science education and ethical values* (pp. 68–78). Washington, DC: Georgetown University Press.

Hopkins, D. (1993). Thoughts on project based learning. *MSTE News, 3*(1), 3–4.

McConnell, M. C. (1982). Teaching about science, technology and society at the secondary school level in the United States: An educational dilemma for the 1980s. *Studies in Science Education, 9,* 1–32.

Miller, G. T. (1990). *Living in the environment: An introduction to environmental science.* (6th ed.). Belmont, CA: Wadsworth.

National Commission on Excellence in Education. (1983). *A nation at risk: The imperative for educational reform.* Washington, DC: U. S. Department of Education.

National Research Council. (1996). *National science education standards.* Washington, DC: National Academy Press.

National Science Board Commission on Precollege Education in Mathematics, Science and Technology (1983). *Educating Americans for the 21st century.* Washington, DC: National Science Foundation.

National Science Teachers Association (NSTA). (1990). Position paper on STS. *Bulletin of Science, Technology & Society, 10*(5,6), 249–250.

Raizen, S. A., Sellwood, P., Todd, R. D., & Vickers, M. (1995). *Technology education in the classroom. Understanding the designed world.* San Francisco: Jossey-Bass.

Rubinoff, L. (1985). Beyond the domination of Nature: Moral foundations of a consumer society. *Alternatives, 12*(2), 37–48.

Solomon, J., & Aikenhead, G. (Eds.). (1994). *STS education: International perspectives on reform.* New York: Teachers College Press.

Soprovich, W. (1990). STS—environment—problem solving. In J. E. Penick and J. R. Stiles (Eds.), *Sustainable development for a new world agenda* (pp. 207–214). Proceedings of the World Environment, Energy and Economic Conference, Winnipeg, Manitoba, Canada.

SSHRC Granting Programs. (1995). *Strategic themes: Applied ethics* (pp. 20–21). Ottawa, Canada: Social Sciences and Humanities Research Council of Canada.

Thier, H., & Nagle, B. (1994). Developing a model for issue-oriented science. In J. Solomon & G. Aikenhead (Eds.), *STS education: International perspectives on reform* (pp. 75–83). New York: Teachers College Press.

Torgerson, D. (1985). The paradox of environmental ethics. *Alternatives, 12*(2), 26–36.

United Nations World Commission on Environment and Development. (1987). *Our common future.* Oxford, England: Oxford University Press.

Yager, R. E. (1994, October). Assessment results with the science/technology/society approach. *Science and Children, 32*(2), 34–37.

Ziman, J. (1994). The rationale of STS education is in the approach. In J. Solomon & G. Aikenhead (Eds.), *STS education: International perspectives on reform* (pp. 21–31.) New York: Teachers College Press.

Zoller, U. (1987). *Problem solving and decision-making in science-technology-environment-society (STES) education.* Columbus, OH: Ohio State University. ERIC Clearinghouse for Science, Mathematics, and Environmental Education. (ERIC Document Reproduction Service No. 300237).

Chapter 12

Baker, D. (1988). Teaching for gender differences. *NARST News 30* (3), 5–6.

Bazler, J. A., & Simonis, D. A. (1990, December). Are women out of the picture? Sex discrimination in science texts. *The Science Teacher 57*(9), 24–26.

Bazler, J. A., & Simonis, D. A. (1991). Are high school chemistry texts gender fair? *Journal of Research in Science Teaching 28,* 353–362.

Canadian Teachers' Federation. (1988, Summer). Female students in math, science, and technology. *B.C. Catalyst,* 12–13.

Cawley, J. (1994, March). Science for students with disabilities. *Remedial and Special Education, 15*(2), 67–71.

Cawley, J., Miller, J., & Carr, S. (1989). An examination of the reading performance of students with mild educational handicaps or learning disabilities. *Journal of Learning Disabilities, 23,* 284–290.

Gagné, F. (1991). Toward a differentiated model of giftedness and talent. In N. Colangelo & G. A. Davis (Eds.), *Handbook of gifted education* (pp. 65–80). Boston: Allyn & Bacon.

Hodson, D. (1993). In search of a rationale for multicultural science education. *Science Education, 77*(6), 685–711.

Idol, L. (1994). Editorial. *Remedial and Special Education, 15*(2), 66.

Kahle, J. B. (1988, Summer). Encouraging girls in science courses and careers. *B.C. Catalyst,* 17–18.

Kahle, J. B., & Rennie, L. J. (1993). Ameliorating gender differences in attitudes about science: A cross-national study. *Journal of Science Education and Technology 2,* 321–334.

Kehoe, J. (1984). *Achieving cultural diversity in Canadian schools.* Cornwall, Canada: Vesta.

Keller, E. F. (1983). Is science male? In H. L. Ching, *Proceedings of the First National Conference for Women in Science and Technology* (pp. 21–29). Vancouver, Canada: Society for Canadian Women in Science and Technology.

Keller, E. F. (1985). *Reflections on gender and science.* New Haven, CT: Yale University Press.

Krashen, S. D., & Terrell, T. D. (1983). *The natural approach.* Hayward, CA: Alemany Press.

Mastropieri, M. A., & Scruggs, T. E. (1992). *Guidelines for effective mainstreaming in science.* West Lafayette, IN: Purdue University, Department of Educational Studies.

Mastropieri, M. A., & Scruggs, T. E. (1994, March). Text versus hands-on science curriculum. *Remedial and Special Education, 15*(2), 71–85.

Mastropieri, M. A., & Scruggs, T. E. (1995). Science and students with mental retardation: An analysis of curriculum features and learner characteristics. *Science Education, 79,* 251–269.

National Research Council. (1996). *National science education standards.* Washington, DC: National Academy Press.

Ottawa Citizen. (1997, February 23). The 'problem with boys.'

Peltz, W. (1990, December). Can girls + science – stereotyping = success? *The Science Teacher,* 44–49.

Pollina, A. (1995, September). Gender balance: Lessons from girls in science and mathematics. *Educational Leadership,* 30–33.

Ramos-Ford, V. & Gardner, H. (1991). Giftedness from a multiple intelligences perspective. In N. Colangelo & G. A. Davis (Eds.), *Handbook of gifted education* (pp. 55–64). Boston: Allyn & Bacon.

Scantlebury, K., & Kahle, J. B. (1993). The implementation of equitable teaching strategies by high school biology student teachers. *Journal of Research in Science Teaching 30,* 537–545.

Science Council of Canada. (1984). *Science for every student: Educating Canadians for tomorrow's world.* Ottawa, Canada: Author.

Selin, H. (1993, March). Science across cultures. *The Science Teacher,* 38–44.

Webb, M. (1993). *Roberta Bondar: Leading science into space.* Toronto, Canada: Copp Clark Pitman.

Chapter 13

Armstrong, T. (1994). *Multiple intelligences in the classroom.* Alexandria, VA: Association for Learning and Curriculum Development.

Bell, B. (1995). Interviewing: A technique for assessing science knowledge. In S. M. Glynn & R. Duit (Eds.), *Learning science in the schools: Research reforming practice* (pp. 347–364). Mahwah, NJ: Erlbaum.

Berenson, S. B., & Carter, G. S. (1995). Changing assessment practices in science and mathematics. *School Science and Mathematics, 95*(4), 182–186.

Bloom, B. (1956). *Taxonomy of educational objectives.* New York: David McKay.

Collins, A. (1992). Portfolios for science education: Issues in purpose, structure, and authenticity. *Science Education, 76*(4), 451–463.

Duffy, T. M., & Jonassen, D. H. (Eds.). (1992). *Constructivism and the technology of instruction: A conversation.* Hillsdale, NJ: Erlbaum.

Ebenezer, J., & Erickson, G. (1996). Chemistry students' conceptions of solubility: A phenomenography. *Science Education, 80*(2), 181–201.

Gabel, D. L. (Ed.). (1994). *Handbook of research on science teaching and learning.* New York: Macmillan.

Gardner, H. (1991). *The unschooled mind: How children think and how schools should teach.* New York: Basic Books.

Gitomer, D. H., & Duschl, R. A. (1995). Moving toward a portfolio culture in science education. In S. M. Glynn & R. Duit (Eds.), *Learning science in the schools: Research reforming practice* (pp. 299–326). Mahwah, NJ: Erlbaum.

Gitomer, D. H., & Duschl, R. A. (in press). Emerging issues and practice in science assessment. In B. Fraser & K. Tobin (Eds.), *International handbook of research in science teaching.* Kluwer.

Lemke, J. L. (1990). *Talking science: Language, learning, and values.* Norwood, NJ: Ablex.

Linn, R. L., Baker, E. L., & Dunbar, S. B. (1991). Complex, performance-based assessment: Expectations and validation criteria. *Educational Researcher, 20*(8), 15–21.

Lorsbach, W., Tobin, K., Briscoe, C., & LaMaster, S. U. (1992). An interpretation of assessment methods in middle school science. *International Journal of Science Education, 14,* 305–317.

Lundberg, R. (1997, January). Student-generated assessment: Having students develop rubrics promotes careful consideration of what constitutes quality work. *The Science Teacher,* 50–53.

McColskey, W., & O'Sullivan, R. (1993). *How to assess student performance in science: Going beyond multiple-choice tests.* Greensboro, NC: SouthEastern Regional Vision for Education.

McMillan, J. H. (1997). *Classroom assessment: Principles and practice for effective instruction.* Boston: Allyn & Bacon.

Novak, J. D., & Gowin, D. B. (1984). *Learning how to learn.* Cambridge, England: Cambridge University Press.

Nussbaum, J., & Novick, S. (1981). Brainstorming in the classroom to invent a model: A case study. *School Science Review 62*(221), 771–778.

Osborne, R., & Gilbert, J. (1980). A method for the investigation of concept understanding in science. *European Journal of Science Education 2,* 311–321.

Peterson, R. F., Treagust, D. F., & Garnett, P. J. (1989). Development and application of a diagnostic instrument to evaluate grade 11 and 12 students' concepts of covalent bonding and structure following a course of instruction. *Journal of Research in Science Teaching, 26*(4) 301–314.

Posner, G., Strike, K., Hewson, P., & Gertzog, W. (1982). Accommodation of a scientific conception: Toward a theory of conceptual change. *Science Education, 66,* 211–227.

Roth, K. J. (1991). Reading science texts for conceptual change. In C. M. Santa & D. E. Alvermann (Eds.), *Science learning: Processes and applications* (pp. 48–63). Newark, DE: International Reading Association.

Shepardson, D., & Britsch, S. (1997, February). Children's science journals: Tools for teaching, learning, and assessing. *Science and Children,* 13–17, 46–47.

Treagust, D. F. (1993). The evolution of an approach for using analogies in teaching and learning science. *Research in Science Education, 23,* 293–301.

Treagust, D. F. (1995a). Diagnostic assessment of students' science knowledge. In S. M. Glynn & R. Duit, (Eds.), *Learning science in the schools: Research reforming practice* (pp. 327–346). Mahwah, NJ: Erlbaum.

Treagust, D. (1995). Enhancing students' understanding of science using analogies. In B. Hand & V. Prain, *Teaching and learning in science: The constructivist classroom.* Sydney, Fort Worth, & Toronto: Harcourt Brace.

Watts, M. (1991). *The science of problem-solving: A practical guide for science teachers.* Portsmouth, NH: Heinemann.

White, R. T. (1988). *Learning science.* Oxford, England: Basil Blackwell.

White, R., & Gunstone, R. (1992). *Probing understanding.* New York: Falmer Press.

Wiggins, G. (1992, May). Creating tests worth taking. *Educational Leadership,* 26–33.

Chapter 14

Aikenhead, G. S. (1987). High-school graduates' beliefs about science-technology-society III: The characteristics and limitations of scientific knowledge. *Science Education, 71*(2), 459–487.

Aikenhead, G. S. (1990). Scientific/technological literacy, critical reasoning, classroom practice. In L. Philips & S. Norris (Eds.), *Foundations of literacy policy in Canada* (pp. 127–145). Calgary, Canada: Detselig Enterprises.

Andersson, B. (1986). Pupils' explanations of some aspects of chemical reactions. *Science Education, 70,* 549–563.

Armstrong, T. (1994). *Multiple intelligences in the classroom.* Alexandria, VA: Association for Supervision and Curriculum Development.

Bruner, J. (1986). *Actual minds, possible worlds.* Cambridge, MA: Harvard University Press.

De Vore, P. W. (1987). Cultural paradigms and technological literacy. *Bulletin of Science, Technology and Society, 6,* 711–719.

Driver, R., Squires, A., Rushworth, P., & Wood-Robinson, C. (1994). *Making sense of secondary science: Research into children's ideas.* London: Routledge.

Ebenezer, J. V., & Connor, S. (1998). *Learning to teach science: A model for the 21st century.* Upper Saddle River, NJ: Prentice Hall.

Ebenezer, J. V., & Erickson, G. L. (1996). Chemistry students' conceptions of solubility: A phenomenography. *Science Education 80,* 181–201.

Ebenezer, J. V., & Zoller, U. (1993). Grade 10 students' perceptions of and attitudes toward science teaching and school science. *Journal of Research and Science Teaching, 30*(2), 175–186.

Fleming, R. (1989). Literacy for a technological age. *Science Education, 73*(4), 391–404.

Gardner, H. (1991). *The unschooled mind.* New York: Basic Books.

Kotz, J. C., & Purcell, K. F. (1991). *Chemistry and chemical reactivity.* Philadelphia: Saunders.

Linder, C. J., & Erickson, G. (1989). A study of tertiary physics students' conceptualizations of sound. *International Journal of Science Education 11,* 491–501.

Marton, F., & Booth, S. (1997). *Learning and awareness.* Mahwah, NJ: Erlbaum.

National Research Council. (1996). *National Science Education Standards—Assessment Standards.* Chapter 5: Assessment in science education (pp. 75–101). Washington, D.C.: National Academy Press.

Osborne, R., & Gilbert, J. (1980). A method for the investigation of concept understanding in science. *European Journal of Science Education 2,* 311–321.

Pedretti, E. (1996). Learning about science, technology, and society (STS) through an action research project: Co-constructing an issue-based model for STS education. *School Science and Mathematics, 96*(8), 432–440.

Pfundt, H., & Duit, R. (1994). *Bibliography: Students' alternative frameworks and science education.* Kiel, Germany: Institute for Science Education, Kiel University.

White, R. T. (1988). *Learning science.* Oxford, England: Basil Blackwell Inc.

Zoller, U. (1987). Problem-solving and decision-making in science-technology-environment-society (STES) education. In K. Riqarts (Ed.), *Science and Technology Education, Education and the Quality of Life 2* (pp. 562–569). Kiel, Germany: IPN Materialen.

Chapter 15

American Association for the Advancement of Science (AAAS). (1989). *Project 2061: Science for all Americans.* Washington, DC: author.

Anderson, C., Sheldon, T. H., & Dubay, J. (1990). The effects of instruction on college nonmajors' conceptions of respiration and photosynthesis. *Journal of Research In Science Teaching, 27*(8), 761–776.

Atwater, M. M., & Riley, J. P. (1993). Multicultural science education: Perspectives, definitions, and research agenda. *Science Education, 77*(6), 661–668.

Ausubel, D. P. (1968). *Educational psychology.* New York: Holt, Rinehart, and Winston.

Bell, B. F., & Brook, A. (1984). *Aspects of secondary students' understanding of plant nutrition.* Leeds, England: Children's Learning in Science Project, Centre for Studies in Science and Mathematics Education, University of Leeds.

Bybee, R. (Ed.). (1986). *Science-technology-society. 1986 NSTA yearbook.* Washington, DC: National Science Teachers Association.

Bybee, R. (1993). *Reforming science education: Social perspectives and personal reflections.* New York: Teachers College Press.

Cobern, W. W. (1991). Science education and the external perspective on science. In S. Hills (Ed.), *The History and Philosophy of Science and Science Education,* (Vol. I, pp. 175–186). Kingston, Canada: The Faculty of Education, Queens University.

Driver, R., Asoko, H., Leach, J., Mortimer, E., & Scott, P. (1994). Constructing scientific knowledge in the classroom. *Educational Researcher, 23*(7), 5–12.

Ebenezer, J., & Erickson, G. (1996). Chemistry students' conceptions of solubility: A phenomenography. *Science Education, 80*(2), 181–201.

Edwards, D., & Mercer, N. (1987). *Common knowledge: The development of understanding in the classroom.* London: Methuen.

Glasersfeld, E. von (1989). Cognition, construction of knowledge, and teaching. *Synthese, 80,* 121–140.

Hodson, D. (1993). In search of a rationale for multicultural science education. *Science Education, 77*(6), 685–711.

Keller, E. F. (1985). *Reflections on gender and science.* New Haven, CT: Yale University Press.

Kuhn, T. (1970). *The structure of scientific revolutions.* (2nd ed.). Chicago: University of Chicago Press.

Latour, B., & Woolgar, S. (1986). *Laboratory life: The construction of scientific facts.* (2nd ed.). Princeton, NJ: Princeton University Press.

Lemke, J. L. (1990). *Talking science: Language, learning, and values.* Norwood, NJ: Ablex.

Longino, H. (1990). *Science as social knowledge: Values and objectivity in scientific inquiry.* Princeton, NJ: Princeton University Press.

Marton, F. (1981). Phenomenography—describing conceptions of the world around us. *Instructional Science, 10,* 177–200.

Marton, F. (1984). Towards a psychology beyond the individual. In K. M. J. Lagerspectz & P. Niemi (Eds.), *Psychology in the 1990s.* (pp. 45–72). Amsterdam: North Holland.

Marton, F., & Booth, S. (1997). *Learning and awareness.* Mahwah, NJ: Erlbaum.

Orpwood, G. (1984). *Science for every student: Educating Canadians for tomorrow's world.* Ottawa, Canada: Science Council of Canada.

Osborne, R., & Freyberg, P. (1985). *Learning in science.* London: Heinemann.

Piaget, J. (1973). *The child's conception of the world.* St. Albans, England: Paladin.

Popper, K. (1979). *Objective knowledge: An evolutionary approach.* Oxford, England: Clarendon Press.

Raizen, S. A., Sellwood, P., Todd, R. D., & Vickers, M. (1995). *Technology education in the classroom: Understanding the designed world.* San Francisco: Jossey-Bass.

Roth, K. J., & Anderson, C. W. (1985). *The power plant: Teacher's guide.* East Lansing, MI: Institute for Research on Teaching, Michigan State University.

Simpson, M. (1984, November). Teaching about digestion and getting the system to work. *Aberdeen College of Education Biology Newsletter, 44,* 15–22.

Simpson, M., & Arnold, B. (1982). Availability of prerequisite concepts for learning biology at certificate level. *Journal of Biological Education, 16*(1), 65–72.

Solomon, J., & Aikenhead, G. (Eds.). (1994). *STS education: International perspectives on reform.* New York: Teachers College Press.

Sutton, C. (1992). *Words, science and learning.* Philadelphia: Open University Press.

Suzuki, D. (with McConell, A.). (1977). *The sacred balance: Rediscovering our place in nature.* Vancouver, Canada: Greystone Books, Douglas and Mcintyre.

Toulmin, S. (1972). *Human understanding: An inquiry into the aims of science.* Princeton, NJ: Princeton University Press.

Tuana, N. (Ed.). (1989). *Feminism and science.* Bloomington, IN: Indiana University Press.

Parting Message

Bell, B. (1994). Editorial. *International Journal of Science Education, 16*(5), 493–495.

Ebenezer, J. V., & Erickson, G. (1996). Chemistry students' conceptions of solubility: A phenomenography. *Science Education, 80*(2), 181–201.

Erickson, G. (1991). Collaborative inquiry and the professional development of science teachers. *Journal of Educational Thought, 25*(3), 228–245.

Gunstone, R. F., Slattery, M., Baird, J. R., & Northfield, J. R. (1993). A case study exploration of development in preservice science teachers. *Science Education, 77*(1), 47–73.

Hargreaves, A. (1994). *Changing teachers, changing times.* New York: Teachers College Press.

Appendix B

Barton, J., & Collins, A. (1993). Portfolios in teacher education. *Journal of Teacher Education, 44,* 200–212.

Schön, D. A. (1991). *The reflective turn: Case studies in an educational practice.* New York: Teachers College Press.

NAME INDEX

SUBJECT INDEX